THE ENGLISH REFORMATION

THE ENGLISH REFORMATION

A. G. DICKENS

SCHOCKEN BOOKS · NEW YORK

For my colleagues in
the Tudor Seminar
S. T. BINDOFF
C. W. DUGMORE
JOEL HURSTFIELD
PATRICK COLLINSON

OTHER BOOKS BY THE SAME AUTHOR

Lollards and Protestants in the Diocese of York
(*Oxford University Press, 1959*)
Thomas Cromwell and the English Reformation
(*English Universities Press, 1959*)
The Register or Chronicle of Butley Priory (*Warren, 1951*)
Tudor Treatises (*Yorkshire Archaeological Society, 1959*)
Clifford Letters of the Sixteenth Century (*Surtees Society, 1962*)
The East Riding of Yorkshire (*Brown, 1954, 1958*)
The Marian Reaction in the Diocese of York
(*St. Anthony's Press, 1957*)
Robert Holgate (*St. Anthony's Press, 1955*)
Victoria County History, City of York
(*1961; Anglo-Saxon and Tudor sections*)
Lübeck Diary (*Gollancz, 1947*)
Reformation and Society in Sixteenth-Century Europe
(*Thames and Hudson, 1966*)
Martin Luther and the Reformation
(*English Universities Press, 1967*)

FOURTH PRINTING, 1974

First published 1964
This edition published by arrangement with B. T. Batsford Ltd.

Library of Congress Catalog Card Number: 64-22987
Manufactured in the United States of America

PREFACE

I DO NOT BELIEVE that any apology is needed for attempting another general survey of the English Reformation. The religious, cultural and social issues which it raised remain to this day both profound and inexhaustible. It proved, moreover, a seminal episode in world history, since it changed the outlook of Englishmen even as they braced themselves to make their astonishing impact upon western civilisation. Furthermore, research is proceeding apace and even during the last decade our factual knowledge has been greatly augmented and corrected. Any competent specialist can thus introduce materials and ideas as yet unfamiliar to non-specialists, though he can do so only with the proviso that further revisions and additions are bound ere long to become necessary.

In this account I have set myself three special objectives. Since a historian's primary task is to explain why things happened, I have allocated exceptional space—about one-third of the whole—to describing those basic conditions which made possible the dramatic and familiar changes of the years 1529–1559. Again, it has long seemed to me obvious that the development and spread of Protestantism should play a far more prominent rôle than that assigned to it by most modern historians of the English Reformation. In the third place, I have sought to depict the movement as it affected ordinary men and women, who have somehow tended to fall and disappear through the gaps between the kings, the prelates, the monasteries and the prayer books. At the same time, one dare not lose grip of the conventional themes, for governments and leaders remain important; the story will not cohere in their absence. This concern with the man in the street has presented some formidable difficulties for a book of moderate length, and even now I have utilised all too inadequately those rich contributions which local and regional researches can make to the social history of the Reformation. In twenty years' time, when our knowledge—and especially that of Tudor diocesan archives—will be far more complete, a definitive treatment of both social and institutional themes may have come within reach.

Initially, I shall be concerned with currents of opinion rather than with dominant personalities. The Angevin Kings, Henry II and John, were as ruthless as Henry VIII and far less conventional by temperament and outlook. They too had overweening ambitions to control the English Church; they strove bitterly with Rome until at last the kingdom fell under an interdict. Nevertheless, it seems inconceivable that in their day any ruler could have abstracted England permanently, or indeed for many years, from Catholic Christendom. In the England of Henry VIII a very different psychological climate arose and, when the King quarrelled with the Pope over his divorce, a permanent schism did not merely become conceivable; it proved actually manageable without arousing much opposition within the realm. And as the schism developed, it became increasingly clear that this was only the harbinger of changes far more fundamental in the religious and ecclesiastical life of the nation. When, how, and why the climate altered, it must be our objective to determine. As a first step we propose to examine the character of English religion, both popular and sophisticated, during the earlier years of Henry's reign and also during the time of his father, the first Tudor King. Throughout our first five chapters we shall be approaching this vital preparatory period from a number of angles. Sometimes we shall be bound to reach back still further into the past, for some aspects of this ominous situation had developed slowly throughout the fourteenth and fifteenth centuries.

In earlier editions I have recorded my debts to many generous friends: Professors G. W. O. Woodward, G. R. Potter, G. Donaldson and C. W. Dugmore, Drs. T. M. Parker, Edmund Fryde, Patrick Collinson, D. M. Loades and Mr. Peter Heath. My thanks are due also to the understanding and technical assistance of my original publishers, B. T. Batsford. The processes of research and writing over three decades owe far more than I can express to my wife.

Since the first edition of 1964 I have made numerous corrections of detail, but I should have made more extensive use of several recent works had they been originally available. Among them are W. A. Clebsch, *England's Earliest Protestants, 1520–1535* (1964); W. R. Trimble, *The Catholic Laity in Elizabethan England* (1964); D. S. Chambers, *Cardinal Bainbridge in the Court of Rome, 1509–1514* (1965); J. K. McConica, *English Humanists and Renaissance Politics* (1965); J. A. F. Thomson, *The Later Lollards* (1965); J. E. Oxley, *The Reformation in Essex* (1965); D. M. Loades, *Two Tudor Conspiracies* (1965); P. E. Hughes, *Theology of the English Reformers* (1965);

H. Aveling, *Northern Catholics* (1966); Claire Cross, *The Puritan Earl* (1966); P. Collinson, *The Elizabethan Puritan Movement* (1967); Margaret Bowker, *The Secular Clergy of the Diocese of Lincoln, 1495–1520* (1967). Forthcoming works of importance will include one by P. Tyler on the Northern Ecclesiastical Commission, and another by J. J. Scarisbrick on Henry VIII, throwing further light on many problems of the reign, notably on the canon law of the royal divorce. Two interesting articles I overlooked are those by L. J. Trinterud in *Church History*, XX (1951) and XXXI (1962), respectively on the origins of Puritanism and on Tyndale's debt to Luther. An erudite article on Melanchthon's influence on English thought has recently been published by my former colleague, Carl S. Meyer, in *Bibliothèque de la Revue d'Histoire Ecclésiastique*, fasc. 44 (Louvain, 1967).

In this present edition I want to draw special attention to Peter Brooks's *Thomas Cranmer's Doctrine of the Eucharist* (1965), an acute re-examination of this truly involved subject. Dr. Brooks has set Cranmer's complex doctrinal development against the wider background of Continental controversy concerning the eucharist. It seems likely that, having rejected Roman transubstantiation, the Archbishop held firmly to a 'real presence' doctrine conceived in the straightforward terms of Scripture, much as Luther himself seems to have done. Again, Cranmer's later acceptance of the Swiss doctrine of the sacrament by no means made him a disciple of Zwingli, but rather the main English exponent of the 'true presence' doctrine enshrined in the *Consensus Tigurinus* of 1549. That the Archbishop was as eager as any Continental divine to bridge the eucharistic divide between the Lutherans and the 'Reformed' may be readily appreciated from his repeated plea for a 'godly synod' to unite the Protestant cause. In the third place, a significant aspect of his thought depends on the impact of patristic study, much of it gleaned from the writings of Oecolampadius, the humanist Reformer of Basle. At an early and formative stage of his career, Cranmer was prompted to urge Vadianus that 'the writings of every man must be read with discrimination'; and as modern research increasingly clears away the old, exaggerated image of 'doubting Thomas', so it reveals a Cranmer possessed of a scholarly and independent mind.

A. G. DICKENS

Institute of Historical Research,
University of London

CONTENTS

1 Late Medieval Religion

Conventional Cults and Idioms

THERE WAS ONCE a certain knight, whose castle stood upon a highway and who mercilessly robbed passing travellers. Despite his conduct he nevertheless maintained his pious daily prayers to the Blessed Virgin. One day, when it was the turn of a certain holy monk to be stripped by this knight's henchmen, the victim demanded a personal interview with his oppressor, saying he had certain secrets to communicate. Taken inside the castle he asked the knight to assemble his whole household, yet when the knight so obliged him the monk declared that one of its members had absented himself from the assembly. A check revealed that the missing member was a serving man who, when at last located and brought before the monk, proceeded to behave as one insane. Finally he admitted he was no real man but a demon in human guise, who for fourteen years had served the knight by special order of the Devil. The latter had commanded him to watch for the day when his master failed to salute the Virgin in prayer; whenever this fatal moment of neglect should occur, the demon servant would be free to kill the knight and drag his wicked soul to perdition. So far, though ignorant of his precarious situation, the knight had never allowed his devotions to lapse. Now learning the truth he was duly appalled and hurled himself in repentance at the feet of the monk, who commanded the demon to vanish and to trouble the Virgin's devotees no more. With reverence and thanks the knight permitted his saintly deliverer to go free and thenceforth he changed his own life for the better.

This *exemplum*, or story with a moral, was last told not around the year 1200 but by a man who mentions Pope Julius II as still alive. It is one of many such anecdotes in the commonplace book of Thomas Ashby,[1] an Augustinian canon of Bridlington in the days of Henry VII and Henry VIII. This great house had literary traditions dating back to the twelfth century;

more important, it rejoiced in its own saint, Canon John of Thwing, who had died in 1379, received canonisation at Rome in 1401 and continued to attract pilgrims from far and wide even in the time of Thomas Ashby. In no small measure the latter's manuscript centres around these two cults of the Virgin and of St. John of Bridlington. It begins with a long series of items in honour of the former—two rhyming Latin tributes, a group of meditations and prayers centred upon the Virgin and St. Anne, an exposition of the Angelic Salutation, a meditation on the Magnificat. Later on we observe a transcript of the poem *Salve virgo virginum*, and the *exemplum* we have just retold. In St. John and his miracles Ashby's taste for anecdote finds a more extensive scope. We read of the marvellous rescue of the five mariners of Hartlepool, the revival of the dead carpenter, the resurrection of a murdered man who luckily happened to lie unburied because of the coroner's absence. To these miracles, which occur in earlier Bridlington hagiography, Ashby adds another, based on the written testimony of an early fifteenth-century Gascon merchant. This impetuous foreign tourist had failed to wait for the custodian of the shrine and with rash curiosity had presumed to open the capsule containing the head of St. John. In consequence the angry saint had afflicted him with terrible pains in his hand and arm. Journeying south he reached Huntingdon, but his condition worsened and he feared to die. His companions, better instructed in the irascible ways of saints, urged him to return forthwith on an expiatory pilgrimage to Bridlington. Complying he experienced a miraculous cure. The Gascon is then made to end his acknowledgment with an eloquent tribute to St. John, presumably reflecting the exuberant latinity of some Bridlington scribe who drew up the original document.

The local cult is far from exhausted by these items of Thomas Ashby's manuscript. He includes also an office in honour of St. John, records of the canonisation and translation, notes on the foundation of the Priory, and a poem beginning,

Brydlyngtonie prior pie
Imitator caste vie,
Representa nos Messye.

Yet another set of *exempla* illustrates the miracle-working properties of the text, 'In the beginning was the Word'. In Aquitaine there were once two beggars, both demoniacs, one of whom noticed that his companion secured more than his fair share of alms. He therefore resolved to get his competitor cured of this all-too-profitable malady and induced a priest to whisper the miraculous text into the successful beggar's ear. Yet the wary priest insisted on repeating it also to the first beggar, who was shocked to find himself cured as well! Again, relates Ashby, we read that a devil once told a holy man there was a certain text quite terrifying to devils, but naturally he refused to divulge it. The holy man then suggested a series of texts but his adversary returned a contemptuous negative to each suggestion. When, however, the enquirer stumbled upon the first words of St. John's Gospel, the infernal creature vanished with a mighty noise. Also, continues our author, a devil appeared to a certain abbot in the form of a beautiful woman, *alliciens eum ad concubitum* as they were alone together in a pleasure-garden—or so I interpret *in viridario*, though this can also mean a plantation. At all events, when the chaste abbot repeated the same text, the devil disappeared in the manner of his kind, *cum magno strepitu*. These improving tales one might well continue, but those already retold will suffice to indicate that at Bridlington a twelfth-century world lingered on while Machiavelli was writing the *Prince*, while the sophisticated talkers at Urbino were giving Castiglione the materials for his *Book of the Courtier*. And if Ashby cannot be placed among the more sophisticated of provincial Englishmen, his case was far from untypical in a generation of priests brought up on the *Golden Legend* and the *Gesta Romanorum*.

The theological and liturgical sections of his book could equally have occurred at any period of the Middle Ages—an exposition of the Fiftieth Psalm, a treatise on the privileges and rites of various festivals, notes on reading in church, on the four necessities for a dying man, on the symbolism of the episcopal mitre and other vestments, a meditation on guardian angels, verses on how to enter a church, an 'objurgation' against the wretched human body, and a scholastic disputation 'On the Day of Judgment, will men be bare or clothed?' Ashby writes almost wholly in Latin, but he has some English verses in a section concerning the sacrament of the altar, his object here being to enjoin implicit belief in transubstantiation and to allay curious questioning:

The bread is flesh in our credence,
The wine is blood without doubtance.
They that believe not this with circumstance,
But doth themself with curious wit enhance,
To hell pit shall they wend,
There to be torment without end.

This section concludes with supporting patristic texts, especially from St. Augustine, to whom the compiler elsewhere often alludes. On the other hand, he ostensibly cites no author later than Jean Beleth, the eminent French theologian of the twelfth century.

I have adduced Thomas Ashby's book, now in Durham University Library, as one of those many unpublished manuscripts we must investigate in order to gain a more authentic and intimate sense of the popular religion on the eve of the Reformation. A comparable miscellany is that by his younger contemporary John Gysborn, which may be found among the Sloane manuscripts in the British Museum.[2] This cleric, probably a native of Guisborough in North Yorkshire, joined the Premonstratensian order and at first describes himself as a canon of Coverham. Subsequently he styles himself 'curate' (i.e. parish priest) of Allington in Lincolnshire, but he doubtless served there while still remaining a regular canon, since the benefice of Allington belonged to Newbo, another Premonstratensian house. Gysborn's career unfortunately cannot be dated from the Lincoln diocesan records, but the three or four datable documents in his collection range between the years 1520 and 1531. He begins with liturgical notes on the duties of the deacon and subdeacon at mass in his own order. He then provides detailed English questionnaires for use in the confessional, indicating the methods whereby dutiful pastors discovered the more intimate lapses of their flocks. A rhymed prayer to the Virgin is also in English, though with a Latin refrain, and there follow various prayers to the angels, the patriarchs, the apostles, the martyrs. Then comes an historical account of Confession, a report on a miracle at Exeter, a badge of the Five Wounds drawn in pencil and red ink, a couple of sermons, a further note on sins revealed in the confessional, and two spirited accounts of the pains of hell. Unlike Ashby, Gysborn provides a number of secular items, including a sequence of model letters and three acknowledgments of debt, respectively by a Grantham draper, a yeoman of Donnington and a former rector of Allington. In common Tudor style he also records remedies for stone, colic, strangury, pox and plague; he explains how to make aquavite from herbs, how to engrave upon iron or steel, to grind gold for illuminating and to enamel on gold. Altogether Gysborn stands nearer than Ashby to lay life and there is more than a touch of humour in some of his macaronic poems.

Manuscripts like these two are far from embracing the whole gamut of English devotional life on the eve of the Reformation. They nevertheless exemplify many important elements of the popular and conventional religion[3]—its effort to attain salvation through devout observances, its fantastic emphasis on saints, relics and pilgrimages, its tendency to allow the personality and teaching of Jesus to recede from the focus of the picture. That the connection of such writings with the Christianity of the Gospel is rather tenuous could be demonstrated with almost mathematical precision. The point is reinforced by the testimony of Catholic reformers like Colet, More and Erasmus, for Catholicism as it then existed amongst real men and women was far from homogeneous. People who can sing the same creed together are not necessarily practising the same type of religion. There lay all the difference in the world between Thomas More and the friar whom More found at Coventry superstitiously preaching that a sinner could escape damnation by the simple expedient of saying his rosary every day. It would nevertheless be mistaken to imagine that the religion of saint-cults and observances appealed only to poor and uneducated believers. In 1522 the wealthy pluralist Robert Langton, nephew of a bishop of Salisbury and Winchester, published a book on his interminable pilgrimages on the continent, yet it scarcely mentioned any object of interest other than the shrines of saints.[4] The celebrated shrine of St. Mary of Walsingham attracted the highest-born, and the theological learning of Henry VIII did not prevent him from making the pilgrimage in person. Few can have made it in the sarcastic spirit of Erasmus, who in later years wrote a colloquy ridiculing the commercialisation of the shrine and the ignorance of the canons. And even he did not know that Walsingham Priory had become, amid all its wealth and magnificence, one of the least pure and disciplined religious houses in England. This fact was nevertheless well known to Bishop Nix of Norwich and his officials, who inexorably recorded the details in their visitation-records. But there were fashions in saints and the most famous of all in England had proved a waning financial asset for over a century before this time. At Canterbury the receipts of the shrine and the altars are shown by the official accounts of the fifteenth and sixteenth centuries to have become quite negligible in comparison with the golden shower of the high Middle Ages.[5]

Purgatory; Devotional Reading

OUR two 'new' witnesses Ashby and Gysborn scarcely do justice to another debatable feature of late medieval religion—its dogmatic and detailed emphasis upon the horrors of Purgatory and the means whereby sinners could mitigate them. Here again we observe no mere cult of the vulgar. In that most terrible—and magnificently written—passage in his *Supplication of Souls*, More himself makes the suffering dead cry out to the living for more prayers and masses:

> If ye pity the blind, there is none so blind as we, which are here in the dark, saving for sights unpleasant, and loathsome, till some comfort come. If ye pity the lame, there is none so lame as we, that neither can creep one foot out of the fire, nor have one hand at liberty to defend our face from the flame. Finally, if ye pity any man in pain, never knew ye pain comparable to ours; whose fire as far passeth in heat all the fires that ever burned upon earth, as the hottest of all those passeth a feigned fire painted on a wall. If ever ye lay sick, and thought the night long and longed sore for day, while every hour seemed longer than five, bethink you then what a long night we silly souls endure,

> that lie sleepless, restless, burning and broiling in the dark fire one long night of many days, of many weeks, and some of many years together. . . . You have your physicians with you, that sometime cure and heal you; no physic will help our pain, nor no plaister cool our heat. Your keepers do you great ease, and put you in good comfort; our keepers are such as God keep you from —cruel, damned sprites, odious, envious and hateful, despiteous enemies and despiteful tormentors, and their company more horrible and grievous to us than is the pain itself: and the intolerable torment that they do us, wherewith from top to toe they cease not continually to tear us.[6]

This, it should be recalled, was not hell but merely the long prison-sentence which the average man must anticipate, a sentence liable to be much lengthened because other people were slack about buying masses and indulgences to shorten it. This much must be said because so many idealisers of medieval religion have supposed that the equally inscrutable Deity of the Calvinists represents some sinister novelty, or that fifteenth-century religion had a childlike gaiety and optimism reminiscent of some sweet group of saints by a Sienese master. On the contrary, medieval men were faced by quite terrifying views of punishment in the life to come; it was small wonder that they felt more comfortable with the saints than with God, or that they came to regard the Blessed Virgin as a merciful mediatrix for ever seeking to placate the divine wrath of the Son as Judge. When they discovered the slightness of its scriptural basis, Protestant zealots like Tyndale crudely denounced the doctrine of Purgatory and indulgences as a worldwide plot by the priesthood aimed at fleecing poor and rich alike. Yet whatever the credentials of this doctrine, it was sincerely held, and it showed at least an uplifting sense of community with former generations of Christians. Some Englishmen felt profound offence when the government of Edward VI forbade organised intercession for their dead parents and benefactors; they hastened spontaneously to restore the practice when the accession of Queen Mary made it safe. Within this penumbra of Christian doctrine, there lay edification and sincerity as well as superstition.

A vivid impression of the last generation of medieval English Catholics can be gained from the numerous manuscripts of a younger contemporary of John Gysborn—Robert Parkyn, curate of Adwick-le-Street near Doncaster.[7] This man took priest's orders some time before 1541 and soon proved himself an assiduous student and copyist of Richard Rolle and other mystical authors. He subsequently wrote sermons, pious verses and an interesting guide to the contemplative life,[8] which is overwhelmingly medieval by inspiration even if it shows traces of influence by the Jesuit-inspired Dominican, William Peryn. Parkyn also admired More and his fellow-martyr Bishop John Fisher, making copies of their more intimate meditations. Under Queen Mary he wrote a narrative of the Reformation,[9] deploring the English

Prayer Books and the Edwardian abrogation of Catholic ritual. All the same, he continued to hold the curacy of Adwick throughout all the ecclesiastical revolutions until his death in 1569. By this time he had begun to make literary contact with the exiled English writers of the Counter Reformation, but there is no sign that he resisted the Elizabethan Settlement or considered relinquishing his office. Robert Parkyn did not live in a private world. His career and beliefs are closely paralleled by those of his neighbouring colleague William Watson, curate of Melton-on-the-Hill, some of whose letters were fortunately preserved among Parkyn's own papers. They show that in November 1555 these two conservatives independently revived the pre-Reformation practice of saying a trental, or series of thirty requiem masses.[10]

It was indeed a harsh and rigid Protestantism which desired to outlaw convictions so deeply grounded. Yet when the old popular religion encountered the Protestant demand for Biblical evidence, it exposed more vulnerable aspects than a belief in the multiplication of intercessory masses. Amongst the manuscript works of this same Robert Parkyn is a versified *Life of Christ*,[11] over 10,000 lines in length and written in seven-line stanzas; he composed it between the years 1548 and 1554, intending it for public readings before his parishioners. With some narrative skill, though in the creaking versification of the period, he combines the materials of all four Gospels and then proceeds to cover the first two chapters of *Acts*, ending with Pentecost and the going forth of the apostles to preach. At the outset Parkyn vociferously claims that he will affirm nothing except what can be proved from the scriptural text, and he does in fact often distinguish between the latter and the mere conjectures of patristic and medieval commentators, among whom his favourite is the great Spanish Dominican St. Vincent Ferrer. Despite these good intentions he nevertheless devotes many stanzas to the pretty legends. We are told, for example, that angels informed the Virgin of the temptation in the wilderness, inviting her to send food to the Lord; she did so, but with the request that they should return to her the fragments. Again, Parkyn devotes three equally apocryphal stanzas to the detailed subject-matter of the disputations in the temple. Most reprehensibly of all, since he fails to reveal their lack of scriptural basis, he invents long discussions between the apostles as they await Pentecost, and here he deliberately makes the Virgin appear the dominating figure of the nascent Church. When we reflect that as late as 1550 a virtuous, sincere and by no means uneducated parish priest could so manipulate these passages, we perhaps begin to comprehend, though not necessarily to admire, the impatience of the Reformers. They were dealing with a failure to understand the meaning of evidence, with an invincible addition to time-honoured fable, with an obstinate denial of the principle which had its origins in humanism —that belief must be based upon a close scrutiny of original sources rather than upon the unsupported authority of medieval doctors or upon writers of pious fiction. Robert Parkyn's intellectual superiors amongst the Catholic clergy may seldom have perpetrated such major lapses, yet they certainly lost influential support through their undue attachment to those 'unwritten verities' which the contemporaries of Erasmus had come to suspect. Here we encounter one of the greatest issues of the Reformation, and it remains an issue upon which modern writers cannot be expected to achieve close agreement. Yet in the present writer's view, the Catholic party lost the struggle in England not simply because they temporised with Henry VIII but also because, in an age when an increasing number of men were thinking for themselves, the intellectual slackness of much late medieval religion played into the hands of Protestant critics.

Our picture of conventional religion arising from these little-known sources finds confirmation in the analysis of printed books made thirty years ago by Dr. Pierre Janelle.[12] Behind these books we sense a considerable body of pious readers and, if we know almost nothing about the number of copies printed, the many editions of certain works testify to their popularity. Of the seventy-four books edited by Caxton from 1470 to 1490, at least twenty-nine are works of edification. In the next decade his chief successor, Wynkyn de Worde, published thirty such religious works in a total list of fifty-four, and this high proportion continues throughout English publishing at least until the decade 1530–40. Between 1490 and 1530 at least twenty-eight editions of the *Hours of the Blessed Virgin* were printed in England. Myrc's *Festial*, the chief English collection of pious legends and miracles, achieved nineteen editions from 1483 to 1532. The delightful but still heavily fabulous *Golden Legend* by Jacob of Voragine was published in 1483 by Caxton who, so far from pruning its luxuriance, added seventy new lives of saints. Its well-maintained popularity is attested by further editions in 1485, 1493, 1498, 1503, 1512 and 1527. During this period books centring around the saints immensely outnumbered any other type of religious book. Myrc and Voragine had several rivals in this field. Wynkyn de Worde published John of Tynemouth's *Sanctilogium Angliae* in 1516, while the Bridgettine monk Richard Whitford compiled the last of the great English hagiographical collections, the *Martiloge*, and saw it published in 1526.

Over and above this steady native output, a large number of similar books came to England from the presses of France and the Netherlands. Guides to appropriate preaching on the various festivals comprise a smaller but still considerable group of publications; of these, *Manipulus Curatorum*, *Pupilla Oculi*, *Exornatorium Curatorum* and others often find mention in the wills of Tudor clergymen. The mystics are represented by several works of Rolle and Hilton, but these writers provided a more *recherché* approach which we shall examine separately. Compared with the public avidity for saints and marvels, both these and the intellectual treatises by scholastic theologians and philosophers account for a tiny part of the labours of English printers. Needless to add, the Bible occupies a negligible place, and the English Bible no place at all. This latter fact was based on the prohibition in 1408 of any translation unless sanctioned by the bishops; it was peculiar to England rather than to Catholic Christendom. Ironically enough, the nation about to be most dominated by the Bible stood as yet among the least directly influenced in the Christian world. In Germany twenty complete translations appeared, together with innumerable partial editions, between 1466 and 1522. In France the first printed translation dates from 1477, while ten years later that of Guiart Desmoulins (1291) was published by Canon Jean de Rély; it was reprinted seven times from 1487 to 1521.

Such works had no printed parallel in England until 1526 when Tyndale published his Protestant New Testament. Here the vernacular Scriptures had been so long associated with the Lollard heresy that our English ecclesiastical establishment would take no chances with either official or private translations. This insular conservatism received an uneasy support from Sir Thomas More who was satisfied to place the whole blame upon Wycliffe.[13] However surprising it may seem today, his attitude was widely shared by responsible people, but by the time Tyndale broke the deadlock there were obviously great numbers of laymen who thought that such reasoning unduly simplified one of the most vital issues of the Christian life. Here we are confronted by one of the great formative factors in the origins of the Reformation. The gradual yet portentous growth of a literate laity, already discernible in fifteenth-century sources,[14] was far from being limited to the gentry and the richer merchant classes. In the long run it was bound to involve not merely critical attitudes toward the Church but also more constructive intellectual and religious ambitions which could not be excluded from the sphere of religion.

Since we seek to explain the progress of the Reformation, we have chiefly concentrated upon what we suppose to have been the vulnerable aspects of the conventional religion. On the other hand, no reasonable observer would seek to deny that the latter had both inspiring and mitigating features. Above all, it could still inspire lively art and craftsmanship. Despite the decline of glass-painting and the proliferation of mass-produced sculpture by ecclesiastical contractors, the great gothic tradition survived well into the reign of Henry VIII. During the half-century preceding the Reformation numerous splendid churches were still being built or extended. Parish guilds continued to flourish, funds were raised by church ales and other entertainments, devotional and secular life interpenetrated each other and, in a world which afforded the average man little indoor space and privacy, the churches were in a real sense the homes of the people.

Since Pugin idealised medieval art and life in contrast with the commercial ugliness and the cold charity of Victorian times, it has not been easy for Englishmen to attain a just view of the changes which swept across their religious culture during the sixteenth century. A more exact knowledge of the social background of medieval art and architecture has struck some heavy blows at Puginesque sentiment. Were not these attractive creations often commissioned by wealthy magnates anxious to buy their way into heaven, or by superstitious worldlings who subscribed to building funds by buying indulgences? Do not the works themselves show that superstition and legend constantly stood at the elbows of designers and carvers? Where lay communities genuinely supplied the means, did they not pay more regard to pretty fictions about the saints than to the searching demands of Pauline theology? When actually Christocentric, did not popular art and literature concentrate unduly upon such favourite themes as the Passion and the Nativity, to the neglect of a fuller and more balanced presentation of Christ's life and teaching? Such questions have been asked by scholars in their zeal to deflate that absurd Victorian romanticism which threw the age of the Reformation into a false perspective.[15] A converse danger has now arisen, at least for those whose religious beliefs occasion no vested interest in the credit of the Middle Ages. After all, scholarship equally respectable can support the existence of a genuine fervour alongside the admitted mundane and mechanical aspects of late medieval patronage. Such fervour may occasionally appear even in the most workaday sources. As it happens, we still have the accounts for the building of the superb steeple of Louth, which in its three hundred feet of soaring grace still bears witness to the devotion and pride of a little town standing somewhat apart from the mainstreams of Tudor England. This marvellous structure was begun in 1501, and over a period of fourteen years it cost over £305. At last, on the eve of Holy Rood Day 1515 the weathercock was erected, 'there being Will Ayleby, parish priest, with many of his brother-priests there present, hallowing the said weathercock and the stone that it stands upon, and so conveyed upon the said broach; and then the said priests singing *Te Deum laudamus* with organs; and then the kirkwardens garte [made] ring all the bells, and caused all the people there being to have bread and ale, and all to the loving of God, Our Lady and All Saints.'[16] It was surely no calculating heart which dictated these words.

The pre-Reformation decades also retained literary forms at once popular and religious, forms which nevertheless vanished without obvious successors amid the multifarious changes of the sixteenth century. We should enter no controversial ground in expressing an aesthetic preference for the delightful macaronic poems and carols of the fifteenth century as compared with the jog-trot of the metrical psalms inflicted by Sternhold and Hopkins upon the mid-Tudor and later generations of Englishmen. Again, the York, Coventry and Chester mystery plays, though already becoming archaic, survived the first onset of Protestant belief through their genuine popularity among the common townspeople. Ultimately, however, these plays foundered upon the hostility of Elizabethan Puritanism.[17]

Cultural forms die; new ones are born. During the century which followed Elizabeth's accession Protestantism itself was to create a great religious literature. The virility of medieval religious art and drama had lain in their power to present Christian belief in pictorial forms. A dual change occurred during the sixteenth century. On the one hand the attention of both artists and writers was increasingly captured by secular themes and patrons—this not only in Protestant countries. On the other hand, emphasis in religion shifted steadily from the image to the printed word, from pictures to literary ideas. The old idioms hence became progressively isolated from the culture of that expanding group, the literate laity. Such changes of emphasis had no doubt begun to take effect by the early years of the century but as yet they do not appear to have diminished the esteem enjoyed by that supreme dramatic and pictorial cycle, the Catholic liturgy itself. On the eve of the Reformation this liturgy had, as it seems to us, its stronger and its weaker aspects. The Christian year, and in particular Holy Week, had been furnished with a sequence of spectacular services often of moving beauty and pertinence. On the fringes lay many half-secular ceremonies, devoid of genuine antiquity, inessential to Catholic belief and in some cases weakened by obscure symbolism or by over-boisterous congregational support. But apart from persons affected by the Lollard heresy there are few evidences of active demand for liturgical reform until, during the last years of Henry VIII, specifically Protestant ideas began to grip large sections of the nation. Thenceforward clear divisions of opinion became manifest at all social levels. The priest-led western rebels of 1549 dismissed the new English Prayer Book as 'a Christmas game'. Yet under Queen Mary, when the old liturgy was revived, the same phrase (in northern dialect, 'a Yule lark') was used against it by some parishioners of Rothwell in the West Riding, while a man of Brampton in Lincolnshire, seeing his vicar ceremonially opening the the church doors with the staff of the cross, exclaimed, 'What a sport have we towards! Will our vicar run at the quintine (i.e. tilt at the target) with God Almighty?'[18] This proletarian irreverence and popular scepticism, of which mid-Tudor records afford numerous examples, undoubtedly precedes Protestantism and stems at least in part from Lollard influences.

Popular Religious Knowledge

IF the growing intellectual ambitions of laymen and the extension of literacy imposed on the English hierarchy challenges which it failed to meet, one should not assume that the Church left parishioners ignorant of the creeds or of the significance of the mass. It is generally agreed that parasitic beliefs had attached themselves to the latter, but there agreement ends. Were these dubious notions fully rejected by the responsible theologians? How far did enthusiastic preachers and fund-raisers stimulate them? To what degree was the difficult doctrine of transubstantiation misunderstood by men untrained in scholastic philosophy? The factual research demanded by these interesting questions remains incomplete and the emotional partisanship they have always aroused contributes nothing to their elucidation. That certain vulgar errors were widespread is not in dispute, yet we are not entitled to assume that they vitiated the spiritual life surrounding the mass or that they justified the bitterness of Protestant indignation. Popular theology suggested that those who looked on the host would prosper and avoid blindness or sudden death all that day.[19] Special results were expected from a 'trental' or series of thirty intercessory masses. King Henry VII ordered ten thousand masses for his own soul at the rate of sixpence apiece, at least half as much again as the standard fee.[20] Such beliefs clearly threatened the rite with commercialisation and might well cause it to be regarded in terms of merit mechanically acquired by wealthy investors in the future life. The miracle of transubstantiation itself was sometimes misunderstood in gross materialist senses, but in our present state of knowledge it would seem presumptuous to assert that this was generally the case. Earlier generations of the faithful had, it is true, been much regaled upon stories of consecrated hosts exuding blood and upon other miraculous indications of the corporal presence in the elements, yet too much of the Tudor evidence for such materialism seems to derive from prejudiced Protestant witnesses like John Foxe.

The place of books in the religious instruction of the people forms a better-investigated topic, but it also presents uncertainties. The *Lay Folk's Mass Book*, translated from an early medieval French original, had long circulated in a variety of regional dialects. Prymers containing the Hours of Our Lady, the Penitential Psalms and collections of prayers often occur in lay wills over the century preceding the Reformation. We might in fact be tempted to argue too much from these latter books. While over a hundred editions of the Sarum Prymer were printed before 1534, their texts are in Latin, though some of them contain in addition certain English devotions. English prymers can only have made their serious impact after the onset of the Reformation, since between 1534 and 1547 twenty-eight editions were printed wholly in English, alongside eighteen more in Latin.[21] The nervous attitude toward vernacular books which marked pre-Reformation ecclesiastics in England seems here far less intelligible than in the case of the Bible. Did this fear prompt the authorities to 'play down' doctrinal instruction by means of English books or is their paucity just an index of small demand? When James Gairdner wrote that 'no person of any rank or station in society above mere labouring men seems to have been wholly illiterate' he did not, even if his view be accepted, help with this particular problem, for literacy remains a highly imprecise term. And so far as it goes, the bibliographical evidence certainly does not prove that any considerable proportion of the laity followed or studied the mass in books. On the other hand, visiting London churches in 1500, a Venetian ambassador was impressed by the manner in which pairs of pious lay-people recited antiphonally from their prymers the Offices of Our Lady and of the Dead, together with the Penitential and other Psalms, the Litany of the Saints and other collects and prayers.[22]

Despite the limited rôle of English books and the relative infrequency of sermons outside the larger towns, we need not believe that lay people of average intelligence and devotion lacked reasonable opportunities to learn the elements of Catholic doctrine. Ideas were still chiefly communicated by speech, memories still unimpaired by oceans of print. When illiterate Lollards memorised long sections of the Bible, the dissemination of orthodox fundamentals can scarcely have depended upon vernacular books or even upon licensed sermons. Robert Aske, the pious and intelligent leader of the Pilgrimage of Grace, said that his northern men were 'rude of conditions and not well taught the law of God'. Yet even the North cannot so be dismissed in a phrase, for vast differences of opportunity existed between the shepherds of the remote Pennine dales and the citizens of York with their forty parish churches. And especially in relation to the religion of provincial townsmen, modern writers have too little to say of the friars, whose influence was not in fact killed by Chaucer's irony and who remained both active preachers and frequent legatees in wills during the early years of the sixteenth century.

In these vital matters of religious instruction, it seems risky to generalise concerning perhaps three million people whose material and educational backgrounds varied so widely. It may, however, be suggested that the vast majority of Tudor Englishmen were far less interested in theology than most modern books concerning the Reformation would suggest. On the other hand, atheism and agnosticism (as distinct from sporadic doubts about particular doctrines) scarcely existed. The conventional religion may have distorted or neglected some important Christian truths but England nevertheless remained a Christian country. Easily enough we may illustrate the fact that religious belief could not subdue a rampant greed and gangsterism which, having regard to that small population, seem in the legal records to dwarf even the social maladies of our own day. Yet without conventional and institutional Christianity the forces working for refinement and gentleness of spirit would have remained far less effective. If the medieval Church had made slow progress in conditioning this turbulent society, the medieval State had, by the fifteenth century, almost come to a dead stop.

Alongside the Protestant Reformation, the Tudor dynasty undertook another sort of reformation—the conditioning of society to the rule of law. Subsequent historians of this phenomenon have too often adopted a complacent version of the doctrine of progress, whereby God inevitably looked after his Englishmen. Ecclesiastical historians in particular have tended unduly to concentrate upon the battles between Church and State, forgetting that the two were always fighting the moral and social battle side by side. Dante's *De Monarchia* became a somewhat academic book even in its own day, yet its apotheosis of peace and law as necessities for man's spiritual development, its vision of the complementary nature of the functions of Church and State, might have furnished many a valuable lesson to those who have ventured to write of the Reformation without understanding the primary needs of society and the rôle of the State in ministering to those needs. The Tudor rehabilitation of law and government has enormous importance not merely for church-history but also for the religious history of Englishmen.

Mysticism and the 'New Devotion'

OUR reflections upon the orthodox religion have omitted at least one ingredient of much significance and interest—that deepening of the spiritual life in the later Middle Ages usually known as the *devotio moderna*. Though throughout Europe this movement tended to assume the form of a quiet pietism among lay people and secular clergymen, it derived from, and existed alongside, the more austere and exalted mysticism still prevalent within a small élite of the monastic orders. Its chief problem concerned the adaptation of these claustral techniques to life as lived in the rough world. Granting that the higher states of prayer remained difficult of attainment, even for cloistered contemplatives, the writers in the *devotio* tradition claimed that at least the lower steps of the spiritual ladder might, by the use of well-tried exercises, be ascended by men and women obliged to continue in the active life. At all its levels the new devotion aimed at a direct and personal sense of the presence of God. In general, such states of prayer were recognised to involve fleeting contacts with the Divine, though a few specially favoured practitioners might achieve long periods of union, sometimes expressed by the term 'mystic marriage'. Broadly speaking—and simplifying some far from uniform schemes of thought—three major phases of this spiritual journey were envisaged: the purgative way, pursued by means of self-mortification and good works; the illuminative way, a progressive series of 'experiences', often interrupted by periods of dryness and desolation; and the unitive way, begun by advanced contemplatives in this life, yet even by them completed only in the world to come.[23]

From the viewpoint of the Church, the claims of mysticism have always presented problems. Many of its phenomena are not confined to Christians, since analogous techniques and states appear in the literature of Platonism, Buddhism, Taoism, Hinduism and Islam. Moreover in many instances, some of them Christian, a dangerous trend toward pantheism can be detected. This was especially true of Neo-Platonist mysticism, to which the Christian school nevertheless owed profound debts. The notion that God is the whole of Being, that all things have their existence in God, naturally attracted some mystics since it expressed their awareness of absorption into the Divine Being. To cite an extremist, the seventeenth-century Quietist Miguel Molinos thought that the soul should progress through devotion to the Church, then through devotion to Jesus, then into a superior devotion to God alone, so aspiring to a nirvanic union with the Deity. Such tendencies often compelled institutional Christianity, both medieval and modern, to view the contemplative approach with caution. The timid saying, that mysticism begins with mist and ends in schism, enshrines a measure of ecclesiastical wisdom. Yet the Catholic Church always allowed this approach as one of the legitimate ways toward God, provided that it eschewed pantheist extensions and clearly admitted a transcendent God, above, beyond, and infinitely greater than his creation.

Transmitted from Augustine, Gregory and Dionysius the Areopagite across some six centuries to Bernard, Richard of St. Victor, Aquinas and Bonaventura, the tradition assumed an important yet balanced rôle in the versatile religious culture of the high Middle Ages. Then in the fourteenth century it developed one of its most subtle, diverse and influential phases, it refined its techniques and terminology and it began to express itself in a literature capable of emerging from the confines of the cloister. This was the age of the great German Dominicans, Eckhart (died 1327), Tauler (died 1361) and Suso (died 1366); it was the age of the Fleming Ruysbroeck (died 1381), called not without reason the true founder of the *devotio moderna*. In England,[24] the second half of the century saw two great contemplative masters in the anonymous author of *The Cloud of Unknowing* and in Walter

Hilton (died 1396), who as an Augustinian canon of Thurgarton in Nottinghamshire belonged to one of the least mystical orders of the Church. More widely circulated were the voluminous writings of the ardent Yorkshire recluse Richard Rolle (died 1349), a delightful prose-poet of religion but hardly an advanced mystic. These English writers did not confine their message to members of religious orders and Hilton's *Treatise written to a Devout Man* is specifically directed to laymen and secular clergy living 'a mixed life', both active and contemplative. Likewise on the continent, the concepts of mysticism were made social and subdued to pietism through the Brethren of the Common Life, whose schools and charities won such renown, and again through that classic of the new devotion, *The Imitation of Christ*, which soon crossed the narrow seas to rival our native mystics among the devout readers of Yorkist and early Tudor England. On the eve of the Reformation a variety of works inspired by the *devotio* were finding their way into the English printing-presses—not only several editions of *The Imitation* and of works by Rolle and Hilton, but contemporary manuals such as those by the two Bridgettine monks of Syon, William Bonde and Richard Whitford. The latter, among the most prolific devotional authors of the century, was not interrupted by the Henrician dissolution of his house from continuing a succession of books, some of them explicitly designed to help the middle-class laity.

Meanwhile a more heroic asceticism, more ambitious attempts to scale the peaks of contemplation, had characterised members of the Carthusian order, which in England had remained selective and small. The records of their London and Sheen houses display abundant evidence of such activities; even more illuminating are those recently discovered for Mountgrace Priory in Yorkshire. Here, even as late as 1523, worthy recruits continued to compete for each cell as it became vacant.[25] Genuine holiness had even proved a successful business proposition. Since its late foundation in 1396, Mountgrace had built up an annual income of more than £300, and it continued to receive substantial gifts from Lord Clifford and other benefactors almost until the dissolution. Today, as the only well-preserved Carthusian ruin in England, it rewards a visit just as richly as its Cistercian compeers Fountains and Rievaulx. Within sight of the desolate Cleveland moors, set under a steep hill with hanging oakwoods, the great cloister evokes the solitary life of the Carthusian. Throughout the daily round of prayer each monk remained secluded in his private cell with its tiny garden; he received his frugal meals through a hatch placed at right angles in the thickness of the wall, so as to spare him a distracting glimpse of the attendant lay-brother. Between the great and small courts rises the gaunt, undecorated church, the sole daily meeting-place of the brothers. Of all the monastic sites in England this one reminds us the most forcibly that the desert of late monasticism still had its fountains of living water. No wonder that even as late as the reign of James I, Mountgrace remained the object of secret midnight pilgrimages by 'diverse and sundry superstitious and popishly affected persons'. For once the folk-memory did not greatly err.

During the last half-century of monastic life, spiritual adventure at Mountgrace centred on two personalities. Richard Methley, born in 1452 and dying apparently in 1528, wrote in Latin at least five mystical treatises, three of which have survived.[26] In addition he translated into Latin *The Cloud of Unknowing* and *The Mirror of Simple Souls*, a French contemplative work of the thirteenth century.[27] The only one of his writings as yet printed is a spiritual epistle addressed to Hugh the Hermit, probably the recluse who dwelt in the hermitage still to be seen on the hill above the Priory. It is in English, for the recipient was not learned, and it instructs him how to order his day between work and prayer, how to avoid becoming immersed in rural society and how to sublimate his sexual impulses. 'In the beginning', concludes Methley, 'thou shalt feel some penance or pain, but ever after thou shalt live like a throstle-cock or a nightingale for joy, and thank God, and pray for me.'[28]

In his three extant mystical works this Carthusian describes some of the spiritual experiences which, beginning about 1485, befell him from time to time. On 1 August 1485, for example, he had just celebrated mass and was engaged in prayer when,

> God visited me with great force, fot I languished in such love that I almost expired. . . . Love, and the longing for the beloved, raised me spiritually into heaven, so that, apart from death itself, nothing was lacking to me concerning the glory of God, who sits upon the throne. . . . As men in peril of fire are only able to ejaculate the single word 'Fire', so, as the languor of love grew stronger, I could scarce think at all, but merely formed in my spirit the words 'love, love, love'; and at last, ceasing even from this, I wondered how I might wholly breathe out my soul, singing in spirit through joy.

These passages have a fairly close parallel in Richard Rolle's *Incendium Amoris* and describe the sensory experiences concerning which readers are cautioned by *The Cloud* and by Walter Hilton. In passages perhaps aimed against Rolle's emphasis, these greater masters dismiss such experiences as gifts made to weaker spirits and not to be confused with the higher contemplation.

Almost contemporary with Methley was John Norton, who entered the order about 1482, became prior of Mountgrace in 1509–10 and died in 1521 or 1522. This monk is also remembered by three surviving mystical treatises[29] and he too refers to ecstasies occurring as early as 1485. If Methley's experiences do not penetrate far beyond the foothills of contemplation, those of Norton seem to lie still more remote from the peaks of that arduous country. He provides graciously-phrased but rather trite dialogues between his own soul and God, and between his soul and his good angel. These, he says explicitly, took place in the spirit, a phrase which seems to exclude any claim to quasi-physical auditions or visions. Certainly he supposed them to have been divinely inspired. He also believed himself to have been granted visions of Our Lady, likewise *in spiritu*. On one of these occasions, surrounded by an assembly of the heavenly host, she revealed to Norton the salvation attained by a recently deceased Carthusian monk. The details are vividly described and may represent hallucinations or dreams provoked by extreme austerities and by concentration upon Christian imagery. Elsewhere we find clear evidence that Norton fell into trances, and we might well recognise him as at once a saintly religious and a psychopath. While his visions may have kinship with those described by Dame Julian of Norwich, they give rise to reflections far less subtle and interesting than hers. Yet if Norton hardly belongs to the cool and bracing world of Walter Hilton, it would be presumptuous to comprehend him wholly within the terms of psychiatric medicine, which has not advanced far in its analysis of such cases. Alongside Prior Norton's autobiographical passages one might place Maurice Chauncy's description of the rigours, visions and the occasional cases of desperate hysteria amongst the last generation of Carthusians in the London house of the Salutation.[30]

As in London, so at Mountgrace, the tradition survived until the Dissolution. The monk Robert Fletcher, who edited Norton's treatises and was also reported to have enjoyed visions, appears in 1539 on the final pension-list of the house. And four years earlier, when the noble London Carthusians were suffering martyrdom, some of their Mountgrace colleagues also fell under suspicion of treason. They were thought to have inspired George Lazenby, a simple Cistercian of Jervaulx, who conversed with Our Lady and had strange dreams, yet who heroically suffered death rather than accept the Royal Supremacy.[31] And one cannot mention these men without recalling the case of that other victim of Henry VIII, the Maid of Kent, who despite her trances and visions was almost certainly an epileptic, and far more clearly a psychopath, than any of the persons we have hitherto named. Yet all of them are related in some degree to that unfortunate tendency of late medieval mysticism—the tendency to attract emotional and idiosyncratic characters and to expect violent psycho-physical phenomena as signs of divine favour. Such characteristics became especially obtrusive among saintly nuns like Angela of Foligno, Bridget of Sweden and Dorothea of Prussia; while on a lower level they appear in our own Margery Kempe of Lynn. These were devotees who fell into foaming trances, interviewed angels, enjoyed charming if rather vapid *causeries* with Our Lady, or were helped to roll out altar cloths by the Christ Child in person. None of the acknowledged masters regarded such events as essential accompaniments of the contemplative life, while even the most sympathetic of modern authorities tend to see them as contaminations of the pure stream, as aberrations impeding progress toward the higher mystical states. Certainly if the reader turns from these sensationalists to Walter Hilton, he will at once feel himself in a very different world and in contact with an obvious spiritual aristocrat —lucid, sane, exquisitely discriminating, the exponent of an utter selflessness, a soul truly directed toward God and rejecting not only self-advertisement but that last infirmity of noble minds, the temptation to luxuriate in the memory of 'experiences'.

Mysticism and the Reformation

THE hysterical tendencies of the new devotion proved by no means its only weakness when it sought to diffuse religion throughout society, and one may feel a deep attraction to this movement without believing that it entertained any solid chances of averting the Protestant Reformation or of capturing the forces and aspirations which made the latter possible. Like Lutheranism, the *devotio* offered a personal, heartfelt and fundamentally non-scholastic religion. During the first two or three decades of the sixteenth century it remained, though within restricted circles, a lively influence. This much we know from the activities of its publicists and from certain well-documented biographies—for example, that of Sir Thomas More, who spent some years of his training with the London Carthusians and in whose household the graces both of humanism and of the *devotio* can so clearly be discerned. Nevertheless, the demands of contemplation remained too exacting and too technical for ordinary men. If one were to make encouraging progress, one needed somewhat exceptional powers of prolonged concentration, not to mention a measure of asceticism, detachment, self-criticism and charity beyond the resources of moderately devout men amid the bustle, squalor and lack of privacy outside the cloister. Despite the optimism of its devotees concerning a 'mixed' life, mysticism could hardly form the basis for a popular religious idiom; such a basis was more likely to be found in the saint-cults and observances or in Lutheranism, which (in theory at least) left everything to God and did not rely upon a 'method' or psychological expertise. One could not graduate to contemplation through the cults; they had to be thoroughly exorcised and unlearned, for they involved a clutter of imagery and creatures. 'Do that in thee is', says *The Cloud*, 'to forget all the creatures that ever God made and the works of them. . . . Yea, in this work (i.e. contemplation) it profiteth little or nought to think on the kindness or the worthiness of God, nor on our Lady, nor on the Saints or Angel in heaven, nor yet on the joys of heaven.'

Again, the *devotio* did not prove well equipped to inspire a Catholic resistance movement against the claims of Henry VIII. In lay society at least, it tended to create quietist individuals rather than schools of thought or propaganda. In England it gave birth to no organisations, no official leaders. It was not adapted to the militant principles of the Counter Reformation; it avoided rancorous disputation and its orthodoxy was not much concerned with credal asseverations or with such principles of church-government as the Papal Supremacy. To the age's expanding intellectual curiosity it remained hostile, and its manifestoes united to condemn learning as vanity, to dismiss rationalism, scriptural research and scientific knowledge as broken reeds in the world of the spirit. In the words of *The Imitation*:

> For though thou didst know the whole Bible by heart and the sayings of all the philosophers, what doth it profit thee without the love of God and without his grace? . . . Surely an humble husbandman that serveth God is better than a proud philosopher that, neglecting himself, laboureth to understand the course of the heavens.

These were not the accents of men likely to steer the course of the sixteenth and seventeenth centuries, whether in Catholic or in Protestant countries. Amid the growing spiritual conflict and chaos, the *devotio* supplied no fighting creed. That small section of the English opponents of Henry VIII who were its beneficiaries—More, for example, and the London Carthusians—did not base their resistance upon its principles but upon a series of historical and rational assertions centring around the ideal of a Christendom united under papal leadership. Elsewhere, despite its intrinsic orthodoxy, the diffused pietism of the *devotio* is at least as likely to have prepared ordinary minds to receive Protestantism as to receive reformed Catholicism, since it had diverted interest from cult-observances, from the hierarchical chain of command, from the legal mechanisms and the organisation-men of the Church. Yet in the last resort a movement so retiring cannot be thought to have supplied decisive reinforcement to either Reformation or Counter Reformation. The genius of the new devotion has sometimes been compared with that of Quakerism. From our English viewpoint the story of the nation would have been poorer without either of these movements, yet neither of them noticeably deflected the march of our history.

Protestant England lacked niches for the mystical life and for the types of piety which were its derivatives. Despite his admiration for Tauler and for the Brethren of the Common Life, Luther propounded a basically different solution for the dilemma of mankind. Still more remote was Calvinism, and as the later Reformation developed under this second influence, English Protestants were unlikely to take even an academic interest in mystical contemplation. On the other hand, amongst Catholic Englishmen the old arts did not abruptly perish. In the reign of Mary, Richard Whitford was still publishing, and the Yorkshire priest Robert Parkyn still writing, devotional essays with affinities to Rolle, Hilton and *The Imitation*. During the same years the Dominican William Peryn also retained lively impressions from his medieval guides. Yet Peryn, a more characteristic figure of the mid-century than either Whitford or Parkyn, closely based his spiritual exercises upon the work of the Fleming Nicholas van Ess, whom he had met when in exile at Louvain.[32] Here he stood at the parting of the ways, since van Ess had introduced him to a devotion far more 'modern': that of St. Ignatius Loyola, whose ordered thematic meditations and vivid use of mental imagery stand so sharply distinguished from the methods and values of medieval contemplation.

The most remarkable of the English Catholic *émigrés* to continue in the older tradition was the Capuchin Benet Canfield (died 1611), an original mystic who instructed Père Joseph, the 'Grey Eminence' of Richelieu and many other notable Frenchmen, but exercised little influence in England.[33] Not long afterwards Father Augustine Baker (died 1641)[34] was still introducing his English nuns at Cambrai to Richard Rolle and Walter Hilton, yet he was remarking that by now a Latin translation would help them to understand Hilton's antiquated English! Baker himself wrote a famous guide to the spiritual life; toward the earlier mystics it often shows insight as well as scholarship. Yet his original experience and personal achievement were exaggerated by his Benedictine biographer Serenus Cressy, the chaplain of Lady Falkland and after the Restoration a servant to Queen Catherine of Braganza. Cressy (died 1674) may be claimed as the last enthusiastic student of the old tradition before the long period of neglect. By his generation we are dealing with antiquaries rather than practitioners; indeed, in this field of mysticism the whole seventeenth century has an air of revival rather than one of survival. Inexorably the delicate flowers of medieval spirituality had been uprooted by the river in spate and borne away to remote crannies in a backwater of our national life.

2 The Abortive Reformation

The Rise of Lollardy

THAT JOHN WYCLIFFE and his followers anticipated many of the key-doctrines of Protestantism has never been in dispute. The man himself remains in some respects a mystery; we know so much of his thought, so little of his thoughts, so little of the inner sources of his radicalism. An obstinate North-Country mind endowed with the subtleties of the Oxford schools; a combination of disappointed careerist, temperamental rebel, sincere reformer of immense moral courage; all these and yet further complexities seem to dwell side by side.[1] During his last six years (1378–1384) Wycliffe was no longer a mere academic radical or a mere revivalist. By all the standards of his time he had become a manifest revolutionary and heresiarch. He accepted the Bible as the one sure basis of belief and demanded that it should freely be placed in lay hands. Improving upon the predestinarian doctrines of Archbishop Bradwardine (died 1349), he restricted the true Church to those persons whom God had predestined to salvation. He rejected the doctrine of transubstantiation as a historical novelty and as philosophically unsound, urging that the body and blood of Christ were present in the eucharist not corporally but *sacramentaliter, spiritualiter et virtualiter*. In some passages he seems even to approach receptionism—the doctrine that the efficacy of the consecrated elements depends upon the spiritual state of the communicant. He shared most of the bold anticlerical and erastian doctrines for which, very shortly before his birth, Marsiglio of Padua had been excommunicated. Upon the Papal Supremacy Wycliffe had long cast doubts; he had likewise advocated clerical marriage, denounced monasticism and placed fanatical emphasis upon the need to disendow a rich and mundane clergy. Anticipating the Lutheran glorification of the godly prince, he elevated temporal rulers above human laws and invested them and other lay magnates with the sacred duty of reforming the Church. Perhaps the only major doctrine of the sixteenth-century Reformers which Wycliffe cannot be said to have anticipated was that of Justification by Faith Alone.

Upon the Reformation abroad he exerted appreciable if indirect influences. John Huss, though affected also by continental predecessors, clearly acknowledged his own teaching to have been inspired by that of Wycliffe; in any case his extensive and often verbal borrowings from the Englishman prove this fact to the hilt. The Hussite Reformation in Bohemia appealed vividly to Luther's generation, which saw in it the sole example of a kingdom which had not only overturned the age-old structures of Church and State but had continued in defiance for a century. Appalled by the anticlericalism of the English Reformation Parliament, Bishop Fisher was quick to recall this warning precedent. On the other hand, the direct influence of Wycliffe's works upon the German and Swiss Reformers cannot be regarded as crucial, even though his name was not forgotten by them, and though in 1525 his *Trialogus* was printed at Basel.

Meanwhile in England Wycliffe's teaching underwent strange modifications and vicissitudes.[2] Despite its complex and scholastic exposition in his Latin works, it soon found vulgarisers and translators who wrote *The Wycket* and other English pamphlets falsely ascribed to Wycliffe's own pen. Within a very few years of his death these doctrines developed a widespread appeal among townsmen, merchants, gentry and even among some of the lower clergy. There were limits to their appeal. The economic restiveness of the peasantry did not in general disturb their doctrinal conservatism, while the revolutionary character of the Wycliffite manifestoes, together with the attack on transubstantiation, alienated the great majority of the ruling and propertied classes. John of Gaunt, who had formerly utilised Wycliffe in a political campaign against the bishops, seems to have protected him while he wrote the last works in his rectory at Lutterworth, yet neither John nor the other magnates were now prepared to back the heresiarch, as in earlier years they had backed the anticlerical reformer. Thus, despite the enthusiasm of a group of knights at court, the Lollards lost any real chance of laying their hands upon the levers of the State. Not in fact until the death of Henry VIII was any Protestant group destined to gain full control of this mechanism.

The earliest Wycliffite cell consisted of the Oxford clerks headed by Nicholas Hereford, who is thought to have made the first Lollard translation of the Scriptures, a deliberately literal and therefore rather unreadable version. In November 1382 these men were forced into submission by Wycliffe's old enemy Archbishop Courtenay, who drove Hereford into exile. There harsh experiences broke his spirit, and when in later years he returned, it was only to recant. At the moment of Courtenay's triumph in Oxford, the term 'Lollard' was applied to the sect in a sermon by the Irish Cistercian Henry Crump; a Middle Dutch word meaning 'mumbler' or 'mutterer' of prayers, it had long been applied to the Beghards and other Netherlandish pietists whose orthodoxy was suspect. In this same year a new and predominantly lay group developed around Leicester, where the message had been brought by Hereford's friend Philip Repingdon, an Augustinian canon of St. Mary's in the Fields near that town. Though Repingdon himself soon conformed and ultimately became a persecuting Bishop of Lincoln, the heresy continued to spread in the Midlands and the Home Counties. Wycliffe's own secretary John Purvey furthered its progress by compiling a much more approachable translation of the Bible, the basis of the Lollard versions which were to continue circulating in manuscript until the middle years of Henry VIII.

In the last decade of the fourteenth century there emerged in the House of Commons a vocal group of Lollard partisans counting among its backers several of the household knights of the young King Richard II. It was this parliamentary group which in 1395 formulated the 'Twelve Conclusions', the first manifesto of what had now become far more than an academic heresy. The document, significantly drawn up in English, deserves attention as a statement of those Lollard teachings which were to linger so tenaciously into the period of the Protestant Reformation. It condemns the subordination of the English Church to Rome, together with transubstantiation, clerical celibacy and its untoward moral consequences, the consecration of physical objects (as akin to necromancy), prayers for the dead, pilgrimages, images and the excessive preoccupation of the Church with the arts and crafts. In addition it denounces the work of prelates as temporal rulers and judges, declares all forms of warfare contrary to the teaching of the New Testament and denies that confession to a priest is necessary for salvation.

The 'Twelve Conclusions' are a list of reform-demands and hence fail to stress the two chief positive teachings now axiomatic to Lollard partisans—that the clergy should emphasise preaching rather than the sacraments and that the vernacular Bible should be freely placed in the hands of the laity, learned and unlearned alike. These numerous denials and assertions cover the large majority of charges which we find brought against Lollard heretics in the records of the ecclesiastical courts. The summaries attempted by later anti-Lollard writers like Thomas Netter and Bishop Reginald Pecock also correspond, allowing for their inevitable hostility, with the 'Twelve Conclusions'. It should not, however, be supposed that every Lollard defendant was charged with a wide selection from these beliefs or that all the Lollard groups and individuals showed uniform emphases. Persecution forced Lollardy to become a surreptitious congregational sect, lacking effective national leaders and hence precise formularies. Moreover, like most religions which inclined to Biblical fundamentalism and encouraged judgment upon the Scriptures by unqualified persons, it inevitably developed a fringe of cranks. Here, however, we reach a difficult subject, for in some court-cases the articles of accusation were doubtless based upon the testimony of foolish or malevolent witnesses. Both ecclesiastical and lay courts often showed gross unfairness toward defendants of any sort. Another difficulty arises when we attempt to distinguish between the genuine Lollards and the sceptics who may have been encouraged by Lollardy yet were motivated by incredulity rather than by religious idealism. Altogether, the weak features of the movement become apparent enough, though a certain strength shines alongside its weakness. It zealously sought to recover from the Scriptures an authentic sense of the person and spirit of Jesus. It argued with force that the materialism, the pride, the elaborate ritual and coercive jurisdiction of the Church found no justification in the lives of Christ and his disciples as recorded in the New Testament. It made a special appeal to the underdogs of feudal and ecclesiastical society by permitting them a far more active rôle in the management of their religious lives. In short, it had many of the lively features which characterised the English sects of the Stuart period.

This proletarian character of Lollardy developed rapidly during the earlier decades of the fifteenth century, when the movement was stripped of its political aspirations. From their advent the Lancastrian kings backed the bishops in a fresh campaign against heresy. In 1401 Purvey was forced to recant, William Sawtre burned and the Statute *De Heretico Comburendo* passed through Parliament. These steps failed, however, to crush the Lollard parliamentarians, who produced bills nine years later to soften the laws against heresy and to distribute the surplus wealth of the Church between the King, a newly-created nobility and such useful institutions as hospitals. Then, in the early days of 1414, catastrophe intervened when Sir John Oldcastle, a leading convert imprisoned for heresy, escaped and planned a Lollard march upon London from all parts of the kingdom. Easily overthrown by Henry V at St. Giles' Fields, this rash gathering resulted in numerous arrests of leaders and suspects. Deprived of influential backing the cause was obliged to move underground. Though a Lollard political plot came to official notice as late as 1431, the devotees of the fifteenth century had in general abandoned their hopes of winning over the dominant classes of the realm. Lollardy became a pertinacious rather than a heroic faith, occupying quiet groups of tradesmen and artisans, but here and there attracting a few priests, merchants and professional men. From the mid-century the record of prosecutions becomes less frequent, and we are left wondering whether the number of adherents had declined or whether in that troubled period Church and State lacked the opportunity and the zeal to persecute. If, however, a real decline occurred, there must certainly have followed a marked revival in the last decade of the century. From about the year 1490 we hear with ever-increasing frequency of Lollard heretics and of official attempts to obliterate the sect. This fact has an obvious interest for historians of the English Reformation.

Lollard Survival

THE former tendency to overlook the evidence for early Tudor heresy was in some measure due to the distaste of once-fashionable historians[3] for the most informative of our sources, the *Acts and Monuments* of John Foxe. The martyrologist, who was a large-scale compiler rather than a fastidious historian, showed immense industry in amassing documentary information even if his standards of accuracy are not those of modern scholarship. When all due reservations have been made, it cannot sanely be maintained that Foxe fabricated this mass of detailed and circumstantial information about early Tudor Lollardy. To have done so would have necessitated diabolical inventive powers and erudition, including a study of the parish registers of Buckinghamshire, in which a large proportion of the surnames and several of the actual persons occur. Such wholesale forgery would also have been highly foolish at a date (Foxe was collecting these materials from about 1552 onwards) when so many of the people and the events remained well within living memory. Again, no forger would have given, as Foxe gives, a host of precise references to episcopal records. In some cases he receives detailed support from surviving documents; in others his sources have clearly been lost. That this view involves no guesswork can be illustrated from the situation in regard to the York archiepiscopal records. In this diocese we have details of well over seventy cases brought against heretics during the reigns of Henry VIII and Mary, but of these only some half-dozen come from the archbishops' formal registers. The rest are mainly derived from certain surviving act books of the court of audience.[4] Yet in most dioceses the equivalent of these York act books are today completely or almost wholly missing. At Lincoln, for example, there are no longer act books covering those periods of persecution by Bishops Smyth and Longland which Foxe describes; hence Foxe cannot for a moment be charged with fabrication simply because the surviving Lincoln records do not provide close corroboration.

Bishops' registers are indeed most selective compilations and usually preserve only a few 'model' cases. Nevertheless we should expect, if Lollardy were indeed common, to find in them at least a number of scattered cases. This in fact we do find. The present writer is acquainted with seventeen or eighteen episcopal registers of the period 1490 to 1530, and every one shows at least some Lollard cases.[5] Fresh examples are continually coming to light in hitherto unknown registers and court books, while other sequences of information occur in the London chronicles, in the significations of excommunication at the Public Record Office, in the State papers and many other secular sources. Even if Foxe had never written, we should still know a great deal concerning Tudor Lollardy, some of it unknown to Foxe himself. Our complaint against Foxe should not be one of exaggeration but one of incompleteness, a charge which might incidentally be supported by the fact that at least eighteen known Lollard martyrs do not appear in his pages.

We now stand in a position to attempt a summary sketch of the distribution and nature of heresy in early Tudor England. That its inspiration was overwhelmingly Wycliffe, at least until about 1530, would not for a moment be disputed by anyone who read the original texts and who had even an elementary acquaintance with earlier Lollard processes.

In the early decades of the sixteenth century the most striking group of Lollard communities was to be found in the Chiltern area of Buckinghamshire, then near the southern extremity of the great diocese of Lincoln.[6] Amersham, a prominent centre in 1414, 1425 and 1461, had again developed into a considerable focus of Lollardy by 1495. In 1506 or 1507 Bishop Smyth dealt with over sixty heretics here and over twenty at Buckingham. All these recanted and did penance, except two who were ultimately burned. There were further abjurations in 1508, while some of the Buckinghamshire heretics are known to have attended Colet's sermons at St. Paul's and expressed warm approval for his reforming views. In 1521 Bishop Longland attacked them on a larger scale. Nearly 350 persons were accused before him in the long and complex proceedings preserved in such detail by Foxe. We do not know how many of these people were convicted, but the martyrologist records six as executed (four of whom appear also in the significations) and about fifty abjurations. Perhaps the real severity of the blow arose from the demoralised recriminations amongst the accused. By far the greater number of the accusers were themselves reported as heretics; wives and husbands informed against each other; parents accused their offspring and vice versa; several people gave evidence against their instructors in Lollard doctrine. It says something for the substantial integrity of Foxe that he did not 'edit' this material, for it furnished a Protestant hagiographer with singularly feeble propaganda. The heretical doctrines he mentions had all been familiar since the earliest days of Lollardy—disbelief in transubstantiation, reading the English Scriptures, using rude expressions about church bells, saints' images, pilgrimage, purgatory and the claim that the Pope could release souls from the latter on the payment of money. Dissent was sometimes expressed in coarse, home-made terminology. One heretic called the image on the rood 'Block-almighty'; another, referring to transubstantiation, said that he threshed God Almighty out of straw; a third, hearing the bell in a country steeple, said, 'Lo, yonder is a fair bell, an it were to hang about any cow's neck in this town.'

Further important heretical cells existed in the diocese of London, both in the city itself and in the county of Essex.[7] The London chroniclers report a steady succession of offenders going to the stake or doing public penance throughout the reign of Henry VII. Bishop Fitzjames prosecuted at least forty offenders in 1510 and another thirty-seven in 1517, on each of these occasions two relapsed heretics being burned. Of these four victims, three abjured, were reconciled to the Church and then consumed by fire amid the consolations of the faith. Meanwhile in 1514 the affair of Richard Hunne, the heretical merchant who was found hanged in the episcopal prison at St. Paul's, convulsed the city and provoked a crisis between Church and State which we must reserve for another context. This scandal does, however, throw some light upon the position of the Lollards. We cannot doubt that formal heretics as yet constituted a tiny part of the city population, yet the immense uproar which followed the murder shows that the citizens abhorred Bishop Fitzjames and his officials infinitely more than they abhorred a strong suspicion of heresy brought against an otherwise respectable neighbour. And when his chancellor was arrested for the murder, Fitzjames besought Wolsey to help him, 'For assured I am [that] if my chancellor be tried by any twelve men in London, they be so maliciously set in favour of heretical pravity that they will cast and condemn my clerk though he were as innocent as Abel.' And that the bishop did not say this in momentary anger appears from the fact that he repeated it some weeks later in the House of Lords, adding with gross exaggeration that if the obstinate jurymen went unpunished, 'I dare not keep my house for heretics.'

In the years succeeding the death of Richard Hunne a leading figure amongst the activist Lollards in London and Essex was John Hacker, known as 'old father Hacker', a water-bearer of Coleman Street and a convert of some years' standing. About 1520 this man was distributing heretical books at Burford and in 1521, being then also involved with the Buckinghamshire Lollards, was compelled to abjure by the authorities of the diocese of Lincoln. Associated with him, and more prominent in the subsequent years, were John Stacey, also of Coleman Street, and Lawrence Maxwell, of Aldermanbury parish close by. These two were prominent members of the Tilers' and Bricklayers' Company and had wide contacts both inside and outside London. Stacey kept a man in his house 'to write the Apocalypse in English', the costs being met by John Sercot, a grocer. From this Lollard background Stacey and Maxwell graduated in later years to Lutheranism and took a prominent part in distributing imported Lutheran books. Coleman Street itself, though within a few yards of Guildhall, was in fact destined to become for many years the centre of various heretical sects. Hacker's group had close connections with the Lollards of Colchester and of Buckinghamshire but its ultimate importance lay in the fact that it provided a ready-made organisation to promote the Lutheran book-trade of the late twenties. Another of Hacker's disciples was the leather-merchant John Tewkesbury, whom Bishop Tunstall persuaded to recant Lollard opinions but who went on to encounter actual Lutheran propaganda in Tyndale's book *The Wicked Mammon*, copies of which he proceeded to sell to others. Robert Necton, another Londoner who sold imported books in and around London, also had previous connections with the Lollards accused before Bishop Longland of Lincoln in 1521. By the mid-twenties the situation in the London diocese had become so notorious that Tunstall and his successor Stokesley were forced to attempt an extensive purge. Between 1527 and 1532 more than 200 heretics are alleged by Foxe (who gives the names and particulars) to have abjured after conviction in the diocesan courts. Of these people about half came from the city and half from Colchester, Steeple Bumpstead, Birdbrook and other places in Essex. By this time substantial foreign influences had begun to merge with Lollardy, yet the evidence strongly suggests that the old English heresy remained for years afterwards the basic, perhaps the predominant, element. Such few commendations of Lutheranism as we find in these circles prove no more than that Lollards had recognised kindred teachings in the German heresiarch and that they derived courage from the news that orthodox beliefs and ceremonies were being abolished overseas.

In Kent, especially around Tenterden, Cranbrook and Benenden, several Lollard communities were denounced to Archbishop Warham, who in 1511–12 received nearly fifty abjurations and delivered five offenders to the secular arm for burning. Here Foxe receives detailed support from the unusually informative register kept by the Archbishop.[8]

One of the less specific stories of Foxe concerns a 'glorious and sweet society of faithful favourers' in Berkshire. This had existed for some fifteen years when, soon after 1500, six or seven score of its members were forced to abjure at Newbury and three or four burned. Foxe obviously knew very little about this community but the diocesan registers of Salisbury show various penances done by Berkshire Lollards in 1499, eight cases being recorded for Reading, six in and around Faringdon, five in Wantage and one at Hungerford.[9] In the west Midlands, Coventry maintained its former preeminence. Foxe, who had lived there, gives a very precise account of seven 'godly martyrs', including a widow, who in 1519 suffered burning.[10] One of the fugitives from this group was captured on his return and so went to the stake alone. Concerning this and other west Midland groups, the recent discovery at Lichfield of a court book of Bishop Geoffrey Blythe has added substantial information.[11] In 1511–12 about seventy-four heretics (a third of them women) appeared before the diocesan court and their names include some given by Foxe. A few also came from Birmingham where the congregation may have been an offshoot of the larger one at Coventry. One of the Birmingham offenders is said to have associated with many heretics in Bristol, and some scattered references to heresy in this latter city occur elsewhere. To the late efflorescence of the Lollard heresy in the towns and cloth-making districts of Yorkshire and Nottinghamshire we shall shortly return.

Our sources afford much information on the social status of the Lollards. All save a few belonged to the common people—weavers, wheelwrights, smiths, carpenters, shoemakers, tailors and other tradesmen, 'of whom', writes Foxe, 'few or none were learned, being simple labourers and artificers, but as it pleased the Lord to work in them knowledge and understanding by reading a few English books, such as they could get in corners'. Craftsmen and town-workers bulk larger than mere husbandmen; as a class they were more mobile and enjoyed more contacts inside and outside their various trades. A small handful of secular priests, an odd friar and a schoolmaster also appear, while in London some merchants and middle-class men became involved. Of the four London heretics who resorted to a conference at Amersham, one was a goldsmith and one, Thomas Grove, a well-off butcher, able to give no less than £20 to Dr. Wilcocks, vicar general of the diocese of London, to avoid doing open penance. In general, however, the social background bore much resemblance to that of the seventeenth-century congregational dissent to which late Lollardy had such marked religious affinities. Of these people many must have been unable to read, yet illiteracy was then quite compatible with a measure of doctrinal and scriptural knowledge. Some of the Buckinghamshire heretics knew the *Epistle of St. James* by heart; this practical, down-to-earth book was a general favourite amongst Lollards, though the *Apocalypse* certainly nourished their visionary moods. Not a few were specifically charged with possessing, reading and hearing the vernacular Scriptures. Of other suspect works we hear most of *The Wycket*, though all English books, even the more innocent-seeming *Prick of Conscience* and the *Shepherd's Calendar*, tended to bring suspicion upon proletarian owners.

Without question, the influence of Lollardy extended beyond those areas where organised Lollard congregations existed. As already suggested, the diocesan records at York have recently yielded numerous hitherto unknown trials for heresy under Henry VIII and Mary. This enormous diocese comprised Yorkshire, Nottinghamshire and, until 1541, parts of Westmorland, Cumberland and Lancashire. In general, it can be described as conservative in religion and social outlook; certainly it contained none of the major centres of heresy. Between 1500 and 1528 records of only three cases of Lollard heresy have been discovered, though this low figure is doubtless due in part to the absence of diocesan act books during this period. Here, however, such cases may still have remained rare in that the Lollard 'revival', so apparent in many other parts of England, may not have spread to the North during the first two decades of the century. Whatever be the case, from 1528 the recorded situation alters and by the end of the reign about thirty cases of heresy appear, some in the registers proper but most in the act books of the court of audience, which effectively survive from 1534. Only in three cases amongst all these does the least sign of Lutheran or Zwinglian belief occur, and of these two concern priests. The rest, all of them involving proletarian offenders, continue to exhibit conventional Lollard beliefs and in no detail would the groups of charges seem out of place in a record dating from the year 1510, or indeed from 1410. By this second half of the reign of Henry VIII everyone had heard of Luther, yet this did not make every heretic a Lutheran, let alone an informed Lutheran.

The northern heretics during the later years of Henry VIII afford a spectacle of surprising complexity. Old Wycliffite tenets are beginning to merge with the new continental beliefs; meanwhile the crude radicalism, to which we have already alluded, repeatedly asserts itself, but almost always as an obvious derivative from well-known Lollard teachings. One man, objecting to saints' days, made ill-mannered aspersions on the moral character of St. Mary Magdalen but was so unwise as to broadcast them under the parson's window by the church of All Saints, North Street, York. Another case is that of William Bull, a young clothworker from Dewsbury, who went off to ply his craft in Suffolk and returned in 1543 with violent if now old-established views on holy water, extreme unction and the confessional. 'The font', he remarked, 'is but a stinking tarn, and he had rather be christened in the running river than in the said tarn, standing stinking by half a year, for when God made the world, he hallowed both water and land.' And why, he continued in substance, should I confess to the priest when I have 'japed' a fair woman? If he got the chance, the knavish priest would always be ready to use her the same way. But if I recite the creed and confess directly to God, calling to God with a sorry heart for my offence, God will forgive me. This is not only the authentic proletarian accent; if a trifle coarsely illustrated, it is also a true expression of Lollardy. Such authenticity did not, however, amuse the judges of the court of audience at York. The plain-spoken young man suffered a spell in the unsavoury archiepiscopal prison and after his recantation was doubtless glad to keep his pungent views to himself.

John Foxe tended overmuch to see Lollardy through prim Elizabethan eyes and to see it as a local phenomenon involving organised and informed groups with clear-cut beliefs. In certain areas such groups admittedly existed, yet outside them heretical ideas circulated freely about the countryside, in the cities and ports, in the little weaving-towns. These ideas were widely held, sometimes by people without special claims to piety, often by those who lacked pretensions to any heretical system of belief. Their importance may well have lain in their ability to sharpen in many minds the vaguer but widely diffused anticlericalism of the age, for whatever Lollardy involved it always involved anticlericalism. Such an atmosphere was described in the court at York by Richard Flynte, parish clerk of Topcliffe in the North Riding, who had refused to confess to his priest from 1540 to 1542. Charged with this offence, he admitted 'he was not confessed by the said time, saying the cause moving him to the same was that there was a saying in the country, that a man might lift up his heart and confess himself to God Almighty, and needed not to be confessed at a priest'. When the judges, anxious to trace the disseminators of this old saying, asked from whom he had heard it, Flynte replied 'that as he shall make answer to God, he knoweth not, nor yet in what place'. Likewise in Bishop Fisher's register, the Rochester joiner John Dissenger is found to remark, 'I have heard say in the city of London that we should not worship saints, but God only . . . also I have heard say that a man should not show his confessor all his sins that he had done.'[12] It seems of real significance that such opinions were circulating even in the slow-moving areas, while Henry VIII continued staunchly to uphold the confessional. Certainly it would be an exaggeration to call such men as Flynte and Dissenger Lollards, or to suppose them converts to Lutheran novelties. Such old heresies had been floating in solution, now here, now there, for generations; they had been attracting people because of the desire of many laymen (and indeed of some priests) to be free of hierarchical control and canon law, to become responsible for their own souls before God. As for Lollardy, the prime mover of this shifting world, it boasted its congregations, its preachers, even its heroes, yet in general it was an evasive, unheroic and underground affair. It lay far too low in society to achieve a Reformation unaided, yet through this very fact it could avoid obliteration by the judicial machinery of Church and State.

We have suggested that late Lollardy suffered grave disadvantages by its lack of national organisation. On the other hand, the inference should not be made that the scattered Lollard areas lacked means of inter-communication. Lollardy had its missionaries, one of whom we have already encountered in the person of John Hacker. A still better example is that of Thomas Man, who in March 1518 suffered burning at Smithfield as a relapsed heretic.[13] As early as 1511 he had been imprisoned by Bishop Smyth of Lincoln for denying transubstantiation, auricular confession, extreme unction and image-worship. Man was also alleged to have claimed that the holy men of his own sect were priests, that pulpits were priests' lying-stools and that the popish Church was not the Church of God but a synagogue. After a long term in the episcopal prison he recanted and underwent further confinement for penance in Osney Abbey. Contriving in due course to escape from the diocese of Lincoln he lived among the Lollards of Suffolk and Essex, but this area seems to have formed merely a base for his missionary sorties. At the time of his second trial and conviction a witness testified that Man had 'been in divers places and countries in England, and had instructed very many, as at Amersham, at London, at Billericay, at Chelmsford, at Stratford-Langthorne, at Uxbridge, at Burnham, at Henley-on-Thames, in Suffolk and Norfolk, at Newbury and divers places more'. Man himself confessed that at Windsor he had discovered a Lollard group formed by fugitives from the persecutions at Amersham, 'a godly and a great company, which had continued in that doctrine and teaching twenty-three years'. From this and other clues we can deduce that certain periods at least saw a flow of information and ideas between the communities of Buckinghamshire, of East Anglia, of London and the Thames Valley. Tudor provincial society contained large mobile elements and the part played by wandering cloth-workers in the dissemination of heresy has already been observed. The case of the young Yorkshireman William Bull suggests how the counties of Suffolk, Essex and Kent (where both native and continental heresies flourished in the reign of Henry VIII) were enabled to stir up sympathy in remoter and more conservative parts of England. Actual contagion as well as similarity of background seems to account for the fact that in Yorkshire late Lollardy and early Protestantism both became prominent in the clothing-areas of the West Riding and especially in Halifax and Leeds.

Connections between Lollardy and Lutheranism

WHAT evidence can be found of contact between the Lollard groups and early Lutheranism? How often did the Lutheran book-agents, who were active in England from the late twenties, find backers in people with established Lollard affinities? Considering the secret character of these transactions, it is surprising how many instances of them can be produced. We have already found substantial examples of transition from Lollardy to Lutheranism in the Coleman Street group centred around the persons of Hacker, Stacey and Maxwell. Many others can be added. The chief vehicle of early Lutheranism was Tyndale's New Testament of 1526 which, printed in Antwerp, was soon finding eager buyers among the native dissenters. In 1527 an Essex Lollard, John Tyball of Steeple Bumpstead, related in court how he and a friend had visited that leading colporteur, the Augustinian friar Robert Barnes, in order to acquire a copy. In Barnes's chamber at the Austin Friars in London they found several callers including a merchant reading a book. They hastened to establish their bona fides with Barnes and related how they had begun to win over the curate of Steeple Bumpstead to their views. They even produced a copy of their old Lollard manuscript-Bible:

> . . . certain old books that they had: as of four Evangelists, and certain epistles of Peter and Paul in English. Which books the said friar did little regard, and made a twit of it, and said, 'A point for them, for that they be not to be regarded toward [i.e. compared with] the new printed Testament in English, for it is of more cleaner English.'

Barnes proved himself a competent salesman, and he ended by inducing them to buy a copy of Tyndale's version for 3s. 2d. (about a week's wage for a skilled craftsman) 'and desired them that they would keep it close'.[14]

From what he calls a 'register' of Bishop Longland dated 1530 Foxe collected a story indicating a different aspect of the contact between Lollards and Lutheranism. In the house of John Taylor of Hughenden a group of eleven men, mainly from West Wycombe and Chesham, had met to hear one Nicholas Field of London who had recently been in Germany and had returned with fascinating reports. He first 'read a parcel of Scripture in English unto them', and then

> expounded to them many things; as that they that went on pilgrimage were accursed: that it booted not to pray to images, for they were but stocks made of wood, and could not help a man: that God Almighty biddeth us work as well one day as another, saving the Sunday; for six days he wrought, and the seventh day he rested: that they needed not to fast so many fasting days, except the ember days; for he was beyond the sea in Almany, and there they used not so to fast, nor to make such holy days.

Field also asserted that monetary offerings to the Church did no good and were not needed by their recipients. When one of his audience objected that offerings maintained God's service, he replied, 'Nay, they maintain great houses, as abbeys and others.' He then went on to declare that men should say the Paternoster, the Ave Maria and the Creed in English, and again that 'the sacrament of the altar was not, as it was pretended, the flesh, blood and bone of Christ; but a sacrament, that is, a typical signification of his holy body.'[15] With the single exception of this last expression (which suggests Zwingli, perhaps *via* Tyndale), there is very little in Field's discourse which a Lollard audience can have found novel. We are left wondering how much

Lutheran theology an agent like Field had in fact absorbed. Was he a Lollard who had merely acquired a superficial smattering of the continental ideas or did he in fact expound the central Lutheran doctrine of Justification by Faith, only to have it forgotten by these country Lollards who remembered the more familiar elements of his teaching? In his case, we shall presumably remain ignorant of the precise situation, but that some men of heretical leanings did establish direct yet wholly superficial contacts with Lutheranism can be illustrated from other anecdotes.

The diocesan records of Lincoln contain an interesting narrative concerning a group of Hull seamen, which helps to illustrate these mental complexities of the transition.[16] After returning in 1527 from a long visit to Netherlandish and German ports, these men talked too much and fell under suspicion of heresy, yet their examinations show that they had only skimmed the surfaces of continental heresy. In the words of one, they tarried five weeks in Bremen and found that 'The people did follow Luther's works, and no masses were said there, but on the Sunday the priest would revest himself and go to the altar, and proceeded till nigh the sacring time, and then the priest and all that were in the church, old and young, would sing after their mother tongue, and there was no sacring.' Asked whether he had visited Germany to learn Luther's opinions, this man answered: 'Nay, and they were not nigh Luther, not by fifty Dutch miles.' There are hints indeed that some of these seamen had already acquired an interest in unorthodox ideas before their visit to Germany, yet once there they had seemingly learned little about Lutheran doctrine. This type of contact is precisely what one would expect to find on the popular level. Yet one of them had acquired a copy of Tyndale's recently published New Testament and it seems probable that such a man would begin to understand continental Protestantism from the prefaces which Tyndale attached to the scriptural text.

As our examples have indicated, the old heresy and the new began to merge together from about the time Tyndale's Testament came into English hands. From this stage onward the turmoil of anti-Catholic teachings prevalent in Germany began to be paralleled in England, and if we seek to tabulate and classify individual heretics by means of neat textbook-labels we are clearly parting from realities. One cannot tabulate the waves of the sea. Nevertheless, for decades after the coming of Lutheranism, numerous prosecutions took place in the ecclesiastical courts, during which the accused exhibited a whole group of very characteristic Lollard beliefs and showed no sign whatsoever of the justificatory and sacramental teachings peculiar to Luther or Zwingli. In 1541 the English merchant Richard Hilles told the Swiss Reformer Bullinger that a young man supposedly burned for Lutheran heresies had in fact held the opinions of 'our Wycliffe'.[17] In the exceptionally well-documented diocese of York the prevalence of this neo-Lollardy remains marked not only throughout the later years of Henry VIII but even in the reign of Mary. One of the Marian offenders is even charged with the *crimen Lollardiae*, which in this official context probably represents something more precise than the vulgar equation of 'loller' with 'heretic'. Though this situation may be especially characteristic of heresy in the remoter and more conservative provinces, where Anglican and other modern Protestant forces were slow to infiltrate, the late survival of Lollardy even in London and south-eastern England has been spontaneously noticed by more than one local historian. Though Amersham gave a warm welcome to John Knox when he visited the place in the reign of Edward VI, the former Lollard areas of Buckinghamshire tended to resist both Anglicanism and Calvinism during the days of Elizabeth; instead they proceeded to evolve a congregational dissent bearing the suggestion of local continuity from the medieval past. In various parts of East Anglia and south-eastern England, even in the North at Halifax, a strongly Puritan or dissenting tradition seems to show continuity of growth from local mid-Tudor radicalism based mainly on Lollardy.

Though the survival of Wycliffite elements can thus be traced in the annals of English dissent into and beyond the reign of Mary, their latest manifestations lack any great significance in our national history. By 1530 they had already accomplished their two main services to the Reformation. In the first place fifteenth-century Lollardy helped to exclude the possibility of Catholic reforms by hardening the minds of the English bishops and their officials into a sterile, negative and rigid attitude toward all criticism and toward the English Scriptures. The predicament of Bishop Fitzjames amongst his unaffectionate flock of Londoners forms no more than an extreme example of a widespread situation. If their fear of heretics impelled them to refuse even the legitimate aspirations of a new age, the bishops would become more dependent than ever upon the King, and he more than ever enabled to bend them to his will. The second and more important function of the Lollards in English history lay in the fact that they provided a spring-board of critical dissent from which the Protestant Reformation could overleap the walls of orthodoxy. The Lollards were the allies and in some measure the begetters of the anticlerical forces which made possible the Henrician revolution, yet they were something more, and the successes of Protestantism seem not wholly intelligible without reference to this earlier ground-swell of popular dissent. The Lollards demonstrably provided reception-areas for Lutheranism. They preserved, though often in crude and mutilated forms, the image of a personal, scriptural, non-sacramental, non-hierarchic and lay-dominated religion. For good or ill, these emphases were prophetic. On the other hand, such a sect almost inevitably fell victim to its own qualities. Its hostility to institutions led many of its adherents or potential adherents into negativism, unbelief and incoherence. Moreover its apparent threat to social and ecclesiastical stability deprived it of power to capture the ruling classes. A Bible-religion, it lacked access to the printing presses until after 1530. So limited and debarred, it could become no more than an abortive Reformation. It created an underground and there awaited the appearance of liberators. When liberation finally came, it was compelled, like any underground resistance, to yield the leadership to regular armies with heavier and more modern equipment.

That Lollardy thus survived and contributed in some significant degree toward the Protestant Reformation is a fact based upon massive and incontrovertible evidence. This was, moreover, the impression of informed contemporaries. At the moment when the gradual transition to Protestantism was beginning, no one knew more of these matters than Bishop Tunstall. When in 1528 he licensed Sir Thomas More to read heretical books, Tunstall coupled the two heresies together: 'There have been found certain children of iniquity who are endeavouring to bring into our land the old and accursed Wycliffite heresy, and along with it the Lutheran heresy, foster-daughter of Wycliffe's.'[18] But five years earlier he had put the matter more directly and accurately in a letter to Erasmus: 'It is no question of pernicious novelty; it is only that new arms are being added to the great crowd of Wycliffite heresies.'[19] And that the clergy in general were still concerned with the old heresies as late as 1536 may easily be ascertained by a perusal of the *mala dogmata* then alleged by Convocation 'to be commonly preached, taught and spoken . . . to the slander of this noble realm, disquietness of the people, damage of Christian souls, not without fear of many other inconveniencies and perils'.[20] This long list of evil doctrines proves on examination little more than a splendid anthology of old-established Lollard opinions, mostly given in the crude terms of uneducated heretics. By no stretch of the imagination can the list of *mala dogmata* be thought an anti-Lutheran or anti-Zwinglian document. To the recent advent of Anabaptist doctrines, then limited to foreign immigrants, it may refer under two or three heads, but this element also remains subordinate. Altogether, if the English clergy were perturbed in 1536 by any doctrines save those of neo-Lollardy, they made extremely little of the fact. Conversely, by this time Protestant intellectuals had begun to see Lollard writings as serviceable additions to their arsenal of Reformation-propaganda.[21] Between 1530 and the death of Henry VIII, at least nine Wycliffite treatises are known to have been set forth in print by Gough, Redman, Bale and other publicists, who preceded Foxe in realising the usefulness of a religious pedigree, especially one of an all-English character.

3 Scenes from Clerical Life

Wolsey and Rome

WHEN HENRY VIII quarrelled with Pope Clement VII over his proposed divorce, the Church of England lay like a broad, rich and somewhat defenceless province between the contending hosts of Crown and Papacy. But long before the first shots of this campaign had been fired, the members of the English Church itself had also become locked in a series of tensions ostensibly related little to the main struggle but in the end exercising no small influence upon its result. Of such internal maladjustments the most spectacular and the most recent were those occasioned by the truly fabulous career of Thomas Wolsey, for whom the mass of Englishmen, clerical as well as lay, had developed an intense dislike. His tactlessness and financial demands in Parliament, his repression of the nobility, his development of Chancery jurisdiction at the expense of the influential common lawyers, his costly and ineffective foreign policy, his failure to execute radical reforms in the Church, his voracious appetite for other clergymen's privileges, the Roman basis of his authority as Legate, each of these features attracted powerful enemies. Above all, his personal arrogance, his enormous wealth and splendid ostentation were resented and freely contrasted with his origin as the butcher's son from East Anglia. To an increasing extent Wolsey's policy became based upon his legatine office; in England the justification for his unique powers would disappear the moment he ceased being able to manipulate papal jurisdiction. Hence he strove to keep Rome out of hostile hands, or at least to stand well with whichever European power might threaten to dominate the Papacy. And when at last in 1527–8 his King demanded of him the supreme act of manipulation, his fatal moment had arrived, for it so happened that another hand was now inexorably closing upon the controls—the hand of the Queen's nephew, the Emperor Charles V.

Though the enormous concentration of secular and ecclesiastical powers in the hands of the Lord Chancellor and Cardinal Legate came to offend the whole nation, the unprecedented extent of his legatine privileges gave rise to a special hatred amongst churchmen. The intensity of this feeling is but thinly disguised by their servile respect. He was not even Archbishop of Canterbury, but as *legatus a latere*, a special envoy of the Holy See, he had elevated a vast range of emergency powers into a permanent system centred upon his own person and offices. He could reform all clergy however eminent, reduce them to honest living, correct, chastise and punish them by himself or by deputy; he could grant degrees in theology, arts and medicine, dispense with canonical impediments to holy orders, appoint to benefices, legitimise bastards, absolve people from excommunication and other ecclesiastical sentences and penalties: all this notwithstanding any former restrictions placed upon legatine authority. Never had such a tyranny been seen in the English Church. It was small wonder that the University of Oxford addressed Wolsey as *majestas*; small wonder again that the chronicler of Butley Priory, one of the last of our monastic annalists, wrote of *gaudium humanum*, when at last he heard that the upstart from nearby Ipswich had died in disgrace.[1] And while in fact ecclesiastics were the main sufferers under Wolsey's system, it provided also a lurid theme for anticlerical demagogues, who did not stop to reflect that the King must bear chief responsibility for this portentous phenomenon.

Whatever its ultimate causes, the misuse of ecclesiastical wealth and privilege provided a heavy bludgeon to beat churchmen. Here Wolsey had not behaved with conspicuous tact. His natural son Thomas Wynter while still a schoolboy was dean of Wells, provost of Beverley, archdeacon of York, archdeacon of Richmond, chancellor of Salisbury, prebendary of Wells, York, Salisbury, Lincoln and Southwell, rector of Rudby in Yorkshire and of St. Matthew's, Ipswich. And to make the youth a trifle more secure as he grew up, he was handed further preferments until his annual revenues amounted to about £2,700, then over 250 times the income of a poor country parson.[2] It is true that his father prudently retained much of this fantastic income in his own hands leaving Thomas to live upon an allowance of £200, yet even this represented the income of a well-off landowner.

Wolsey's career exerted a dramatic influence upon that of Archbishop William Warham and hence upon the initial crisis of the English Reformation. A typical civil service prelate, Warham had in 1504 been promoted to Canterbury over the head of the more distinguished Richard Fox. This move to secure a subservient primate had distant repercussions which would have surprised its author Henry VII, since Warham's respectable mediocrity is among the important negative factors of our story. Flattered as an intellectual leader by the adroit Erasmus, he patronised humanists without participating in their scholarship. A considerable nepotist in his own right, he displayed no sense of urgency over Church-reform at a stage when reform need not have entailed revolution. From 1515 the jurisdiction of Canterbury was in large part superseded by Wolsey's legatine powers, and during the next 15 years Warham seemed even in his own eyes the mere shadow of an archbishop. As a long-standing devotee of Thomas Becket, he conceived on Wolsey's fall an ambition to tread the perilous path of his martyred predecessor, yet his resolution proved fleeting. At the moment of its confrontation by the naked force of the temporal power, the English Church had at its head no Becket to fight for its ancient privileges, but an old and broken man bred in the service of the King and long inured to personal impotence.[3]

As the manager of Roman authority in England, Wolsey undoubtedly stimulated the dislike of his fellow Englishmen for Roman jurisdiction. When Wolsey was hated, inevitably some measure of that hatred became directed against Rome. 'All his grandeur', wrote Wolsey's colleague Cardinal Campeggio, 'is connected with the authority of the Holy See.' Accordingly the outbursts of a hostile but still Catholic nobility were directed against Roman legates and cardinals in general. When on his fall he wailed to the Duke of Norfolk, 'My authority and dignity legatine is gone, wherein consisted all my high honour', the Duke was swift to answer, 'A straw for your legacy! I never esteemed your honour the more or higher for that.' Lord Darcy, though ardent in his attachment to the old faith, proposed a statute that no further legate should ever be admitted to the country. The Duke of Suffolk was mutton-headed enough to express the viewpoint of less exalted people: 'It was never merry in England while we had cardinals among us!'[4]

This attitude cannot be attributed solely to the malign influence of Wolsey. In English eyes the decline of papal prestige since the Avignon Captivity and the Great Schism had not been repaired by the triumph of the Popes over the Conciliar Movement. Even Sir Thomas More doubted in earlier life the arguments for the Papal Supremacy over the Church, and he claimed to have been reconverted by the King himself in that famous royal book against Luther. Though there is no evidence that ordinary Englishmen spent their time grieving over the sins of the Borgias, there were those who, like Wolsey's own secretary Richard Pace, saw Rome at first hand and were duly shocked. Cuthbert Tunstall, one of the most doctrinally conservative of Henry VIII's bishops, resented papal taxation and remembered witnessing the overweening pride of Julius II: 'I saw myself, being then present thirty-four years ago, when Julius, then being bishop of Rome, stood on his feet and one of his chamberlains held up his skirt, because it stood not as he thought with his dignity that he should do it himself, that his shoe might appear, while a nobleman of great age prostrated himself upon the ground and kissed his shoe.'[5]

While the love-hate complex of educated Englishmen toward Italy may perhaps already have been operating at the expense of the Papacy, we should attach far more significance to that ingrained chauvinism of the common people, which had blazed up so often in medieval London and which again so savagely displayed itself in the 'Evil May-day' riots of 1517. This indiscriminate emotion could readily turn, or be turned, against any foreign power. When Rome fell in 1527, alleges Hall, 'the King was sorry and so were many prelates: but the commonalty little mourned for it, and said the Pope was a ruffian, and was not meet for the room: wherefore they said that he began the mischief, and so he was well served'.[6] Such a mentality did not represent serious thinking about the Papal Supremacy, yet it must have provided fertile ground for the later suggestions of the London anti clerical pamphleteer Simon Fish, that the realm had for centuries 'stood tributary unto a cruel devilish bloodsupper' at Rome.

Whatever may have been the case in the remote reign of Henry III, this financial charge was quite untrue in the time of Wolsey. Peter's Pence, the only papal tax paid by the laity, amounted to less than £200 annually for the whole of England. The clergy paid larger, yet still far from astronomical, taxes. About twenty religious corporations yielded a regular *census* in return for privileges granted by Rome, while some 500 bodies, including cathedral chapters and religious houses, paid very small sums as 'procurations' or wages to the papal collectors. Much more important was the fluctuating income accruing to Rome from clergy who received papal provisions to benefices. In the cases of the bishops and great abbots a whole series of payments and fees became due under this head, the chief being annates or first-fruits. Between 1485 and 1533 the average annual total of all these, and some other minor taxes, stood at about £4,800. The hypocrisy, conscious or otherwise, of the Acts which abolished these 'intolerable and importable' payments, became manifest when Henry VIII, the new head of the English Church, proceeded vastly to increase its financial burdens. Whereas on the eve of the Henrician changes King and Pope together collected about £17,300 annually from the national Church, the King between 1535 and 1547 probably amassed an annual sum in the region of £47,000.[7] That the clergy were not in fact ruined, that a large part of this money came from richly beneficed clerics and that the real value of these payments had fallen rapidly with the inflation, these facts must also be conceded. All the same, it remains impossible to regard the early Tudor Church as a milch-cow of the Papacy or to deny that its 'liberation' from Rome resulted in a new and heavier financial bondage.

The Bishops and Higher Clergy

SOMEWHAT outside the intoxicating world of Wolsey and his favourites stood the bishops, whose normal functions in society were those of civil servants, ambassadors and royal councillors. They spent their lives working for the king—somewhat uneasily, it is true, for several tried to make amends by spending their last years in their dioceses. After Richard Fox had been supplanted at court by Wolsey he passed the last twelve years of his life at Winchester. He wrote to Wolsey in 1517 that he had utterly renounced 'meddling with worldly matters, specially concerning the war or anything to it appertaining: whereof of the many intolerable enormities that I have seen ensue by the said war in time past, I have no little remorse in my conscience, thinking that if I did continual penance for it all the days of my life, though I should live twenty years longer than I may do, I could not yet make sufficient recompense therefor'. Yet how difficult Fox sometimes found this renunciation of the great world! Within a few days he confesses to Wolsey that he is forever thinking of state affairs, as if 'I were daily attending upon you in the King's Council'.[8] This anomaly affecting the bishops does not, however, represent one of the more overt ecclesiastical tensions; neither does the occupation of English sees by foreign absentees. That of Worcester, it is true, was held successively by four Italians from 1497 to 1534; but this situation cannot be paralleled elsewhere during the same period. Apart from the small Lollard minority, who rejected episcopal authority outright, the mass of Englishmen were hardened to the absentee system by centuries of usage; it was not this aspect of episcopal power which they most deeply resented.

While the bishops spent so much time on the king's business, their dioceses did not in fact go untended. They delegated their spiritual functions to suffragan bishops, who in the early Tudor years were numerous; in almost every see they are found confirming, consecrating and ordaining. These were relatively humble figures, often friars and graduates in theology. The bishop's chancellor, a graduate in civil or canon law, was his chief legal adviser and by this time normally held in addition the office of official principal, presiding as such over the consistory court of the diocese. The sequestrator-general or commissary-general was the collector of the bishop's spiritual income, an important part of which arose from sequestrated benefices—those which fell into the bishop's hand during vacancies or when legal coercion was being applied to their refractory holders. Many dioceses had a sequestrator in each archdeaconry. The bishop's temporal revenues, forming a more substantial part of his income, needed their own hierarchy of stewards, bailiffs and receivers. Outside this very self-sufficient secretariat, the galaxy of episcopal, archidiaconal and peculiar courts ground through their ancient routines, keeping the morals of all men under observation; their notaries scribbled down the sins and quarrels of society in spidery hands across those countless thousands of pages with which modern historians are gradually becoming more familiar. The system was hard, mechanical and institutional. It held every temptation to avarice and careerism, and the lavish rewards, whether in the King's service or in that of a bishop, went to clerics who were primarily lawyers by training and never concerned themselves in any real sense with the cure of souls. It would not necessarily have been humanised by the more frequent presence of the bishops, since they stood far less close to their clergy and people than do their modern counterparts. Despite their heavy expenditure in the royal service most diocesan bishops were wealthy lords, each with several residences, a host of underlings and a long rent-roll. The curtailment of episcopal revenues under the Tudors was no doubt carried to excessive lengths, yet it probably benefited the spiritual health of the Church. And had the surplus revenues, together with the monastic lands, been more constructively employed by the Crown, England could have been made a charitable and educational Elysium.

The behaviour of the English bishops during the Henrician schism seems in no small degree to have been conditioned by their academic backgrounds. Few were theologians and most had undergone legal training. Of the lawyers, a small minority were canonists and by far the greater part had taken degrees in the civil law. Here lay perhaps the gravest weakness in the spiritual leadership of the English Church and one of the reasons why its whole thinking became pervaded with legalism and denuded of missionary spirit. This civilian emphasis harmonised admirably with the bureaucratic and diplomatic employment of the bishops; more important, it helps to explain why, almost to a man, they followed King Henry when he severed relations with the Papacy. They were already well attuned to the claims of the sovereign State. That the dispute over the Supremacy did not seem to them primarily one of doctrinal import may be seen in the active adherence to the royal cause of conservatives like Gardiner and Bonner, who followed Henry with alacrity but went to prison rather than accept Protestant doctrine under Edward VI. The claims of Caesar failed to alarm men nourished upon Justinian, and even a Royal Supremacy as sweeping as that envisaged by the tendentious theologian on the throne did not lie outside their intellectual orbits. Such academic influences seem to have continued in operation throughout the subsequent years. With the fall of the monasteries the episcopal bench obtained several new recuits in the form of distinguished ex-monks, most of them university-trained theologians. Like the few other theologically-educated bishops these men tended to become Reforming

Henricians, while their colleagues trained in the law generally adopted the standpoint of Catholic Henricians. Yet the significant fact remains that both groups marched behind the King.[9]

Just below the bishops, yet towering high above the rank and file of the parish clergy, stood a group of civil service pluralists—deans, prebendaries and archdeacons, who dominated the two Convocations and whose unflagging royalism contributed so much to the triumph of the Henrician Reformation. Of these we may take as an example Thomas Magnus, a striking figure in northern administration and diplomacy throughout the half-century preceding his death in 1550 at the age of 87. Born of middle-class parents at Newark, Magnus rose as a protégé of Archbishop Savage and took a doctorate at some foreign university. He held the archdeaconry of the East Riding from 1504 to 1550, a canonry at Windsor from 1520 to 1547 and another at Lincoln from 1521 to 1548. By the mid-thirties he was also master of St. Leonard's Hospital at York, master of the wealthy college of St. Sepulchre's near York Minster, master of Sibthorpe College, Nottinghamshire, vicar of Kendal, rector of Bedale, Kirkby-in-Cleveland and Sessay. At this time his eight benefices in the York diocese alone yielded him the enormous income of £814 per annum. Yet these great emoluments had not been bestowed upon Magnus in vain, for he ranks among the most devoted servants of the dynasty. For a time he served on the Privy Council; he worked as treasurer with the northern armies and participated in at least five diplomatic missions to Scotland, achieving close personal relationships with James V and Queen Margaret.

When in 1525 Henry VIII sent his natural son the Duke of Richmond to be titular head of the Council in the North, Magnus served as that Council's surveyor and receiver-general, rescuing its accounts from the confusion into which lay incapacity had plunged them. He was also the agent who in 1531 impelled the restive northern clergy to pay the King a large fine in order to avoid charges under the Statute of Praemunire. In 1533, now assisted by Bishop Rowland Lee, that indefatigable champion of law and order in Wales and the Marches, Magnus induced the northern Convocation to accept the unpopular royal divorce. Already at this time he wrote that his 'old body is now so oft clogged with infirmity and unwieldiness' and he had already begun to make his peace with a higher Sovereign by founding a grammar school and a song school at Newark. His last years were nevertheless to be spent in the less congenial reign of Edward VI. Despite his untiring devotion to the Crown he can have had little sympathy with Protestantism since, when his will came to be proved, it provided that a chantry should be founded to pray for the souls of his father, mother and sisters. But this clause had now been rendered void by the recent dissolution of all chantries. His executors also failed to gratify his wish to be buried in York Minster beside the superb tomb of his long-dead patron Archbishop Savage. Instead he sleeps beneath a fine portrait brass in the chancel of the parish church of Sessay. Should one wish to sense in one life the inwardness of the Henrician revolution, one should study Thomas Magnus rather than Thomas More.[10]

The Parish Clergy

TURNING to those lesser animals within the great ark of the Church, the parish clergy, we observe a body so heterogeneous as to defy generalisation. If they tended to lack spiritual and intellectual distinction, this fact, as both Dean Colet and More forcibly stated, was to some extent the fault of the bishops. 'All who offer themselves', wrote the former, 'are forthwith admitted without hindrance. Hence proceed and emanate those hosts of both unlearned and wicked priests which are in the Church.' 'I wot well', comments More, 'there be therein many very lewd and naught [i.e. wicked]. And surely wheresoever there is a multitude it is not without miracle possible to be otherwise. But now if the bishops would once take into priesthood better laymen and fewer (for of us be they made) all the matter were more than half amended.'[11]

The growing concern felt by the founders of Cambridge colleges for the professional education of the secular clergy has been stressed by Janelle, who also notices the anxiety of many humbler testators to ensure that their pious instructions should be executed only by priests of good moral repute.[12] And by no means all senior ecclesiastics were complacent over the situation. Apart from Colet one of its critics was William Melton, who had been John Fisher's tutor at Michaelhouse, Cambridge, and who served from 1496 until his death in 1528 as chancellor of York Minster. About the year 1510 this learned dignitary published a *Sermo Exhortatorius* on the vexed subject of clerical education and it was accompanied by an *imprimatur* from Colet himself. Melton here stresses the extreme responsibility and dignity of the priest's office, which in these days has been degraded by crowds of rude and stupid clerics. At ordination every aspirant should have a moderate grasp of Latin and be in a position to make further progress merely by private study. Otherwise, experience has shown that he will continue in notorious ignorance to his dying day. Here, declares Melton, lies the reason why so many country clerics take to dicing, drinking, hunting and wenching; if they begin in ignorance, how can they ever profit or delight in sacred studies?[13] This thesis cannot be dismissed as the prejudice of a former don, since Latin was in every respect the gateway to that mental life without which any rural clergyman was more than likely to run to seed. Melton's argument forms a strong indictment of the system whereby the direct study of the Scriptures had been sealed from non-Latinists, while nevertheless numbers of very poor Latinists were permitted to enter holy orders. Despite such strictures, some contemporary diocesan records show bishops ordaining several hundreds of men a year in circumstances apparently excluding the possibility of thorough examination and without due thought to their subsequent employment. Melton writes as if examination were a serious business, but in his own diocese, in the years 1510–11, 1,107 men were ordained to various orders, 265 of them to the priesthood, 248 as deacons and 296 as subdeacons. In the diocese of Lincoln at least 700 men were ordained to the priesthood from March 1514 to December 1520 and while on paper about 600 benefices became vacant during that period, a large number of these were held in plurality, so that nothing approaching 600 became available for the new ordinands.[14] It should, however, be stressed that such hasty over-production was exceptional; on what might be regarded as an average occasion, less than 30 clerics presented themselves before the bishop and serious questioning could well have occurred. The names of the rejected were not registered, but occasionally we hear of a candidate being told to study for a year or so before reappearing.[15] While many prominent clergy showed increasing concern for these matters from the early years of the century, Convocation began to propose effective measures only in 1529, when lay interference already loomed large.

While the Church could boast too little by way of vocational selection, many ordinands tended to be thrust into a clerical underworld, since they were ordained without adequate 'title', or spiritual function carrying a financial competence. Again, some clerics lingered permanently in minor orders, lacking the status and most of the functions we now associate with the term clergy, yet still apt to bring discredit on the whole profession. And amongst so large a body of celibates there were inevitably enough sexual lapses to give some substance to the meaner types of anticlerical propaganda. The lurid contrast between the exalted functions of the priesthood and the behaviour of a mundane (and often lightly punished) minority gave genuine offence to the pious as well as dangerous ammunition to the malevolent and the hypocritical.

For many a country parson life on six days of the week was not markedly different from that of a substantial yeoman. He farmed his glebe of forty or sixty acres in the common fields. He ploughed and reaped with his neighbours, and when he drafted his will it was as full of sheep and pigs and wains and sacks of malt as that of any layman. A vicar was paid in kind by the small tithes; he shared with his parishioners in the yield of the land and he suffered its asperity in time of dearth. Both before and after the Reformation tithes nevertheless produced an astonishing number of lawsuits and in the aggregate they must have made a marked contribution to popular anti-clericalism. A classic exemplar may be found in the quarrel of 1530 between the parishioners of Hayes, Middlesex, and their vicar Henry Gold. For various reasons, Gold also had his backers inside and outside the parish. The matter soon proceeded to large-scale riots and, with the parishioners coming armed to church, the Star Chamber took cognizance of the dispute as a threat to public order. The detail, exceptional only in scale and in complexity, occupies over forty fascinating pages of Dr. Elton's *Star Chamber Stories*.[16] Tithes had long lost their personal and quasi-sacred character; even before the Reformation, they were commonly farmed out to laymen and regarded as a mere rent. All things considered, the economic situation of the country priest was by no means richly privileged. While on the one hand he owed no services to the lord of the manor, on the other local custom might expect him to keep a bull and a boar for the use of the parish. His income might be burdened by the pension of a predecessor, which he had agreed to pay before presentation to the living. If his tithes were substantial, he often found them difficult to collect in full and he paid higher taxes than laymen of similar means. In a farming economy his lack of a family may have proved on balance an economic disadvantage.

By no means all the parochial clergy fitted into this pattern. The system of appropriations, once well-intentioned but now so harmful in its results, produced one sort of exception. A religious house to which a benefice was appropriated usually ordained a vicarage, endowing the vicar either with a stipend or with the small tithes and other minor revenues, while itself retaining the greater tithes. It might, especially if it were one of the numerous houses of regular canons, appoint one of its own members to act as vicar. On the other hand, it might appoint a mere unbeneficed chaplain or curate, paying him a small annual salary and thus making him dismissable at the will of the house. Both these latter two procedures seemed to outsiders, especially to critical laymen, modes of exploiting to the last penny the ancient endowments which should have gone to find educated and efficient ministers. In Lincolnshire 311 out of the 628 parochial benefices were appropriated on the eve of the Reformation, while Yorkshire then had about 622 parish churches of which 392 were appropriated. In the latter county the position was probably worse than in any part of England, since of th' 392 more than 100 were served by these poor, removable priests in place of vicars.[17]

The monasteries were the most flagrant but by no means the sole converters of parish endowments to new purposes. The Church was little touched by egalitarian concepts and in not a few cases the lucky recipient of several livings had nothing to recommend him save high connections. And while pluralities and non-residence sometimes provided the means whereby young men were enabled to undertake a prolonged university education, such grants were too often unlimited by considerations of need. Notable beneficiaries of the system, such as John Colet and Reginald Pole, came of wealthy families which could easily have provided for their maintenance. The royal physician Thomas Linacre likewise received several rich benefices years before he was even ordained priest.[18] Such cases were nevertheless exceptional. Though in certain episcopal visitation-records the absentees comprise anything between a tenth and a quarter of the total beneficed clergy, the great majority of them were licensed to be absent for what early Tudor opinion considered adequate reasons. Most were bishops' chaplains, diocesan administrators and ecclesiastical lawyers. Others were chaplains to noblemen, clerics afflicted by physical incapacity or licensed to go on a pilgrimage. We naturally hear most of those cases (no doubt a small minority) where parish affairs went badly astray under a neglectful *locum tenens.* And in general we should certainly blame the system rather than the rapacity of individual clerics. It says little for the mental flexibility and the pastoral sense of kings, bishops, founders and patrons that they could evolve no better method for the support of monasteries, clerical officials and students than one liable to injure the spiritual life of the common people. Yet by the same token the failure of their post-Reformation successors to achieve anything more than a slow and piecemeal improvement forms an equally depressing spectacle.

In addition to the poorer vicars and chaplains, the unprivileged section of the late medieval church contained several thousand chantry priests and—especially in the sparsely-populated uplands of the North—priests who served in small chapelries dependent upon a mother church. A chantry was normally a private endowment in real property to ensure masses for the soul of the founder and his kin, but often it had other functions which we propose to discuss at some length in a later chapter. The great majority of these thousands of stipendiary curates, chantry and chapel-priests worked for very small salaries ranging between £4 and £7 per annum; these already represented proletarian incomes and were destined soon to fall swiftly in purchasing power under the stress of inflation. Many rectors and vicars had little more; there was no economic difference between the unbeneficed and the poorest of the beneficed. An analysis has been made recently by Mr. Heath of the annual values attached to parochial livings by the great survey of 1535. In the fairly typical diocese of Coventry and Lichfield there appear 210 rectories and 187 vicarages. Of these 397 livings, 87 per cent were worth less than £20 per annum; 79 per cent less than £15; 60 per cent less than £10 and 10 per cent less than £5. Half the rectories and 72 per cent of the vicarages fell below the £10 level: the level at which, said Latimer a few years later, a parson 'is not able to buy him books, nor give his neighbour drink'.[19]

Observers of the period did not differ concerning the low intellectual quality of an underpaid parish clergy. Archbishop Edward Lee of York wrote to Thomas Cromwell in 1535 that many of his priests were so uneducated that they simply could not understand, let alone accept, the arguments advanced in favour of the Royal Supremacy. 'Doubtless many of our curates can scant perceive it. Many benefices be so exile, of £4, £5, £6, that no learned man will take them, and therefore we be fain to take such as be presented, so they be honest of conversation and can competently understand that they read, and minister sacraments and sacramentals, observing the due form and right. . . . And in all my diocese I do not know secular priests that can preach, any number necessary for such a diocese, truly not xii, and they that have the best benefices be not here resident.'[20]

Except in London and some neighbouring areas the resident parish clergy contained a minute percentage of graduates; armed with a modest grammar school latinity the average priest learned his job by the empirical methods of apprenticeship. Yet the very varied educational standards of the parish clergy did not necessarily correspond with the values of their benefices. Of this we may cite mid-Tudor examples amongst Archbishop Lee's own clergy. Marmaduke Atkinson, rector of Bainton (a very good living worth £35 per annum) was accused of incompetence in the Archbishop's Court of Audience by his own curate Edmund Pepper. The curate had seen Atkinson lingering at the altar unable to find the gospel for the day. When Pepper at last sent up the parish clerk to show him the place, 'he would not of long time believe it was the gospel for that day, and said unto the clerk that he thought that it had been longer.' Pepper had also heard him read out *nobis* for *vobis* and 'sound the accusative case for the ablative case and one case for another'.[21] At the other extreme in the same diocese there stood the relatively learned Robert Parkyn, whose curacy at Adwick-le-Street afforded him a stipend of less than £6 a year, since it had been appropriated to Hampole Priory. It is fair to remark that this assiduous student and writer inherited some family lands and that his brother, a fellow of Trinity College, Cambridge, sometimes sent him parcels of books by the carrier.[22]

When the time came to propound new schemes of church-government, these lower clergy confronted the government with an important but problematic class. From the viewpoint of Henry VIII they were not as 'safe' as the bishops. The unlearned had the conservatism of immobility, while even the educated, especially outside London and the south-eastern counties, were by no means familiar with books and theories (erastian, Protestant, humanist, or civilian) conducive to change or even to open-mindedness. And despite their limitations, despite the rancour which often existed between clergy and laity, the former continued to be a key-class upon which at least rural laymen relied in large part for the transmission of ideas. So long as the doctrine of transubstantiation found general acceptance, the humblest or most sinful priest, by whose hands the actual body of God was ministered to the faithful, preserved a certain distinction which set him apart from the common run of men. In the event of his treason this distinction did not, it is true, preserve him from the common hangman's rope and knife, yet the weapon of terror needed to be used but sparingly during the process of the Reformation, since the problem of seditious priests was rendered by various factors less formidable than might have been expected. Not a few of the clergy became involved in treasonable speeches or helped to lead the Pilgrimage of Grace, the Western Rising of 1549 and other rebellious movements. Yet these men constituted a tiny proportion of the whole body. We cannot doubt that a far larger group detested theological and liturgical innovation but nevertheless obeyed governmental orders. Robert Parkyn's narrative of the Reformation shows that he promptly executed commands which he regarded as heretical under Edward VI, while he died in office after a further decade of obedience to the commands of Elizabeth. Tudor government was not primarily concerned to open windows into men's souls and the parish clergy were in general modest and timid men, blessed at least in the sense that they were poor in spirit. Well aware of the limitations of their learning they remained content to follow in the wake of their bishops and archdeacons. They varied widely in their devotion to principles and in their degree of detachment from merely secular calculations. The changes of the age broke upon them but gradually, and during the whole reign of Henry VIII they had to swallow—apart from the overthrow of the Papal Supremacy—no doctrinal changes of substance. As for that Supremacy, the numerous other factors we have already mentioned and the lapse of time since its effective exercise in England continued to weaken its appeal. What little we know of the private thoughts of conservative priests suggests that changes in ritual and in sacramental doctrine, together with the abolition of requiem masses, troubled them far more than the severance of the Roman bond.

Above all, unless they were led by their superiors, the parish clergy had no mechanisms for making protests or planning resistance. In the two Convocations the archdeacons and other *ex-officio* members outnumbered the proctors of the parish clergy, but these proctors also tended in fact to be safe and senior men. The custom-ridden conservatives to whom the sharp-tongued John Bale gave the collective title of Doctor Dodypoll[23] were not potential martyrs for a Catholic ideal. And the upper reaches of the Christian Church have at most periods of its history been well populated by Dodypolls.

The Religious Houses

IF the secular clergy have received too little notice from historians of the Reformation, the regulars have perhaps received too much. It is indeed easy to overestimate the scale of English monasticism towards the end of the middle ages, since the shell had become too big for the oyster. The huge and romantic piles of masonry left on such sites as those of Fountains and Rievaulx or such immense converted buildings as those at Durham or Peterborough can prove highly misleading. Indeed, the tendency of English monks to overbuild in a manner quite disproportionate to their numbers had long ago presented them with one of their major economic problems. The total number of English and Welsh religious persons, which fell from about 12,000 in 1500 to 11,000 or less in 1534, was quite insignificant compared with, say, the immense and ever-growing armies in Spain. The nuns in particular represent a startingly small group; they numbered over 2,000 in 1500, falling to about 1,600 at the time of the Dissolution, and living in about 136 communities. An exhaustive survey for England and Wales shows at the Dissolution about 825 religious houses of all types.[24] Consequently a house of average size numbered about twelve actual religious persons, but even this figure gives little notion of the difficulties attaching to excessively small establishments, where discipline so often proved hard to maintain. A recent calculation by Dr. G. W. O. Woodward deals with 205 of the 'lesser' monasteries dissolved in 1536, for which we happen to possess actual or approximate totals. In these houses the total of religious persons lies between a maximum of 1,651 and a minimum of 1,557. This suggests a national average for the lesser houses of between 7½ and 8.[25] A good many places fell below this figure and certain of those which Wolsey suppressed in favour of his own new colleges boasted only one or two monks.

Needless to say, all these figures take no account of the lay officials and personal servants or of the corrodians—lay people who had bought the right to live as pensioners in monasteries. At the larger and wealthier houses the number of servants had tended to become by any standards excessive. At Rievaulx there were 122 for only twenty-two monks; at Gloucester eighty-six for twenty-six monks. The detailed household-list of 1538 for Butley Priory shows what a smaller but well-endowed house could do; it had only twelve canons but two chaplains, eleven domestic servants, a master of the children, seven children 'kept on alms to learning', three cooks, a slaughter-man, a sacristan, a cooper, three bakers and brewers, two horse-keepers, two maltsters, a porter, six laundresses, two bedemen and some thirty-four workers of all sorts on the home farm and gardens. The whole community at Butley thus numbered some eighty-four persons.[26] Despite such figures, it now appears that in the past we have tended to exaggerate this feature of late monastic life. Many of these dependents, especially the husbandmen, obviously cannot be accounted as evidence of luxurious living. Moreover, there exist numerous establishment-lists of the lesser monasteries made at the time of their dissolution in 1536 and these show a far more modest picture. In these poorer houses the domestic servants scarcely outnumber the monks and canons, whilst in the case of the smaller nunneries they number less than half the total of actual nuns. It would therefore seem erroneous to suppose that the rank and file of religious persons were lavishly attended or that the financial difficulties of the monasteries sprang primarily from the burden of swollen staffs. When, however, their reform or dissolution came under discussion, scandal tended to matter more than statistics. The term 'abbey-lubbers' had come into general circulation to denote the supposed hordes of idle and vicious servants surrounding the monasteries. And like all medieval servants, those of the great monasteries had a strong *esprit de corps* which could lead them into long-standing feuds with neighbouring townsmen and others.

At the suppression the annual revenue of all houses of men and women was returned at £136,362, a sum which probably covered about half the total wealth of the English Church and seems all the more impressive since for over a century the monasteries had received extremely few major benefactions. Yet, as usual, the gross figure conveys a false impression of the average actualities. The whole of the nunneries account for only £15,000, while the 'lesser' houses, constituting nearly half the total number, enjoyed less than one-ninth of this total income.[27] In their dimensions as in their discipline and social importance, the individual religious houses display extreme variations. St. Mary's of York with its superb buildings, its far-flung estates and its gross revenue of more than £2,000 a year lay only a few miles distant from Nunburnholme, with a tiny group of nuns living on an annual income of £10.[28] In material attributes and worldly influence the two resembled each other as little as a London department-store resembles a village shop. Again, the friars, who still mattered in the devotional life of society, were 'non-possessioner religious' and lacked landed estates or notable wealth of any kind. Not surprisingly, a number of radical thinkers and Protestant Reformers arose from their ranks.

Despite the controversies which have always surrounded the problems and the fate of the monasteries, they may nevertheless be regarded as the least mysterious and best-documented section of the Church. We know all about them we could reasonably expect to know, and reputable historians are nowadays not seriously divided about the facts. Our knowledge of the disciplinary conditions depends in no sense upon the reports of government hirelings; it depends upon a variety of more trustworthy documents and principally upon the frequent episcopal visitations to which most of the orders were subject. At least three large printed collections of visitation records cover the decades immediately preceding the Dissolution. They refer respectively to the dioceses of Lincoln[29] and Norwich,[30] and to the Premonstratensian houses,[31] which had their own visitors. In addition, several visitations of individual houses and of smaller groups have been published.

These materials need careful handling, for it is their business to record sins and faults. The hasty reader has every temptation to gloss over the many enquiries which reveal no shortcomings of importance and to bestow his attentions upon episodes more lurid and picturesque. Moreover, these are confidential enquiries unintended for the delectation of inquisitive outsiders like ourselves. The bishop usually saw each monk privately, and each lay under an obligation to reveal the shortcomings, great and small, of his fellows. Neither laymen nor secular priests have ever been so remorselessly dissected, and in their position any other group might have looked worse. The great majority of houses bore little resemblance to those sinks of iniquity which Protestant propagandists once believed them to be. In most visitations faults relatively venial come to light; there was, for example, a widespread tendency for monks and nuns to own articles of private property and to assume lay dress. Amongst the monks of Norwich, for example, we encounter some with exquisite purses and one with red silk bows on his shoes. The latter did not, says the record, blush to lift his frock before the prior and the junior monks so as to display his elegant footwear, while some of the novices appeared in top boots and hats with satin rosettes. Even the abbot of St. Mary's, York, was charged with sartorial magnificence, while the canons of Warter Priory were reproved by the Archbishop for wearing 'silken girdles ornamented with gold and silver, and gold and silver rings'.[32] Abbots and priors commonly maintained expensive separate households and luxurious tables; they often failed to present accounts or to consult the brethren on important transactions; sometimes they assigned leases and offices to lay relatives, who might exercise undue authority or prey upon the monastic revenues. Chronic disharmony between heads of houses and their subordinates proved by no means rare, though here we must beware of deducing a serious feud whenever a monk dutifully exposed the faults of his brethren to the bishop. Again, it would be unjust to assess late medieval monasticism from its voluminous documentation after the year 1530. During these final stages the threat of catastrophe hung in the air, morale ran low and many of the heads themselves were government nominees selected for their pliancy rather than for their monastic virtues.

When all these many qualifying factors have been taken into account, one is still tempted to think that no major section of the early Tudor Church stood more grievously in need of reform and fresh inspiration than did the regular clergy. That even the better houses had their few chronic misfits cannot occasion surprise when so many immature persons were accepted without serious tests of vocation and when no machinery functioned adequately to discard the failures. The pressure of episcopal authority proved unequal and spasmodic; a grossly inefficient or secular-minded monk could easily continue to hold important offices even after his failings had become notoriously apparent. A small house which happened to acquire a corrupt head could easily degenerate into violence and vice, yet the number which might thus be described was small and one might well marvel that it was not greater.[33] The difficulties did not arise solely from poor selective and disciplinary routines. The religious orders had never solved a more basic problem —how to find suitable and constructive employment for their members outside the hours of prayer and praise. Monks did not personally construct buildings or till the land; extremely few had ever illuminated manuscripts or created works of art; the Tudor successors of the great monastic chroniclers were both rare and professionally degenerate. The minority of monks fitted to undertake university courses (357, including friars, appear in the Oxford registers from 1505 to 1538[34]) tended to huddle for long years in the houses of study supported at Oxford and Cambridge by the more important monastic orders. When they at last returned, they found little scope for their academic talents.

Outside the universities monks played an almost negligible rôle in early Tudor education. As for the schools in certain of the greater houses, these comprised a small fraction of the national school-population and in any case usually employed secular priests as teachers. Spiritual ministration to the laity was likewise not the function of the majority of religious orders, though an important exception was formed by the preaching friars and by those regular canons who served the parish churches pertaining to their houses. For the ordinary monk or canon life had become in many respects more comfortable than the laborious, often squalid lives of labourers, artisans and small merchants; for the heads of the large houses life had become by any standard lordly and luxurious. Perhaps the most subtly disturbing of all Tudor monastic documents is the journal of William More, prior of Worcester from 1518 to 1536.[35] Hence there emerges no vicious character but a gracious, easy-going country gentleman, generous to his relatives and a popular figure in county society. Avoiding the life of the cloister he moves between his several manor-houses, immersed in secular business, always extremely attentive to his own health and comfort. William More was indeed no monk in the sense demanded either by St. Bernard or by the religious orders of our own day, yet for many years he guided without notoriety the fortunes of one of the renowned cathedral priories of England.

Then as now, it was too easy for outsiders to speak in censorious tones, and the blame for all these shortcomings should not be attributed solely to the monks and to their ecclesiastical superiors. On all sides the enforcement of discipline was hampered by selfish and interfering laymen who contended for monastic stewardships and leases, built up their factions within the cloister or the abbot's household and engaged in drinking-parties and sports with the denizens of poorly-ruled communities. The religious houses were accepted as long-standing members of local society; people sponged upon them, quarrelled with them in endless lawsuits, hobnobbed with them and distracted them from the life of religion. Until their very last years there are no signs that the laity desired or anticipated a general dissolution and a scramble to buy monastic lands. On the other hand, the evidence does not suggest that most monasteries were conspicuously beloved by their surrounding populations. Even during the ostensibly pro-monastic Pilgrimage of Grace there occurred, according to the extant records, as many local instances of ill-will as of good-will on the part of the rebels toward the northern houses.

With certain exceptions, there seems no strong reason why the monks should have commanded the unmixed affections of their neighbours. To the latter they appeared in everyday life as landlords, receivers of rents and tithes, rival traders, unsatisfactory proprietors of churches, which they seemed to regard as investments, to the neglect of the fabric and the parishioners. In relation to their tenants they were not noticeably more generous than lay lords and, as Wolsey's enquiries of 1517 showed,[36] some had already joined in the tendency to enclose lands and expel tenants. When Sir Thomas More protested against harsh enclosures, he placed among the worst offenders 'certain abbots, holy men no doubt'.[37] One of the bitterest passages in Jerome Barlow's anticlerical *Burial of the Mass* (*c.* 1527–8) is directed against rent-raising by abbeys.[38] In 1517 the Abbot of Peterborough became involved in fierce and unscrupulous legal contests with the local townsmen on account of his forcible enclosures of parts of the fens,[39] whilst in 1526 the men of Orford rioted against enclosures made by Butley Priory on what they claimed to be common land.[40] What with repairs to over-elaborate buildings, royal taxation and other heavy overheads, most houses stood in debt and simply could not afford to practise quixotic landlordism. In any case, their agrarian policies must often have been framed by the laymen who acted as their stewards and understewards.

In the more thinly-populated areas of England monastic hospitality benefited travellers of all types; it was dispensed to everyone from dukes to beggars and not based upon fine calculations of social need or moral desert. At the time of the Dissolution royal commissioners and other laymen praised the beneficence of certain individual houses,[41] and their passing must have had its effect upon the amenities of their districts. At the same time middle-class disdain for indiscriminate charity had begun to pervade the atmosphere and to blame religious houses for fostering rogues and vagabonds. In the *Valor Ecclesiasticus*, the great survey of ecclesiastical incomes made in 1535, the monasteries appear to bestow less than three per cent of their income in alms,[42] but charges of ungenerosity based upon such percentages are to be deprecated, since the royal commissioners for the *Valor* allowed the houses to submit only those alms which they were legally obliged to disburse by the provision of benefactors. How much the monks gave casually out of general income or in the form of food and broken meats, we shall never be able to compute, but their spontaneous giving can hardly have made a major impact upon the national problem of pauperism. Needless to add, English monasticism had failed to initiate charitable, teaching, nursing and missionary orders and organisations such as those which were beginning to appear in Germany and Italy and were soon to figure among the chief glories of the Catholic Counter-Reformation.

To this spectacle of an uninspired and lukewarm establishment contemporaries rightly acknowledged three notable exceptions—the Franciscan Observants, the Carthusians and the Bridgettines, all numerically small orders, maintaining close relations with each other, holding a strong allegiance to the Holy See and a consequent disposition, when the Henrician crisis arrived, to reject the King's new claims. With very few exceptions, the genuine monastic martyrs came from these restricted circles. The Observants, who alone among the orders in England represented a recent reform-movement, had only seven houses here, and of these the royal foundation at Greenwich had become the most important. Not only did it enjoy the King's direct patronage but it also supplied confessors to Queen Katherine and her daughter Mary. More aristocratic, intellectual and wealthy was the single English Bridgettine house of Syon, near Isleworth.[43] This was in effect a double house, with some sixty nuns and twenty-five brethren, the latter acting as chaplains and directors to the former. Among them were many Cambridge graduates and after 1500 at least six former fellows of colleges in that University. Syon boasted a reputation for strict observance, a remarkable library, a strong interest in the English mystics and important contemporary devotional writers in William Bonde and Richard Whitford.

Even more exacting in its vocational demands was the Carthusian order. Its nine houses in England (seven of them founded between 1340 and 1414) all maintained to the Dissolution an unblemished name for devotion together with a magnificent corporate spirit which sometimes verged upon spiritual pride. Alongside its saints it also found room for a number of tormented and restless characters whose devotional capacities fell short of their romantic aspirations. In this regard the famous London house of the Salutation was unfortunate to leave as its historian the superstitious Maurice

Chauncy, who seems so unable to distinguish genuine spirituality from hysteria.[44] Yet even through the eyes of this inept hagiographer we receive a vivid impression of the balanced sanity, the sweet rigour of Prior Houghton, the gallant faith and selflessness of that part of his community which in 1535 followed him to the gibbet or died in chains. If they did not, as Froude oddly imagined, die for religious freedom, they died for a conviction as sincerely felt as the love of God which had first led them along the hard and high paths of the Carthusian life. The Tudor age bred no nobler Englishmen than these, and the inhumanity of their punishment must remain among the fouler blots upon the record of Henry VIII. Of Mountgrace, the Charterhouse second in importance to that of London, we have already said more than a little and said it perhaps in too captious and critical a spirit. In expressing reserve concerning the spiritual penetration of monks like Richard Methley and John Norton, we were inevitably placing them alongside great contemplatives like Ruysbroeck and Hilton. With these exalted standards they cannot for a moment pretend to compare, yet they, and no doubt most of their brethren, exhibited a standard of devotion far above that of the mass of contemporary English monks. Owing to its situation Mountgrace could not radiate an influence comparable with that of the London house, yet it did not fail to command wide veneration throughout the North. Had the average rural religious house displayed half its virtue, the attitude of Tudor Englishmen toward monasticism would have been vastly different from that which prevailed at the meeting of the Reformation Parliament.

The Situation of the Church

SUCH, then, in bald outline was the situation of the English clergy during the early decades of the sixteenth century. Their power and influence in society was more apparent than real. They were beginning to lose their once effortless intellectual ascendancy. They stood in no favourable posture to wage any conflict against the growing pretensions of the laity and of the State. Their leaders lacked inspiration, unity and loyalty to the supranational concept of Christendom. While the Papacy as yet needed to reform itself before it could inaugurate reform within the national churches, our English Church remained too full of conflicting interests, too complacent in its conservative and legalist routines to reform itself. During the reign of Wolsey its internal chasms widened. One of these lay between the Cardinal Legate and the bishops, another between the upper and the lower clergy, a third between the seculars and the regulars. Of the chasm which was steadily growing between clergy and laity we have already said something and shall shortly be bound to say more. Whereas the secular clergy tended to encounter resentment as an unduly privileged caste within the national society, the monks now found themselves seated upon an even more precarious limb of the tree of commonwealth. Nevertheless, when we reflect upon the causes of the Reformation, it is easily possible to exaggerate the importance of particular tensions and personal failings. Had Wolsey experienced a fiercer urge to reform, even his immense legal powers could scarcely have accomplished more than gradual and superficial changes. But the hour was later than most men supposed and reforms on this scale would not have availed to prevent either the state-revolution of Henry VIII or the subsequent conquests of Protestantism.

Writers who feel no personal attraction toward Protestant concepts have often tried to explain the advance of Protestantism too purely in terms of these tensions and weaknesses we have just described, sometimes merely in terms of fainthearted and confused bishops faced by a grasping and turbulent laity. However great weight may be attached to these negative factors, it should never be forgotten that Protestant beliefs exercised positive claims upon certain types of mind, that they have steadily continued to exercise such claims and that most of their holders cannot be dismissed as rebellious neurotics, politicians, or self-deluded profiteers. Some men were drawn to Protestantism by understanding and love; some by hatreds and heady enthusiasms; some by the belief that it was an escape-route from the broad road to damnation. But the magnetic process was real enough and it came to operate quite extensively throughout English society. Whatever our various confessional allegiances, we can scarcely begin to understand the Reformation without some sober and sympathetic effort to examine Protestantism from the inside. Any other approach is in danger of ignoring some of the plainest realities in our national history. Like the old Lollardy before it, the new Lutheranism floated upon a tide of negative criticisms, yet its positive affirmations were well trimmed to catch the winds blowing through the sixteenth century. These affirmations now demand our notice.

4 Lutherans and Humanists

Justification by Faith: Luther and Zwingli

WARMLY AS WE MAY reject the notion that all the essential ingredients of the English Reformation were made in Germany and Switzerland, we are bound to recognise that from the third decade of the century our religious history became closely interlocked with the great turmoil on the continent. The personal story of Martin Luther, necessary as it is to explain some aspects of his theology, cannot here concern us in detail. By any criterion, he is a mountainous phenomenon in the history of religion and his flanks are littered with the corpses of incautious climbers who thought to scale him with a few pieces of simple equipment—Anglican, Catholic, Freudian, Marxist—or for that matter Lutheran![1]

Between 1517, when he denounced indulgences in his ninety-five theses, and 1520, when he published his three revolutionary manifestoes, Luther formulated both his doctrinal and his practical programmes. He summoned the German princes to undertake the reform of the Church, to abolish papal taxation, to dissolve the religious orders, to abrogate pilgrimages, clerical celibacy and masses for the dead. He also denied the doctrine of transubstantiation, though he proceeded to replace it by a far from simple or radical alternative. He limited the sacraments to the scriptural two, baptism and the eucharist, while to the laity he assigned communion in both kinds. But the keystone of his doctrine, one unparalleled in Wycliffism, was the doctrine of Justification by Faith Alone, or solifidianism. This he based in the main upon the teaching of St. Paul, though he found for it a considerable measure of support in the anti-Pelagian writings of St. Augustine and in his favourite fourteenth-century German mystics, Johann Tauler and the anonymous author of the *Theologia Germanica*. Moreover, he stated this doctrine with all the fervour of a liberated soul, for it had proved his own way of escape from an intolerable predicament of the spirit. Whatever its merits, we gravely underestimate this doctrine if we think of it as yet one more theological proposition added to the multitude. Once understood it developed an intimate power to alter both the inner lives and the religious habits of the millions who came to accept its message. Justification by Faith can best be understood by re-reading that early masterpiece of Christian theology, the *Epistle to the Romans*, followed by Tyndale's *Prologue to the Romans*, which is a translation from one of Luther's own commentaries. This *Prologue* acquires all the more interest when recognised as the actual vehicle which brought Luther's salient doctrine to the first generation of English Protestants.

The antithesis between God and man presented by Luther, and indeed by the Apostle himself, is stark in the extreme.[2] On the one hand stands the Deity in his unutterable majesty and justice; on the other languishes man in his corrupt self-centredness; his wretched nature being curved inward upon itself, he remains unable even to approach the divine standards by his own pitiful observances and good works. But if God's righteousness is terrifying, his loving purpose toward man is boundless. In the Son he has furnished man with the sole means of transcending this awful inadequacy. God will justify men—put them in a right relationship with himself—only if they abandon all reliance upon personal merit and place their whole trust in the merits of Christ. Truly, good works are an inevitable outcome of this faith, yet in themselves they contribute nothing to justification and salvation; they can form a dangerous stumbling-block to misguided men, who take pride in them as a title to redemption. To this sequence of thought St. Paul repeatedly returns, and Luther took it as the very heart of early Christian theology.

> For (again from Scripture) 'no human being can be justified in the sight of God' for having kept the law: law brings only the consciousness of sin. . . . Therefore, now that we have been justified through faith, let us continue at peace with God through our Lord Jesus Christ, through whom we have been allowed to enter the sphere of God's grace, where we now stand. . . . Israel made great efforts after a law of righteousness, but never attained to it. Why was this? Because their efforts were not based on faith, but (as they supposed) on deeds. . . . For they ignore God's way of righteousness, and try to set up their own, and therefore they have not submitted themselves to God's righteousness. For Christ ends the law and brings righteousness for everyone who has faith.

These are not Luther's words, but those of *Romans* (iii, 20; v, 1–2; ix, 31–2; x, 2–4). The Apostle pursues a similar course in *Galatians* (ii, 16; iii, 11–12) and nowhere does he (or his follower) make the point more concisely than in the second chapter of *Ephesians*. Having dwelt on the redemption of the flock from the death of sin by the quickening power of Christ, the writer concludes: 'For it is by his grace that you are saved, through trusting him; it is not your own doing. It is God's gift, not a reward for work done. There is nothing for anyone to boast of. For we are God's handwork, created in Christ Jesus to devote ourselves to the good deeds for which God has designed us.'

Reiterated with force by St. Augustine, the doctrine of Justification by Faith had not, of course, been ignored by medieval theologians, yet they had shown, rightly or wrongly, a marked indisposition to accept it without reserves. On the one hand, elements of human merit had been implicitly and explicitly introduced in the scheme; on the other, it had been too lightly assumed that the Apostle referred to grace as conveyed by the sacraments. Again, the Pauline conception of faith had come to be identified with intellectual assent to credal propositions. Interpreting St. Paul, Luther is especially insistent upon the distinction between *assensus* and *fiducia*; it is the latter we need, the infinitely humble, yet infinitely confident trust of the sinner in God's redeeming mercy. The hesitations and qualifications of Luther's predecessors and opponents are, of course, intelligible enough. There were other passages suggesting modificatory trends in New Testament thought, notably the *Epistle of St. James*, with its stress upon good works, which Luther dismissed as 'an epistle of straw'. More important, the doctrine seemed above all others hard to accept in its fullness, for it shattered every man-made notion of justice and morality. The response of the conventional moralist could only be that of the Good Brother in the parable of the Prodigal Son: 'You know how I have slaved for you all these years; I never once disobeyed your orders; and you never gave me so much as a kid, for a feast with my friends. But now that this son of yours turns up, after running through your money with his women, you kill the fatted calf for him.' But now all this moral accountancy was thrust aside by Luther. God is no longer seen as weighing up a man's life; no longer does God stand like an innkeeper, chalking up the items and the prices to be paid for them. His grace is in no sense a prize for the pupil with the highest terminal total of marks. And all this is only the first unpalatable draught to be swallowed by the naturally law-abiding, by the people who have that insidious gift, a 'good conscience'. So whole-hearted an emphasis upon the unaided rôle of God in justifying and saving certain undeserving men (but not others!) obviously entails a doctrine of predestination. Well aware of this necessity St. Paul proceeds in *Romans* to sketch a predestinatory system, and he is none too happy in his attempts to reconcile it with human free will (*Romans*, viii, ix). Once again this element, elaborated by St. Augustine, received full acceptance from Luther and in due time was to achieve a rich yet debatable development at the hands of Calvin.

In the early sixteenth century a heavy emphasis upon Justification by Faith was bound to play havoc with the cults of the popular religion. It struck at the foundations of saint-worship, pilgrimages, formal penances, pardons, indulgences, intercessory masses, chantries and a host of other institutions, since not merely the abuses and superstitions associated with them, but even the beliefs underlying them became suspect; they seemed to be futile attempts to build up human 'merit' and distractions from the creation of the new relationship between God and man. To Luther the main purpose of the mass itself was to strengthen the faith of the individual communicant. He could see in the Scriptures no reason for regarding it as a 'good work' from which other persons might benefit. To regard it as in any sense a sacrifice merely derogated from the all-sufficiency of Christ's unique sacrifice on the Cross. Everything in scholastic theology which lacked a direct basis in the Scriptures now fell under suspicion. Aristotle, the high priest of medieval rationalism, suffered dethronement as a pagan influence; the old truth, as docketed in Aristotelian pigeon-holes, was cancelled in favour of a new truth both personal and subjective. Here, in short, was a prototype of modern existentialism and if it proved destructive of many medieval concepts it was destined to stand at least equally opposed to the comfortable sub-Protestant liberalism of the eighteenth and nineteenth centuries.

Hard upon the heels of Luther's teaching came news of the independent Reformation carried out by Huldreich Zwingli at Zürich and imitated at Bern, Basel and elsewhere. Switzerland's lack of effective central government and episcopal control, its central position and multilateral culture, made it an ideal focus for religious experimentation. Between his call to the Great Minster at Zürich in 1518 and his heroic death fighting against the Catholic cantons in 1531, Zwingli with the aid of the council abolished the old worship with a thoroughness greater than that advocated by Luther. He was at once a humanist teacher and the most radical of the century's major reformers. More tolerant than either Luther or Calvin, he believed that salvation lay in believing the essentials of the Gospels, not in assent to formulae devised by any Church.[3] He allowed great personal freedom to interpret the Bible, yet he was careful to guide such interpretation by a hitherto unparalleled torrent of instruction from the pulpit. In the appeal to European radicalism he had certain advantages over Luther through his clear-headed simplicity; if he did not speak so grandly of salvation, he enunciated a sacramental doctrine more comprehensible than that of Luther and one more in line with popular heterodoxy like that of the Lollards. Luther while rejecting transubstantiation had in 1520 illustrated his concept of the real presence in the elements by the famous analogy of the fire and the iron. When the two are combined, the fire communicates heat and light to the iron, yet neither loses its original identity. 'While both bread and wine continue there, it can be said with truth, This is My body; this wine is My blood, and conversely.' On the other hand, Zwingli dismissed all notions of a change in the elements at consecration and taught that 'a sacrament is a sign of a sacred thing, that is of grace which has been given.' While he took very seriously the communicant's preparation to receive the sacrament, he believed the latter 'nothing else than a commemoration'. In the words, 'This is my body', he interpreted the word 'is' as 'signifies'. To disprove both Catholic transubstantiation and Lutheran consubstantiation he used the argument that, since the Ascension, Christ's body had been in heaven.

At the outset, we may add that the influence of Zwingli upon the earliest English Reformers still needs disentanglement. Men like William Tyndale and John Frith were attracted by his doctrines, while the present writer recently encountered his sacramental teaching in the case of an obscure Yorkshire parish priest charged with heresy in 1535. At the same time, before we proceed to study English Protestants, we must again be on our guard against attaching tidy 'Lutheran', 'Zwinglian', 'Calvinist' and other labels to these very eclectic Englishmen; we must beware of compartmentalising the torrent of doctrines which by 1530 was flowing into England.

Within the teaching of both Luther and Zwingli lay an outspoken emphasis upon the claims of the individual Christian conscience, an emphasis which contained at least the elements of religious liberty and toleration. Hardly, however, had such notions been formulated when enormous claims to a direct spiritual inspiration were made by idealists like Carlstadt and Müntzer; they horrified Luther and henceforth impelled the 'moderate' Reformers to fight with decreasing tolerance on two fronts. This new and more radical drive for Reformation assumed most formidable power in the varied groups broadly known as Anabaptists, which owed something to late medieval pietistic traditions but which are usually regarded as coming to birth in 1523 at Zürich under the shadow of Zwinglianism. During the subsequent two decades Anabaptism spread throughout Europe and, as we shall observe, achieved by about 1550 a certain significance in regard to the English Reformation. Yet the initial impulses underlying the new Protestantism in England sprang predominantly from Luther, to a far lesser extent from Zwingli and as yet scarcely at all from the radical sectarians on the continent.

Christian Humanism

DESPITE its inherent attractions, the first successes of Lutheranism in England are not self-explanatory. The ground had been prepared for its reception not merely by Lollard doctrines but by various forces more subtle and intellectual. We have already seen that the *devotio moderna* had tended to deflect interest from the cults and ecclesiastical institutions in favour of an interior and personal religion. In addition, Luther's replacement of scholastic theology by biblical theology had been preceded by the slow discrediting of the whole structure of scholasticism. To the process of attrition the nominalist philosophy of William of Occam had contributed a powerful solvent. This companion of Marsiglio had argued impressively enough that man depended purely upon revelation for his knowledge of theological truths. Even the existence and attributes of God were not discoverable by reason but must be accepted by blind faith. The Occamists denied the whole scholastic assumption that reason must harmonise with faith, philosophy with theology, Aristotle with Christ. Thanks to them and to other internal influences, the scholastic world stood in no position to defend orthodoxy when Luther made his challenge. He in fact received his training from Occamist teachers; though he finally parted from them, they helped to inspire his tendency to treat faith and reason as antitheses and his demand that the 'blind pagan teacher' Aristotle should be banished from the universities.[4]

The rôle of nominalism among the English Reformers deserves more investigation than scholars have yet provided. Nevertheless, we are unlikely ever to regard its influence as comparable with that other longstanding solvent of scholasticism—the humanist approach to the problems of literature, history, religion and the art of living. Why, by the third decade of the sixteenth century, were so many educated Englishmen prepared to abandon their class-prejudices against heresy and listen to Lutheranism, or even to more radical emphases? Certainly, if the Lutheran comet had appeared above the English horizon twenty years earlier, the watchers would have raised very different cries. This preparatory change of atmosphere is often loosely called the New Learning and in its origins owes much to the influence of the Italian humanists, who even before Petrarch's day had abandoned scholastic philosophy and theology in favour of literary, historical and philological studies. By the time of Reuchlin, Erasmus and Colet, this approach had been fully transferred to the study of the Scriptures. In English theological life the shift of standpoint and method showed itself clearly in 1496–7 when Colet returned from Italy and delivered his famous Oxford lectures on Paul's *Epistle to the Romans*. It may be granted that the future dean of St. Paul's did not deduce nearly as much as Luther deduced from this same book. Yet in comparison with its medieval predecessors his commentary cannot but impress by its freshness, its common sense, its breadth of outlook, its relative modernity.[5]

Colet brushes aside the old treatment of the Bible as a verbally-inspired arsenal of texts; he will have nothing of the schoolmen's neglect of the literal sense in favour of allegorical, tropological and anagogical interpretations. He looks at the book anew, and his lectures are anything but the usual *catenae* of subservient references to patristic and medieval exegetes. He applies the humanist critique to the Bible as fearlessly as to a text of Cicero or Virgil. He is interested in the book as a whole; he is plainly fascinated by the life and mind of Paul; he realises he is dealing with a real man in a real historical setting and he reaches down his Suetonius in order to discuss the social background of Paul's Roman congregation. Humanists were seldom profuse in acknowledging the help they derived from others and it would be mistaken to suppose Colet was unaided by any trends in medieval exegesis. During the late Middle Ages there stood among the most widely read of Biblical commentators that famous doctor of the Paris schools, Nicholas of Lyra (*c.* 1270–1340), whose work reappeared in many editions from the early days of printing. Nicholas had made outspoken attacks upon those who had multiplied the mystical senses of Scripture so as to choke the plain, literal sense; his radicalism in this regard caused him at last to become notorious as an alleged inspirer of Luther: 'If Lyra had not lyred, Luther would not have danced.' Unjust as this saying may have been, Lyra's influence upon the early Tudor period is no mere surmise; his books appear quite frequently in the wills and inventories of English clergymen between 1500 and 1550. To many of these men they must have been more familiar than the sermons of Colet and they perhaps contributed materially toward the triumph of the humanist approach as the new century advanced.

Certain of Colet's emphases are admittedly akin to those subsequently forthcoming from Luther. Nowhere does he speak with more warmth than when urging, with St. Paul, that 'rites and ceremonies neither purify the spirit nor justify the man'. Again, he turns aside from discussing Paul's collections for famine-relief and contrasts their voluntary character with the 'money extorted by bitter exactions under the names of tithes and oblations'. Not without intrepidity Colet contrasts the covetous tithe-seekers of his day with the example of Paul, who chose to 'get his living by labouring with his hands at the trade of tentmaking, so as to avoid even suspicion of avarice or scandal to the Gospel'. Nevertheless, Colet's exposition of *Romans* cannot be regarded as more than a half-way house toward that of Luther. He paid little attention to Paul's determinism; unlike Luther, he specifically upheld the free agency of man, whose will was 'secretly accompanied' but not forcibly coerced by God's providence. Man's guilt and not God's will supplied the cause of his condemnation. The strongest influences upon Colet were the Neoplatonists Ficino and Pico della Mirandola, whose thinking did not lead in Luther's direction. The corruptions of the Church and of society strike Colet not so much as universal and inherent in the fallen nature of man but rather as disorders from a more perfect norm. Again, unlike Luther, he will not oppose violent perversions by counter-violence; if, as is possible, he began in his last days to consider Luther's criticisms and remedies, he must surely have felt misgivings as well as some measure of approval. Yet if Colet lacked the demonic force of Luther, he was more sternly independent and forthright than Erasmus. He apparently believed in transubstantiation, held the mass to be a propitiatory sacrifice, accepted all seven sacraments and accompanied his denunciation of papal scandals by an acknowledgment of the Papal Supremacy. Nevertheless, one cannot be surprised that he was admired by the Lollards and accused of heresy by Bishop Fitzjames. He is a Catholic with a special place in the history of Protestantism. The latter was above all a Biblical religion, and Colet's chief distinction lies in the fact that he stressed, well before Luther and Tyndale, the extreme relevance to contemporary religious problems of the Scriptures, historically, humanly and literally considered. He stands both among the causes and the symptoms of that climatic change which swept across English intellectual life during the early decades of the century.

In this same process the writings of Erasmus can also claim a formative rôle; despite immense differences of temperament, of teaching, of fundamental aims, there remain some elements of truth in the cliché: 'Erasmus laid the egg that Luther hatched.' The influence of Erasmus, and of his counterparts among the German humanists, extended beyond their ridicule of ecclesiastical corruption and superstition, beyond the application of humanist methods to the Scriptures. From them there also emanated a modishness which captured even natural conservatives like Thomas More. As a result of their propaganda one had to accept humanist values or risk becoming a figure of fun as an obscurantist. Convinced or not, one had to be very old, very obtuse or very courageous to avoid turning one's back on the past and joining the movement. Its compulsion lay not merely in the intrinsic worth of the new approaches but in the mounting conviction that a golden age of enlightenment had at last arrived. Here was a new era because it so firmly believed itself to be a new era. This mood of confidence did not last long, but it accomplished wonders while it lasted, and Lutheranism entered into its heritage. Whatever the power of his shoulder Luther had not to shift the dead weight of what we now call 'medieval tradition'. While we cannot doubt that the European impact of Erasmus accomplished no small part of this primary task, the narrower problem concerning his influence upon the earlier stages of the English Reformation still admits of argument and might repay further investigation. The earliest known society of English Lutherans originated about 1520 in Cambridge, where in 1511-14 Erasmus had worked upon the Greek text of his New Testament and revised the Latin version formerly inspired by Colet. Yet none of the known personal associates of Erasmus in Cambridge was destined to prominence among the Reformers. On the other hand, there remains ample evidence that his New Testament, especially the Latin version, exerted a powerful influence upon the Lutheran cell in Cambridge and upon its offspring at Oxford. To cite one of several known cases, Thomas Bilney confessed that he sought eagerly for a copy, allured in the first place by the Latin rather than by a desire to attain Christian truth. And we shall shortly encounter another case in Anthony Dalaber, who turned to Erasmus's Latin Testament in his hour of peril.

The Erasmian climate pervaded in varying degrees the minds of many European intellectuals throughout the succeeding decades. It became a natural tendency in a classically-educated age to co-ordinate the teaching of the great pagan moralists with that of the New Testament, to see in Christianity a mode of this life rather than a way of salvation for the next, even to envisage a cool, reasonable religion, a Christianity without tears. But the present writer finds himself unable to join the distinguished Dutch historian who takes Christian humanism to be the 'major Reformation' as opposed to the 'minor Reformation' of the Protestants.[6] To regard the former as an integrated movement in the same sense as the latter would be to ignore the great complexity and the rather impalpable character of humanist trends after the death of Erasmus. To call these thought-tendencies a Reformation only creates semantic confusion. They did not create churches or closely shape the religious lives of ordinary men. Even upon statesmen their influence is hard to define and establish. Henry VIII did not dissolve the monasteries because Erasmus ridiculed monks. By any reckoning and by comparison with any movement, there was nothing 'minor' about the Protestant Reformation. One should not inflate the historic claims of Christian humanism by exaggerating its modernity, by supposing it to be more in accord than Protestantism with our own world, by falsely investing it with the paternity of modern scepticism, liberalism, agnosticism, or scientific materialism. Millions of people are still Lutherans, Calvinists and Anglicans but few are Erasmians or Christian humanists in the Renaissance meaning of this now ambiguous term. The ideas of Galileo and Harvey, of Shakespeare and Milton, of Descartes, Newton and Voltaire were no mere developments from the ideas of Erasmus. We shall later have occasion to observe the increasing range, versatility and secularism apparent in the Elizabethan outlook. Yet this process cannot properly be labelled Christian humanism: it sprang from many causes and it cannot be fitted into conceptual moulds fashioned from the cultural history of the Netherlands.

Early Lutheran Circles

IF modern admirers of early English Protestantism desired to establish a national shrine, they could select none better than the little Cambridge church of St. Edward, King and Martyr. It still contains the small pulpit, made about 1510, from which Barnes, Bilney and Latimer preached. It was the church of Trinity Hall and Clare, the colleges of the two latter Reformers, and its parish contained (on the site now appropriately occupied by the Cavendish Laboratory) the Augustinian Friary whence Robert Barnes went forth on the travels which ultimately led him to the feet of Martin Luther. In a later age the first Cambridge edition of the Authorised Version was printed in this parish by Thomas Buck, whose memorial survives there along with those of two of the translators. Most notably of all, St. Edward's parish also included the White Horse, sardonically called 'Little Germany', where Cambridge scholars first gathered to discuss the new German doctrines.

Of these meetings we know very little save the meagre traditions recorded by John Foxe, who does not attempt to date the origins.[7] They could have begun before the year 1520, since the first holocaust of Lutheran books in Cambridge seems to have taken place at the end of that year or early in the next. On 12 May 1521 a far more magnificent burning took place at St. Paul's in London, where, before an enormous crowd, Wolsey took the chair under a canopy of cloth of gold, attended by a brilliant throng of peers, bishops and foreign ambassadors. Yet these events are by no means the earliest evidence of Lutheran studies in this country. In February 1519 two of Luther's correspondents separately told him that his books were being exported to England, while later in the same year Erasmus informed him that certain very great people in England were admiring his writings. The identity of these mysterious *maximi* can only be a matter for conjecture. A more solid fact appears in the daily ledger of the Oxford bookseller, John Dorne, who sold some dozen books by Luther between 29 January and late December 1520. It was nevertheless in the other university that the first and most influential group of Lutheran intellectuals developed.

The great majority of the men who led the first generation of English Protestants were in residence at Cambridge during the years when the White Horse meetings were in progress. This is true of Tyndale, Joye, Roy, Barnes, Coverdale, Bilney, Latimer, Cranmer, Frith, Lambert, Ridley, Rowland Taylor, Thomas Arthur, Matthew Parker and many others who preached, wrote, accepted high office or embraced martyrdom in the cause. One cannot doubt that in this informal setting most of them first encountered and discussed Lutheran doctrines. The usual chairman was Robert

Barnes, then prior of the Augustinians. Bishop Stephen Gardiner, who in his youth probably attended some of the meetings, later described Barnes as 'a trim minion friar Augustine, one of a merry scoffing wit, friar-like and as a good fellow in company well beloved of many'.[8] On the strength of this tart testimonial from a bitter opponent, certain modern historians have depicted a public-house wrangle presided over by the loudest voice. There is no real basis for this image. Whatever his indiscretions Barnes was a very serious and dedicated Reformer who dared everything for his religion and died at the stake. He had already studied at Louvain and was a distinguished teacher of the classics; he was soon to lecture on the New Testament of Erasmus and to become involved in serious trouble for denouncing the pomp and splendour of Wolsey.[9]

Not for long was English Lutheranism the preserve of Cambridge intellectuals. That groups of London businessmen should soon interest themselves was only to be expected. We have already observed the continuity from Lollardy to Lutheranism in these circles and we shall shortly contemplate the London anticlericalism which centred around the murder of Richard Hunne, that scandal which stank continuously in the nostrils of Londoners until the Reformation Parliament. In addition, the large community of foreign traders in the capital contributed to the spread of the new heresy. Early in 1526 several of the Hanse merchants of the Stilyard were prosecuted for holding Lutheran heresies and importing Lutheran books when they returned from their periodic visits to their own country. About a year later two of them abjured and did penance at St. Paul's along with Robert Barnes.[10]

From this time onwards English merchants in both London and Antwerp began to play a crucial part in the drama. The share of the trading communities in other ports received clear acknowledgment in 1530 from Bishop Nix of Norwich who wrote, 'I am "accombred" with such as keepeth and readeth these erroneous books in English and believe and give credence to the same, . . . the gentlemen and the "commenty" [commonalty] be not greatly infect[ed], but merchants and such that hath their abiding not far from the sea.'[11] Reformation history cannot be converted into a mere shadow of economic and social history, for the same religious ideas embraced countries where the economic and social structures differed markedly from their English counterparts. Nevertheless, the spread of Protestant doctrines was greatly facilitated by the international connections, the anticlerical outlook, the mobility and relative political immunity of the merchant classes throughout Europe. Ideas, not in themselves economic, advanced naturally along the lines laid down by economic men; trade often built the circuits, if it did not supply the generators and the current. Alongside the heretical ex-friars and other university men we have always to reckon with resolute and moneyed groups in the larger trading-centres. Compared with the contribution of these two groups to the Reformation, that of the squirearchy has often been overestimated, and nowhere more than in England where ownership of land has been commonly regarded as conferring intellectual influence.

William Tyndale

UNQUESTIONABLY the most remarkable figure among the first generation of English Protestants was William Tyndale.[12] Born in Gloucestershire about 1495, he took his M.A. from Magdalen Hall, Oxford, in 1515. Thereafter he also studied briefly at Cambridge, yet there is no certainty that he joined the group at the White Horse. His whole career shows a stark independence of groups, fashions and hero-worship. Mentally as well as physically he was an austere man, devoted to an idea and infinitely laborious in acquiring the technical equipment needed for its realisation. Buschius, one of the humanists who contributed to the *Epistolae Obscurorum Virorum*, referred to him as 'an Englishman . . . who is so skilful in seven tongues, Hebrew, Greek, Latin, Italian, Spanish, English, French, that whichever he speaks, you would think it his native tongue'.

While serving as tutor in the household of Sir John Walsh at Little Sodbury, Tyndale preached on College Green in Bristol and fell foul of the local priests, whose ignorance he despised, and of the archdeacon of Gloucester. At this time he had resolved at all costs to translate the New Testament, in his own words, 'because I had perceived by experience how that it was impossible to establish the lay people in any truth except the Scripture were plainly laid before their eyes in their mother tongue, that they might see the process, order and meaning of the text'. This work he offered to do in the household of Cuthbert Tunstall, Bishop of London, but the prelate replied that his household was full and advised him to seek patronage in the city. This proved in the event the most fateful of many miscalculations by the English bishops in the matter of biblical translation. Tyndale resentfully took Tunstall's advice and went to labour day and night for six months in the house of a very different patron, the rich cloth merchant Humphrey Monmouth. Here he entered the obscure world of the 'Christian Brethren'. Soon afterwards this term was used of the secret society of London merchants engaged in subventing and importing books by English Protestants on the continent; it was also loosely applied to Lollards and we have already observed this older tradition among the merchants. On the one hand,

Humphrey Monmouth and his associates belonged to the international world of Lutheranism; on the other, they were certainly linked with men of Lollard background in the distribution of these forbidden books from abroad. When in 1524 Tyndale went on to Wittenberg and met Luther, Monmouth was transferring money to Hamburg for his use, and Tyndale's subsequent publishing work can scarcely be explained except upon a basis of large-scale subsidisation by English merchants. The connection became overt in later years when Tyndale resided mostly in the English house of the Merchant Adventurers at Antwerp. He was only the first of a series of Protestant scholars and translators to operate under this patronage, and Europe's greatest commercial city became in a very real sense the cradle of the English Reformation.

Along with his amanuensis, the ex-Observant Friar William Roy, Tyndale began in 1525 printing his New Testament at Cologne. Though forced to flee by the local magistrates, he completed it at Worms, a Protestant city, before the end of the year. Copies began streaming into England by March 1526; the efforts of Warham, Tunstall and More to check their spread proved almost uniformly fruitless. The successive editions of the work (revised 1526, 1534, 1535, and having a number of so-called pirate editions published in the Netherlands) provided a text at once splendid and homely in character, a text which has dominated all successive translations until our own day, for nine-tenths of the Authorised Version itself derived from Tyndale. Both here and in his original writings Tyndale showed himself a prophet of our language; he divined the genius of a predominantly teutonic tongue and so remained more readable and less 'dated' than most other writers for the next two over-latinised centuries. His translation owed most to the Greek Testament of Erasmus: it was philologically sound and careful, yet we cannot blame the authorities of that period for finding it tendentious. Admittedly, he was right in translating *μετανοεῖτε* by 'repent' instead of by the official 'do penance' (*pœnitentiam agite*). On the other hand, when he gave 'congregation' for *ἐκκλησία*, and 'senior' (later 'elder') for *πρεσβύτερος*, he was making no secret of his subversive intentions towards the visible Church and the priesthood. He firmly believed that the Bible came first and should invariably determine the doctrines, institutions and ceremonies of a Church which had come to bear little or no relation to that of the New Testament. In such cases as these he therefore studiously chose terms which were philologically accurate, yet could not be used to bolster up current ecclesiastical usages. It had been exciting for learned men when Erasmus had similarly utilised such basic terms; it was now revolutionary to hand laymen a Bible which seemed not even to mention priests or the Church. Yet the charge of intellectual dishonesty should never have been made against Tyndale; he was brutally honest—and even more radical than his orthodox critics have supposed! In the famous octavo of 1526 his prefaces were based on Luther's but he avoided marginal notes, and his work might well have been more effectively done had he continued this policy. To later editions, while improving his text, he added an array of marginal notes crudely attacking the Pope, the hierarchy and the priesthood. Likewise his translation of the Pentateuch (1530), though in itself an almost equally remarkable contribution to English Protestant scholarship, was disfigured by similar glosses, making Scripture a vehicle for a partisan position rather than allowing it to speak for itself.

Whatever the effect of such garnishings, the New Testament made a triumphant entry into the field. There is every reason to believe that many readers of moderate or even conservative views studied it with eagerness over the next decade. Perusing contemporary records one encounters it in the most unlikely places. Robert Plumpton, scion of a Lincolnshire and Yorkshire family later distinguished for its loyalty to Catholicism, wrote in 1536 from the Inner Temple to his mother: 'If it will please you to read the Introducement, ye shall see marvellous things hid in it. And as for the understanding of it, doubt not, for God will give knowledge to whom he will give knowledge of the Scriptures, as soon to a shepherd as a priest, if he ask knowledge of God faithfully.' Plumpton even cites the preface which Tyndale added to his 1534 edition and makes specific references to the famous *Prologue* to *Romans*. Besides the copy he sent his mother, it appears that his father already had another at home in larger print. In a second letter, Robert continues: 'Dearly beloved Mother in the Lord, I write not this to bring you into any heresy, but to teach you the clear light of God's doctrine.... Mother, you have much to thank God that it would please him to give you licence to live until this time, for the gospel of Christ was never so truly preached as it is now. Wherefore I pray to God that he will give you grace to have knowledge of his Scriptures.'[13] It was in the next year 1537 that Edward Fox, Bishop of Hereford, addressed the assembled episcopate: 'Make not yourselves the laughing-stock of the world; light is sprung up, and is scattering all the clouds. The lay people know the Scriptures better than many of us.'[14]

Our own age can only by an effort of imagination grasp the full impact of the vernacular Bible upon a generation more ardent and narrow in its Christianity than our own, yet from which the private study of the Scriptures had been so rigorously withheld. It is hard indeed to recapture that blissful sense of release and new awakening. But it was a dawn made doubly poignant by tempest and sudden death. In May 1535 Tyndale himself was tempted by the squalid betrayer Henry Phillips (who posed as one of his converts) to pass outside the immunity of the English House in Antwerp. At once he was seized by agents of the Council at Brussels and imprisoned in the Castle of Vilvorde. After long disputations he was condemned in August 1536 for obstinate heresy and in the following October strangled, his body being consigned to the flames. Biased contemporaries like the chronicler Edward Hall blamed the machinations of English bishops, yet much as the news may have pleased these sorely-tried officials, their actual participation cannot be proved or fairly presumed.

Despite his courage and integrity, his selfless devotion and fine linguistic sense, William Tyndale lacked those endearing qualities which are fostered by human affections. Like many another dedicated Protestant he grievously underestimated the more reputable of his opponents and the religious achievement of the centuries preceding his own. He supposed that the greater part of medieval institutional Christianity was a priestly confidence-trick based upon avarice. For his conservative adversaries he had little better to say than that they were 'dreamers and natural beasts, without the seal of the Spirit of God; but sealed with the mark of the beast and with cankered consciences'.[15] To most men who met him privately Tyndale seemed a gentle creature, but in public life he was an able, angular and bigoted controversialist who gave and expected no quarter. He had suffered and seen his friends suffer. The combat had become mortal and, in an age of abusiveness and overstatement, he received few examples of temperance from the other side. While it would be pointless to look for modern liberalism in the pamphlet-war between Tyndale and Thomas More, this dreary verbosity, this infrequency of true intellectual and spiritual penetration shows neither disputant at his best. On both sides there looms not only a closed mind, a refusal to admit any legitimate differences of doctrinal viewpoint, but a personal uncharity so bitter that it seems to blunt the weapons of controversy themselves. The clash of these two good men stands among the most depressing spectacles of the English Reformation because it involved the imposition of that century's least Christian habits upon its most devoted minds.

Until 1530 Tyndale followed Luther's theology, but from the time of his work upon the Pentateuch he laid increasing stress upon law, alongside Luther's stress upon gospel. The sinner is indeed justified by faith before God, but he then justifies himself before men by obedience to the moral law, while God covenants himself to show mercy toward the law-abiding. This bi-focal scheme doubtless qualifies for a place among the many progenitors of that complex phenomenon: English Puritan theology. Tyndale's political thought represents a link between Lutheran theory and the English Schism as effected by Henry VIII. The German Lutherans mounted the chariot of the godly prince not merely because they recognised his shining countenance alongside those of the prophets in Old Testament history but also because they had no other strong political allies. Where political necessity enjoined a course of action, one could always discover the relevant scriptural texts. And where the godly prince did not exist, it was clearly necessary to invent him, or at least to collaborate with one less transparently inspired, and hope he would make a tolerable substitute. What practical alternative existed? Lutheranism could expect little support from the prelates; it dare not ally itself with the popular visionaries, with the hopeless economic agony of peasant-rebellions or with the predatory kites and crows among the doomed neo-feudal classes. Its natural and actual allies, the urban traders, could not rule great regions and—despite the very independent policy of certain great Imperial cities—also had ample incentives to collaborate with the princes. Yet when one stops to reflect, almost all these phrases, these basic elements of the German picture, could apply also to the England of Henry VIII.

It seems therefore natural enough that Tyndale's political deductions, even when framed with England in mind, should assume a close conformity with those of Luther. His *Obedience of a Christian Man* (1528) is an unflinching exposition of the divine right of kings, who should hasten to shake off their thraldom to the Church and whose subjects are bound to obey them as a matter of religious duty. 'He that judgeth the King, judgeth God and damneth God's law and ordinance . . . the King is, in this world, without law; and may at his lust do right or wrong, and shall give accounts to God alone.' Here Tyndale preached with immense conviction, yet he preached more than he practised. When the royal divorce-suit developed, he soon began to condemn the King's proceedings. Subsequently he repelled the blandishments of Thomas Cromwell, refusing to become a royalist literary champion until Henry VIII should introduce Lutheran principles into England. It was safer to argue with the godly prince when one lived outside his dominions! In this inconsistency Tyndale did but prophesy future changes of attitude among non-Lutheran Protestants in many parts of Europe, including England: prince-worship was not in fact to be their permanent habit. But for the time being the apotheosis of monarchy had become general: it seems almost as prominent among doctrinal conservatives as among Lutherans. In England itself the distinguished anti-Lutheran Stephen Gardiner was about to embrace royal autocracy in terms as eloquent and whole-hearted as those of Tyndale. An age sick of anarchy and near-anarchy was quoting amid general approbation the adage, *The Wrath of the Prince is Death.* For most men life was short and hard even in times of political peace and order, and it would ill befit a twentieth-century critic to begrudge them their limited version of social security.

With his assistants Tyndale had some curious experiences. Friar Roy, born of Jewish stock in Calais, had joined the Observants at Greenwich and ultimately fled to matriculate at Wittenberg. He gave Tyndale useful mechanical help during the crucial months of 1525 but was too open-mouthed and could only be disciplined when he had no money. Dismissed for his indiscretions he somehow obtained funds, translated a Protestant tract and employed another fugitive friar from Greenwich, Jerome Barlow, to write the *Burial of the Mass*, a scurrilous attack in verse upon the ecclesiastical establishment in general and upon the public and private life of Wolsey in particular.[16] Tyndale's grave dislike for these frothy characters and methods was amply justified by the outcome. On Wolsey's fall Barlow begged the King's permission to return home and did atonement by assaulting his former friends in a *Dialogue against the Lutheran Factions*. Meanwhile William Roy disappeared from the Netherlands and from history, though it was later rumoured that he managed to get himself burned for heresy in Portugal about the year 1531. A more substantial figure in Tyndale's entourage was the former fellow of Peterhouse, George Joye,[17] who assisted the master in the controversy with More, and may have written *The Supper of the Lord*, usually attributed to Tyndale himself. Joye produced his own translation of the Psalms (1530) and certain other books of the Old Testament but these inferior productions derived merely from the Latin of Zwingli and others, since Joye, unlike Tyndale, had little knowledge of Hebrew. The friendship between them finally collapsed when in 1534 Joye pirated an edition of Tyndale's New Testament with some impudent emendations of his own. He had still a long career before him as a minor publicist but he never began to compare in importance with Miles Coverdale, the chief legatee and successor of Tyndale. This former Augustinian friar, once a follower of Barnes at Cambridge, went out in 1529 to meet Tyndale by appointment at Hamburg and there worked under him on the Pentateuch. Coverdale then seems to have followed his chief back to Antwerp, where in 1534 they were certainly in company and associating with John Rogers, another important future translator of the Scriptures. Hence, on the eve of his betrayal, Tyndale had found disciples capable of carrying his labours to full fruition. It was a sure instinct which prompted him to cry out at the stake, 'Lord, open the King of England's eyes.' The remaining tasks were indeed as much political as literary, and they called for men with more tact and instinct than Tyndale.

Garret, Frith and Bilney

DURING Tyndale's activities at Antwerp, such English Lutherans as Robert Barnes and Thomas Garret were selling his New Testament wherever they could elude the vigilance of the bishops. They were helped by a most heterogeneous set of allies. Amongst those prosecuted in 1528 for distributing Tyndale's Testament and certain Lutheran writings were Jeffery Lome, a former porter of St. Anthony's School, Sygar Nicholson, a Stationer of Cambridge, and John Raimund, a 'Dutchman' who had brought 500 copies of the Testament into England. But the story of Garret and his friends at Oxford remains the most intimate and appealing of those preserved.[18] This young cleric pursued a successful academic career both at Oxford, where he proceeded M.A. in 1524, and at Cambridge, where he later achieved his doctorate. Long before this last stage he had entered the Protestant book-trade. In December 1525 Erasmus mentions him among the booksellers to whom he sends greetings, and the following year, supplied by the London bookseller Gough, he was back at Oxford selling both Latin texts and Tyndale's New Testament. In 1527 he also visited Reading Abbey, corrupting the prior (as conservatives alleged) by selling him over sixty books. At this time he was also curate of the London church of All Hallows, Honey Lane, but his parochial duties do not appear to have prevented him from taking the Thames Valley as his parish. In 1527 Dr. John London, then Warden of New College, wrote to the Bishop of Lincoln that 'this unhappy Mr. Garret was in Oxford at Easter and after that . . . he sought out all such that were given to Greek, Hebrew and the polite Latin tongue, and pretended he would learn Hebrew and Greek, and bought books of new things to allure them: after that he procured a great number of corrupt books and secretly did distribute them among his acquaintance in sundry colleges and halls.' Under this stimulus the Oxford Protestant cell had swiftly developed. Dr. London went on to relate how Garret's young friend Anthony Dalaber had confessed to borrowing a number of Lutheran books from John Clark, an associate of Garret and one of the Cambridge men recently transferred by Wolsey to his new Cardinal College in Oxford. To London, a deep-dyed Oxonian, the true reason for these dark developments had now become only too obvious. 'Would God my Lord's Grace had never been motioned to call him [Clark] nor any other Cambridge man unto his most towardly College!' Meanwhile Dr. Cottisford, commissary of the Bishop of Lincoln, set about the task of destroying this nest of heretics.

In later years Anthony Dalaber wrote an affecting account of his encounter with Garret when the latter, now a hunted fugitive, sought refuge in Dalaber's rooms at Gloucester College. Both were understandably agitated, since Garret had already been captured once and had just escaped from a locked room, while the commissary was at evensong.

> But now, with deep sighs and plenty of tears, he prayed me to help him to convey him away; and so he cast off his hood and his gown, wherein he came unto me, and desired me to give him a coat with sleeves, if I had any; and told me that he would go into Wales, and thence convey himself into Germany, if

> he might. Then I put on him a sleeved coat of mine, of fine cloth in grain, which my mother had given me. He would have another manner of cap of me, but I had none but priestlike, such as his own was. Then kneeled we both down together upon our knees, and lifting up our hearts and hands to God, our heavenly Father, desired him, with plenty of tears, so to conduct and prosper him in his journey, that he might well escape the danger of all his enemies. . . . And then we embraced, and kissed the one the other, the tears so abundantly flowing out from both our eyes, that we all be-wet both our faces, and scarcely for sorrow could we speak one to another. . . . When he was gone down the stairs from my chamber, I straightways did shut my chamber-door, and went into my study, shutting the door unto me, and took the New Testament of Erasmus translation into my hands, kneeled down on my knees, and with many a deep sigh and salt tear, I did with much deliberation read over the tenth chapter of St. Matthew's Gospel; and when I had so done, with fervent prayer I did commit unto God . . . our dearly beloved brother Garret.

The commissary, pale with anxiety over the escape of his prisoner, was soon seen consulting with the Dean of Cardinal College and with Dr. London. He had Dalaber's room searched, thoroughly cross-questioned the young accomplice and finally set him in the stocks, where his fellow-Protestant Clark encouraged him to bear the persecution with thankfulness. These steps did not, however, locate the fugitive Garret. London himself relates how the commissary, 'being in extreme pensiveness, knew no other remedy but this extraordinary [one]; and caused a figure to be made by one expert in astronomy, and his judgement doth continually persist upon this: that [Garret] fled in a tawny coat south-eastward, and is in the middle of London and will shortly to the seaside'. This divination was shrewd but as it happened wrong, for Garret had started off westward and was soon captured by the proctors in the neighbouring village of Hinksey. He saved himself for a future martyrdom by abjuring and carrying a penitential faggot in open procession along with Dalaber down the High Street. Afterwards they were imprisoned for a time at Osney until Wolsey magnanimously gave Garret work—the innocuous task of copying documents. But Clark and several others of the Oxford group had less reason to feel gratitude. The prison of Cardinal College into which they were thrown was also the storehouse for the salt fish and, what with its stench and a constant diet of fish from February to August, Clark, Sumner and Bailey died of some infection. Perhaps Wolsey, amid the pressure of affairs, merely forgot to have them released; perhaps he felt no urgency, since these men had gravely marred the beginnings of his beautiful new college.

Another of these much-abused Cambridge intruders into Oxford managed during the débâcle to arrange a speedy withdrawal to the continent. He was John Frith, seemingly among the most interesting personalities to emerge from the records of early English Protestantism.[19] Escaping to Marburg, he first helped Tyndale, and then in 1529 published a tract called *Antithesis, wherein are compared together Christ's acts and our holy father the pope's*, an antithesis not unexpectedly made to the marked disadvantage of the latter. Subsequently in *A Disputation of Purgatory* he answered with cool precision, but without vituperation, More's *Supplication of Souls*. Frith's return to England in 1532 led, after various adventures, to his imprisonment and the betrayal to More of a discourse on the sacrament, written for a friend but not for publication. More reported that this work 'teacheth in a few leaves shortly all the poison that Wyclif, Oecolampadius, Huss, Tyndale and Zwinglius have taught in all their books before'. Everything we know of Frith's writings and reputation suggests a mind of high ability and independence; had he survived, his must have become one of the great names of the age.

That More had good reason to place this antagonist well to the left of Luther can be proved by reference to Frith's writings, by his discipleship to Oecolampadius (who held Zwinglian views on the eucharist) and by records of the examination which led in 1533 to Frith's martyrdom at the stake. He was examined upon two articles, purgatory and transubstantiation, yet in his own submission he did not die for any rigid denial of these two doctrines but for the principle that a particular doctrine on either point was not a necessary part of a Christian's faith. 'The cause of my death is this', wrote Frith, 'because I cannot in conscience abjure and swear that our prelates' opinion of the sacrament (that is, that the substance of bread and wine is verily changed into the flesh and blood of our Saviour Jesus Christ) is an undoubted article of the faith, necessary to be believed under pain of damnation.' To a greater extent than any other of our early Protestants, Frith thus upheld a certain degree of religious freedom. To make all dogmas equally binding, to abolish the distinction between an article of faith and a thing indifferent, had indeed become ever more characteristic of medieval orthodoxy, especially where the findings of Thomist Aristotelianism had been accorded a special reverence. The attack on excessive dogmatism was not original to Frith; it had already become a tenet of the more liberal Lutherans and was soon to become a leading concept of the intellectuals surrounding Thomas Cromwell.

In their reaction against what they considered the arrogance of the schoolmen, Luther made and Melanchthon developed the important distinction between necessary and immutable things, and *adiaphora*, things indifferent.[20] The concept was one of genuine antiquity, since it could be based upon several texts in St. Paul (e.g., *Colossians*, ii, 16–20; *I Timothy*, iv, 1–5; *Galatians*, ii, 3–5: v, 13–15). It also claimed support from Augustine's letter to Januarius and from the most liberal opinion of the fifteenth century, including that of Gerson, John of Wesel and Wessel Gansfort. However attractive we modern observers with a similar cast of mind may find adiaphorism, we should also acknowledge the limited nature of its effectiveness under sixteenth-century conditions. Certainly it provided no easy track towards reunion. When men had agreed to place such obvious things as holidays, fasts, and vestments under the heading *adiaphora*, how much more could be included? How many would go so far as Frith and include purgatory or even transubstantiation? The challenges presented by the concept to the charity and scholarship of Christians remain permanent, but at the Reformation it remained a forlorn hope of a world little prepared to accept its broader implications.

In the gallery of early English Protestants Thomas Bilney should be placed somewhat apart from the rest.[21] He was an independent reformer whose spiritual struggles had much in common with those of Luther, but his heresy, if such it can be called, involved little more than a denial of intercession to saints and of the current purgatorial doctrines. A Norfolk man, born about 1495, he received ordination from Bishop West of Ely in 1519 and at some later date took his LL.B. from Trinity Hall, Cambridge, being elected a fellow there. Using the New Testament of Erasmus at first for its Latin, he went on to reflect more deeply on its substance and to experience a personal conversion. 'Immediately, I seemed unto myself inwardly to feel a marvellous comfort and quietness, insomuch as my bruised bones leaped for joy.' This feeling arose from his acceptance of the Pauline doctrine of Justification by Faith, from which, again like Luther, he deduced the vanity of a religion based on external observances. To his dying day he remained orthodox on the Papal Supremacy, the authority of the Church, the doctrines of transubstantiation and confession. With regret Foxe himself admits Bilney's substantial orthodoxy. When people with more decidedly Protestant leanings like Robert Barnes and John Lambert were 'converted' by Bilney, this may mean little more than the fact that he first brought home to them the full meaning of a personal religion. Nevertheless, when he converted Hugh Latimer in 1524, this did in fact make Latimer cease attacking the Lutherans. Bilney at this time entertained puritanical scruples against strong language and even against music. On the other hand, he distributed his goods to the poor and the prisoners, often visiting the lazar houses and the equally foul prisons of Cambridge. In Latimer's words he was 'meek and charitable, a simple good soul, not fit for this world'.

In July 1525 Bilney was licensed to preach throughout the diocese of Ely, but he did so elsewhere, disputing with a friar at Ipswich concerning the veneration of images and being twice hauled out of the pulpit at Norwich by people who thought his views heretical. About 1526 Wolsey summoned him for denouncing saint-worship and caused him to take an oath that he did not hold, and would not disseminate, Luther's doctrine. In November 1527 he came again before Wolsey, from whom Tunstall of London took over the case. During this trial he freely admitted that Luther was 'a wicked and detestable heretic' and claimed that he himself had not wittingly taught Luther's doctrine. On the evidence of hostile witnesses Tunstall declared him convicted of heresy and then refused to reopen the case and hear favourable testimony. The Bishop nevertheless twice postponed judgement to allow the accused an opportunity of recanting. This Bilney finally did under pressure from his friends, though he appears to have made it clear that he doubted his own guilt. Having been imprisoned in the Tower for a year he reaffirmed his recantation and was allowed by Wolsey to return to Cambridge. His melancholy temperament had been deeply affected by these experiences, and his companions were afraid to leave him alone. For two years he tried to live with the conviction that he had betrayed his principles. Then he announced that he was going 'up to Jerusalem', meaning that he intended to court martyrdom. This he did effectively enough by field-preaching in Norfolk and by giving the anchoress at Norwich a copy of Tyndale's New Testament. Approached by Bishop Nix's officers he was soon condemned, degraded and handed over to the secular arm by Dr. Pellys, the diocesan chancellor. Before going to the Lollard's Pit at St. Leonard's Hill in August 1531, he heard mass, received the eucharist, accepted confession and absolution. The future primate Matthew Parker, who was an eye-witness, denied the official story that he made a recantation at the stake, but the dispute over this point remains academic, for he had little of substance to recant.

While Latimer and Dr. Edward Crome, also examined about this time, could be saved by influential favour, the case of a relapsed heretic like Bilney remained hopeless. As in the secular courts, the position of an unpopular defendant in the hands of the Church was always perilous. The charge of heresy could too easily be brought against any critic of ancient practices and privileges; it had even been made by some enthusiasts against that stout Catholic Dr. Standish, when in 1515 he had championed the King's claims in a merely juridical dispute. The case of poor Bilney shows the rigid, merciless legalism of the system at its worst, yet in a sense he also fell victim to his own impatient scrupulosity. Had he waited a very few years, he would have been given nearly all he wanted by the conservative King and bishops. By his martyrdom he perhaps accomplished less than he might have done by continuing the simple call to faith and repentance, the mission to individuals he had already shown himself so well equipped to conduct. Bilney's memory and example worked fruitfully in the minds of a few friends, but among the people the affair occasioned no great scandal, since his earlier recantation had given him the repute of a relapsed heretic. The critics of the Church did not exploit his case as they had exploited that of Hunne; they needed broader targets and were already finding plenty elsewhere.

Frith and Bilney were by no means the only educated Reformers who failed to adapt themselves neatly to Luther's patterns. Amongst the most influential figures in Cambridge during the later twenties was George Stafford, a young Fellow of Pembroke Hall, who refused to base his New Testament lectures on the time-honoured *Sentences* of Peter Lombard, or to waste time upon figurative and anagogical interpretations.[22] A hearer of his expositions of St. Paul recalled that 'he seemed of a dead man to make him alive again and . . . to set him forth in his native colours'. This method lay well within the tradition of Colet; both Stafford and his friend William Warner (later actually called the Cambridge Colet) could probably have joined Bilney and Latimer in disclaiming the influence of Luther. This did not save Stafford from being reported for heterodoxy to the Cardinal, but before encountering trouble from that quarter he died of the plague—which he happened to contract through his zealous efforts to extricate another Cambridge scholar from the toils of black magic!

So far from simplifying the pattern of the conflict, the advent of continental Protestantism soon made it more involved. Observing the thirties we cannot profitably think in simple terms of a Protestant-versus-Catholic struggle, since both sides, and especially the former, show profound divisions. The welter of beliefs and emphases had now become almost as confusing as in central Europe itself. This new decade, which in England saw the decisive political and confiscatory measures, remained, doctrinally speaking, an indecisive period of argument and uncertainty. Meanwhile a political, legal and expropriatory Reformation went ahead without tarrying for theological agreement. The fixed point in a shifting world was the essential harmony between King and Parliament. But on the eve of these momentous changes it seemed perfectly possible that the King himself might inaugurate a sudden religious move to the left. When, late in 1528, Cardinal Campeggio returned to England in order to hear the royal divorce-suit, he was appalled to find Lutheran books freely circulating at court and to hear talk of a negotiation between the King and the Lutherans. At this time the Defender of the Faith was not above hinting that, in the event of his divorce being refused, he might embrace such radical notions. And as late as December 1529 he told the Imperial ambassador Chapuys that if Luther had limited himself to inveighing against the vices, abuses and errors of the clergy, instead of attacking the sacraments of the Church and other divine institutions, everybody would have followed him and written in his favour. 'Nevertheless', continued Henry, 'though the said Luther had evidently mixed up a good deal of heresy in his books, that was not a sufficient reason for reproving and rejecting the many truths he had brought to light.'[23] As we now know, the King was interested in putting pressure upon Rome and never seriously intended marching alongside the Lutherans. Quite apart from his Catholic doctrinal convictions, he always meant to be master in his own house rather than the junior partner and paymaster of some international theocracy. Nevertheless, his mood in December 1529 presaged ill for the Church, and his loyal lay subjects, at this time assembled in Parliament, were only too eager to help in paring down the voluminous privileges of the clergy. Before, however, we survey this first climax of the revolution, we have one last expanse of background to scan—the earlier story of tension between Church and State, together with its companion-movement, the rise of secular anticlericalism in England.

5 Erastianism and Anticlericalism

The Growth of Erastianism

THE ENGLISH PROTESTANT REFORMATION arose and grew largely in opposition to the will of Henry VIII. Yet for his own reasons the King soon initiated a second Reformation, which was bound ere long to affect the course and character of the first. During the thirties he consummated a dual revolution, severing the English Church from the Papacy and subjugating it to the control of the Crown in Parliament. This act of state was made possible by the many influences we have already described, in particular by the weak hold of the Church upon public opinion. Once executed, the royal revolution became in itself a causal influence and did not fail to exert marked effects upon the religious, intellectual and social history of the nation. Had Henry patched up his quarrel with the Papacy in 1533, the spread of English Protestantism would probably have been retarded; some sort of concordat with Rome, however insecure, might for a time have been maintained. Powerful forces were nevertheless at work to promote drastic action at Government level, and only exceptional forbearance on both sides could have avoided a desperate crisis. The conflict between Church and State did not centre solely around the problem of the royal divorce; it was a conflict with its own involved history, its own compulsions. This being the case, the revolutionary measures of the Reformation Parliament cannot be understood without reference to certain earlier crises, which had lacked neither bitterness nor memorable qualities and which had already imposed some conspicuous statutory limitations upon the English Church. And alongside the more dramatic episodes we must not fail to observe something more fundamental—the gradual, exacerbating growth of anticlerical and erastian[1] opinion amongst Englishmen. Such opinion had, in addition, an academic background. When the powerful states of Renaissance Europe sought various forms of control over the churches within their power, they could find in medieval theory a plenitude of justificatory arguments. In Dante, in the publicists who espoused the cause of Philip IV of France against the popes, in Marsiglio of Padua and in Wycliffe, there abounded erastian notions drawn from biblical, theological, philosophical and historical sources. Wycliffe was neither the greatest nor the most original of the medieval erastians; moreover, it can clearly be shown that he was not the one who provided the main fund of these ideas to the defenders of Henrician Reformation in England. All these distinctions may be claimed with some confidence for Marsiglio, the most portentous of medieval rebels.[2] Both medical doctor and theologian, he won renown in those schools at Paris and Padua which also gave birth to the chief medieval forbears of modern natural science. In 1326, two years after the anonymous publication of his notorious work *Defensor Pacis*, his authorship became known and he fled to the service of the excommunicated Emperor Louis of Bavaria, with whose cause he remained closely involved until his death in 1342. Marsiglio's own excommunication at the hands of Pope John XXII can have surprised few contemporaries, since the *Defensor* was the most able, audacious and elaborate attack ever made upon the pretensions of the medieval Church. Arising from a reconsideration of Aristotelian doctrines it ended as a prophetic forerunner of the Protestant erastianism of the sixteenth century, the democratic theory of the nineteenth and the State-worship of the twentieth. Briefly, it saw the secular State as the only cohesive force which could create a civilised life for man on earth, and it strove to exclude the Church from all worldly power and jurisdiction. The State is omnipotent, self-sufficient and entirely responsible for supplying the needs of its people for this present life. It derives its authority from the whole people, who retain the ultimate right to decide upon its institutional forms. The Church, on the other hand, is clearly bidden to centre its thought and action upon the next world. Here on earth it can claim no rights, no property, no jurisdiction save those which the State sees fit to lend it.

Marsiglio explicitly compares the functions of the clergy to those of physicians. They must celebrate religious rites, admonish the wicked, instruct men how to achieve everlasting life and to avoid damnation. But Christ's teaching gave them no authority to impose temporal punishment for sin or even to assign penances. Heresy, if punished at all in this world, should only be punished as a civil offence. The clergy should be subject, equally with laymen, to all the provisions of State-law; they can claim no prescriptive rights to tithes or tax-exemptions unless the State thinks it expedient to grant them such privileges. Moreover, all church-officials from popes and bishops downward receive their offices from civil rulers; so long as they obtain their emoluments, they can legitimately be compelled by these rulers to perform their religious duties, and if found unsatisfactory can be deposed by civil action. The Church consists of the whole people; it is simply the citizen-body organised (and organised as simply as possible) for other-worldly purposes. Marsiglio at least begins to approach the Lutheran notion of the priesthood of all believers when he says that laymen are also churchmen, *viri ecclesiastici*. While Christ instituted the priesthood, such offices as those of pope and bishop remain of human institution and their holders have no spiritual qualities or rights beyond those of simple priests. The Pope can claim no authority as the successor of St. Peter; even Peter himself enjoyed no pre-eminence over the other apostles; he is not called a bishop, and indeed there exists no adequate historical proof that he was ever in Rome. The ecclesiastical primacy of Rome obviously arose, argues Marsiglio, from the fact that the city was the capital of the Empire. This being so, papal decretals and canon law in general have no binding force except in so far as the State may sanction them. Christian doctrine and conduct have only one sure basis—the New Testament.

Marsiglio was the boldest thinker of an age when many thinkers had been provoked to erastianism by the excessive claims of Boniface VIII and by the succeeding Avignonese Captivity, which, incidentally, had a parallel in the Habsburg captivity of the sixteenth century. Some of his views had been anticipated by Dubois and John of Paris; many were shared by his associate in the imperial service, William of Occam, or were to be elaborated in the next generation by Wycliffe. They did not suffer oblivion amid the more moderate and statesmanlike efforts of the Conciliar Movement, and in some directions they were reinforced by the irreverent humanist scholarship of the fifteenth century. Even Marsiglio had believed in the Donation of Constantine, the forged document whereby the Papacy imagined itself to have derived a vast jurisdiction from the Emperor. His unquiet spirit might have rejoiced almost a century after his death when Lorenzo Valla, later on to become himself a great papal official, conclusively proved the spurious character of the Donation.

It would be easy to exaggerate and to misunderstand the impact of fourteenth- and fifteenth-century theorists upon the Reformation at home and abroad. Early Tudor Englishmen did not in general develop erastian and anticlerical views through reading authors like Marsiglio and Wycliffe. Such views arose in the main through practical abuses, quarrels, scandals and conflicts of interest. Theory tended to remain in the storehouse until the political situation demanded its production and its use as propaganda. This, as we shall observe, was particularly the case with Marsiglio of Padua, who enjoyed his heyday in England only when the propagandists supporting the actions of Henry VIII found in the *Defensor* a valuable armoury of weapons. Until the King of England actually found himself in a situation analogous to that of the Emperor Louis, the views of Marsiglio played little part in the formulation of English opinion or in the conduct of Anglo-Papal relations.

Tensions between Church and State

WITH marked success over long periods, medieval Europe had maintained a compromise between the notion of a Universal Church, governed at the centre by its own popes and councils, yet at the many points where it touched and comprehended secular life yielding large areas of jurisdiction and influence to the various states. This division of authority did not lie along the lines which modern minds would regard as dividing the spiritual from the temporal. In England as elsewhere the church courts dealt, as one would anticipate, with heresy, blasphemy, contempt of clerical authority, absence from church services, dereliction of duty by the clergy. Yet they also dealt with perjury, slander, drunkenness, sorcery, incontinence, adultery, matrimonial disputes and the probate of wills. On the other side, the King's courts had resolutely maintained their jurisdiction over all matters involving the real estate of the Church, including the important sphere of advowsons. The State never relaxed its view that all benefices and ecclesiastical corporations owed their physical existence to royal and noble benefaction, while the King never forgot that he was lord of all the land in England. Again, after those lurid scenes in which the figure of Thomas Becket bulked so large, a relatively stable compromise had been achieved concerning jurisdiction over criminal clergy. Other compromises had been forced upon kings and popes by plain common sense. Whether or not, for example, a diocesan bishop was a royal minister, he always retained extensive secular duties and feudal obligations. It was hence highly desirable (and usually the case after Edward II's reign) that chapters should consult the King, and the King the Pope, concerning the choice of persons to occupy episcopal sees.

Nationalism within the English Church grew in strength throughout the medieval centuries; one could list many prominent clergy whose actions proclaim that in all practical matters they considered themselves primarily Englishmen rather than subjects of the Roman Pontiff. All the same, the common medieval term *Ecclesia Anglicana* never meant 'Church of England' in the post-Reformation sense of an independent national Church claiming parity with that of Rome. Whatever its material reservations, the medieval English Church acknowledged the spiritual overlordship and jurisdiction of the Papacy. It administered in its courts a body of law based upon papal decrees and upon the canons of international church councils. Only on its fringes—for example, on matters concerning tithes and testamentary jurisdiction—had this law been modified by English national custom.

So far as the persons and property of the clergy were concerned, the balance of real power had fluctuated along with the political exigencies of the realm and of the papacy. At the end of John's reign and under Henry III the measure of papal control stood high. Under Edward III and Richard II, when the prestige of a reputedly pro-French or divided papacy sank to its nadir, the actual powers of the Crown rose in marked degree and the English bishops looked increasingly to the King as their master. This was the period distinguished in England by the statutes of Provisors and *Praemunire*.[3] The former statutes, of which four were made from 1351 to 1389, were framed to curb papal 'provisions', or appointments to vacant English benefices over the heads of ordinary patrons. Disregarded even by Edward III himself, they did little to diminish the frequency of such provisions, which continued numerous until the Reformation. The three *Praemunire* statutes (1353, 1365, 1393) were designed to check papal encroachments against the rights of the Crown; they were likewise the outcome of temporary situations and speedily disregarded. They culminated in the so-called Great Statute (1393) and, since this was the law to be used by Henry VIII with such paralysing effect against the English clergy, we should note here its original intentions. The Great Statute involved in substance a protest against two hostile manœuvres by Pope Boniface IX. He had threatened to excommunicate English bishops who enforced decisions of the King's courts regarding advowsons; he had also criticised the acceptance of secular offices by certain bishops and had threatened to shift them from see to see, thus shaking a government heavily dependent upon clerical ministers. The Great Statute was a political manifesto meant to impress the Pope with the determination and unity of the kingdom. It did not prohibit the entry of all papal bulls or otherwise threaten the wholesale exclusion of papal jurisdiction from England; it merely threatened with forfeiture of land and goods all persons who should introduce papal bulls in order to execute these two specific threats against the bishops. The particular quarrel was soon healed, and for many years relations were resumed as if the Great Statute had never been enacted. So loosely, however, had its text been drafted that in subsequent times lay lawyers began to envisage its use as a multi-purpose weapon against ecclesiastical jurisdiction. Humphrey Duke of Gloucester attempted to employ it in order to weaken his rival Cardinal Beaufort, while later in the fifteenth century Crown lawyers invoked certain of its passages to suggest that the Church courts were of dubious legality, as representing a 'foreign' jurisdiction. While no responsible statesmen then anticipated either a severance from Roman jurisdiction or a drastic interference with the age-old operations of the canon law, the two-handed engine continued to stand without, still capable of smiting, even were its mechanism rusted and its original purposes largely forgotten.

This period of royal ascendancy continued under the Lancastrian kings, who banished or even executed rebellious bishops and who thrice compelled prelates to refuse cardinalates, even though duly nominated in Rome. Meanwhile on a lower level, fifteenth-century common lawyers did all they could to encroach upon the jurisdiction of the church courts. But the advent of the Tudor dynasty formed no landmark; the reign of Henry VII was far from presaging major crises in Anglo-Papal or Church–State relations. On both fronts, it appears in retrospect one of the more harmonious chapters in the long story. The King and the Pope behaved as wily managing directors combining to dominate the supine body of shareholders known as *Ecclesia Anglicana*. To the English bishops and senior clergy the reign cannot indeed have seemed a honeymoon between the temporal power and the clergy. The royal policy seems riddled with minor anticlerical actions, mostly financial in character; in particular, the recognizances exacted from the bishops during Henry's later years left them owing enormous debts to the Crown. Even in relations with the popes, the balance of tangible advantage had now tipped decisively to the side of the King, who extracted many privileges from Rome but suffered little hard cash to leave England for the papal coffers. No pope disputed his nominations to English preferments, which were always made with strict regard to the interests of the Crown. Seldom if ever before had the episcopal bench and the more sumptuous benefices been more solidly packed with royal administrators and diplomats. On the other hand, like his Lancastrian forbears, the King ostentatiously displayed his abhorrence for heresy, and on one occasion he even troubled to convert a Lollard at the stake before burning him, *pour encourager les autres*.

The two Church–State tensions which then assumed prominence would have attracted little subsequent notice but for their sequels under Henry VIII. Their appearance under both kings was nevertheless more than accidental, because both related to that most basic task of the dynasty—the imposition of law and order upon a turbulent people recently torn by civil strife. The two problems were those of sanctuary and benefit of clergy. Exemption from the harsher punishments of secular justice had in former times been extended not only to clerics in major and minor orders but even to such laymen as were supposedly capable of receiving ordination through their ability to read Latin. The requirement commonly involved stumbling through a so-called 'neck-verse'; after which modest feat the criminal, delivered to the bishop, might succeed in purging himself by oath-helpers or in escaping with a relatively mild penance. Perpetrators of treason and of certain felonies had already been debarred from claiming benefit, and the innovations under Henry VII merely resulted in a slight enlargement of these excluded categories. The statute of 1489 provided that any felon claiming clerical privilege should be branded on the thumb and that, if he claimed it a second time, his plea should be refused unless he could prove himself actually in holy orders. A second statute (1497) deprived a layman of the claim if he had committed petty treason by murdering his lord or master. So far as concerned the right of sanctuary,[4] the severest problems arose in connection with great chartered sanctuaries like those of Durham and Beverley. By taking refuge here many serious criminals escaped justice, since—unlike those who sought sanctuary in an ordinary church—they were not required to abjure the realm after forty days but might linger there unpunished for life provided they took oaths of obedience to the lord of the jurisdiction. Once subject to him they could not be made answerable for further crimes, even those committed outside the sanctuary-area. In 1487 the judges held in the case of Humphrey Stafford (who had tried to start a rising against Henry VII) that sanctuary did not avail in cases of high treason, a development later supported by a papal bull. When, however, these various measures are taken together, they constitute a very modest advance of the State into the domains of the Church. The claims of the first Tudor might have been made by any late medieval King; they can hardly be regarded as a prelude to the work of the Reformation Parliament.

During the later years of the reign, it is true, certain royal officials developed radical views. One of these was the King's notorious agent Edmund Dudley, destined along with his colleague Sir Richard Empson to be thrown to the wolves by Henry VIII. The modern interest in Dudley's book *The Tree of Commonwealth*[5] may seem antiquarian in character; while written in 1509–10 during its author's imprisonment in the Tower, it lay unprinted until a century ago, and hence cannot rank in the sequence of erastian books which helped to form Tudor opinion. It nevertheless throws light upon those trends of thought among early Tudor lawyers and officials which foreshadowed some aspects of the coming Royal Supremacy. Long before men had heard of Luther and his godly princes, Dudley argued that church-reform was an urgent task which must be pursued under royal guidance. The King was by right not merely the protector but the overseer of the Church, for he appointed the bishops and was responsible for making them conscientious in the punishment of wrongdoers. Moreover, he should foster concord within the realm by adjudging disputes between the clergy and the laity. 'And no man', concludes Dudley, 'can do it but the Prince.' At the time these words were written, the new King was but nineteen years of age, his mind filled by antique notions of military glory on the fields of France. If then, or for several years to come, he ever heard his servants talking along Dudley's lines, he is unlikely to have reflected upon their full implications. In Sir Thomas More's pregnant phrase, the lion did not yet know his strength.

The Hunne Affair and its Sequels

To a modern reader, the ecclesiastical history of Henry VIII's first year does not lack some prophetic notes. When Archbishop Warham called a provincial council for January 1510, the text of his summons dwelt upon the hostile attitude of the laity toward the clergy and the rights of the Church. And if one did not know their date, one would attribute his lurid phrases to the period of the Reformation Parliament twenty years later. Dean Colet, chosen to preach the inaugural sermon, placed the blame for this lay malevolence upon the 'evil life' of the clergy themselves. 'Ye will have the Church's liberty, and not be drawn before secular judges, and that also is right . . . but if ye desire this liberty, first unloose yourself from the worldly bondage.' With puritanical severity, Colet then thundered against their moral laxity, greed, immersion in secular business, and he called for a series of specific reforms—stricter examination of candidates for orders, the gift of benefices to worthy men, rehabilitation of the religious orders, more frequent provincial councils, strictly canonical elections to bishoprics, injunctions against simony, non-residence, dissolute clerics, the wasteful use of episcopal revenues and the 'filths and uncleanliness' of ecclesiastical courts. After this rousing start the gathering proceeded to an anticlimax. Its reform-committee included strong personalities like Colet himself, Bishop Fisher and Bishop Nix of Norwich, but it managed to produce only three constitutions directed against unruly stipendiary priests, simoniacs and improper clerical costume. No real programme of reform emerged, and the provincial council soon fell back into wearisome jurisdictional disputes of the sort which had bedevilled the careers of bishops and their officials throughout the Middle Ages.[6]

Early in the new reign serious discussion still centred on benefit of clergy, and in 1512 its scope was again somewhat circumscribed by an Act of Parliament which removed benefit from persons not in orders, if they committed murder or felony in churches, were guilty of murder or robbery on the highway, or robbery accompanied by murder or violence in private houses. Even this moderate reform still lay *sub judice*, since the Act was couched as a temporary one, to operate only until the next Parliament. In May 1514 a further complication arose when the Pope promulgated a declaration that no layman had authority over a cleric by any law, human or divine—a position which seemed to threaten even the compromises attained in England centuries ago. Yet before this matter could be revived in Parliament, it became merged in the graver series of disputes which arose from the murder of Richard Hunne. To this astonishing story, concerning which some important discoveries were published as recently as 1961, we have hitherto made only passing allusions. Since it forms a landmark in the development of erastian and anticlerical opinion, it now demands a steadier glance.[7]

Richard Hunne was a merchant tailor and freeman of the city of London with a hitherto good personal reputation. As we now know, his troubles began not a few months but three years before his death. In March 1511 his infant son died in the parish of St. Mary Matfelon, Whitechapel, and the rector Thomas Dryffeld demanded the bearing sheet by way of mortuary dues. Hunne refused, on the ground that the sheet belonged to him and not to the baby. In April 1512, rather sordidly, the rector instituted proceedings at Lambeth and there on 13 May Cuthbert Tunstall (then Warham's chancellor) decided the case against Hunne. In January 1513 Hunne brought a charge of slander against the rector's assistant priest, Henry Marshall, alleging that in the previous month Marshall had refused to conduct evensong in his presence, since he was 'accursed'. This slur, it was claimed, had injured Hunne's credit with his business associates. The slander-case was never settled but went through a series of adjournments until Hunne's death. Meanwhile, in Hilary Term 1513 Hunne instituted another suit, also in the King's Bench, against the rector Thomas Dryffeld and others, the charge being that they had offended against the *Praemunire* Statutes. He was not the first litigant to attempt such a counterstroke against the church courts, but there may have been a measure of truth in More's characterisation of Hunne as 'a man high minded and set on the glory of a victory'. It is now apparent that this *Praemunire* suit was also never in fact settled; it was repeatedly adjourned on a point of law, the last adjournment being from Michaelmas 1514 to Hilary 1515, by which latter date Hunne was dead.

In view of the hostility of the secular courts, Hunne's use of this weapon was naturally regarded as provocative by the clergy, and at this stage the Bishop of London, Richard Fitzjames, took a hand. He was an elderly but venturesome prelate, ready to go to any lengths in the defence of ecclesiastical interests. Sir Thomas More's later references to him are surprisingly polite, considering that he had persecuted Colet and that Erasmus thought him the worst type of superstitious reactionary. In this affair he lived well up to his reputation and augmented his already marked unpopularity in London.

On the bishop's order Hunne was arrested and a search of his house yielded some heretical books, including a Wycliffite Bible. Pending his trial he was confined in the Lollards' Tower at the south-west corner of Old St.

Paul's. On Saturday 2 December 1514 he was taken to Fulham for examination by Fitzjames. Brought back to the prison he was discovered the following Monday morning hanging in his cell. A coroner's jury refused to return a verdict of suicide, since the body and the state of the cell showed signs that Hunne had been strangled before his neck had been broken. After a long examination of those able to trace the movements of the persons involved, the jury found a verdict of wilful murder against the Bishop's chancellor, Dr. Horsey, and against two of Horsey's henchmen. One of these was the gaoler Charles Joseph who had been one of the defendants in Hunne's *Praemunire* suit. Joseph subsequently confessed that he and others had strangled Hunne; the usual story that he made this admission under duress depends merely upon the assertion of Fitzjames, an unsupported assertion which involves various improbabilities.

The three were duly indicted, but the ecclesiastical authorities managed to prevent their being brought to trial, an outcome which convinced London lay opinion that they had indeed perpetrated a murder of revenge and intimidation. When a court presided over by Fitzjames pronounced Hunne a contumacious heretic and handed over the body to be burned at Smithfield, the atmosphere became still further poisoned, since this judgment literally reduced his family to pauperism, entailing as it did the forfeiture of his property to the Crown. From the legal viewpoint this was rightly thought a strange judgment, for Hunne had not been convicted in his lifetime and no just inference of his final contumacy could be made. The London diarist Wriothesley summed up the impression of the man in the street when he wrote that Hunne 'was made a heretic for suing a *Praemunire*'. Here we may leave the personal aspects of Hunne's case, though not without a word of warning against most of the literature which has accumulated around it. The conflicting accounts by More, Hall and Foxe, written long afterwards by highly-prejudiced propagandists ignorant of the documents, remain all but worthless. Of Gairdner's equally prejudiced attempt to exculpate the churchmen,[8] the less said the better.

The grave disturbances raised in London by the scandal of Hunne's death represent no sudden and isolated upsurge of anticlerical feeling on the part of his fellow-citizens. We have commented elsewhere on the importance of tithe-disputes as a background against which ill-feeling between clergy and laity should be viewed. Especially is this true of the Londoners.[9] For at least two centuries they had engaged in periodic but often bitter conflicts with their parish priests over the assessment of their tithes, and the city records show that this struggle had again reached one of its more chronic phases. Quarrels, law-suits, negotiations and short-lived awards dragged on until 1534, when Thomas Cromwell and other high officials arbitrated on the dispute and had their awards confirmed by Act of Parliament. In addition, other prominent cases concerning mortuary dues and offerings occurred in London both before and after the case of Hunne. The city remained small enough to allow the personalities of the contestants to become widely known, yet it was large enough to develop a formidable volume of mass resentment, whether against foreign traders, exacting clergymen or any other group whose interests were distinguishable from those of the citizen-body.

For our purposes, the political sequels of the Hunne affair are far more important than its resemblances to detective-fiction. When in February 1515 the Commons met under its shadow, they staged a passionate counter-attack upon benefit of clergy and soon attempted to renew the temporary statute of 1512. At this juncture Richard Kidderminster, the distinguished and scholarly Abbot of Winchcombe, preached at Paul's Cross that such a measure contravened the law of God and the liberties of the Church. Whatever the force of his arguments they were at least in harmony with the recent papal declaration. The temporal Lords and some of the Commons retorted with an appeal to the King, who, never averse to take part in a display of learning, arranged a disputation on this issue. Here the Church was represented by Abbot Kidderminster, the King by Dr. Henry Standish, warden of the Greyfriars and a favourite court-preacher. The latter denied that a papal decree upholding the immunity of clerics in minor orders could apply to England. When the Abbot quoted the text 'Touch not mine anointed', Standish tried in the manner of the humanist generation to put the Psalm into its historical context. Parliament adjourned in April, but the dispute died down only to revive on its reassembly in November. It was then that Standish received a summons to appear before Convocation and, foreseeing an imminent charge of heresy, appealed for protection to the King. In the wrangles which followed, the temporal Lords, the Commons, the justices and the common lawyers all viewed the immunities of the clergy against the emotional background of the Hunne case. Some of their opponents, equally uncompromising, went so far as to deny long-established English law by asserting that a cleric could not even be brought to answer, let alone be tried, in a secular court. Dr. Standish and his supporter Dr. Veysey, dean of the King's chapel, replied that this claim manifestly defied ancient practice. In a subsequent dispute at the Blackfriars, the judges widened the scope of the debate by accusing Convocation of a breach of *Praemunire* and by asserting that the King could hold a Parliament without the Lords spiritual, who had the right to appear merely by reason of their temporal possessions. The judges made clear their view that Parliament was not only the highest court of the realm but derived its authority from lay sources alone.

The final meeting of the series was held at Baynard's Castle, and here Wolsey (whose dual position commands some sympathy) presented an apology for the churchmen, urging that they had not thought of diminishing the royal prerogative. On the other hand, he petitioned that the dispute over benefit of clergy might be referred to Rome; he and everyone else well knew which way judgement would there be given. When the King told the bishops that Dr. Standish had answered their points, Richard Fox, then on the point of resignation from political life, exploded in fury, 'Sir, I warrant you Dr. Standish will not abide by his opinion at his peril.' This was an open threat which allowed Standish to gain sympathy by another dramatic appeal for royal protection. 'What should one poor friar do alone', he cried, 'against all the bishops and clergy of England?' While the King had no intention of handing over his champion to the mercy of the bishops, he was still young, conventional and dependent on a great ecclesiastic as his chief minister. Having reasserted the freedom of English kings from any earthly superior, he assumed the rôle of peacemaker and allowed the struggle to end with honours even. Horsey appeared in the King's Bench, pleaded not guilty and obtained his discharge, while Standish was likewise dismissed by Convocation. Henry caused his parliamentary agents to drop the bill which stripped benefit from minor clerics; he also allowed the attack on mortuary dues to languish. But with equal significance, he refused to remit the matter to Rome, and in 1518 he made Standish Bishop of St. Asaph.

The precise importance of this crisis of 1514–15 remains far from easy to assess. To regard it as a dress-rehearsal of the Henrician Reformation would be misleading, but it did to some extent foreshadow the initial stages of the Reformation Parliament in 1529–32, when reforms were being pressed upon the Church yet without schismatic designs against Rome. In 1515 the rival armies of Church and State had been drawn up in full battle order; they had exchanged loud shouts of defiance and even a few blows. Nevertheless, their generals had no intention of allowing serious bloodshed, pitched battles or extensive conquests. Wolsey, the most influential amongst them, was a *condottiere* engaged for high fees by both sides. Yet this mustering of the forces did not lack significance, and the King was left to meditate at leisure upon the spectacle. Should Church–State relations threaten in future to become strained, he would know in advance the muster-rolls both of his followers and of his opponents.

Apart from a strong erastian faction amongst the knights and burgesses of the Commons, the whole legal fraternity from the judges downwards had now shown itself more than willing to assault the ranks of clerical privilege. From this same profession there soon arose the earlier anticlerical and royalist pamphleteers, while the Inns of Court, always a great formative force in Tudor life, were also to contain in the late twenties something regarded by the King with far less favourable eyes—a strong Protestant cell. Even so, the crisis we have described lacked any immediate sequel. Apart from that of the year 1523 there were no Parliaments for the remainder of

Wolsey's ministry and so fewer chances of another frontal clash. The King was anything but a natural revolutionary, and for many years to come he had no personal motives to exercise his strength against the Church. In 1521 he published his book *Assertio Septem Sacramentorum*, denouncing the heresies of Luther; it sold well in numerous Latin, English and German versions and, dedicated to Leo X, earned for its author and his successors the title *Defender of the Faith*. Yet while the events of 1514–15 remained so vividly alive in the minds of Londoners until the Reformation Parliament, Henry himself can scarcely have forgotten their lessons. The historian Polydore Vergil, then London agent of the papal collector, had written that the people were 'raging against the clergy, or would be if the King's Majesty were not curbing their fury'.[10] What an enviable position for a King, and how unenviable for the Church and the Papacy, should the latter become unable to give an increasingly egotistical King what he most wanted in the world!

While the Cardinal's ministry attracted hatred against Wolsey in person, it also increased the violence of indiscriminate anticlericalism, which began to develop into general attacks upon the Church even before Wolsey vanished from the scene. 'Nearly all the people here hate the priests', wrote Chapuys a month after the assembly of the Reformation Parliament in November 1529. Both the lay grievances of the twenties and the clerical reaction are clearly recorded by the chronicler Edward Hall in his account of its first session.[11] Here Sir Henry Guildford declared that he had paid the enormous sum of 1,000 marks to the Lord Cardinal and the Archbishop of Canterbury for probate of the will of Sir William Compton. With heavy sarcasm other members claimed that the clergy, such was their charity, would take a dead man's only cow from his beggared children rather than forgo their mortuary dues. Ecclesiastics, they alleged, were also exacting landlords, grinding the faces of poor husbandmen; abbots kept tanneries and traded in wool like temporal merchants; beneficed clergy resided at court and in the households of lords; they took everything from their parishioners, leaving them without preaching and instruction, to the peril of their souls; unlearned priests held ten or twelve benefices, while learned scholars at the universities lacked the means to study. When the unfortunate clergy heard this parliamentary chorus, it seemed to them as if the whole lay world had been suddenly inspired by the Devil to turn and rend them. 'My lords', exclaimed Bishop Fisher in the Upper House, 'you see daily what bills come hither from the Commons House, and all to the destruction of the Church. For God's sake, see what a realm the kingdom of Bohemia was, and when the Church went down, then fell the glory of the kingdom: now with the Commons is nothing but down with the Church: and all this, me seemeth, is for lack of faith only.'

These jeremiads, reported to the Commons, only served to enhance their rage and make them exclaim that they were slandered as heretics in the presence of the Lords. Their Speaker set off with thirty members to the King's presence. 'Are we infidels, are we Saracens, are we pagans and heathens, that the laws which we establish should be thought not worthy to be kept by Christian men? I beseech your Highness to call that bishop before you, and bid him speak more discretely of such a number as be in the Commons House.' The King, careful as ever not to cross them, soon brought about a superficial reconciliation, and Fisher had to explain away his irate words. During these exchanges the faults of both sides appear with painful clarity. The Commons generalised unjustly from the darkest aspects of canon law and church-administration. The ecclesiastical hierarchy thought nothing so important as the maintenance of every privilege and source of income which churchmen had gained in very different times. Meanwhile, some of their more incautious officials managed to keep alive the bitter memories of Hunne's case. The best-known of these follies arose in relation to the will of a Gloucestershire gentleman, William Tracy of Toddington. When this document came in 1531 to be proved in the Prerogative Court of Canterbury, Tracy was found to have used the form which later became common in Protestant wills; he had written that he trusted to be saved only by the merits of Christ and did not rely upon the works of men, or upon saints or masses.[12] After Archbishop Warham had consulted Convocation as to the will's orthodoxy, Tracy was pronounced a heretic and orders were sent to Dr. Parker, chancellor of the Worcester diocese, to exhume the corpse from consecrated ground. Not only did Parker comply, but he also burned it, a childish blunder, for it was agreed that only the King's officers could burn a heretic, dead or alive. Informed of this offensive zeal the King sent for Parker, who pleaded the Archbishop's orders. But Warham was now dead; the plea availed nothing and the offender was compelled to forfeit the very large sum of £300 to gain his pardon.

St. German and Simon Fish

THESE hostile exchanges meanwhile had their analogies in the literary field. Here we encounter one of the founders of Henrician legal and political theory in Christopher St. German, who unlike his luckless contemporary Edmund Dudley, survived not only to utilise the press but also to participate in the actual crisis of the struggle.[13] Born about 1460, the son of a Warwickshire knight, educated at Oxford and the Inner Temple, St.

German was already an old man when he came to prominence in the controversies surrounding the Henrician revolution. As a jurist he took little interest in religious dogma, to which his approach was conservative. This made him the greater menace to the clergy, who found themselves unable to pin him down by a colourable charge of heresy; it allowed him free rein to indulge his grand passion, for he was the very embodiment of the old hatred felt by the common lawyers for ecclesiastical jurisdiction. After 1532 he was to become a thoroughgoing defender of each new position occupied by the King, but his earlier works antedate the revolutionary years and may claim a conspicuous place among those which prepared public opinion for drastic change.

St. German's first book, published in 1523, was called *Dialogus de fundamentis legum et de conscientia*, being an academic discussion in Latin between a doctor and a student concerning theories of law and equity and their relation to the law of England. In 1530 St. German published a second dialogue, this time in the vernacular; then in the following year came a free translation of the first dialogue and an appendix of thirteen 'Additions' containing some important views on the powers of Parliament in relation to the Church. The English version and its extensions, together known as *Doctor and Student*, not only enunciated anticlerical doctrine but also exerted a prolonged influence on English thought, since they formed a guide for law-students up to the time of Blackstone. Also among St. German's formative works stands his *Division between the Spirituality and Temporality*, published in 1532 and often regarded as part of a royal propaganda-campaign then in its initial stages. In fact, no documentary proof indicates a connection at this date between the author and the government. The *Division* attracted the attentions of Sir Thomas More, who devoted much of his *Apology* to an attack upon it. When in 1533 St. German replied with his *Dialogue betwixt Salem and Bizance*, More again intervened and closed the controversy with his *Debellacyon of Salem and Bizance*. This sharp conflict did not, however, exhaust the energies of the formidable septuagenarian, who then produced three more controversial pamphlets, keeping well abreast of the governmental advance and seeing with exceptional clarity and prescience the full implications of the newly-enunciated Royal Supremacy.

From the first, St. German had much to say about abuses of ecclesiastical jurisdiction; he always entertained an exalted conception of the rights of the State and came near to equating the English common law with the Law of Reason itself. Nevertheless, the modernity of his earlier views could easily be exaggerated. Repeatedly he refers to Gerson (who had died a century earlier) to prove that canon law is far from being identical with divine law and, again, that jurisdiction over all temporal things belongs to the secular State. If he does not mention Marsiglio of Padua by name, his debt to that patriarch of radical erastianism becomes clear when, for example, he says that the clergy 'undoubtedly make not the Church, for the whole congregation of Christian people maketh the Church'. Again, St. German's theory of English law is closely based upon Sir John Fortescue's *jus politicum et regale*—the notion that a King of England must obtain the consent of his subjects in order to legislate. With this traditional background he can never think in terms of a royal autocracy, and in *Doctor and Student* he stresses the necessity of parliamentary consent to English law-making. It is in this emphasis upon parliamentary sovereignty and statute law that the earlier works of St. German most obviously foreshadow the changes about to be executed by the Reformation Parliament. From 1530–32 St. German was claiming for Parliament cognizance of all matters affecting property, goods and money; it may justly, he argued, legislate upon mortuary-dues, prevent the further transference of lands into mortmain or prohibit bishops from charging visitation fees upon religious foundations. One startling passage of the *Division between the Spirituality and Temporality* even assigns to Parliament an absolute power to redistribute all temporal things between subjects, whether laymen or clergy. On the other side, St. German will not allow to the church courts the right to decree the forfeiture of the goods of a heretic. Likewise, if a man be excommunicated in a church court for debt or trespass, he may forthwith sue for a writ of *Praemunire facias* against his ecclesiastical opponents. In *Doctor and Student* the author would leave the Church with jurisdiction only in the narrow category of 'mere spiritual things'. Though he puts his case with more precision and verve than his predecessors, he is nevertheless in his earlier works carrying old ideas to extremities rather than inventing new ones. The *Division* does not go far beyond the dialogues, and together they cannot be said to constitute a wholly revolutionary theory of Church and State. They assert that the Church has often exceeded its legal authority in relation to English statutes and customs and in relation to the divine law. They glorify the common law and assert the omnicompetence, even the infallibility, of Parliament in all causes concerned with property and temporal things. On the other hand, they as yet present neither an attack upon the Papacy nor the suggestion that ecclesiastical jurisdiction in England derives from the Crown. These later and more advanced phases of St. German's thought proceeded *pari passu* with the actual statutes of the Reformation Parliament.

Sir Thomas More ridiculed St. German's grave and judicial pose as a 'pacifier' of these disputes, and his trick of avoiding specific charges against the clergy by prefacing his anticlerical stories with the phrase, 'Some say'. 'All his some says', retorts More, 'be of his own saying.' The first criticism seems to have substantial justice, for the tears of St. German over clerical misdeeds are indeed those of the crocodile. The second has less justice, since in those times a man could not, without fear of plague-ridden dungeons, make specific charges against bishops and ecclesiastical courts. And however slight the sincerity behind his professed solicitude for the Church, St. German's polemical methods seem urbane in comparison with those of the London rabble-rousers to whom we now turn. Into this Grub Street category Simon Fish must fall, though he was also a lawyer with the same professional prejudices as St. German. His *Supplication of Beggars* can scarcely be claimed as a serious Protestant pamphlet; it exemplifies anti-clericalism in its most virulent, unprincipled and eloquent form. Driven into exile through a quarrel with Wolsey, Fish subsequently helped to distribute copies of Tyndale's New Testament; he was also circulating his *Supplication* in London as early as 1529. According to a picturesque story in Foxe, Anne Boleyn introduced it to the King, who 'kept the book in his bosom for three or four days'. Henry then made contact with Mrs. Fish and persuaded her to produce her husband, who lay in hiding only a mile from the court. If we may believe an anecdote almost too good to be true, the King then 'embraced him with loving countenance', took him hunting for several hours and gave him his own signet to protect him against the hostility of the Chancellor, Sir Thomas More. Whatever the accuracy of these stories, the contents of the book were calculated to please Henry, who no doubt saw in Fish a potentially valuable henchman should the threatened struggle develop. Unfortunately for such a design, the pamphleteer died of the plague in the following year, 1531. His wife must also have felt strong religious convictions, since she then married the son of a Gloucestershire knight, James Bainham, one of the Protestants allegedly whipped by order of Sir Thomas More in his garden. Whatever the truth of this other dubious story, Bainham was certainly burned at the stake in 1532.

In the *Supplication* Fish makes none of St. German's pretensions to judicial calm and conciliation.[14] Every punch is as hard as the author can make it and not a few are directed below the belt. We must attempt to summarise Fish's argument in something like his own manner, since a polite synopsis of full-blooded Tudor propaganda would miss the point. This argument is couched in the form of a supplication coming from the outcasts of society and directed to the King. The lepers, the sick, the needy, the impotent, complain to the King that they die of hunger, because of these holy beggars and vagabonds—bishops, abbots, priests, monks, friars, pardoners and summoners, who have taken into their hands a third of the kingdom. Even the poor tithe-paying housewife must account for every tenth egg or be taken as a heretic. And what money they pull in by probates, mortuaries, pardons and fines! Above all (and here the figures rise well into the realms of fantasy) a vast income of over £40,000 goes to the begging friars. Is it any marvel that secular taxes can be levied only with great difficulty? The Turk himself would never be gaining ground in Christendom if he had to cope with such a horde of locusts within his realm. What are the holy thieves doing with these annual exactions from the people? Nothing, except translating all rule, power, lordship, authority, obedience and dignity from your Grace to themselves. 'Since the days when King John was made tributary to Rome, your most noble realm (alas for shame!) has stood tributary, not unto any kind of temporal prince, but unto a cruel devilish blood-supper, drunken with the blood of the saints and martyrs of Christ ever since.' And what do they more? Truly, nothing but apply themselves, by all the sleights they may, to corrupt every man's wife, daughter and maid, that licentiousness should reign over all your subjects, that no man should know his own child, that their bastards should inherit every man's possessions to the disinheritance of the right-begotten children. Lured by their superfluous riches into unclean lust, they carry disease about the realm; some even boast among their fellows that they have meddled with a hundred women. Some have run off with men's wives and goods as well, reducing whole families to beggary.

Where is your sword, the poor people ask the King, where is your power that should punish such felonies committed by this generation? How many more people would there be in the realm if these celibates had married? What woman will work for threepence a day, if she can have at least twenty pence for gratifying a monk or friar? What honest person dare take into his service any man or woman who has been at school with a spiritual man? Who can get justice against the clergy, when all the learned men of the realm are paid fees by them? If poor Richard Hunne had not sued a priest, he would have yet been alive. Did not your noble predecessors provide statutes against mortmain? Yet notwithstanding, have not the clergy gotten into their hands more land than ever? What law can be made against them? In return for all these riches, they can only claim to deliver our souls out of purgatory by their prayers. Yet, as learned men now declare, there is no purgatory; it was a thing invented by the covetous spirituality. In any event, they will pray for nobody unless they are given money. People who protest against the system are called heretics, forced to do penance or burned at the stake. Christ submitted himself to temporal government, gave Caesar his due, and taught that the higher powers must always be obeyed. To conceal these teachings, the clergy will not allow the New Testament to go abroad in the mother tongue. And did not Dr. Allen, the Cardinal's chancellor, seek to deprive your Grace of such pleas as belong to your high courts and to withdraw them to the church courts? Did not Dr. Horsey murder Richard Hunne when he sued for your writ of *Praemunire*? And your own Lord Chancellor, hitherto always a cleric, will take care to maintain his own ecclesiastical kingdom, even though all temporal kingdoms in the world should be destroyed. What remedy is there for us, the poor and the sick? Should men found more hospitals? No, the more the worse, for always the fat of the whole foundation hangs on the priests' beards. If your Grace will build us a sure hospital, take from these oppressors all their ill-gotten gains. Set these sturdy lubbers to work, to get them wives of their own, to earn their livings by the sweat of their faces! Tie these holy thieves to the cart's tail, to be whipped naked about every market town till they fall to labour and cease to take the bread from our mouths! Then shall the profligates decrease; then shall these exactions end; then shall your own power no longer be filched from you; then shall idle people be set to work, matrimony be better kept, population and wealth increase; then shall the gospel be preached and we shall duly pray to God for your most noble estate long to endure.

These were cruel, unjust and wildly exaggerated attacks, yet since clerical avarice and immorality were far from totally fictitious, the *Supplication* retained just that substratum of truth which made it dangerous. Tavern-talk had now found open and eloquent expression. No lay politician with half an eye could fail to see the uses of such invective, should the worst come to the worst. If the King in fact carried the pamphlet about in his pocket, this was not because he believed it to be an impartial report on the state of his realm.

When such prime examples of anticlericalism have been fully described, many sides of a complex phenomenon continue to elude our grasp. When Bishop Fisher exclaimed 'All this, me seemeth, is for lack of faith only', he may have been using inaccurate terminology, yet he was sensing a real change of spirit. The younger generation, the one which had become adult during the reign of Henry VIII, was not yet deeply pervaded by formal heresy. Even if it had sickened of those clerics who raised the cry of heresy whenever laymen pressed for church-reforms, it had not yet committed itself to Protestant doctrines. Nevertheless, it had lost interest in numerous attitudes and observances which had meant much to Fisher's generation. These mid-Tudor people differed as much from their fathers and grandfathers as we differ from the Victorians. The growth of anticlericalism was but one symptom of a shift in values. Another was that large-scale secularisation of chantries and other minor foundations which in all parts of England marked the thirties and forties. Many Englishmen felt no more compunction in diverting chantry-funds to practical uses, both public and private, than we should feel in demolishing the once-mighty Bethesda Chapel in some depopulated area of an industrial city. The subjects of Henry VIII tended to be unsentimental and mundane, both in their charities and in their greed. This change of spirit was not initiated by Henry VIII or Thomas Cromwell, let alone by continental heresiarchs. At no time in Christian history has the world stood as still as elderly churchmen have wished: even when they are saints they cannot stop it moving and, if they seek a measure of influence upon public life, they must attempt to understand its ambivalent values. The year 1530 was not an opportune moment for prophecy. Some of the men of destiny were already presenting their claims, yet some had not yet shown their faces. At this moment John Calvin had not finally broken with Rome, and Ignatius Loyola had not yet founded the Society of Jesus. Had Fisher been able to see ahead thirty or forty years, he would have witnessed, alongside the immense growth of secular interests, a world which had by no means lost its interest in the Christian faith, a world which still felt fiercely on theological matters, yet a world in which all the protagonists, even those who revered his memory, had at least agreed to discard his own fifteenth-century patterns of thought.

First Stages of the Reformation Parliament

When Parliament at last met on 3 November 1529 the reform of ecclesiastical abuses, including the removal of Wolsey, was obviously anticipated by the government, the members and the public alike.[15] But not even the most sanguine anticlerical can have foreseen the magnitude of the revolution to be consummated during the following six years. At the outset no one cause inspired the calling of this Parliament. Though the new Lord Chancellor Sir Thomas More began the session with a bitter attack on Wolsey, Parliament was not called especially to deal with the latter by attainder, since when the writs went out the normal processes of law had scarcely been initiated against him. It was not summoned for urgent legislation on the royal divorce, which it did not even discuss until 1533. And since it made no grant of supply until 1534, it seems not to have been assembled to solve a financial crisis. Yet more than six years had elapsed since the last session. Ecclesiastical problems apart, many secular ones demanded legislation; how many can be seen from the enormous list of statutes passed by this Parliament. Despite occasional interference with by-elections by ministers and magnates, the Reformation Parliament was not 'packed' to any significant extent: it did not need to be, since all Tudor parliaments contained a solid phalanx of office-holders and other members wholly reliable in the eyes of the government. If anything, this Parliament was remarkable for the number of occasions on which it displayed a spirit of independence, even for the extent to which it was flattered and cajoled by the King and his ministers. Nevertheless, to assert that the

Commons accurately represented the will of any classes other than the gentry and the merchant-oligarchies would be a rash assertion; this would also be rash if made concerning any parliament before 1832!

We may scarcely doubt that at this moment the problem of the divorce lay uppermost in Henry's own mind. He was already considering indirect methods by which Parliament could be made to strengthen his hand. During the previous year the King's agents, Stephen Gardiner and Edward Fox, had already been threatening Pope Clement VII with the possibilities of an English schism and a General Council of the Church. In 1528, however, Henry had still maintained optimism regarding his divorce; however anxious to spur on the Pope he had no real desire to proceed to extremes. As yet he had not finally parted company with Wolsey, the resplendent symbol of papalism. Now, however, the nemesis of a persistent failure to control Rome had overtaken the Cardinal, and a few days before Parliament met, a bill of indictment under *Praemunire* was preferred against him in the King's Bench. It accused Wolsey of specific offences under the common law—for example, presenting to the livings of other patrons, annexing the testamentary jurisdiction of other bishops and using his legatine authority to extract pensions from abbots. The resultant spectacle—the most powerful legate in English history humbly acknowledging the right of the King's court to try him for illegal exercise of his papal powers—shook the edifice of clerical privilege to its foundations.[16] The time had also come to put much heavier pressures upon Clement by giving parliamentary anticlericalism its head. Over the next three years there followed a sequence of statutes which, though still carefully avoiding schism, involved the most serious curtailment of ecclesiastical privilege since the fourteenth century. Mortuary dues and probate fees were closely regulated by scales of charges according to the means of the payer. Pluralities were limited, beneficed priests forbidden to accept chantries and clerics forbidden to indulge in trading. Those below the order of sub-deacon now forfeited benefit of clergy, should they be charged with murder, treason, arson, burglary or highway-robbery. Of this legislation by far the most interesting and prophetic item is that clause of the Pluralities Act (21 Henry VIII cap. 13) which invalidates any present or future papal licence 'contrary to the present Act'. A ready assumption of the power of statute to debar the operation of papal jurisdiction in England thus appeared in the very first session of the Reformation Parliament.[17]

In 1530 the King also allowed his legal advisers to put the Statute of *Praemunire* to a test even greater than that involved in the prosecution of Wolsey. There resulted a somewhat complex operation, the nature of which has been lately reconsidered.[18] In the summer of 1530 writs of *Praemunire facias* were issued against eight bishops and seven other prominent divines, the charge being that they had aided Wolsey in his offences by assigning to him a part of their incomes. Though the fact was notoriously true, the suggestion of guilt remained absurd. Almost all churchmen from archdeacons upward had been in the habit of making these peace-offerings, not to enhance the power of Wolsey but simply to prevent him from infringing their privileges by means of his omnicompetent papal powers. But before this suit against the fifteen defendants had reached any conclusion, the plan of attack was broadened into a crude and sweeping accusation against the whole of the English clergy. Edward Hall and other contemporaries say that they were charged with accepting Wolsey's legatine powers, but the subsequent Act of Pardon alleges that they had exercised ecclesiastical jurisdiction 'contrary to the form of the Statutes of Provisors, Provisions and *Praemunire*'. As we now know, however, Bishop Stokesley reported that certain councillors had altered the text of the pardon, a fact which might possibly account for this discrepancy. Whatever the case, when the Convocations met in January 1531, they accepted this preposterous situation by resolving to bribe off the Crown. In return for their pardons, the clergy of the Province of Canterbury offered £100,000 and those of York £18,840. The King graciously allowed them to pay by instalments spread over five years but, when invited to define the future scope of *Praemunire*, he refused. The most hardened of his lawyers might indeed have felt some embarrassment if asked to explain this legal fairyland. 'But we will provide', said Lord Chancellor Audley to Gardiner, 'that the *Praemunire* shall ever hang over your heads and so we laymen shall be sure to enjoy our inheritance by the Common Laws and Acts of Parliament.'[19] From Henry's viewpoint the beauty of the weapon lay in its complete vagueness; he was not likely to debar himself from further arbitrary aggressions by telling his clergy just what they could and could not do. Flushed with his success he urged them in the following month to acknowledge his sole right to the title 'Protector and Supreme Head of the English Church and Clergy'. Not yet entirely subservient, they insisted on adding the clause 'so far as the law of Christ allows', thus making an acknowledgment considerably more limited than the one they came to accept two years later.

The Divorce

THESE advances against the English Church had appreciably augmented Henry's power but, when he paused to think of his own original purpose, he must have felt bitter disappointment. Bullying his English clergy had failed to produce from Rome the divorce he had been seeking for the last four years. Concerning this theme, we need not here follow the interminable analyses of diplomacy and litigation compiled by historians; for our present purpose the upshot has much significance, the day-to-day exchanges very little.[20] Detestable as were the King's monumental egotism, his moralising self-deception, his inhuman treatment of Katherine, one finds it hard to avoid the impression that the ecclesiastical historians have accorded him rather less than justice. Not for long can his case be intelligently discussed as that of a private man anxious to rid himself of a stale and ageing spouse. He could have lived as licentiously as Charles V or Francis I without troubling about divorce and remarriage. Even the phrase 'reason of state' seems rather inadequate to convey his motive, for nothing less than the fate of the nation lay in the balance.

The work of the dynasty remained fragile; neo-feudal reaction and the old spirit of lawlessness were by no means broken. The King had a sickly daughter, but the last female sovereign had been Matilda, whose experiences afforded no great comfort to historically-minded Englishmen. Desperately, indeed, any kingdom of that period needed a strong and mature male heir, for the worst fate which could befall it would spring from irresolute rule, from a minority, from a disputed succession. Moreover, even before Anne Boleyn was born, there had existed genuine doubts among the canon lawyers of Europe concerning the validity of the unusual dispensation by which Julius II had permitted the child-marriage of Henry and Katherine. On far less plausible grounds rulers and magnates had gained decrees of nullity. Louis XII had arranged one in order to marry the heiress of Brittany. In 1527 a divorce had been granted at Rome on the flimsiest of grounds to Henry's immoral sister, Queen Margaret of Scotland; the following year Clement VII confirmed the earlier divorce (obtained under highly dubious circumstances) of his brother-in-law the Duke of Suffolk. Had Henry's plea been indecently weak in law, had his wish to remarry rested purely on private grounds, had not Rome over many years alternately encouraged and repelled him, he would have had little cause for bitterness and less claim for sympathy.

By the time of the Church–State crisis the divorce presented no novel issue. The role of Katherine as a permanent, active and in fact formally-accredited ambassador of Spain had long since occasioned tension between the royal pair, and in 1514, when her father Ferdinand had betrayed English interests, people believed that Henry intended forthwith to repudiate the Queen. Yet the crucial factor in the collapse of the marriage was that extraordinary succession of miscarriages, stillbirths and infant deaths which accounted for all their offspring apart from the Princess Mary. Katherine's last failure occurred in 1518, and the following year her desperate but still hopeful husband vowed to lead a crusade against the Turk if he could be granted a male heir. No English King had lost so many children, and an age which saw the hand of God in far less remarkable coincidences was not slow to remember the curse of childlessness pronounced by *Leviticus* against a man who should marry his brother's wife. That Henry himself came to believe this we have no reason to doubt. By 1525 he had given up hope, though he was still only 34; he began to study the theology and canon law of divorce, concerning which, wrote the Papal Legate Campeggio, he soon knew more than any divine. He and his Council even considered entailing the succession upon the little Duke of Richmond, the natural son who had been so styled with deliberate reference to the title of Henry VII before Bosworth. In March 1527 the King began serious legal proceedings. It is not known whether he already planned a marriage with Anne Boleyn; certainly he was doing so by the following autumn, when he sent Dr. William Knight to procure a dispensation to that end. His famous love-letters date from about this time; the unwonted depth of his affection added not a little to his rancour as move succeeded hopeless move and stalemate gradually confronted him.

The key to Henry's problem lay not in the merits of his legal case but in the military control of Rome by the Emperor Charles V, and this control had been intermittently but steadily tightening ever since 1527, when the imperial armies had subjected the papal city to such appalling sack and slaughter. Clement VII, despite his own conciliatory character, had no freedom to grant Henry a divorce against the will of his political master, who had no special affection for his aunt but had to placate the intense pride of his Spanish subjects in their national monarchy and their royal family. In England itself the position had become all too clear by 1529, when Campeggio left England, the now useless Wolsey was cashiered and Henry understood that the verdict would go against him if he allowed the case to be transferred to Rome. Wolsey had now been replaced by an inferior triumvirate. The Duke of Norfolk was a competent soldier and negotiator, unprincipled except in his loyalty to the King but without originality as statesman or administrator. Henry's brother-in-law and boon-companion the upstart Duke of Suffolk was a less competent soldier but a good sportsman and a fine figure on ceremonial occasions. The Earl of Wiltshire was Anne Boleyn's father and so grandfather of our greatest Queen; even so, he remained a nonentity. Though as early as January 1531 Norfolk told Chapuys that papal jurisdiction was invalid in England,[21] he and his colleagues lacked the legal and political expertise to take the revolutionary steps indicated by the failure of their pressures upon Rome. The years of their ascendancy saw the frenzied search for favourable patristic texts and papal decrees, the consultation and bribery of universities throughout Europe, the bombastic citation of legend to prove the self-sufficiency of

English jurisdiction. As a richly characteristic scene, we can picture Edward Carne and William Bennet, Henry's agents in Rome, frequenting the Vatican Library on a plea of disinterested research, but in fact ransacking the papal registers in their master's cause, while the suspicious librarians followed them from volume to volume in an attempt to discover exactly what they were about.[22]

Like the rest of the King's researchers these agents found singularly little comfort to their master, whose attitude toward Rome became deeply and permanently poisoned; all the more deeply since he entertained an inflated notion of his former services to the Holy See. Sick of trying to conduct the game according to the ancient rules, he resolved at last upon more heroic remedies, and he called in a new type of minister, one ready to work out a merely national solution of the problem, one ready to pass far beyond the divorce into new concepts of political organisation, one who possessed a fully professional knowledge of legal instruments and the apparatus of propaganda. This virtuoso of statecraft was Thomas Cromwell.

The place of the royal divorce in the history of the Reformation will always remain a subject for argument. Protestant writers have tended to dismiss it as a mere 'occasion' rather than a genuine cause; Catholics have sometimes regarded the divorce as the chief cause of the cataclysm and supposed that, had it not been pressed, England might well have remained a Catholic nation. To the present writer neither of these views seems wholly acceptable. The Protestants have too readily assumed the inevitability of a Reformation similar in timing and in character to the one which actually occurred. The divorce was something more than a mere 'occasion'; without it the schism would not have been consummated by 1533–4. Had Henry either abandoned or obtained his divorce he would most likely have tried, and with success, to hold his realm in some sort of spiritual allegiance to Rome, though it seems inconceivable that he or his people would tamely have reverted to any earlier situation. We may well agree with Pollard that the Pope's refusal of the divorce 'alienated the only power which might have kept in check the anti-papal and anti-sacerdotal tendencies then growing up in England'.

On the other side, we must avoid the temptation to equate the Henrician Schism with the Protestant Reformation. The divorce-suit did not create either Protestantism or those anti-papal and anti-sacerdotal forces which smoothed its path. That such forces were diverse in origin and deep-laid in society we have endeavoured to indicate in our earlier chapters. That by the thirties they had reached a critical intensity throughout the dominant classes and regions of England cannot be doubted. And so far as the new beliefs are concerned, it must be acknowledged that, irrespective of his relations with Rome, Henry VIII could not have frozen the English in their religious posture of the year 1530. Even during the last seven years of his reign, when he was attempting to check Protestantism, it was spreading more rapidly than ever before, and it captured the government immediately upon his death. When we are tempted to underestimate its expansive capacities, we should recall that in the Netherlands, in Scotland and elsewhere, it soon played havoc with the plans of kings and governments. At the death of Henry VIII Calvinism still lay, so far as England was concerned, in the womb of the future; but its new challenge, politically more formidable than that of Lutheranism, was bound to be made some day, whatever the complexion of future English governments. Moreover, the special attractions of Protestantism for the ruling classes rapidly manifested themselves; Henry VIII was not immortal and a strong chance remained that future rulers of England would be captured by Protestant beliefs. The most knowledgeable among us cannot speculate with much profit regarding the probable courses of history, had the divorce-problem been solved in Rome or had it never presented itself. Yet was the divorce anything more than one of the many dangerous reefs which English Catholicism had to circumnavigate? And English Catholicism, despite its gilded decorations, was an old, unseaworthy and ill-commanded galleon, scarcely able to continue its voyage without the new seamen and shipwrights produced (but produced far too late in the day) by the Counter-Reformation.

Over and above these considerations, the divorce and its attendant schism arose from a European pattern destined to persist for another century—a pattern which continually set English nationalism at loggerheads with English Catholicism and which at any stage was liable to plunge the latter into disaster. This pattern consisted of a powerful Spain, seeking not only to curb the Atlantine enterprises of the north-European peoples but to control the Mediterranean, the Italian peninsula and with them a reluctant but often rather powerless Papacy. In that age political and religious controls could not be kept apart, and one finds it impossible to imagine a people as tough, as active and as independent as the Tudor English acquiescing for any length of time in a Christendom organised along these Habsburg lines. In some sense, national schisms like that of England became more possible from 1503, when Spain overran the kingdom of Naples and began to establish its long dominance over central Italy. Even if Henry VIII had remained a model of matrimonial respectability, even if the ministers of Edward VI had been converted by a stray Jesuit, even if Queen Mary had survived for another decade, it still requires a vivid imagination to envisage the English as dutiful children of the Holy See at the end of the century. And amongst the many forbidding obstacles, Philip II and Calvin are the two which first catch the eye.

6 Statutes and Bibles: The Henrician Revolution

The Rise of Thomas Cromwell

THOMAS CROMWELL, who laid the legal foundations of the national Church, was in every sense one of the 'new men' brought to the fore by the increasingly flexible outlook of the sixteenth century.[1] That his character showed a certain hardness can only be expected of one who received his training in hard schools, of a *parvenu* who rose to precarious eminence amid a court-society riddled with intrigue and snobbish pretensions. He was born about 1485, the son of a turbulent person who combined the businesses of brewer, fuller and blacksmith at Putney. His sisters married well, and the elder gave birth to that Sir Richard Williams who took the name of Cromwell and is remembered as great-grandfather of the Protector. In his late teens Thomas adventurously sought his fortune abroad and is said to have served in 1503 with the French army at the disastrous battle of the Garigliano. Drawing the obvious conclusions he then entered the service of the banking family of Frescobaldi and worked in northern Italy for two years or more. Armed with this experience he accompanied some English traders to the Netherlands and there became a business-consultant, making reports to London merchants on the all-important state of the Antwerp market. Cromwell's early backgrounds were hence as intensely urban, lay and non-feudal as any in Europe; he enjoyed every opportunity to free himself from the blue-blooded and ecclesiastical prejudices of a moribund yet far from dead medieval world. He was no boor; he had the sense not only to brush up his Latin but to acquire a grasp of Italian literature and ideas which educated contemporaries acknowledged to be far more than superficial. His most familiar portrait is very far from conveying the whole of his personality. He could talk amusingly and he showed good taste in furniture, books, pictures, food and wine; having made his fortune he lived with discretion and elegance, avoiding the grandiose style which had attracted such hatred against Wolsey.

In Antwerp, the greatest commercial and financial capital since ancient times, Cromwell perfected the knowledge of commerce and finance which he displayed to such advantage during his years of power. From Italy he seems to have derived even more fundamental lessons. Unlike the great majority of his fellow countrymen, he learned to think in terms of function and efficiency, to disregard hidebound traditions and all-embracing philosophical systems, to discard that canting rationalisation of self-interest in terms of religious duty which became an embarrassing feature of the outlook of Henry VIII and many mid-Tudor Englishmen. On the other hand, he was no agnostic and, in so far as his cool temperament allowed, he appears to have been genuinely attracted to the ideas which stemmed from Luther. There are numerous improbabilities in Reginald Pole's story that, as early as 1528, four years before the publication of *The Prince*, Cromwell was propounding cynical doctrines based upon that work. If we seek for a fundamental book on Church and State which helped to inspire Cromwell's revolutionary ideas, we are more likely to find this in the *Defensor Pacis* of Marsiglio.

We have already summarised the conclusions of a work too profoundly rebellious to be accepted by its own century, yet destined to exercise widespread influence upon the age of Renaissance and Reformation. Its adoption by Cromwell and his circle remains no matter of guesswork. In the years 1533–5 Richard Sampson, Edward Fox and Thomas Starkey [2] explicitly used Marsilian doctrines to justify the overthrow of papal jurisdiction in England, and the last-named was under direct Cromwellian patronage. More important, in 1535 Cromwell personally supplied the money to another henchman, William Marshall, in order to finance the first English translation of the *Defensor Pacis*.[3] Two years earlier Cromwell had already summarised its doctrine in a few masterly phrases of his Act of Appeals.[4] 'This realm of England is an Empire . . . governed by one Supreme Head and King having the dignity and royal estate of the imperial Crown of the same, unto whom a body politic, compact of all sorts and degrees of people divided in terms and by names of spiritualty and temporalty, be bounden and owe to bear, next to God, a natural and humble obedience.'

On the other hand, though he is said once to have quoted in council the old civilian adage, 'What pleases the Prince, has the force of law', there is no real evidence that Cromwell based his measures upon the authoritarian principles of the civil law. By training and outlook he and his followers were common lawyers. And at every stage his public career was concerned with the House of Commons, through which he consistently worked. Hard as he strove to make the Crown rich and powerful, his supposed intention to make Henry VIII an irresponsible despot may be regarded as a myth, for no statesman ever sought with more zeal to express sovereignty in terms of laws and institutions. When all has been said of Italy and Antwerp, another vital development of Cromwell's education came after his return to England.

This event occurred about the year 1512, when he married a woman of gentle background and settled in London. During the obscure years which followed, he must have embarked upon an intensive study of the common law, since by the period 1520–24 he had already become a solicitor entrusted with important business by Wolsey and other personages. He sat in the Parliament of 1523, from which year dates a long parliamentary speech on foreign policy written in the hand of one of his clerks. We cannot prove that he delivered this oration, but it shows that Cromwell was already thinking for himself on the leading issues of national policy. It is as much of an opposition-speech as any made at that time in the Commons. While criticising Wolsey's expensive and hazardous plans for a campaign in France, it gives priority to the task of uniting England and Scotland.

Despite such views, within a year or two Cromwell became one of the leading members of Wolsey's enormous household and he was soon employed upon the Cardinal's most enlightened project—the suppression of some twenty-nine monasteries in order to found colleges at Oxford and Ipswich. This was in itself a task of no small magnitude, since while none of these houses boasted more than ten members, two of them (Daventry and St. Frideswide's, Oxford) had annual incomes exceeding £200 and three others incomes between £189 and £125. Here the newcomer displayed that infinite capacity for taking pains which in later years impressed all observers. The opportunity to change some aspect of an outworn system always brought forth his single-minded attention to detail, and in a world of amateur administrators he began to shine forth as superbly professional. Though he later claimed to have received few material rewards from Wolsey, he cannot have neglected his numerous opportunities for receiving fees and presents. The will which he drafted in 1529, a few weeks before Wolsey's fall, shows that he possessed very considerable resources and proposed to make a number of lavish benefactions to London charities. Likewise when he came to power, Cromwell showed himself both grasping and generous. If, like any other Tudor minister, he disdained no gift in return for his favours, he also fed two hundred paupers daily at his gate, spent his means in the service of the Crown, gambled like a gentleman and was always ready to oblige an old friend or to win a new one.

On the dismissal of Wolsey he stood in obvious danger as the known lieutenant of that unpopular minister, but after a moment of weakness, even of tears, he resolutely rode off from Esher to London, gained the favour of the King and through the good offices of Sir William Paulet entered the first session of the Reformation Parliament as member for Taunton.[5] Here he defended Wolsey's remaining interests with a conspicuous if finely-calculated loyalty, which gained him far more credit from contemporaries than from his ungenerous modern biographers. By January 1531 he was sworn of the King's Council and within two years held the appointments of master of the King's Jewels, clerk of the Hanaper and chancellor of the Exchequer. None of these could then be called an important office but together they enabled him to begin the rehabilitation of Crown finance and to attract the attention of the King. In 1534 he became principal secretary, an office which he was allowed to extend into a ministry of all affairs, and from this point his surviving state papers leave an impression of laborious omnicompetence hardly rivalled by any other minister in English history.

The Political Context

OUR present concern is with Cromwell's ecclesiastical policy, yet it should be recognised that this policy becomes intelligible only in a general setting of administrative reform. The problems of Church, State and society at large were then closely intertwined. The eight years of Cromwell's ministry form a truly notable episode in the history of the English State. In that of the English Church they are equally revolutionary years, in part destructive, in part as highly constructive. And it cannot reasonably be questioned that Cromwell supplied their chief guiding force. Like Wolsey before him, he received from the King enough independence to be able to set his personal seal upon the period of his ministry. By contrast, outside these eight years, the reign of Henry VIII has scarcely a single creative or revolutionary achievement to its credit. The King's will-power, his courage, his decisiveness, his immense capacity to inspire adulation, these preserved the integrity of the kingdom and paved the way for the long Elizabethan peace which Englishmen were to enjoy amid a chaotic Europe. But otherwise his personal touch proved sterile; he was too egotistical, too emotional, too interested in kingly pleasures, too conservative to initiate new techniques of government, new paths of progress for English society. Yet between the years 1532 and 1540 all is different. Creation, destruction and change are visible on all sides; something like a planned revolution issues from the mind of a minister who is known to have reflected not merely upon practical administrative reform but upon the theory and ultimate purposes of government. Cromwell had his own clear vision of the sovereign State as transcending the turmoil and division inherited from both the defects and the death-struggles of feudal society. While he was subjugating the Church to the Crown in Parliament, he was also curtailing feudal liberties and sanctuaries, bringing a new order to crime-troubled Wales and conciliar justice to the North, where a Percy still counted for more than a Tudor. Again, he was overthrowing the Geraldines in Ireland, striving to build up co-operation with the Scots, initiating the Tudor poor laws, attracting the cloth-trade from the Netherlands to England, checking the export of coin and reforming the whole complex of the financial courts. By the time it was dissolved in 1536 the Reformation Parliament had passed about seventy social and economic statutes, besides another thirty-seven concerning the reform of the law, both criminal and civil. Above all Cromwell proved himself a great manager of Parliament and a great drafter of statutes, the common lawyer who dominated a period of legislation far more intensive and more complex than that of any earlier Parliament or ministry.

Never before had the estates of England been called upon to execute so prolonged, so integrated, so radical a programme, or one more likely to affect the lives of common Englishmen. Beginning with the restricted problem of the divorce, Cromwell ended by reshaping the multilateral relationships of Crown and Parliament with the clergy, the gentry and the common people. Through and with Parliament he resolved the mounting tensions of earlier Tudor society into a new equilibrium which survived the stresses placed upon it by bigotry and incompetence and which in its essentials outlasted the dynasty.

The Henrician Statutes

THE first year of Cromwell's ministry saw the destruction of the legislative independence of the English Church, a process which had effectively commenced with the drafting of the Supplication of the Commons against the Ordinaries. The origins, gradual development and ultimate purposes of this document are still debated;[6] it survives in several versions, the dating of which presents some intricate puzzles. The earliest apparently belongs to the year 1529, when Thomas Cromwell as an ordinary member is thought to have drafted it on behalf of the House of Commons. Do the revisions of 1532 indicate a spontaneous resurgence of anticlerical zeal in the Commons, or should the Supplication be regarded from this point as the instrument of a government-sponsored attack upon the Church? This question has been closely argued, but the evidence may never allow of a precise answer. In any case its broader significance should not be exaggerated. By 1532 Cromwell and other ministers were using the document, yet it remains equally clear that the rank and file of the Commons had lost none of their hostile spirit of 1529 and that they responded swiftly to the lead from above. The actual text of the Supplication[7] represents a fusion of their multiple grievances with the narrower designs of the Crown. As redrafted in 1532, it cleverly links together two main themes which in everyday life were not very intimately connected —the legislative action of the Church, which the King wanted to control, and the practices of the ecclesiastical courts, from which the laity desired to liberate themselves. It begins by blaming discord and heresy upon the uncharitable activities of ecclesiastical officials, and it then descends to 'particular griefs', though without citing names, dates and events. The first is the power of Convocation to make ecclesiastical laws without the consent of the laity, and at their expense, particularly since those laws are not set forth in English and may so be infringed out of mere ignorance. The Supplication then enlarges upon the inordinate delays, prosecutions over trivialities and high fees current in the church courts, the vexatious examinations and imprisonments of offenders, the subtle traps set for people unlucky enough to be charged with heresy. For good measure, some miscellaneous accusations are thrown in: payments are extorted by some priests for administering the sacraments; nepotism still results in the presentations of minors to benefices; the excessive number of holy days conduces to 'execrable vices' and 'wanton sports'.

On 18 March 1532 the Speaker, Thomas Audley, presented the Supplication to the King, who after a curious delay sent it on 12 April to Archbishop Warham, requesting a speedy answer. This challenge came at a moment when the ecclesiastics were showing a real disposition to resist and even to inaugurate reforms on their own account. The previous February Warham had made a formal protest against all acts of the present Parliament derogatory to the Roman Pontiff, to ecclesiastical power or to the privileges of the See of Canterbury.[8] In March he had excommunicated Hugh Latimer, then in favour at court, on charges of heresy, and in reply the government had trumped up a charge under *Praemunire* against Warham, on the technical ground that he had consecrated Dr. Henry Standish before the latter had done homage to the King. Meanwhile in January and February Convocation itself had at long last begun to develop an impressive programme of reforms. Though its new canons centred around the theme of heresy, they also included measures to ensure closer examination of the credentials and education of ordinands, to compel beneficed clergy to reside, to increase the penalties imposed on clerics who committed fornication or indulged in scandalous field-sports and even to impose a weekly minimum of six hours' scriptural study upon incumbents.[9] This development cannot have seemed welcome to the more bitter opponents of the clergy. It is hard to avoid the suspicion that there were now many laymen who no longer sincerely wished to see the Church set its own house in order and who were correspondingly eager to press on with the reduction of its powers before it could recover prestige.

On receiving the Supplication, Warham transmitted it to the Lower House of Convocation, whence there soon emerged a lengthy Answer of the Ordinaries,[10] inspired in large part by Bishop Gardiner. This defence naturally pointed to the unspecific nature of the charges made in the Supplication and to the injustice of blaming a long-accepted system for the faults of isolated individuals. So far did lay malice extend, that divers of the clergy were even being subjected to physical violence, 'so injured in their own persons, thrown down in the kennel in the open street at mid-day, even here within your own city and elsewhere'. The Answer concluded with a moving appeal to the King as protector of the English Church, but the clergy were soon to discover that they had to buy his protection with something more tangible than fair words. On 30 April Henry handed their reply to the Speaker along with a heavy hint. 'We think their answer will smally please you, for it seemeth to us very slender. You be a great sort of wise men; I doubt not but you will look circumspectly on the matter, and we will be indifferent between you.' Having thus encouraged the Commons to maintain their attack he proceeded on 10 May to deliver his own, and confronted Convocation with these demands—that it should pass no new legislation unless he licensed it to do so, and that existent canons should be referred for approval or disapproval to a royal commission of thirty-two members, half of them laymen. The next day he again summoned and addressed the Speaker and a deputation of the House: 'Well-beloved subjects, we thought that the clergy of our realm had been our subjects wholly, but now we have well perceived that they be but half our subjects; yea, and scarce our subjects; for all the prelates at their consecration make an oath to the Pope, clean contrary to the oath that they make to us, so that they seem to be his subjects, and not ours.' So saying, he handed them copies of these two customary oaths, which the Speaker later caused to be read in the House itself.[11]

The matter as well as the manner of this oblique menace to the clergy is worthy of note. The demand for a single sovereignty and an undivided allegiance savours strongly of the known convictions of Thomas Cromwell; moreover, the whole design to fetter clerical legislation stems from the first section of the Supplication of the Commons, also attributable to that minister. The King was already being guided into a territory unfamiliar to his predecessors on the throne of England, into far-reaching and fundamental doctrines which passed well beyond his immediate and personal aims. From this stage we cannot understand Crown policy if we continue to envisage Thomas Cromwell as merely a smart lawyer who made his fortune by solving the King's matrimonial problem. For good or ill, he is a figure of far greater significance in our history.

Whatever doctrines underlay the royal tactics, they proved immediately effective. At this point the clerical front suddenly crumbled, and on 15 May Convocation acceded to all the royal demands by the document known as the Submission of the Clergy. Only seven bishops, it is true, actually attended the crucial session; of these, three consented only with reservations, while one (Clerk of Bath and Wells) refused his support. Yet Warham himself stood among the submissive, and we can give no clear explanation for the sudden collapse of his resistance. Here was a tragic anticlimax, for the Primate can hardly have come overnight to believe in this degree of surrender; he had little to lose and could have made matters very difficult for the King. His death the following August came somewhat as a happy release from a situation even more intolerable than his former place under the shadow of Wolsey. By Sir Thomas More the Submission seems to have been accepted as a landmark; at all events, his resignation of the Chancellorship the following day is not thought to have been purely due to his ill-health, the proffered excuse. In due course he was succeeded in office by Thomas Audley, a prominent agent in the same transactions. For the clergy in general, the Submission represented a further appeal to the King against the Commons. By giving him control over their law-giving functions they avoided the hazard of a far worse fate—the wholesale destruction of their courts and their legal privileges at the hands of Parliament. The King proved less anticlerical than his subjects, and in the last resort he honoured his promise to stand between the laity and the clergy. Having used the Commons as a bugbear to frighten Convocation into handing him its legislative power, he then showed no enthusiasm concerning the rest of the lay demands and refrained from that radical overhaul or abolition of ecclesiastical jurisdiction to which the Commons aspired. Henry VIII was in fact the manipulator, not the creator, of anticlerical sentiment. Neither he nor his successors would follow it to the point of destroying the legal functions of the Church in society, and his situation in 1532 dimly foreshadows that of Elizabeth, standing half a century later between her puritanical Commons and her sorely-pressed Church.

While the Submission of the Clergy applied only indirectly to the divorce-suit, the year 1532 did not pass without some intensification of the direct pressure upon Rome. Annates were now conditionally withheld, pending negotiations for their abolition, and the Act effecting this also stated that should the Pope delay or deny bulls of consecration, bishops might be consecrated by English authority alone. Should he respond by excommunication or interdict, the King and his subjects might 'without any scruple of conscience' continue to enjoy the sacraments and services of the Church, any papal censures notwithstanding. Early in 1533 this threat extorted from Rome the necessary instruments for the consecration of the King's strange candidate for the See of Canterbury, Thomas Cranmer.

Also in 1533 Cromwell produced his most critical piece of legislation—the Act in Restraint of Appeals, containing that famous preamble we have already observed. By here calling England an 'Empire', Cromwell designated it a sovereign state, with a King who owed no submission to any other human ruler and who was invested with plenary power to give his people justice in all causes. In the sense of full temporal sovereignty, the claim to Empire had been repeatedly made by medieval kings and, long before quarrelling with the Pope or the Emperor, Henry had attributed to himself an imperial title. Throughout Europe humanists had been applying the word *imperium* to the rule of kings, but in England its use was more than semantic. Here men seriously believed the legends whereby their kings descended from Arthur, who in turn descended from the Emperor Constantine and his allegedly British mother, Helena. In addition to divorce-precedents, Carne and Bennet had been ordered to seek in the papal archives any acknowledgment of an imperial authority held by Henry's predecessors. In his conversation of January 1531 with Chapuys, the Duke of Norfolk also alluded to these venerable British traditions in remarks which passed well above the head of his ill-informed hearer. About a year after the passing of the Appeals Act, Polydore Vergil, the Italian archdeacon of Wells, published his famous *Anglica Historia*, asserting that an imperial crown had descended on modern English kings in an unbroken line from Constantine. Henceforward the claim was to be made in a steady succession of Tudor statutes, while before the end of the century the term Empire began also to be applied to the overseas expansion of the English State. Its importance in relation to the Reformation should not, however, be overstated. It is true that during the drafting of the Act of Appeals, the King for a time suggested that he should claim to derive his spiritual jurisdiction from this imperial authority, but he found that the claim could not be substantiated by reference to the Holy Roman Empire or to other precedents. He thus ultimately refrained from pressing this emotive but historically circumscribed term, and instead he based his spiritual jurisdiction upon a special claim to a Royal Supremacy over the English Church.[12]

In the text of the Act of Appeals the assertion of Empire is vaguely based upon 'divers sundry old authentic histories and chronicles' and accompanied by the Marsilian definition of spirituality and temporality. The claim to sovereignty once made, the rest of the Act proceeds in a lower key to practical considerations. That part of the body politic called the spirituality or the English Church, it continues, have always had sufficient 'knowledge, integrity and sufficiency of number' to settle spiritual causes without appeals to Rome. Such appeals, despite the laws of former English kings, continued to cause the present King and his subjects cost, vexation and delay. Henceforth all cases concerning matrimony, testaments and tithes shall be finally settled in England. In ecclesiastical suits, appeal shall be from the archdeacon to the bishop's court and from the latter to the archiepiscopal court. But in matters concerning the King and his successors, an appeal shall go to the Upper House of Convocation, without traversing the lower courts. In some parliamentary circles this government measure proved unpopular, though its known critics were disturbed not by its doctrinal corollaries but by the fear that the Pope might organise a European trade-embargo against England. Such misgivings were ably handled by Cromwell, and shortly after the passage of the Act in March 1533 he received open acknowledgment as the King's chief minister.

Far-reaching as were the consequences of this decisive measure, its immediate purpose was to grasp the nettle of the divorce and to make way for the King's speedy re-marriage. This had become urgent, since Anne Boleyn was already known to be pregnant; she actually gave birth to the Princess Elizabeth the following September. By May, after some careful lobbying, Cromwell secured large majorities in both Convocations for two propositions. The first stated that the Pope had possessed no legitimate power to permit the marriage of Henry to Katherine of Aragon, after she had consummated her former marriage with his brother Arthur. The second alleged (despite Katherine's own denial) that such consummation had been adequately proved. On this basis the new Archbishop, long a whole-hearted adherent of Henry's cause, could complete the work. He was licensed to hear the suit, and before the end of the month had declared Katherine's marriage to Henry null and void from its inception. Katherine refused to appear before him, yet under the recent Act her counsel were checkmated and could now appeal no further.

Having thus cut through the tangled skein of the divorce Cromwell was left free to elaborate a new legal relationship between Church and State. With remarkable expedition he produced a series of statutes to this end, and passed them through Parliament during the two crowded sessions of the year 1534. The so-called Act in Restraint of Annates had a far wider significance than its title would suggest. It not only withdrew annates from Rome but also forbade Englishmen to procure papal bulls for the consecration of bishops. Moreover, it instituted the process whereby at each vacancy a cathedral chapter was obliged to elect as bishop the person nominated by the King in his letters missive, accompanying the royal *congé d'élire* or licence to elect. Failure to do so, or failure on the part of the Archbishop or bishops to consecrate the person elected, would expose the offending parties to the dreaded penalties of *Praemunire*. Revived by Queen Elizabeth, the procedure continues to this day, and the durable character of the Henrician legislation is illustrated by the fact that this very situation is still causing disquiet in the Anglican Church, which now might well be credited with enough maturity to select its own bishops. These misgivings seem the more intelligible since that odd legatee of Henry VIII, the prime minister of the day, who could be an atheist, selects bishops for the Sovereign's nomination. Another feature of our day which would have seemed even stranger to Henry is the rôle played in the selection by the patronage secretary of the prime minister.

The Dispensations Act finally stopped all payments to Rome and then stipulated that dispensations (licenses to allow departures from the canon law) should be issued by the Archbishop of Canterbury. Characteristically enough, Cromwell also forestalled by lay controls the possibility that extortionate fees or unreasonable refusals would be occasioned by the Archbishop's officials. Fixed fees for every sort of dispensation would now be agreed and made public, and all grants daily recorded by the clerk of the Chancery. Should a dispensation not emerge upon a reasonable claim, then the Lord Chancellor might issue a writ enjoining the Archbishop under penalty either to grant it or to explain his refusal in Chancery.

The Act for Submission of the Clergy put the existing submission into statutory form by forbidding Convocation to legislate except by the licence of the Crown; it permitted the King to appoint a committee to allow or disallow canons passed by that body. Another clause prohibited all appeals whatsoever to Rome and allowed appeals from the archiepiscopal courts to the Court of Chancery. The first Succession Act vested succession to the Crown in the heirs of Henry and Anne, making it treason to slander the marriage and enjoining that every subject of full age should take an oath to uphold this Act. The latter clause Henry soon showed himself ready to use against eminent opponents of the divorce. When Bishop Fisher and Sir Thomas More refused to take this oath, they were sent to the Tower. They did not dispute the right of Parliament to settle the succession, but they rejected the Royal Supremacy and the assertion that the King's first marriage had been unlawful.

During the late session of this same year 1534, the revolution was substantially completed by the passage of three more statutes. The Act of Supremacy recognised the royal headship as already in existence, and specifically assigned to the Crown the power to conduct visitations of the clergy. This was a clear sign from the King that, although he did not claim to consecrate bishops or to administer the sacraments in person, he had no intention of remaining a mere secular protector of the national Church. He meant to exercise certain spiritual functions hitherto pertaining to the Papacy and the bishops; he annexed the power to correct the opinions of preachers, to supervise the formulation of doctrine, to reform the canon law, to visit and discipline both regular and secular clergy, and even (as happened in the case of John Lambert, which we shall describe) to try heretics in person. Henry's theological knowledge and self-righteousness gave his Supremacy a dangerously personal character, and it was well for the future health of the national

Church that his immediate successors were a minor and two women, all less inclined or less able to undertake the personal exercise of caesaro-papalism.

In January 1535 he proceeded to make a most striking demonstration of the latter. Without reference to any other authority, he appointed Thomas Cromwell his vicegerent, vicar general and special commissary by a grandiloquent commission seemingly modelled on those granted by the Papacy to Wolsey. It gave Cromwell unlimited ecclesiastical jurisdiction as representing the Supreme Head of the English Church. Invested with such powers as no lay subject has held before or since, Cromwell proceeded not only to reorganise ecclesiastical taxation and conduct a visitation of the monasteries, but also to take official precedence over the whole episcopate. Early in 1537, for example, he presided over an important doctrinal debate between the bishops, and displayed patent sympathy with the progressives against John Stokesley, Bishop of London, who staunchly upheld Catholic views of the sacraments and of the 'unwritten verities' of Christian belief. We fortunately possess a detailed account of this episode from the pen of the Scottish Reformer Alexander Alesius, whom Cromwell happened to encounter in the street and took along to the meeting.[13] The debate having begun, he did not hesitate to introduce Alesius to the assembled episcopate as 'the King's scholar' and allow him to speak in violent contravention of Stokesley's arguments. Such an event must indeed have brought home to the bishops the revolutionary character of the Royal Supremacy to which they had become subject.

The respective rôles of Parliament and Convocation as partners in the exercise of this royal supremacy cannot be defined in any simple formula by reference to Henrician legislation and practice. Dr. Woodward has rightly suggested[14] that these statutes and their sequels indicate two divergent tendencies. The famous preamble of the Appeals Act seems to envisage Parliament and Convocation as two concurrent powers, each operating within its own sphere. Similarly, the Act for the Submission of the Clergy places Convocation in a direct relation with the King, a relation parallel to that enjoyed by Parliament. In fact, the King issued articles of faith and (in 1536) curtailed the list of saints' days by the advice and assent of Convocation alone. Through his vicegerent he conducted monastic visitations and issued royal injunctions to the clergy without reference to Parliament. Yet alongside this theory of concurrent powers there ran also a marked tendency to regard Parliament as the superior power and statute law as superior to canon law. The Submission accepted by Convocation had to be regularised by Parliament; Convocation's acknowledgment of the supreme headship had ultimately to be restated in statutory form. From 1540 onwards even the clerical subsidies, granted for centuries by Convocation, were steadily confirmed by Parliament. The Annates Acts, invading the spiritual sphere without reference to Convocation, had already decided that the consecration of bishops without papal approval would be valid. Still more strikingly, the Six Articles Act of 1539 imposed doctrine by the sole authority of the King in Parliament. The vicegerent and eight bishops who drafted the Act sat as a committee of the House of Lords, Convocation not being consulted, while a layman, the Duke of Norfolk, introduced this important religious measure into Parliament. Altogether, while the 'concurrent' theory in the Appeals Act may well have been seriously intended, it often receded into the background. The superior function of Parliament, though irregularly exercised, was from the first so often allowed that Henry's successors had little chance of guarding the English Church as a sacred preserve of monarchy and clergy.[15] Henry, confident in his personal ascendancy and religious learning, is unlikely to have foreseen these future implications. Thomas Cromwell, the parliamentarian, the common lawyer, the institutionalising statesman, may well have foreseen them with equanimity.

The Act for First Fruits and Tenths, judged at least by its intentions, looks the most heavy-handed of all Parliamentary measures imposed upon churchmen. If after perusing it they shared that overwhelming gratitude to the King expressed in its magniloquent preamble, they must have been singularly patriotic Englishmen. It not only annexed the first fruits of bishoprics to the Crown, but extended this exaction to all spiritual benefices, high and low alike. Moreover, it demanded a tenth of their net incomes as a fixed annual tax, beginning at Christmas 1535.

This statute immediately involved one of Cromwell's most remarkable administrative exploits—the compilation of the *Valor Ecclesiasticus*, a detailed assessment of all clerical incomes from those of bishoprics down to those of vicarages and chapels. The compilers first took each taxpayer's gross income, then deducted certain allowances to arrive at his net income, then divided the latter by ten. But the allowances were rigorously limited to the following: fees of stewards and other monastic officials; regular rents and pensions; regular alms distributed under the wills of donors; regular diocesan payments. Though now incomplete for some dioceses, this magnificent survey (since printed in six large folio volumes[16]) is by far the most informative single source on the economic history of the Tudor Church, and is worthy in its fashion to be placed alongside Domesday Book. Likewise impressive is the correspondence by which Cromwell guided the army of amateur administrators charged with the great task. Though many under-assessments of income appear to have remained, the sum of well over £40,000 per annum formed a vast addition to the royal revenue. Before 1542 the Crown had never derived so much as this from its landed estates.[17] Fortunately for the clergy, the inflation soon increased the nominal values of rectories and vicarages, whereas Cromwell's successors contented themselves with levying taxation on the assessments of his *Valor*. From Elizabeth's reign as the burden of clerical subsidies grew, that of first fruits and tenths continued to diminish, until by the time of Queen Anne they had become almost negligible.

Cromwell's first Treason Act made it treasonable to desire, even in words, any bodily harm to the King, Queen or heir apparent, to deprive them of their dignities and titles, to declare the King a heretic, tyrant or usurper, or to detain his ships or weapons. The oft-repeated notion that this legislation first made high treason of seditious words has been proved untrue,[18] yet understandably it remained the only one of these measures to arouse real disquiet amongst the gentry and in Parliament itself. Events soon conspired to remove this tension. Within two years the threats of foreign powers and the rise of treason and rebellion at home brought the vast majority of the nation to the royal standpoint. Little objection arose to the Treason Act of 1536, which imposed the penalties of treason upon any clerical or lay official who refused an oath renouncing the jurisdiction of Rome, or to that of 1539, which threatened all persons seeking to go abroad in order to avoid penalties arising from religious disobedience. Even by Tudor standards, extensions to the treason laws looked oppressive in 1534, but they looked far less so by 1536, when the public peril had become genuine enough. Cromwell did not need to browbeat the courts trying persons accused of plots or papalist sympathies. Unasked, jurors now condemned suspects even on flimsy evidence, and a dismayed people made itself his accomplice in defending the Royal Supremacy by every means in its power.

Resistances

THIS chain of events has the inexorable character of tragedy. Once Henry chose the methods proposed by Cromwell, he was bound to encounter a certain measure of resistance from various minority-groups, ranging from noble idealists to backward-looking feudalists. In a state which lacked police forces and a standing army, this opposition inevitably attracted its unpleasant rewards—harsh and capacious treason laws, counter-espionage, violent prosecutors and juries over-anxious to demonstrate their loyalty. From the secular viewpoint, there was no logical alternative to forcible repression, however unsatisfactory the mechanism available. English history of the fifteenth century and continental history during the sixteenth combined to instil one obvious lesson—that civil war ranked as the worst disaster which could befall a people in this world. To Cromwell, his mind perhaps mainly on the Wars of the Roses, the lessons of history left no room for hesitation, and the reader curious to follow his thinking need only turn to the preamble of the first Succession Act with its insistence upon the 'great effusion and destruction of man's blood', which would spring from the 'sinister appetite and affection' of overmighty subjects arrogating to themselves the right to determine the succession. The majority of the Tudor English abhorred the fanaticism which would plunge a nation into blood upon an issue of religious dogma or canon law. If they clumsily executed too many innocents, blunderers and idealists along with the political traitors, at least they did not, with Alva, burn hosts of heretics or, with Charles V and the German princes, slaughter deluded peasants in their tens of thousands. By comparison with these events, or with many episodes in the so-called Wars of Religion, even the tragic crisis of Henry's reign represents mercy itself in terms of the actual volume of human suffering inflicted. The King was far from compassionate by temperament, and he bears the moral guilt for not a few avoidable executions, including those of his two greatest servants, Thomas More and Thomas Cromwell. Yet in the last resort he fully understood the psychological risks of mass-killing in an English landscape. And only the uninformed critics of Thomas Cromwell have imagined that the minister was a Robespierre. There is no evidence to show that he enjoined severity upon the King and, if a readiness to shed blood had really been a part of his impassive nature, very much more would have been shed during his years of power.

The opposition was not a party. It displayed all the tints of the spectrum without their co-ordination. At its bright end was Sir Thomas More,[19] who as a former minister grasped the civilising duties and achievements of the dynasty, yet on the highest principles found himself obliged to put first the unity of Christendom under papal headship. More was never other than a Catholic, but within that broad definition he showed distinct changes of emphasis. He had his monastic Middle Ages with the London Carthusians, his critical Renaissance with Erasmus, his Counter-Reformation when (on his own showing) he was converted to papalism and actively persecuted the heretics. Alongside him were the Carthusian and Observant victims, understanding far less of the political perils of the day, but beyond criticism in the purity of motive which led them to the gibbet or the dungeon. Somewhat less close than often imagined stood John Fisher, whose saintly personal character should not obscure the extreme unwisdom of his treasonable conversations with the Imperial ambassador Chapuys, that devoted friend of Queen Katherine and equally devoted organiser of sedition.[20]

The reactionary elements of the nobility are ranged in various positions toward the dark end of the spectrum. These magnates formed a menace to the security of the nation, since they could not understand that Tudor England had outgrown the mad bloodshed and faction, the king-making and king-breaking of the fifteenth century. They included active neo-feudalists like Lord Abergavenny, Sir James Griffith ap Howell, Lord Edmund Bray and Lord Darcy; they included also some more mildly disloyal and irresolute groups like that of the Courtenays and the Poles, broken up in 1538 by the discovery of the so-called Exeter Conspiracy.[21] Few of all these men can command much sympathy, because they were destructive anachronists rather than religious objectors. Amid the ruling classes there developed in fact no split along doctrinal lines. Those magnates who did most to preserve Henry's throne amid sedition and rebellion—the Duke of Norfolk and the Earl of Shrewsbury—nevertheless held Catholic beliefs, detesting Cromwell and all those of Reforming outlook. Amongst the higher clergy the impressive feature is the virtual unanimity with which they followed the lead of the King. Only one, John Fisher, accepted martyrdom over the Supremacy. Only one divine of eminence, Reginald Pole, chose exile on account of his beliefs. Those heads of monasteries accused of treason or complicity in rebellion may, with one or two exceptions like Abbot Cooke of Reading, be classed as unlucky victims rather than as deliberate martyrs. The parish clergy, as we have already observed, were in general modest men who quietly accepted the decisions of their superiors, yet their preponderant influence was in the direction of conservatism, and a number of them certainly helped to stir up the group of risings known as the Pilgrimage of Grace. It is also through this latter, one of the best-documented episodes of Tudor history, that we learn most concerning the nature of opposition amongst the laity.

Exactly how far was this most formidable of all the challenges to Henry VIII an anti-Reformation rebellion?[22] It remains hard to answer the question with brevity and precision. The voluminous sources point in many directions, and their problems are complicated by the fact that there were four different risings. The Lincolnshire rebellion of 1–12 October 1536 had virtually collapsed before the northern men rose. The main Pilgrimage under Robert Aske affected Yorkshire, Lancashire and the north-eastern counties. It lasted from 9 October to 5 December 1536. The accompanying revolt in Cumberland and Westmorland (which flared up a second time in the January of 1537) is agreed to have been a social and economic affair, little related to any aspect of the Reformation. The second Yorkshire rising occurred under the leadership of Sir Francis Bigod, no Catholic but a violent Protestant and critic of the monasteries. In January 1537 he brought out his tenants and neighbours, not to oppose the Reformation but to rearm the North against the royal retribution which he saw must needs follow upon the main rising. Our present interest thus centres upon Aske's rebellion and, to a lesser extent, upon the trouble in Lincolnshire. The latter was a chaotic, ignominious and rather sordid affair which can scarcely be dignified as the protest of a Catholic society against the Reformation. Its leaders, headed by 'Captain Cobbler', were simple men. The local gentry joined only when pressed by the commons, and at the first chance they strove to allay the trouble. The general hatred was directed chiefly against an unpopular bishop and his officials and against the collectors of a royal subsidy. While the Lincolnshire insurgents feared the material consequences of the dissolution of the smaller monasteries, they were motivated still more powerfully by wild rumours that the King intended to suppress many parish churches and to confiscate church plate. As for the Royal Supremacy, it receives mention but once in the Lincolnshire records,[23] and this only in order to be accepted by the rebels.

The main Pilgrimage shows a more exhilarating but even more complex list of motives. Led by an attractive religious idealist, it was joined—though often involuntarily—by most of the leading gentle families in the North. Despite some disorder and looting (even at the expense of the monasteries) a large army was assembled in orderly fashion on the banks of the Don, an army more powerful and inured to warfare than the royalist levies sent to oppose it. The conservative North was more dangerous than the conservative West Country, since it was kept in good military training by the Scots and since so many of its gentry were attached in clientage to the feudal houses of Percy, Neville and Dacre, which had traditions of rebellion. Many of the leaders of the Pilgrimage were paid servants of the Percys and felt as a notable grievance the disinheritance of Sir Thomas Percy by his brother, the childless sixth Earl of Northumberland, who had willed the great Percy estates to the King. Another quasi-feudal figure was the aged Lord Darcy, a deeply-trusted servant of the Crown who had long plotted with the imperial ambassador Chapuys and who, at the outset of the revolt, surrendered the key-fortress of Pontefract and joined the rebels. The Pilgrimage was not a White Rose movement, though it might have developed this character had Reginald Pole, a member of the House of York, succeeded in returning to lead it. The northern gentry, like those of Lincolnshire, hated the recent Statute of Uses, which forbade them to settle portions on their younger sons and, by making mortgages illegal, greatly decreased their ability to borrow cash. Many of them held lucrative monastic stewardships and hence had a vested interest in the preservation of the religious houses. They all disliked the recent treason-laws and detested Cromwell for trying the grand jury of Yorkshire in the Star Chamber, on the ground that it had wrongfully acquitted a murderer.

Below these levels, the grievances of the masses were heavily and quite demonstrably economic. In a time of bad harvests and cattle-plagues they suffered additional irritations from hard landlords like the Earl of Cumberland, whose enclosures and entry-fines had provoked an extensive riot the previous year amongst his tenants in the Yorkshire dales. The northerners also suffered from a lack of coin and, seeing the smaller monasteries in process of dissolution, they feared a further drain of currency to non-resident southern landlords, who might succeed the monks. As we shall see, this did not happen on any great scale, but the fear was intelligible enough. According to the clear statement of Robert Aske, this was the main reason why the mass of his followers disliked the Dissolution of the monasteries.[24]

At this moment only some fifteen small houses had in fact been suppressed in Yorkshire. Though in a few cases monks were restored by rebel sympathisers, some mobs showed hostility to their local houses, while the great majority of the monks kept aloof from the movement. As elsewhere in England, the royal divorce was unpopular in the North, but many simpletons went on to imagine that innocent, bluff King Hal was being misled by the parvenu Cromwell and a knot of heretical bishops. Though the northern gentry and clergy were not wholly untouched by Protestantism, conservative religious and social views still predominated at all levels. The common people, as Aske remarked, were 'rude of conditions and not well taught the law of God'. Their conservatism was neither theologically informed nor incompatible with a good deal of anticlericalism, yet they were sufficiently taught by their priests to dislike the idea of heresy. One cannot doubt that most of them heartily approved that clause in the rebel articles which criticised heretical books and doctrines. On the other hand, there is little evidence that the problem of the Supremacy interested the laity, while the senior clergy, ordered to discuss this matter by the leaders of the Pilgrimage, were equally divided over the claims of King and Pope until Aske broke into their meeting and urged them to support the latter. They finally agreed that the King might retain the title 'Head of the Church' but that he could not exercise spiritual powers, even that of visitation.[25]

Rationalising historians have too often neglected the irrational elements observable in popular rebellions, and the Pilgrimage of Grace is in this respect no exception. It was riddled with rumour, fable, folklore and prophecy, particularly by those prophecies concerning the rise and fall of kings which are traceable to the writings of Geoffrey of Monmouth and which had appeared on former occasions, for example in the days of Hotspur and Henry IV. Even educated men took those superstitions seriously. Wilfrid Holme, the Protestant squire of Huntington near York, wrote a long poem on the Pilgrimage of Grace within a few months of its occurrence, his main object being not so much to deride the prophecies as to prove that they could not refer to the reign of Henry VIII.[26] Richard Morison, one of Cromwell's most gifted humanist writers, attacked the 'Welsh' prophecies and then proceeded to develop counter-prophecies in favour of Henry, basing them upon the *Book of Esdras*.[27] Even, however, if its picturesque vagaries be disregarded, one may scarcely maintain that the Pilgrimage of Grace had practical or moral claims to form an alternative government. The ability to formulate a list of grievances did not give it genuine coherence. The gentry, themselves divided by bitter factions, had complaints essentially different from those of the commons. Reluctant to join the movement, they were only too glad to believe the promises made on the King's behalf by the Duke of Norfolk and to go home and discourage any further tendencies to revolt.

Paradoxically, the Pilgrimage could not succeed until it failed, since only the legal Tudor government could mitigate any of its grievances and since legal government could not function until rebellion had been patently repressed. A monarchy based on prestige and little else could not usefully have continued as a puppet of rebellion. Henry VIII, who understood Tudor rule better than his modern critics, could not sleep soundly in his bed until some routine of punishment had been applied to at least a few of the ring-leaders. Having induced the great host to disperse by vicarious promises, he stood in the dilemma of Machiavelli's prince—he could hardly ensure stable government without infringing the principles of private morality. Yet even if, like any other contemporary ruler, he believed that promises made under duress to rebels had no binding force, he could do little to restore his wounded prestige unless his opponents played into his hands. This they proceeded to do. In January 1537 Sir Francis Bigod renewed the revolt and the gentry, full of terrified second thoughts, vied with each other to suppress him. Soon afterwards, renewed risings in Cumberland also disposed opinion in favour of the government and produced an atmosphere in which not only the recent rebels but many of the original leaders could be brought to trial on slender charges. This spectacle remains unsavoury, yet the facile moralising in which romantic admirers of the Pilgrimage have indulged will not bear serious examination. Most of the subjects of Henry VIII believed that rebellion itself was a sin, and they had excellent reasons—not all of them pragmatic—for taking this view. The fabric of civilised life remained tenuous in the extreme; once shattered, it could not be pieced together so easily as by our modern techniques and by our modern minds, so conditioned to law-seeking. Rebellion aimed at changing the government was emphatically not the Tudor equivalent of a general election; it was a desperate gamble with the very life of a people.

That the events of 1536–7 formed the major crisis of the dynasty and that they bear relevance to the history of the Reformation cannot be denied. Nevertheless, the military success of the Pilgrimage would not necessarily have strangled the new religious movements in their childhood. Its failure did not inevitably entail their triumph. Its complex shapes have too often been trimmed to match modern doctrines and too neatly dovetailed into the story of English religion. Aske himself strove to unite its manifold and conflicting grievances into a sense of religious purpose, and for a few days at least he seems to have been partially successful. Yet viewed as a whole, the Pilgrimage cannot for a moment be fairly summarised as a devout crusade to save the rights of Holy Church, to re-edify the monasteries, to overthrow low-born heretics, to restore England to a papalist Christendom. Even the abilities of Robert Aske could not subdue the jarring discords of northern England into this beautiful symphony. The roots of the movement were decidedly economic, its demands predominantly secular, its interest in Rome almost negligible, its leading repressors not Protestant merchants but the highest nobility in the land, who shared its own hostile views toward heresy. In short, the English remained incapable of staging genuine Wars of Religion.

Parish Registers

THE remarkable body of statutes whereby the government and taxation of the English Church were transferred from Rome to England formed only one part of Cromwell's work as vicegerent. The Dissolution of the monasteries, which one should not allow to bulk too large in his career, poses questions of such complexity that we propose to reserve the whole matter to our next chapter. Another episode, the introduction of parish registers by his injunctions of 1538, must at least briefly claim our attention, since nothing illustrates more clearly that Reformation, as understood by Cromwell, did mean reform as well as confiscation.[28] Several years before this national institution of registers, some few humble but sensible parish priests had independently begun to record baptisms, marriages and deaths. In the absence of other records, and amid the small communities of that period, the possibility of marriage within the prohibited degrees presented a constant hazard. No aspect of ecclesiastical law during the Middle Ages lay in so confused a state as that relating to matrimony. Numerous divorces disguised as decrees of nullity were sought and given on grounds of pre-contracts made in infancy or substantiated only by flimsy evidence. Other marriages fell under dispute on grounds of distant blood-relationship, while a further gratuitous series of complexities arose through the arrogance of canonists who invented rules of spiritual affinity between a baptised person and his kin on the one hand, and his sponsors and their kin on the other. This meant that a man could be prosecuted for incest because he had married as his second wife the god-daughter of his first wife. A Church which adopted these irresponsible fantasies and yet failed to organise baptismal and matrimonial records was indeed inviting forcible reform at the hands of the State. Cromwell did not clean up the whole of this Augean stable but at least he made an important contribution to the task.

Early English Bibles

FAR more profound in its effects than the introduction of parish registers, more profound even than the Dissolution of the monasteries, was Cromwell's patronage of the English Bible.[29] However persistently ecclesiastical historians may have overlooked the evidence, there can be no doubts about his early interest in the matter or about his zeal and effectiveness when it came to setting forth translations of the Scriptures. We can believe or disbelieve John Foxe's story that Cromwell memorised the whole of the Latin New Testament of Erasmus while journeying between England and Rome. This task he may have undertaken primarily in order to improve his Latin, yet if so, a close knowledge of the text, enjoyed by extremely few laymen at that date, could scarcely have remained without some deeper influences upon his mind. In 1527, or earlier, Miles Coverdale, as yet an Augustinian friar, wrote to Cromwell with enthusiasm about his study of the Scriptures, dropping a heavy hint about his lack of the necessary books and mentioning the 'godly communication' between the two of them 'in Master Moorys house upon Easter eve'.[30] This passage refers in all likelihood to a discussion at the house of Sir Thomas More, whom Cromwell knew well and deeply respected up to the time of his martyrdom. Coverdale, soon a figure second only to Tyndale in the early history of the English Bible, does not in fact claim to have been actually engaged in translation as early as 1527, but it is not without interest that he was discussing his preparatory studies with his patron Cromwell five years before the latter's ministry began.

By 1534 the King's former distaste for biblical translators and translations, previously stimulated by Tyndale's defiance, had notably diminished. Under the influence of Cranmer and Cromwell, the Convocation of Canterbury now thought it safe to petition the King 'that the holy Scripture shall be translated into the vulgar tongue by certain upright and learned men, to be meted out and delivered to the people for their instruction'. While Tyndale could not openly be used, another instrument was coming to hand. Without awaiting a change of heart in England Coverdale had been hard at work in exile and in 1535, probably at Zürich, published his Bible with an unauthorised dedication to the King.

This was the first complete Bible to be printed in English, for Tyndale had printed, in addition to his New Testament, only translations of the Pentateuch and the *Book of Jonah*. Coverdale was less well qualified to complete the Old Testament, since he knew little or no Hebrew. Hence he incurred a heavy debt to the literal translation from that language into Latin published in 1528 by the Italian Dominican, Santes Pagninus. On the other hand, he had a complete command of German—it sometimes registers adversely upon his English—and made extensive use of Luther's translation and of another German version (largely independent of Luther) published at Zürich in 1531. Nevertheless, his chief obligation was still to Tyndale, long passages of whose New Testament he reproduced with but minor alterations. For all that, he did rather more than merely complete Tyndale's Old Testament. No translator had a better ear for the well-turned phrase and for the ring of a sentence. His independent talent appears to best advantage in that occasionally inaccurate yet lovely version of the Psalms which can still be read in the Anglican Prayer Book. The Church of England, fortunate at least in its literary instincts, continued to prefer Coverdale's Psalms even after the appearance of the Authorised Version of the Bible; they are accordingly still sung at matins and evensong, and for this particular purpose could not be bettered. Even in their obscure moments they have the mellow beauty of some ancient, familiar window with slightly jumbled glass; one would scarcely have the imperfections set right.

In Coverdale the government had found a collaborator far more amenable than Tyndale. 'I am but a private man', he wrote, 'and am obedient under the higher powers.' Though a former disciple of Barnes at Cambridge, and now forced into exile through his bold preaching against images and the confessional, he did not offend Catholic susceptibilities by loading his margins with abuse, and he even altered his original title-page and prologue so as to lessen the impression of his dependence on the German theologians. An eventful career still lay before this mild-mannered but consistent Reformer. Having been allowed to return to England under Cromwell he spent Henry's last reactionary years abroad, but returned under Edward VI. As Lord Russell's chaplain during the troubled summer of 1549 he preached through the West Country in order to pacify the rebellion. Having been rewarded with the bishopric of Exeter Coverdale stood in peril at Mary's accession, and he may well have owned his life to a fortunate family relationship. During the thirties he took as wife a Scottish gentlewoman, whose sister married the Protestant scholar John Macalpine. The latter, also exiled, had risen to influence with the King of Denmark and now prevailed upon that monarch to intercede with Mary for Coverdale's release. The translator hence gained permission to retire to Denmark, whence he moved on to Germany and Switzerland, returning in time to help in the consecration of Elizabeth's archbishop, Matthew Parker. Having refused his former see he then held a London living, revered as a patriarch by all Protestants. Two years before his death in 1568, he also resigned even this benefice as incompatible with his leadership of the nascent Puritan school of thought. We shall shortly refer to Coverdale's main task for Cromwell—the compilation of the Great Bible, which forms the chief memorial of a major and too often neglected figure of the English Reformation.

Meanwhile in August 1535 the Southwark printer James Nicholson (a Netherlander by origin) begged Cromwell's support for the publication of Coverdale's Bible in England. The minister then presumably urged the King to overcome the resistance of the bishops and, according to an anecdote related in Elizabethan times,[31] Henry asked the demurring prelates whether they could find any heresies in the work. When they replied in the negative, he said, 'If there be no heresies, then in God's name let it go abroad among our people.' Some reason exists for believing that Anne Boleyn may have helped to win his tolerance toward a work by one of his exiled Lutheran subjects. She had indeed a vested interest in the Reformation, but she may well have been a more serious convert than modern simplifiers of character have suggested. Not long afterwards, in July 1536, Cromwell prepared a set of ecclesiastical injunctions which contained an order to every parson to provide volumes of the whole Bible, both in Latin and in English, and to place them in the choir of his church 'for every man that will to look and read thereon'. The laity must be encouraged to read the English Bible 'as the very word of God and the spiritual food of man's soul', but also charitably exhorted not to engage in contention over its meaning. Three copies of the 1536 injunctions have survived containing this bold article, yet about the time of Anne Boleyn's fall Cromwell for the moment erased it from his articles. The enterprising Nicholson was nevertheless permitted to print Coverdale, and so successful did the book prove that in 1537 he issued two revised editions.

At this point a competitor entered the market in the shape of a translation by John Rogers, chaplain to the house of English merchants at Antwerp, who used the pseudonym Thomas Matthew. This so-called 'Matthew Bible' first attracted the attention of Cranmer, who in August 1537 brought it to Cromwell. The latter then prevailed upon the King to allow its sale throughout the Kingdom—another testimony to the remarkable influence of the minister and his liberal policy, since everyone knew that Rogers had worked intimately with both Tyndale and Coverdale and that he was closely involved with the German Lutherans. This translator possessed a sound knowledge of both Greek and Hebrew, but wherever possible he made his New

Testament follow Tyndale's. For the Old Testament he drew much inspiration not only from Coverdale but from Lefèvre of Etaples and from Olivetan of Noyon, the relative and mentor of the young Calvin. In one respect, Rogers stood at the end of a tradition, for his was the last of the English Bibles with prefaces and glosses owing a large debt to those of Luther himself. His text is also provided with more than 2,100 notes, drawing heavily upon those by Lefèvre, Olivetan, Bucer, Tyndale and other well-known commentators but superior to those of Tyndale in point of moderation and charity. Nearly two decades later Rogers won distinction as protomartyr of the Marian persecution. He was burnt at Smithfield in February 1555 in the presence of his Flemish wife, a baby at her breast, and of their ten children. If we may follow Foxe's account, his interrogation by Stephen Gardiner expresses the point at issue in this matter of biblical translation. Gardiner stressed the intermediary rôle of the living Church: 'No, thou canst prove nothing by Scripture, the Scripture is dead, it must have a lively expositor.' Rogers replied, 'No, the Scripture is alive.'[32]

The publisher of the Matthew Bible was Richard Grafton, a grocer of London and a merchant adventurer of Antwerp, whose letters to Cromwell display a rather naïve mixture of piety and business acumen. The great difficulties then attendant upon biblical publishing should not, however, be overlooked. Men like Grafton invested large sums but had no comforting foreknowledge that the Bible would ever become a best-seller. On the one hand, they feared that at any moment Gardiner might overthrow Cromwell and procure a reversal of the royal policy. On the other, they were beset by trade rivals unrestrained by modern laws of copyright. These facts should be remembered as we read Grafton's godly phrases and see him sell Cromwell six copies, beseeching him to grant a copyright for three years and to compel every parish priest to buy a copy and every abbey to buy six. In the event, Cromwell licensed both the cheap Coverdale Bible published by Nicholson and the dearer Matthew Bible of Grafton. Though as yet he did not force either upon the clergy, he urged the bishops to do so, and thus promoted the sales of both publications. A circular letter sent to the bishops early in 1538 urges them to exhort the laity to read the Bible and to fix a date by which every parson must lay forth an English Bible for public reading in his church. The evidence indicates that even the conservative bishops followed this directive. On the other hand, if a report on the diocese of Lincoln in September 1539[33] provides a representative picture, a good many parishes must have been slow to comply, a feature more likely to have been occasioned by administrative slackness or by a shortage of copies or money rather than by any resistance on doctrinal grounds.

The Great Bible

IF one understands Cromwell's neat mind aright, this semi-organised situation would never have appealed to him as other than temporary. For some time he had been planning a new and authoritative English Bible. Early in 1538 he entrusted the revision to Coverdale, the printing to Richard Grafton and his partner Whitchurch. The sequel suggests that he would have been wise to envisage an all-English production, but his thoughts inevitably turned to Paris, since he wanted to complete a work of high technical quality in the minimum time. 'Printing is finer there than elsewhere', he told the French ambassador, 'and with the great number of printers and abundance of paper, books are there dispatched sooner than in any other country.'[34] So Grafton and Whitchurch set off for Paris and by June 1538 were at work with their French printer Regnault. Ironically enough, our ambassador at the French court was Gardiner, who left in the October to be succeeded by Edmund Bonner, his future colleague in the Marian persecution. In mid-December with dramatic suddenness the Inquisitor-General of France stopped the work and summoned Regnault to appear before him, while Grafton and Whitchurch wisely fled to England. Cromwell then delivered a strong protest to the French government, arguing that the proposed Bible could not spread heresy in France, being a mere literal translation to help Englishmen who knew no Latin. He also revealed that he had sunk £400 of his own money in the enterprise.

In relating the sequel Foxe tells his usual good story. 'The Englishmen posted away as fast as they could to save themselves, leaving behind them all their bibles . . . and [would never have] recovered them, saving that the lieutenant criminal, having them delivered unto him in a place of Paris (like Smithfield) called Maulbert Place, was somewhat moved with covetousness and sold four great dry vats of them to a haberdasher to lap in caps, and these were bought again, but the rest were burned.' And he goes on to relate how Grafton and Whitchurch ultimately returned to Paris and obtained permission to bring Regnault's presses, type and workmen to England.[35] The bibliographical evidence in fact suggests that the printing took place in two stages and that the type-setting, apart from that of the *Apocrypha*, had been largely executed in Paris. Considering all these obstacles, the completion of the work in London by April 1539 illustrates the assiduity of these early printers and the driving force with which Cromwell accomplished a task. Foxe's final story seems, however, more debatable. He blames the interference of the French Inquisitor upon 'the hatred of the bishops, namely Stephen Gardiner and his fellows, who mightily did stomach and malign the printing thereof'. This is the type of charge not to be believed on the sole authority of Foxe. Yet Gardiner showed himself a consistent adversary of the open Bible; he was in Paris long enough to set opposition in motion and his warmest admirers would not deny his title to be considered an accomplished political intriguer. On first arriving in Paris Grafton and Whitchurch had written to Cromwell offering to reveal the names of certain persons already complaining against them to the University of Paris, 'and most chiefly of our own countrymen'.[36] Even so, it cannot be proved to the hilt that these objectors were Gardiner's secret agents. As for Bonner, he was at this time a dutiful Cromwellian and gave his chief every support in the matter of the English Bible.

Despite these vicissitudes the Great Bible, as it came to be called, duly appeared in April 1539. A year later it achieved a second edition with a famous preface by Cranmer, and by the end of 1541 it had run through no less than five further editions. A letter written by Cranmer to Cromwell in November 1539[37] indicates the continued personal supervision maintained by the minister. Whitchurch, accompanied by the King's printer Thomas Berthelet, had just called on the Archbishop, and Berthelet had urged Cranmer to have the selling price fixed at 13s. 4d. Whitchurch had nevertheless reminded them that Cromwell preferred a price of ten shillings. If, reports Cranmer, Cromwell would grant the firm a monopoly of the Great Bible, Whitchurch would with reluctance accept the lower figure. In response Cromwell obtained a patent forbidding any printer to print an English Bible without his permission. Under this arrangement he could give Grafton and Whitchurch reasonable protection, but in fact he did not accord them a complete monopoly. In the same year he permitted Berthelet to publish a new translation by Richard Taverner, another of his close adherents[38] and a keen student of the Lutheran commentators. Taverner's Old Testament has little interest, in that he knew no Hebrew but followed Coverdale and Pagninus. On the other hand, his knowledge of Greek was excellent; his rendering of the New Testament is closer to the Greek than those of his predecessors, sometimes anticipating both the Rheims New Testament of 1582 and the Authorised Version itself. His notes and accessories are mainly drawn from the Matthew Bible. Finally, in April 1540 Cromwell also allowed Berthelet to print a cheap edition of the Great Bible for purposes of private reading.

The success of the Great Bible proved no more than its just desert, for it turned out to be Coverdale's masterpiece. Beginning with the Matthew Bible (itself owing a good deal to Coverdale's own earlier work) he improved this with the aid of the New Testament of Erasmus and, more important, with that of Sebastian Münster's able Latin translation of the Old Testament, published in 1535 alongside a Hebrew text. The politic hand of Cromwell appears in a gesture made to placate the affection of Catholics for the Vulgate. When the Vulgate added anything to the Hebrew or Greek text, Coverdale agreed to insert the addition in small type and in brackets. He also toned down a few offensive expressions, yet without essentially altering the Protestant terminology deriving from Tyndale. In general this proved a sober, tasteful and workmanlike production. If it sacrifices some of Tyndale's freshness and force, if its accuracy does not achieve modern standards, it may nevertheless be claimed as more consistent and more exact than its predecessors. Cranmer's preface to the second edition has been rightly praised both for its style and its sentiments, but the use of the term 'Cranmer's Bible' has been among the more absurd of popular misnomers. That the Archbishop took a warm interest in the Great Bible is not in dispute, but literary responsibility for this (and all other early translations) belongs to the English Lutherans in the Tyndale tradition. The political initiative, the planning of publication, the finance, the pressure to impose the Great Bible upon the English Church, these came from the vicegerent Thomas Cromwell.

Effects of the English Bible

THE still-prevalent opinion that Cromwell's attitude to religion was purely worldly, negative and sinister is based not on a serious study of Cromwell's character and designs but on an obsession with the monastic dissolution to the neglect of the innumerable proofs that Cromwell had creative and positive views on ecclesiastical reform. As luck will have it, we can trace his lively interest in the Bible to a point much earlier than his rise to political eminence, while his obvious (and ultimately fatal) leanings toward Lutheranism must have involved an understanding of the principles central to that school of thought. One who reads without prejudice his letters, his injunctions, his final parliamentary speech of 12 April 1540, cannot doubt his positive desire to establish a religion based upon the Bible, a religion eschewing on the one hand blind trust in ecclesiastical tradition and on the other the brawling of self-appointed expositors. But in the mind of such a man this desire was far from remaining unworldly; Cromwell did not think about the vernacular Bible in exactly the same terms as Tyndale. His political task bade him to consider the Bible in its social setting, and here no clear division existed between the spiritual and the temporal. One cannot study his injunctions without sensing his zeal to create a scripturally-educated laity as the backbone of an orderly Christian commonwealth. He had his own statesmanlike reasons for hoping, as Erasmus had hoped twenty years earlier, that the gospels might be read by travellers on their journeys and 'that the husbandman may sing parts of them at his plough, that the weaver may hum them at his shuttle'.

The Reformers, the Erasmians, the Cromwellians who entertained such ambitions would not have been dissatisfied could they have looked forward for a couple of centuries into English history. Concerning the immense influence of the vernacular Bible upon both the religious and the secular history of the English people and their colonial offspring, one cannot write save in the danger of perpetrating cant and cliché. Upon the Bible stood both Anglicanism and Nonconformity. Especially during our golden seventeenth century the Bible worked as a midwife to bring forth a whole great literature. It enabled a tinker of Bedford to write *The Pilgrim's Progress*. In an age when Milton could believe that God had chosen his Englishmen to perform his special tasks, it was the Bible which nerved the arm of Oliver Cromwell and fortified the spirit of the pioneers in New England. Without it we can scarcely imagine English constitutionalism or English imperial expansion. It was a capacious literature which, especially under conditions of unscientific exegesis, could be applied to any human situation and made to yield a quasi-supernatural sanction to many courses of conduct. In short, it provoked and it rationalised the theory and the action of those three great centuries during which Britain placed her stamp upon world history. For the mass of her people, this was the true Renaissance, the creative revival of Antiquity.

The English Lutherans, organised by a lay-minister and applauded by a half-Protestant Archbishop, first provided vernacular Bibles at a time when many of the English hierarchy still opposed so radical a departure from medieval principles. Only a few staunch ecclesiasts have believed that the Henrician bishops would have taken the initiative to provide a tolerable version, or for that matter any version, of the Scriptures. But it remains too easy to be wise after the event and to castigate conservatives like More for their zeal to suppress the Lutheran translations and for their timorous refusal of an alternative. They were merely maintaining an established English policy in a period of crisis which threatened to engulf an ecclesiastical and social order they felt committed to preserve. With more reason we may permit ourselves a smile at the expense of Gardiner, who faced by the failure of total prohibition demanded that many debatable words (and indeed many non-debatable ones) should be wrapped up in Latin neologisms: 'Behold the ancille of the Lord'... 'This is my dilect son in whom complacui.'[39]

The governors of the Tudor commonwealth stood in a position not wholly unlike that of modern liberal governments seeking to extend full democracy to unripe peoples. Over-confident in their little knowledge and their adolescent pride, the learners rush in, to the peril of themselves and of others. Yet the stage has arrived when they can learn only from their own errors, when they can be restrained only by a repression more harmful than the abuse of freedom itself. Their state must become worse before it can become better. That in 1538 there were a good many Englishmen prepared to abuse the liberty of the Gospel became at once clear, yet further attempts to restrict access proved half-hearted and ineffective. Of the several canyons across which Thomas Cromwell led the English nation, this was perhaps the widest and the deepest. If the Cromwellian statutes crippled papalism, the English Bible was destined to cripple caesaro-papalism. It even involved in substance the great debate of eighteenth-century Europe; it involved faith in the capacity of human nature for self-improvement. The demand from below was bound to become progressive; men rapidly sensed that after so many centuries of hierarchical and autocratic Christianity they were only demanding a liberty which early Christians had assumed as a matter of course. A Christian country could not educate its laity and then prohibit their access to the written sources of Christian belief. Tudor laymen had to be treated like adults because they believed themselves to be such. Though the art of State-propaganda was now advancing, Tudor governments could neither suppress the appetite for the Bible, once they had whetted it, nor could they successfully prescribe the conclusions to be drawn from biblical study.

These remoter effects were by no means fully discernible in the year 1538, when the English Bible became an established feature of the national life. Its more immediate effects were of a simpler character. It clinched the victory of the régime over papal authority and over the saint-cults. As it happened, the latter had just received further discredit when John Hilsey, the former Dominican who had succeeded Fisher as Bishop of Rochester, exposed the Blood of Hailes, the Rood of Boxley and other time-honoured frauds. As now expounded, the Scriptures constituted a more fundamental if less sensational attack upon this aspect of medieval religion. It was not merely that the New Testament provided so slight a foundation for these cults, but rather that St. Paul laid such emphasis upon salvation through the merits of Christ. If Bible-reading tended to overstress the Old Testament, it also popularised Pauline theology, that intellectual element of the faith which could not have been spread abroad by the theatrical modes of presentation used by the medieval Church upon a less literate public. And whatever happened in later years, the initial perusal of the Scriptures tended to enhance rather than undermine monarchical power. In the Old Testament one read much concerning godly Kings, while the New Testament at least gave Caesar his due. In both Testaments one might frequently encounter prophets announcing the good tidings, but one could sense singularly little of the medieval or Renaissance papacy. Alongside the much-debated Petrine texts one could even read the prolonged rebuke administered by Paul in *Galatians*, ii, 11–21: 'But when Peter was come to Antioch, I withstood him openly, because he was worthy to be blamed. . . .'[40] Yet in the last resort the most potent effects of Bible-reading are unlikely to have been in this text-hunting, beloved as it was by Tudor theologians. They are perhaps to be found in the general atmosphere of Gospel Christianity. The unaffected simplicity which marked the lives of Jesus Christ and the Apostles stood in bizarre contrast with the immense legal and coercive apparatus, the great wealth and splendid architectural exploits of the later medieval and Renaissance Church. Though this contrast had been expressed by Savonarola and other Catholic reformers, its full force could only be experienced by a man who had read the Gospels for himself.

In the Bible, in the notion of a return to the original spirit of Christianity, in the rebirth of a fragment of the ancient world so infinitely more precious to Christians than the glories of Greece and the grandeurs of Rome, here lay the true strength of the Reformation. One who has never felt this nostalgia, this desire to sweep away the accretions, to cross the centuries to the homeland, can understand little of the compulsive attraction of the New Testament, even less of the limited but real successes achieved by Protestantism, successes which cannot, any more than those of the Counter-Reformation, be explained away by reference to ambitious kings and greedy nobles.

Nevertheless, along this path of biblical study lay some yawning pits into which hapless Christians did not fail to stumble. Too many readers, both educated and uneducated, would not be satisfied to present their conclusions as reasonable hypotheses or as starting-points for fresh thought and investigation. Instead, the old demon of the medieval schools reappeared in more insidious guise—the spiritual pride which, even when faced by the obscurer problems of theology, worked through cocksure ratiocination to precise verbal definition, through counter-dogma to counter-persecution. Offered a vision of the free, the enquiring, the charitable, the tentative and modest mind, they turned their backs upon it and entered a prison cell not very dissimilar to the one they had just left. It began to appear that the Spirit of Truth had denied infallibility to the successors of St. Peter, to Aristotle, to the metaphysicians of Paris, only to bestow this wondrous gift upon the theologians of Zürich, Geneva or Cambridge. Revolutions seldom make large immediate contributions to the liberty of man. If the Reformation in the end augmented our spiritual liberty, it did so slowly and by devious ways which many of its original champions could neither have anticipated nor desired.

7 The Great Transfer

Motives for the Dissolution

'THIS YEAR many dreadful gales, much rain, lightning and thunder, especially in summertime, and at odd times throughout the year; also divers sudden mortal fevers, and the charity of many people grows cold; no love, not the least devotion remains in the people, but rather many false opinions and schisms against the sacraments of the Church.' With these words of doom the Augustinian canon of Butley Priory in Suffolk continued his chronicle in the year 1534.[1] To his troubled spirit even the elements seemed to unite in proclaiming the end of an era.

In this same year Thomas Cromwell and his colleagues discussed a certain scheme for the financial nationalisation of the English Church which would have justified the darkest forebodings of this depressed ecclesiastic. These memoranda, still among the State papers,[2] envisage the dissolution of all monasteries with less than thirteen inmates, the transfer of episcopal lands to the Crown and a staff of salaried bishops. In addition, the King would receive annates and half the incomes of cathedrals and collegiate churches. How seriously Cromwell took this radical scheme we do not know, but in the event it was discarded. Perhaps it seemed to involve too much risk of alienating and uniting the whole clerical order. The Crown was remarkably unprejudiced in its readiness to take money from any possible source, ecclesiastical or lay, yet on mature reflection the monasteries must have seemed by far the safest victims. They had broad lands, compliant heads, hostile critics in the parliamentary classes and among the secular clergy. They did not enjoy anything like that measure of popular esteem which modern romantics have thought to observe. Certainly they were not dissolved because of any dangerous devotion to the Papacy; anyone who believed this of any save an exiguous minority of English monks must have been highly prejudiced or foolish. What of the notion that the purchase of ex-monastic lands would bind a wavering nobility and squirearchy to the Crown? As will appear, some contemporaries did entertain this thought, yet it seems to play a far larger part in modern analyses than in the actual records of the Dissolution-years. While Cromwell was prepared to make some discreet alienations of land to certain key figures, his main aim was to endow the Crown in perpetuity, not to make it a mere channel for the enrichment of others. We should view the Dissolution alongside the remark he made to the King on the eve of his execution: 'If it had been or were in my power to make you so rich as ye might enrich all men, God help me as I would do it.'[3]

Following the unhappy experiences of Wolsey with Parliament, there had arisen financial needs which dwarfed those of the Cardinal himself. The enrichment of the Crown had again become the first and most obvious duty of its servants. In general the nation appreciated the internal order bestowed by the monarchy, while yet lacking all eagerness to pay for this blessing. The great inflation occasioned by American silver had by no means reached its acute stage, yet the expenses of government, especially the cost of ships and cannon, were fast multiplying. The monarchies of Europe staggered under mounting debts and soaring rates of interest; even the great Emperor Charles V on at least one occasion owed the preservation of his throne to the prompt financial support of the House of Fugger.[4] In addition to world trends Henry VIII had his own peculiar problems during the crisis of his Reformation. From 1534 the risk of invasion (a risk admittedly increased by the divorce and the schism) demanded great military expenditure. The defence of the northern marches, the Geraldine rebellion and the Pilgrimage of Grace all cost very large sums, while the Reformation Parliament proved far more lavish in protestations of loyalty than in offers of hard cash. Thomas Cromwell, an experienced member of the Commons, no doubt suspected that parliamentary enthusiasm for the King's causes would flourish in inverse proportion with the lay subsidies demanded by the Crown. Under these circumstances national defence and stable government could scarcely be preserved save by some large-scale exploitation of the resources of the Church. Otherwise, only by the most quiescent of policies, by the utmost good fortune in foreign relations, by a rigorous retrenchment of expenditure, could Henry VIII have avoided a dangerous crisis during the last decade of his reign. The exigencies of his situation have often been concealed from historians by two facts—that he had to hand a minister of exceptional foresight and that he could pillage many rich but defenceless ecclesiastical corporations. In a very real sense, the whole nation was the partner of King and minister in the ruthless enterprise of dissolution.

The enterprise itself has been too well described by Professor Knowles to demand further detailed narratives.[5] Indeed, if we adhered rigorously to our main theme, we might almost avoid this topic, since the fate of the monasteries had only indirect connections with the rise of Protestantism. Even so, if a dissolution motivated by finance had not occurred in the thirties, a dissolution motivated in some measure by religion must have occurred as soon as Protestant teachings were professed by the governing class. Celibate communities which fostered the cult of the saints would have placed an impossible burden upon the meagre fund of Protestant tolerance.

The attitude of Thomas Cromwell toward the monasteries demands a rather more careful appreciation than most writers have accorded it. As an efficient layman he had plumbed the depths of monastic inefficiency, while men of his background had never been imbued with any sense of the historic achievements of monasticism. He evidently regarded the religious orders as beyond reform and without claims to a place in the new society he was planning. In addition, there seems every reason to think of him as more powerfully swayed than most Henrician officials by Lutheran influences, which can only have deepened his prejudices. He may consciously have taken his cue from the policy of dissolution already exemplified by the Lutheran rulers of Germany and Scandinavia. Familiar as were his relations with many individual monks, and little as his impassive temperament allowed of strong hatreds, he set about the destruction of the English religious houses with something resembling alacrity. In the conservative atmosphere of the King's service he was in no position to avow the religious ideas behind his dislike of monasticism; he could scarcely declare that the King desperately needed its wealth. There remained only one basis upon which a general dissolution could publicly be recommended—that of bad discipline and general inefficiency. These features were far from wholly imaginary, yet an objective report upon the monasteries might not have carried conviction in Parliament, and Cromwell never left anything to chance. Under these circumstances the final visitations lacked scruple, and the minister, who has been unjustly blamed for so many alleged offences, must in this case be allotted much of the responsibility. The best one can say is that sixteenth-century politicians and administrators lacked the impartiality which (in Britain at all events) we expect today even from the least sensitive of their successors.

The Process of Dissolution

THE exploits of Cromwell's visitors, the 'satrapic' Legh, the garrulous Layton, the pliable Dr. London and their colleagues have often been recounted in terms of an intelligible distaste. With but few exceptions like the laymen John Tregonwell and John ap Rice, they were careerist secular clergy imbued with a full share of the age-old dislike of seculars for regulars. Their attitude was far from uniformly harsh. They spoke well of some religious houses and often proved mindful of the personal interests of particular monks. Certain of their charges of misbehaviour can be corroborated in those few cases where a recent episcopal visitation can be produced or when some other less tainted source happens to survive. Indeed, the deliberate fabrication of monastic shortcomings and vices does not seem to have been their normal habit. They found little need for pure fiction. As a matter of visitation-routine, monks were accustomed to informing against one another, but by this date the morale upon which this system depended had reached a low ebb. Moreover, by a novel perversion of the traditional procedure, evidence was now also taken from witnesses outside the cloister, many of whom may have been inspired by personal grudges, by rumours and modish tendencies to anticlericalism. Self-appointed experts on monasticism could be found at every corner, and they had received no little encouragement from the too intimate social relations subsisting between many religious persons and their lay neighbours. If an official visitor believed, or affected to believe, half the scandal he heard under these circumstances, he would certainly need no imagination in order to compile an unfavourable report on monasticism. And the speed with which these men perambulated the monasteries was often even greater than that of a hasty medieval bishop, and hence even less likely to have permitted any real sifting of complaints and accusations. The main objective of the Cromwellian team was to complete an unfavourable report in readiness for the Parliament of 1536.

The precise effect of this report has not been adequately recorded. In subsequent years Latimer said in the course of a sermon, 'For when their enormities were first read in the parliament house, they were so great and abominable that there was nothing but "down with them".'[6] This late recollection by a prejudiced witness need not necessarily be accepted as the universal verdict of Parliament, and even less attention need be paid to the contrary tradition (which first appears in Spelman[7]) that Henry secured the passage of the Act by openly threatening to decapitate reluctant members of the Commons. Some debate did occur and certain amendments protected the many interests of the laity, who had no assurance as yet that they would benefit directly or indirectly from the Dissolution. The various phases of the latter from 1535 to 1540 may appear to us smooth and premeditated, yet we cannot be certain that, when drafting the Act of 1536, the government itself anticipated the dissolution of the 'greater' monasteries in any immediate future. If it did so, one may well wonder why it was so incautious as to allow the preamble of this first Act to praise the discipline still maintained in the 'greater' houses. Nevertheless, some parliamentarians seem to have perceived the second stage to be implicit in the first. 'Even at that time', reports Edward Hall, 'one said in the parliament house that these [i.e. the 'lesser' monasteries] were as thorns, but the great abbots were putrified old oaks, and they must needs follow.'[8]

The Act had a smaller immediate impact than its text might suggest. Though in appearance it dissolved all houses with incomes of less than £200, a considerable number of these (about 67 of the 304 covered by the Act) obtained exemptions. To cite an extreme example, in the Yorkshire district of the Court of Augmentations, no less than thirty-three of the fifty houses had incomes below the limit, yet of these only fifteen actually underwent suppression in 1536. The rest were not spared momentarily to placate the northern malcontents, because in fact they were not dissolved until 1539. And though the Crown gained fees (and the Augmentations officials *douceurs*) for such favours, the chief reason for this delay was not financial. It seems to have been an accommodation problem. At this stage religious persons could either take a dispensation to leave religion altogether or else be transferred to another house, and in Yorkshire an embarrassingly large number appear to have made the second choice.[9] Another interesting recent discovery has, however, emphasised the great number of those elsewhere who voluntarily withdrew. A register at Lambeth shows that at least 975 monks and canons took this course, mainly in 1536–7, and were willing to depart without awaiting pensions. Of these men with weak vocations a mere handful seem to have received benefices as secular clergy, and at present we have no information regarding the future of the rest. It would appear that many must have merged without regret into lay life.[10]

The Pilgrimage cannot be regarded as a predominantly pro-monastic rising, yet its failure speeded the overthrow of the greater English monasteries. By a strained interpretation of the law, houses were declared forfeit to Crown when their heads were attainted of treason. Jervaulx, Whalley, Barlings, Kirkstead, Holm Cultram and Bridlington fell under this rule, as if they had been private estates. From this stage there ensued throughout England a steady stream of surrenders by the heads of surviving houses, about 188 of whom took this course between 1537 and 1540. Some succumbed reluctantly to pressure from government agents. Others showed themselves eager to earn their pensions by staging an efficient transfer and obliging Cromwell, who in so many cases had originally chosen them for office. When in 1539 the final Act of Dissolution came to be passed, little remained of the once noble edifice of English monasticism. This Act was framed not so much to dissolve houses as to recognise the surrenders already made and to remove any legal queries concerning the King's title to the monastic lands. On 23 March 1540 the last survivor, Waltham Abbey, made its surrender, and by that date the minister himself had scarcely four months to live.

From the Dissolution sprang an administrative experiment of great interest. In April 1536 Cromwell set up the Court of Augmentations to manage ex-monastic lands and administer their revenues, its organisation being originally based upon that of the Duchy of Lancaster. With its many regional receivers and other officials it soon attained the stature of a national treasury and by 1544 its annual revenues had reached the enormous figure of £253,292, more than doubling the combined incomes of the Courts of General Surveyors, First Fruits and Wards. For a time it seemed to have no powerful rivals. The Chamber, revived by Henry VII to deal with the great increases of Crown revenue, had now fallen into decline, while no one could yet have foreseen the ultimate revival of the long-decadent Exchequer. Beginning with practical problems set by the Dissolution Cromwell thus appeared to have created an institution which might permanently control the Crown lands and dominate the financial structure of the State. Nevertheless, after the death of its creator in 1540, the discipline, integrity and effectiveness of the Court of Augmentations began to show patent signs of decline. Though reformed in 1547, when it absorbed the Court of General Surveyors, the Augmentations never fully recovered its authority. In 1553–4 it fell victim to a new movement of financial reform backed by William Paulet, Marquis of Winchester, and by one of its former officials Sir Walter Mildmay, who envisaged its incorporation (together with Wards, First Fruits and the Duchy of Lancaster) into a reorganised national Exchequer.[11] Almost all the leading officials of the Augmentations were prominent Henrician Catholics: Lord Chancellor Audley, the brothers Southwell, Sir John Gostwick and Sir Thomas Pope. Even the unprincipled Sir Richard Rich, Chancellor of the Court, was at least a conscientious persecutor of Protestants. In the destruction, division and purchase of the monastic lands the lead was emphatically not taken by men of the new faith but by men who hated Luther and Cranmer, men who in time became pillars of the Catholic reaction under Queen Mary.

The Ex-Religious

The provision made for the ex-religious remained thoroughly in character with the mundane, insensitive but by no means grossly inhumane spirit of mid-Tudor England. Drama, heroism and martyrdom were not the lot of the dispossessed, and it has been claimed with some justice that they received gentler treatment than the victims of later dissolutions on the continent. Heads of houses were pensioned on a scale far more lavish than their subordinates, and in many cases they soon rose to bishoprics, deaneries and substantial livings.[12] The average pension of an ordinary monk or regular canon stood at the not unreasonable figure of five or six pounds per annum, which in the years 1540–50 represents the wage of an unskilled workman or the stipend of a poor priest with a single chantry. Here, however, generosity reached its limit. The nuns, whose estates seldom proved extensive, received very small pensions and could not, of course, seek to augment them by any other form of ecclesiastical employment. The King, so scrupulous in these matters, debarred by law the marriage of ex-religious persons and, by the time the government of Edward VI reversed this decision, most ex-nuns must have missed their chances of matrimony.

Here and there among the multitudinous wills of the period we encounter nuns of gentle family settling down comfortably amid their nephews and nieces. Perhaps they were wiser than the few who took advantage of the Edwardian Act permitting marriage, only to be divorced a few years later by Queen Mary. In the Marian court books at York we can trace the stories of a few such victims of governmental inconsistency. In 1554–5 Margaret Basforth of Thornaby[13] was accused of solemnising and consummating marriage with Roger Newstead, gresman of Thornaby. She admitted having professed in the nunnery of Moxby at the age of fourteen and she had been only twenty at its dissolution. The couple were now, nearly twenty years later, ordered by the Archbishop's court to desist from cohabitation—never to meet, save in church or market, never to talk save in the presence of three or four persons. Margaret was also ordered to resume monastic apparel at her own expense, but kindly licensed to live outside the nunnery of Moxby, though it had been disused since 1536 and showed no signs of being resuscitated. By chance we happen to know that this particular story had a fortunate ending. Long years afterwards in 1586 Margaret gave evidence at York in a title-cause involving the lands of her former house, and in her evidence she described how she and the 'other younge nunns' of Moxby had helped there with the haymaking over half a century ago. But she now appears once again as wife to Roger Newstead, gresman of Thornaby!

A less attractive tale is that of Jane Fairfax,[14] a former nun of Sinningthwaite who had first retired to her ancestral home at Nun Appleton, made famous under later Fairfaxes by Andrew Marvell. Then in recent years she had gone to live with her relative Guy Fairfax near Gilling. Perhaps through difficulties arising from their kinship, they had failed to marry, yet now in 1555 they had a three-year-old child. Separated and ordered to do penance the unhappy pair reappeared in court not long afterwards on a charge of renewed cohabitation, but the further outcome remains unknown. Other former nuns, whose lives ran in quieter courses, continue to occur in the official pension-lists of the mid-Elizabethan years. Their pensions were not only small but subject, like rich benefices and higher pensions, to a flat-rate tax of ten per cent. We have, for example, a list of 1573 showing several aged Yorkshire nuns paying four shillings per annum on their pensions of £2 6s. 8d.[15] Under Elizabeth the wheels of Tudor bureaucracy ground no less small than under her father.

The other considerable group without any reason to laud governmental generosity was that of the friars, over 1,000 in number, who were turned out unpensioned. Despite their old reputation for preaching smoothly and winning silver they possessed little property and hence by the standards of the age did not qualify to enter the pension-lists. Their training fitted them for parochial functions though it is by no means certain that they found places more rapidly than the monks and canons. When the Dominicans of Gloucester were dissolved, they numbered only a prior and six friars. The records of episcopal visitations held two years later, and again eight years later, show all these seven men serving as stipendiary priests in parishes within and around Gloucester. At least two of them subsequently secured actual benefices in the area. There are nevertheless reasons for believing that this group enjoyed more than average good fortune.[16]

Like most operations of Tudor officialdom the payment of pensions to the dispossessed involved occasional irregularities and delays but the only known general crisis arose late in the reign of Edward VI. A major enquiry conducted in 1552–3[17] surveyed payments not only to ex-religious but to former stewards, corrodians, chantry-priests and others now on the pension-lists of the Court of Augmentations. The returns extant today cover fourteen counties and possibly about half the total number of such grantees then on the books. Speculation, fraud and sales of patents were all found negligible in extent. On the other hand, formidable arrears of payment had accumulated by the autumn of 1552. Of the 800 ex-religious represented in these lists 406 stood in some sort of arrears. About two-thirds of the unlucky claimants had remained unpaid for one year, one-tenth for eighteen months or longer. It seems fair to add that by this time the government's financial position had become appalling and that the clerical pensioners do not appear to have been singled out for special neglect. Again, in view of the standards of sixteenth-century officialdom and the low tone of politics during the last years of Edward VI, it says something for the relative probity of the English tradition that so elaborate and exhaustive an enquiry should at this moment have been undertaken.

On these official lists the rank-and-file of the laymen who had formerly served the monasteries do not appear, and it has sometimes been supposed that their plight at the Dissolution must have constituted an important part of the social problem set by that event. This claim cannot be substantiated. The majority of such employees were husbandmen and other outdoor workers on the home-farms and such other estates as had not been leased. These people must have been needed by the new owners, and stood in no worse condition than other husbandmen in their localities. Many of the indoor servants, it is true, would have to seek employment elsewhere, but the scattered clues certainly do not suggest that they were set adrift penniless. Certain cases are known where they were paid off with rewards amounting to a year's wages, a settlement ultra-generous by the standards of any society. All in all, though we have still much to learn concerning the transactions of the dispersal and the later history of the dispersed, it seems unlikely that many of the latter, clerical or lay, underwent grievous privations. Where hardship existed, it is more likely to have been psychological, and we should probably reserve most of our sympathies for those of the actual religious who did not feel that secular legislation absolved them from their vows or whose minds were otherwise irrevocably geared to a communal life. These elements may be seen in the alacrity with which a few small groups reassembled during Mary's brief attempt to revive monasticism. We may also detect them in two or three authenticated examples of parties who continued living together after the Dissolution. In July 1558, for example, a little band of the former monks of Monk Bretton, headed by their prior William Brown, still dwelt together at Worsborough, not far from their old home.[18] In their rooms they preserved the large library of their house, which they had bought with their own money and which they now proceeded to catalogue in their disused cartulary. The result forms one of our most valuable late monastic book-lists, yet one would gladly exchange it for a diary describing their lives in retirement, their reflections on the new world, their relations with each other and such fragments of the old life in community they were able to maintain.

Results of the Dissolution

THE *Valor Ecclesiasticus* probably tends to underestimate monastic incomes and it omits a few of the poorer houses. The gross income of all those included amounts to £161,853; their net income after the deduction of allowances to £136,361.[19] The latter figure represents considerably more than three times the income of all the Crown estates on the eve of the Dissolution. About a quarter of the gross income arose from tithes, glebes and other proceeds of benefices appropriated to the monasteries; the rest was ordinary temporal income, chiefly from rural estates. These figures do not include the incomes of colleges, chantries and minor foundations dissolved during the last years of Henry VIII or under Edward VI. In addition to this immense income the Crown acquired a very large lump sum from the sale of bullion, plate and other valuables. The immense loss of patronage sustained by the Church included the innumerable stewardships and other monastic offices which had given ecclesiastics so close a hold over important laymen. The monasteries also possessed the right of presentation to about two-fifths of the parochial benefices in England and most of these advowsons remained with the Crown or were soon transferred elsewhere. In the House of Lords the disappearance of the mitred abbots meant that the clerical vote declined from an absolute majority to a minority.

In terms of material splendour, of pageantry, of iconography, of the type of devotion stimulated by these instruments, the Church now fell into an immense decline. Even though the English cathedrals and parish churches were to be spared that extreme degree of vandalism perpetrated in some continental Protestant countries, every lover of the past and of the arts must regret that more was not saved from the treasures of the monasteries. Perhaps the most irreparable of all this damage was occasioned by the melting-down of reliquaries, images and other splendid examples of medieval metal-work and jewellery. That Protestant Reformers should have welcomed an abatement of the emphasis hitherto placed on the plastic arts, one may find intelligible, and there were Catholic reformers who shared their misgivings. Yet it remains a sad thing that these changes came at a moment when the need of the government for cash had become so insatiable, when public museums did not exist, when disinterested connoisseurship and antiquarianism had not passed their raw infancy in England. The injury to scholarship occasioned by the dispersal of monastic libraries was also extensive, though it has sometimes been overstated. Contemporary scholars and collectors were by no means oblivious to the problems of preservation. Henry VIII, aided by John Leland, made a systematic and apparently personal attempt to acquire the choice items for his own collection; out of the 400 of his books now in the Royal collection in the British Museum, about 250 can be traced back to fifty-five medieval libraries, mainly monastic. The King failed, however, to set up the great national repository of which Leland dreamed, and the immediate work of preservation which has left us several thousands of former monastic books was in the main accomplished by many small local collectors throughout the country. A considerable proportion must nevertheless have been lost, for while we know of 500 manuscripts from Durham, 300 from Christ Church, Canterbury, about 250 from Bury and 250 from St. Augustine's, Canterbury, there remain at the other extreme some 400 medieval libraries, mostly smaller monastic ones, each of which is represented by only ten or less extant books. The destruction appears to have been most complete in the small houses, certain of which can be shown by late medieval catalogues to have had libraries, now entirely or almost entirely perished.[20] Our loss does not lie so much in the total disappearance of important works as in the decreased bulk of evidence available to modern paleographers, whose ability to recreate the cultural relationships of the Middle Ages depends upon the comparative study of actual manuscripts on the largest possible scale.

More obvious but perhaps somewhat less grievous was the loss of fine architecture, since not a few of the greatest examples have survived in the monastic cathedrals and elsewhere. Our gothic cities nevertheless lost much of their beauty and no square mile of England changed with the Dissolution in so spectacular a manner as did London. It contained twenty-three religious houses of importance, the precincts of which presented a forlorn spectacle during the decades of reconstruction. Occupying so much of the city's area, they provided welcome space for that gigantic growth of population and housing which overtook the Tudor capital, but the spate of building in Elizabethan and Jacobean London had a wholly secular character. If Shakespeare's city contained a far more diversified and exciting society than those of the past it had lost many of its most attractive landmarks and refreshing spaces. It had gained little in terms of public order, since most of the lawless immunities were suffered to survive. But while Whitefriars, the haven of debtors, became Walter Scott's 'Alsatia', the franchise formerly belonging to the Black friars made possible the establishment of theatres, in the second of which Shakespeare himself became a lessee.[21] He did not need to leave London to find

Bare ruin'd choirs where late the sweet birds sang.

The planned effects of the suppression proved far from negligible, though they did not correspond with the magnitude of the King's initial designs. At this time he genuinely aspired to increase the number of bishops and bishoprics, and already in 1534 he had begun a scheme for appointing more suffragans. At the Dissolution he sketched in his own hand a plan for the erection of thirteen new sees, based upon former monastic buildings and lands.[22] In the event only six emerged—those of Peterborough, Gloucester, Oxford, Chester, Bristol and Westminster, the last-named to be dissolved in 1550. Meanwhile the monastic chapters of Coventry, Rochester, Winchester, Ely, Durham, Carlisle and Norwich were abolished and replaced by deans and secular canons, these being in many cases the former abbots, priors and monks. Such reorganised cathedral churches received new statutes, and, together with those of the wholly new dioceses, they became known as Cathedrals of the New Foundation.[23] This was a less drastic reorganisation than the circumstances demanded, yet it was a far more fundamental reform than the Church had been able to accomplish for itself in recent centuries. Likewise the common charge that Henry failed to use his new wealth in the cause of education was long ago shown by Mr. Leach to be untrue: 'He did it on a scale which entitles him to the praise of being, in a sense, the greatest of school founders.'[24] At Canterbury, Carlisle, Ely, Norwich, Rochester and Worcester the cathedral grammar schools were amply re-endowed and placed under the patronage of the deans and chapters. At Bristol, Chester, Gloucester, Peterborough and Westminster new cathedral schools replaced old grammar schools of various origin and government; they were also much increased in wealth and henceforth managed by the new secular chapters of those cathedrals. At Oxford Henry carried to completion Wolsey's great scheme of Christ Church; at Cambridge he founded Trinity College, which soon outdistanced all its rivals in either university. At Cambridge in 1540 and at Oxford in 1546 he established the Regius professorships in theology, medicine, civil law, Hebrew and Greek—five in each university, and each one endowed with the handsome annual salary of £40. In addition, it would be easy to draw up a considerable list of private beneficiaries from the Dissolution who later became prominent as founders of schools and colleges. Far more indeed should have been made of this unique opportunity, but the share which went to education cannot justly be called insignificant.

Judged by Thomas Cromwell's main purpose the Dissolution can be dubbed a failure, since it tided the Crown over one period of crisis but failed to endow it with a huge and permanent non-parliamentary income. The pointless irony of Cromwell's overthrow in 1540 was followed by a greater irony—the rapid alienation of a major part of the monastic lands. The Crown did not, it is true, forfeit all benefit from these lands, since the many estates which were sold subject to knight service continued to yield reliefs, profits of wardship and other feudal dues. Yet these sums, however considerable, were small compared with those which would have accrued had the same estates remained in the King's hands. Amid the insecurities of his time, when the monarchy towered like a beacon above the turbulent waters of English society, Cromwell's financial plan made good political sense. Nevertheless, had the monarchy somehow succeeded in retaining these new resources for another hundred years, the rise of English liberty would have been more painful and slow. If the King held unprecedented power at Cromwell's death, this was not due to the recent Statute of Proclamations, which merely regularised a long-existent situation. It was due to the possession of enormous rent-rolls, the true sinews of executive power. Yet within seven years these sinews had withered beyond all chance of recovery. The actual effects of the Dissolution upon our history seem as nothing compared with its potential importance at the moment when it was first consummated.

A more complex and equally significant question remains—what place should we assign to the Dissolution in the social and economic history of

England? Until very recent years, almost every attempt to treat this matter was blatantly invalidated by the religious or other doctrinaire convictions which the enquirer allowed to dictate his factual selection and hence his answers. Today it would be difficult even for a prejudiced writer to produce verdicts so crude. We now possess far more evidence and, if much of it proves complex and even contradictory, it is real evidence. We no longer generalise about economic developments on the mere basis of contemporary pamphleteering or pulpit-literature, much less upon that formed by the conjectures of Spelman, Fuller and William Cobbett. The present incomplete state of research still leaves little room for dogmatism, but it has already destroyed the simple black-and-white pictures still being painted only thirty years ago, when some reputable writers had not yet ceased propounding the 'catastrophic' view of the Dissolution. They told of monks and nuns reduced to beggary, up to 80,000 monastic dependents deprived of their daily bread, the 'proverbially liberal' abbots replaced by lay landlords, who rack-rented their poor tenants, enclosed for pasture, drove men off the land and destroyed villages and rights of common. One well-known author even attributed to the Dissolution both the economic troubles of the Tudor towns and the general rise in commodity prices. While the present writer is very far from idealising the subsequent squirearchic period of English social and economic history—it was inevitable rather than equitable—he remains wholly convinced that this tragic view attached to the fall of monastic ownership was based upon no valid contemporary evidence, that it is today held by no competent economic historians and that it will never re-establish itself in the field of serious scholarship.

The mid-Tudor preachers and pamphleteers who denounced enclosers and rent-raisers were in general not economists but moralists. Even the genuine analysts of the known economic data did not understand all the factors causing poverty in England and they were certainly at loss to explain the true causes of the European price-rise. This antedated the fall of the monasteries, which cannot be taken even as one of its minor causal factors. As we now know, two enormous causes were at work: the pressure of Europe's rising population upon her relatively static production and subsequently the inrush of silver, especially that from Peru in the forties and afterwards. Compared with these factors, even Henry VIII's debasement of the English coinage probably takes a minor place in the story. Yet even so, the moralists make very little of the monasteries. With the partial exception of Brinklow[25] (who merely hated the new landlords even more than he hated the old monks) this English literature is remarkable for the lack of emphasis which, in seeking to analyse the causes of poverty, it places upon the Dissolution. The Doctor in the *Discourse of the Common Weal*[26] specifically denies that the Dissolution was a major cause of high prices, while even Latimer's famous denunciations of covetousness are far from being solely directed against landlords.[27]

The Dissolution occurred at a time when the demand for wool was still high, but this fell off from 1550, with the result that the urge to convert arable to pasture diminished. Yet even earlier, much enclosure had been directed to other purposes; it often resulted in great increases of productivity and it did not necessarily involve the substitution of sheep for men. Sometimes it was actually carried out by yeomen and other peasant-farmers. Though Tudor enclosures affected a small proportion of the land, they admittedly continued to have their place among the causes of agrarian discontent, at all events in the Midlands. But their lack of connection with the suppression of the monasteries appears chiefly in the now certain fact that the chief damage had been done long before this suppression. Professor Beresford has shown that the real spate of rural depopulation by enclosure lay between about 1440 and 1520.[28] This was already an old grievance when Henry VII and Wolsey tried to check its progress by legislation and special commissions. We have seen that monastic landlords, who were not in fact 'proverbially liberal', had taken part in it. Certainly there seems no reason to suppose that the retention of religious houses would have checked its continuance.

If the Dissolution did not ruin England by releasing a rush of ruinous enclosures, it cannot be shown to have produced an orgy of rack-renting. Rent cannot be discussed in isolation from its actual purchasing power, from prices. Now prices began to rise throughout Europe as early as 1510; between 1540 and 1560 they roughly doubled and they continued to rise thereafter. Hence a landlord who failed to raise his rents and entry-fines would have been a fool or a saint. Rent-raising is hence far from equivalent to predatory landlordism. The controversy over rent does not much concern lords who ground the faces of the poor. It does not much concern the genuine poor at all; it concerns the relations of landlords with tenant-farmers, who were prospering through the exceptional boom in the prices of farm produce and who naturally wanted the best of both worlds—the new high prices they received, together with their old low rents. But the rising number of these tenants who saw large profits in extended farms meant ruthless competition between them to gain leases and hence an opportunity for landowners to raise rents and so keep themselves abreast of the price-rise. Under these circumstances then, it would seem reasonable to begin talk of rack-renting when we see landlords enhancing rents at a faster rate than that of the rise in food prices, which latter determined the ability of their tenant-farmers to pay their rents. Again, ethical verdicts against the owners might perhaps be justified could it convincingly be shown that their excessive demands, duly passed on by farmers to the consumer, were a main originating factor of the price rise. Though during recent years we have obtained a fair amount of evidence regarding the movement of rent and prices during the sixteenth and earlier seventeenth centuries, neither of these charges can be substantiated.

Until recently most authorities supposed the contrary: that rents lagged behind prices, to the impoverishment of many landlords. The Knight, another of the speakers in the *Discourse of the Common Weal*, makes this claim on behalf of his own class.[29] Professor Trevor-Roper and others have shown that our preoccupation with the 'rise of the gentry' in the period 1540–1640 should not blind us to the converse fact that many gentry-families fell in the economic scale. They ran this danger, it is claimed, especially if they were 'mere' landlords, unable to supplement normal agrarian incomes by professional, official or mercantile earnings or by exploiting mineral resources.[30] Many landlords were indeed hampered in their efforts to keep abreast of the inflation by something more than a traditional and unbusinesslike outlook; they were hampered by the inelasticity of tenures, by the fact that some of their tenants enjoyed long leases or were copyholders safeguarded by law against increases of rent. Recent research into the movement of rent has, however, tended to take a more optimistic view of the position of Tudor and early Stuart landlords. It has been indicated that no simple formula applies and that, while some landlords adopted a commercial attitude, others were more interested in the social patronage and power arising from land.[31] Rents and fines (which latter play an ever-increasing part) rose very unevenly as between different places and different types of land, but the prosperity of the tenant did not necessarily advance at the expense of the lord.

Mr. Kerridge has found some unusually reliable evidence on Wiltshire rents, which for the most part rose quite impressively; the Herberts, the main family here involved, kept pace with the rise of food prices. Here and elsewhere, however, this rise of rents does not begin with the period of Dissolution, currency debasement and early influx of silver. During the twenty years *before* the Dissolution the Herberts had already more than doubled their rents per acre for new leases, and the process continued, though more slowly, during the succeeding century. Miss Finch's interesting study of five Northamptonshire families[32] also shows that land could prove a very sound long-term investment, yet that it failed to yield the spectacular profits so often arising from trade, finance and public office—profits which commonly formed the original means of acquiring landed estates. Here there existed a substantial identity of interest between landlords and tenants; enclosures did not in general develop amid struggle and hardship. The single oppressive landlord, Sir Thomas Tresham, must be regarded as untypical, since recusancy-fines had made his financial situation desperate. A still more recent contributor, Dr. Alan Simpson,[33] has based his rent-researches on certain East Anglian estates; he concludes that 'mere' landlordism could with care be made to pay here, that in the great majority of manors inflexible tenures did not gravely prejudice the owner's position, that farmers were able to take rising rents in their stride, that alongside the spectacular successes and failures most landed families maintained a solid if moderate prosperity. Pending still more studies, confident generalising should perhaps be avoided, but it seems already clear that in this cooler and more scientific atmosphere the rack-renting ogre and the starving tenant have evaporated into the same limbo as the 'proverbially liberal' abbot; as we shall shortly see, they are not the only figments of the former doctrinaire approach to be threatened with that fate.

The theory that the suppression of the monasteries was a major cause of urban poverty has nothing to commend it. All urban historians would agree that the severe strain besetting the old corporate towns had both general and local causes, most of them operative and the subjects of loud complaint well over half a century before the Dissolution. If, for example, we look at the case of York, one of our best documented municipalities, we find 'decay' on the lips of the citizens by the first years of Henry VIII, or earlier. When mid-Tudor and Elizabethan mayors of York give detailed analyses of industrial decline,[34] they do not even mention the fall of the religious houses, though there had been many in the city. From York to Bodmin townsmen had often looked with hostile eyes upon their local houses and had been indisposed to idealise them at any stage. But the lands and economic interests of the monasteries were overwhelmingly rural, and with rare exceptions it is outside the sphere of town life that the main effects of the Dissolution must be sought.

The Successors of the Monks

WHO received the monastic lands and on what terms? The original grantees in the patent rolls can easily be listed, numbered and, after a fashion, classified. Dr. Savine's account of the original grants is well known.[35] It shows that Henry VIII refrained from making many quixotic gifts of land to his favourites. Of the 1,593 original grants made in his reign, only forty-one were gifts, while another twenty-eight were combinations of gift with sale or exchange. The lucky few were great magnates like Norfolk, Suffolk and Shrewsbury, who had just preserved the throne, or leading officials like Cromwell, Audley, Rich and Pope, who had rendered notable services to the Crown. By no means all the grants to these few were gifts; some on closer examination prove to be exchanges and purchases. The great majority of the grantees paid good money.[36] In December 1539 a commission to sell lands to the clear yearly value of £6,000 was issued to Cromwell and Sir Richard Rich; this lays down a minimum purchase price of twenty times the annual rent, which was in fact the normal price asked and received in the great majority of transactions under Henry VIII. It also appears that a few buyers fared better than this during the last years of the reign, when a buyer's market existed and the King needed money more urgently than aspiring purchasers demanded land. Certainly the Crown profited less than would have been the case had it been able to sell more gradually and so avail itself of the steady rise in land values.

We know when and why the monastic lands were sold by the Crown. Despite the commission of December 1539 little of the land was alienated before Cromwell's fall. The rush to sell began with the new commission of May 1543 and according to Savine's calculation about two-thirds of the whole had been alienated by 1547. Broadly speaking, these lands went to pay for the war of 1542–6 against Scotland and France. This is estimated to have cost over £2,000,000, and in addition to these ex-monastic properties other valuable Crown lands were sold off during its course. This was the period when small men joined together in purchasing-syndicates. In October 1544, for example, seventy-seven Londoners (including seventeen brewers, ten cloth-workers, five tallow-chandlers, five bowyers, six innholders and a varied assortment of leather-sellers, girdlers, dyers, stationers, cutlers and doctors) bought monastic lands for £843.[37] Even more, it was the period of obscure individual buyers like Richard Andrews of Woodstock, who bought and sold, sometimes alone, sometimes with one or more of a variety of partners, monastic estates worth many thousands of pounds. These groups and individuals, who re-sold almost immediately, were in some cases mere speculators, yet the notion of an orgy of speculation has been challenged with force by Professor Habakkuk. The fact that values stood so steadily at twenty years' purchase is indeed difficult to reconcile with such a supposition. Again, resale no doubt often occurred merely because purchasers found they had bought more than their resources warranted or because they discovered more profitable investments elsewhere. There appear strong reasons for supposing that many of these obscure buyers, who so swiftly re-conveyed their purchases to better-known men, were really mere proxies acting for the latter and not the true purchasers. Since the sales were conducted in London, it was doubtless useful to be represented by agents who knew the procedure and were given discretionary powers to acquire temporarily under their own names. Exactly the same phenomenon occurred a century later, when buyers of confiscated lands under the Commonwealth made extensive use of agents and trustees.

Whatever the extent of speculative buying, a large proportion of the original grantees possess little interest for the social and economic historian. They were here today and gone tomorrow; they were not the owners who stayed on the land and governed the lives of the yeomanry and peasantry. Savine's well-known classification of the grantees under Henry VIII hence tells us little of the more settled pattern of ownership which emerged from these years of greatest flux. For what they are worth, his figures run somewhat as follows. Spiritual corporations—deans and chapters—seem to occupy a prominent rôle with grants worth £20,000 out of a total of £90,000. Since, however, nearly all these transactions involved mere exchanges of land with the Crown, this particular figure has little significance. Some thirty-eight peers account for £16,000 annual value; courtiers, £7,000; royal officials, £14,000; lawyers, £1,500; 'industrials' (? industrialists), £6,000. Of a total of £90,000 annual value, some £23,500 is reckoned as going to people of uncertain status, mainly gentry. Needless to remark, these categories remain arbitrary, since a large proportion of the grantees could be placed at will under two or more classes. Most courtiers and the more prominent Crown officials were also country gentry. From these not very meaningful figures we must turn to questions more weighty but more difficult to answer with precision.

Into what type of ownership did the monastic lands settle within twenty years of the Dissolution? From what social groups were these longer-term owners drawn? What circumstances are likely to have guided their policies as landlords? Though we cannot answer these questions with complete confidence, we have at least learned to regard with scepticism the uninformed generalisations of our predecessors. Only by undertaking many patient regional and local studies can we hope to achieve more accurate knowledge. For example, Dr. R. B. Smith's detailed survey of economics and society in the West Riding in the decade 1535–46[38] has shown within that area no less than five major regions with differing agrarian conditions, social structures and monastic elements. Likewise the relatively democratic Fenland farming described by Dr. Joan Thirsk[39] and the 'peasant aristocracies' in Dr. Hoskins' Midland villages[40] do not fit into the conventional squire-dominated picture of post-Dissolution landlordism. Neither the monastic economy nor its successors can rightly be covered by any crisp formula applicable to all the districts and regions of England.

In addition to that of Dr. Smith certain other regional surveys are also pertinent to our enquiries, notably that made by Mr. Hodgett for the Lincolnshire ex-monastic lands[41] and that by Dr. Youings for those of Devon.[42] In Lincolnshire three great noblemen, Suffolk, Rutland and Clinton, all prominent for their services to the King, initially gained substantial grants, but these were in part exchanges. Moreover, they did not seek to consolidate their holdings in that county, and all three afterwards parted with substantial portions of their grants. In addition to the local gentry the early buyers included certain prominent Augmentations officials and royal servants. But several of these enterprising functionaries, such as Sir Thomas Henneage and Robert Tyrwhitt, also belonged to the Lincolnshire gentry and might with equal sense be placed in either class. Typical of the more permanent elements among the purchasers were three Henneage brothers, whose ancestors had held manors in Lincolnshire since 1435. Both before and after the Dissolution they and their descendants figure on all the commissions of the peace, for sewers and for gaol delivery. A fourth brother was dean of Lincoln. A Henneage was high sheriff of the county in 1576, 1585, 1598 and 1629. In these later times members of the family adhered, like the Tyrwhitts, to the old religion; they suffered for their recusancy even though their fortunes had been enhanced by the Reformation. Here, it may be added, is a pattern by no means uncommon also amongst the gentry of Yorkshire and Lancashire. Local gentlemen with well-known names but lesser opportunities—many owned only one or two manors—also bulk large among the Lincolnshire purchasers. Other early grantees were obscurer men, whose surnames and small parcels of land strongly indicate that they belonged to the more substantial of the local yeomanry. But relatively few of the direct grants from the Crown went to yeomen. Many more of this class purchased at second and third hand; not infrequently they bought parcels which they already held as leaseholders. Very few corporate bodies acquired Lincolnshire monastic land, a minor exception being the corporation of Boston, which acquired property inside the town belonging to several local houses. An exceptionally interesting group is formed by the few big operators. In Lincolnshire by far the largest of these were John Bellow (who narrowly escaped murder in the Lincolnshire rising which inaugurated the Pilgrimage of Grace) and his associate John Broxholme. These men, though usually accounted London businessmen, came of Lincolnshire families and obviously possessed valuable local knowledge. By some means unknown they were able to raise capital on a very large scale. Between July 1545 and November 1546 Bellow and Broxholme paid the Crown £7,800, but, judging from the number of licences to alienate afterwards granted to them, they were speculating or acting as agents for others rather than seeking to found great estates in their native county. In Lincolnshire as elsewhere there appear very few indications that a new type of landowner was settling upon the land. The story is that of a transfer into the hands of a large body of men already well established in the county, men varied in means and status—richer gentry, small gentry, younger sons and yeomen, but almost all of them settled members of an agrarian society and conversant with its opportunities, customs and obligations.

In the case of Devon Dr. Youings has edited and analysed the group of records which promises most to modern questioners—the Particulars for Grants in the Augmentations records, which can be made to yield a picture of development over the decades succeeding the Dissolution. In Devon the great majority of grants consisted of property valued at under £20, most of it sold at the rate of twenty years purchase, or more. Gifts were few in number, much the most important being the donation to the Russell family which the King deliberately made great in Devon in order that it should replace the fallen Courtenays and provide reliable leadership in a potentially troublesome area. Some heads of the older families managed to raise capital; often, it would appear, with great effort. Larger purchasers were Devon-born lawyers and royal officials, several of whom had been monastic stewards and already possessed an intimate knowledge of the lands they bought. A very small proportion was acquired by merchants, though those of Totnes bought some rural land and those of Exeter some urban property. London merchants proved a negligible factor amongst the Devon purchasers. In this county, resales, whether for speculative or other purposes, assumed far less prominence than in Lincolnshire and other more accessible areas.

By 1558 a pattern is observable in Devon. The Russells and the canons of Windsor owned between them nearly a quarter of the property so far alienated by the Crown. Less than a tenth was held by people who had come in from outside Devon. The ostensibly 'new men' were not in fact strangers; they were of Devon gentry-stock, younger sons or heads of junior branches of well-known families, men who had earned money by active careers, often in the royal service. Monastic lands in Devon did not go to a handful of very rich men; they increased the number of moderate-sized estates. They neither made the rich much richer nor did they create a new species of landowner. By 1558 these lands had been distributed, mostly in small parcels, amongst a very considerable number of persons, though even now no large proportion was owned by yeomen or tradesmen. At every stage of the story we hear little or nothing of that figure beloved by doctrinaire historians—the absentee landlord emancipated from the need to keep face in the county and armed with a merchant's greedy ideas on profit. The merchant-turned-landlord cannot be dismissed as a myth but, so far as the present writer's observations in various other areas extend, he was an exceptional figure, and there seems every likelihood that his outlook and practices were speedily assimilated to those of the established class. The same presumably applies to the clothiers who bought monastic lands, for they were substantial men and landowners already. A few among this interesting group are incidentally known to have converted monastic buildings to industrial uses. An Oxfordshire clothier applied for properties of Abingdon Abbey on the ground that he already employed 500 workmen and could employ more, given suitable premises. William Stumpe, another big industrialist, actually established a rudimentary factory in buildings of Malmesbury Abbey.[43]

In the West Riding Dr. Smith has traced the stories of the twenty-one purchasers or families who held sixty per cent of the ex-monastic land in 1546 and who include all the larger grantees.[44] Of these twenty-one no fewer than ten were the heads of established landed houses, even though at this moment the northern gentry, who lacked ready cash, were not pressing forward in large numbers. The ten included four peers, Cumberland, Shrewsbury, Wharton and Latimer, together with Sir Gervase Clifton of Nottinghamshire, Guy Fairfax of Steeton, Thomas Malleverer and Arthur Kay of Woodsome. Of the other eleven, younger sons of established northern families numbered four, or rather seven, if we include younger sons who had risen on the basis of legal and official careers. In this group we might place the tough lawyer Sir Leonard Beckwith, whose Yorkshire interests before the Dissolution had been but small, but who, after triumphing over charges of fraud, died in 1557 with estates worth £360 per annum. His position as county Augmentations receiver was not unconnected with his ascent. Yet by no means all these younger sons founded branches of lasting importance in the area. One purchaser, Richard Paver, was a yeoman-farmer who achieved a considerable measure of success in his efforts to rise into the gentry. The remaining three grantees might indeed be called townsmen. One was a Londoner, presumably an agent or speculator, who disappears shortly afterwards, while another, Richard Pymond of Wakefield, had no children and also failed to found a landed family. The third was the financier Sir Richard Gresham, a Lord Mayor of London, preserver of the London hospitals and father of the even more famous Sir Thomas Gresham. Parts of his purchases still remained with the family in the Elizabethan period. Altogether, this seems a most undramatic picture and exceedingly discouraging for the theory that the Dissolution introduced a new type of landlord to the countryside. We need more such regional surveys, and when they are forthcoming some may show divergences from these three. It will nevertheless be surprising if they radically change the broad pattern we have just observed.

At this stage it also seems appropriate to stress the irrelevance of this transfer of land to the controversy between Protestants and Catholics. As observed, Henry VIII granted or sold off the greater part of the monastic lands between 1539 and his death in 1547. During the whole of this period most forms of Protestantism remained proscribed. So far as I have observed, not the slightest evidence exists that conservative doctrinal beliefs caused men to desist from buying monastic lands or that a leaning to Protestant beliefs increased their eagerness to purchase. Some of the greatest recipients, for example the Duke of Norfolk and the Earl of Shrewsbury, stood among the leaders of religious reaction. And we have already observed examples of families with consistent Catholic traditions, families soon due to suffer for their faith, which nevertheless made extensive purchases of abbey-lands. This absence of doctrinaire control is everywhere characteristic of the whole process of the transfer. 'It is indeed worthy of comment that of the leading figures concerned in the Dissolution in Cornwall, not one was a Protestant: Sir Thomas Arundell no more than Sir John Tregonwell, neither Prideaux nor Prior Mundy. The sympathies of each were unmistakably Catholic.' So concludes Dr. A. L. Rowse after examining the chief Cornish purchasers.[45] Encouraged by this spectacle Protestant controversialists might well urge that the chief denouncers of property-speculation and greedy landlordism were Protestant utopians and moralists like John Hales and Hugh Latimer. Even so, they would be unwise to press these claims too far, since selfish and socially reactionary politicians were soon to cash in upon the Protestant movement, tarnishing its reputation for economic and social idealism. From first to last, the acquisition of monastic lands suggested itself to men of all opinions in terms of strict business. The compunction, the sentiment, the nice scruples, the superstition that an evil destiny awaited the buyers, these were invented by later and more poetic generations. In general, it would seem reasonable to envisage the commonest and most typical successors of the monks as gentry of established local families, conservative-minded churchmen but loyal servants of the monarchy, not necessarily rich but always anxious to maintain or to build up a good reputation with all classes in the shire. We know the minds of these people fairly well. Their ambitions and their place in society seem unlikely to have allowed them to resemble the rack-renting absentee landlords of nineteenth-century Ireland.

Some 'New Monastics'

THANKS to the standard collection of Tudor economic documents, generations of students have taken as typical of the 'new monastics' Sir John York,[46] who in 1553 attempted to raise the rents of twenty-seven tenancies in the liberty of Whitby Strand from the old monastic total of £28 to a new figure of £64 per annum. By this stage of the inflation the old rents must have become absurdly low, and the tenants were doubtless now receiving nearly double the old prices for their produce. Even so, this landlord had tried to progress faster than most and presumably deserved to be taken to court. The story is one of a notoriously ambitious owner of unusual background. Though the grandson of a mayor of York, Sir John was a financial agent of the Crown, a leading merchant, an absentee in London and a politician; he was in fact in the Tower for complicity with Northumberland's plot when his Whitby tenants brought their case. More important, the matter ended happily for the tenants, since he immediately promised to abandon his claims to higher rents during their leases. The case thus illustrates little more than the fact that some tenants could get redress in the courts; if the transition to lay landlordism is to be given a dramatic air, many cases more disturbing than this will need to be discovered! But there is no reason whatever to make Sir John York a typical image—we have in fact others which might serve better.

In order to be sure of these situations, we need more than the one-sided evidence of a landlord's opponents in a single law-suit, but as yet the more intimate and balanced pictures emerge in relatively few cases. One of these is the case of Sir William Petre,[47] who accomplished the remarkable feat of remaining Secretary of State from 1544 to 1557. During this period he built up two great estates—in Devon, his native county, and in Essex, where his wife had brought him the nucleus of the Ingatestone estate. It is certain that his growing prosperity was not financed by rent-raising. His accounts show that by 1556 his assured return on his outlay in Essex amounted to only five per cent per annum, to which another one or two per cent could be added for 'casualties', e.g. income from manor courts and the sale of timber. Not until his last years (he died in 1572) were rents giving him a return of seven per cent on his original capital—a low rate of interest by Tudor standards, and lower still when we take into account the immensity of the inflation during the thirty years covered by Petre's investments in land.

When working some years ago in Washington, the present writer happened to find amongst the Loseley papers in the Folger Library a memorandum on estate and household management by Sir John Gostwick, treasurer of First Fruits and Tenths and a close associate of Thomas Cromwell.[48] In all his obvious attributes this man seems to form a shining textbook-exemplar of the Crown official who entered into the heritage of the monks. Of old but hitherto undistinguished county stock the diligent Gostwick had risen to high administrative office and to important territorial status in his native county of Bedford. A buyer of monastic lands, he was at the same time largely Catholic in doctrinal belief. He protested to Cromwell against anti-ecclesiastical propaganda, and in later years he incurred the wrath of the King for speaking against Cranmer's heresies in Parliament. About 1540 Gostwick wrote for his heir these careful instructions concerning his chief manor at Willington. Here he actually urges his successor not to levy fines on the entry of new tenants at a greater rate than the customary minimum of one year's rent. He again adjures him never to increase the rents of his tenant-farmers unless he sees the latter imposing increases upon their own subtenants—a humane and stabilising principle and a further salutary reminder that a landlord's policy affected in the first place substantial tenants now making hitherto unparalleled profits. Gostwick then urges that a certain tenant, who had contracted to supply wheat and peas, should not be released from his bargain: 'He may bear it very well, for he hath a goodly farm of you.' Sir John is indeed quite hard-headed; he demands efficient service from his miller (who must not be a married man) and from his farm-hands. He sternly refuses to allow leases of more than twenty years. On the other hand, he is a fair employer and he knows that it pays to be fair.

> If he be a good herdsman, let him have good wages, for he may soon save his wages; and let him have livery such as you give carters. Let Sottill never go from you . . . for ye shall never have a better herdsman . . . And let Henry Wild have the keeping of the pastures with certain milch kine, which will help him, his wife and his children, for God knoweth, he can make but little shift for himself.

Behind all this lies Gostwick's desire to gain credit among the neighbours as well as to remain in good odour with God and the King.

> Item, I charge you of my blessing to get the good will and favour of all your neighbours, as well in Willington as in the whole shire, and to do for them and help them in all other causes according to your power. And in your so doing you shall please God and also have the love of them.

And as if in order to become the quintessential example of his type, Gostwick ends with the political creed which the Tudors and their great ministers sought to implant.

> And be true to God, the King and your friend. And if your friend do open his mind and secret counsel to you, I charge you if it be to keep counsel . . . open it not, for if you do, you are not to be trusted with no man:— unless your friend should open to you felony or treason. Then I charge you not to keep his counsel, but open it to two or three of the next justices of peace which dwelleth next unto you, or else to one or two of the King's most honourable Council, if you may get unto them. But in any wise, utter it as soon as is possible, for the longer you keep it, the worse it is for you, and the more danger toward God and the King's Majesty.

Here, it would seem, is the so-called 'new man', the leader of society brought increasingly to the fore by a multitude of changes. He is no ogre, no economic abstraction; his is no impersonal management; to him workmen and tenants are real people; though far from oblivious to the main chance he still lives in a custom-governed rural society. For such a climber, in a world still affected by aristocratic ideals, excessive avarice and grasping innovations would prove merely self-defeating. Altogether, Sir John Gostwick has obvious limitations, but he looks to me an improvement upon the leaders of the former bastard-feudal society. Pending fuller knowledge, why should we not view this rising class in terms of known facts and probabilities rather than in terms of ideology and melodrama? And if we must indulge in this dubious mental pastime of building images or types, there seem good reasons to accept the rather benevolent Sir John Gostwick as more typical than the over-thrustful though not very horrific Sir John York.

The Rise of the Gentry

WHILE the Dissolution did not ruin the humble or dramatically alter the character of English landlordism, it clearly helped to change the balance of social groups within the nation. The decline of clerical wealth and territorial influence, the corresponding rise of large elements among the gentry, as acquirers of land, tithes and advowsons, these are far-reaching developments which certainly owed much to the Dissolution. The causes and implications of this shift, political, social and economic, have for many years been the subject of heated debate, a debate which can never be resolved to universal satisfaction. The broad thesis of change was expounded as early as the mid-seventeenth century by James Harrington. Power, he urged, gravitates towards the groups which hold a preponderance of land. The division of great monastic and baronial estates amongst the gentry and yeomanry enriched and enlarged this group.[49] Indirectly it thus created the demand of the House of Commons for political and constitutional change which, though fended off for a while by the romantic appeal of Queen Elizabeth, ultimately led to the Civil War. However great Harrington's simplifications and the inaccuracies of his modern misinterpreters, the broad sense of this hypothesis continues to command respect. Yet should we not think at least as much of the numerical expansion of the landed gentry as of their individual enrichment? Unless many heralds' visitations are uniformly misleading, the century which followed the secularising of church lands saw in every shire a remarkable multiplication of gentle families and of the more substantial yeomen-farmers from whose ranks new gentry were constantly being recruited.

Around the year 1600 Yorkshire had a total population of about 300,000 but it contained nearly 600 gentle families, each of which (since the gentry married young and bred rapidly) might have dozens or scores of living representatives.[50] Camden's visitation of Warwickshire in 1619[51] produced over 230 gentle pedigrees; the visitations of Surrey from 1530 to 1623[52] show about 240 and those of Lincolnshire between 1560 and 1660[53] nearly 1,000. In the two latter cases not all these families existed simultaneously, yet on the other hand the lists are incomplete, and they naturally omit all yeoman-families, even though some of these were more ancient and wealthy than many gentle families. The editor of the Lincolnshire pedigrees comments on the enormous rise in their number between 1562 and 1634. The pedigrees in the Essex heralds' visitations increase from 144 in 1558 to 336 in 1634.[54] The same impression is given by the vast number of applications for the grant or confirmation of arms during the Elizabethan period and the seventeenth century.[55] In general, these multitudinous successors of the monks inhabited superior farmhouses, not stately dukeries. Nothing can be more misleading to students of Tudor and Stuart England than a visit to Burghley House, to Montacute, to Audley End, to Hardwick Hall. These superb piles did not belong to gentlemen of anything resembling average resources. For obvious reasons the growth in numbers hastened the decline of clientage to great noble families; it extended the relations of the gentry not upwards, but downwards and outwards into the professional, the farming, the trading classes. The disruptive force of clientage, still dangerous under Edward VI, was gradually exchanged for something far more creative, yet equally difficult for governments to handle—a huge gentry and near-gentry, law-abiding, yet capable of absorbing puritanical and legal theories opposed to a powerful monarchy.

On the local level the effects of these changes also appear impressive. While collectively the gentry began to gravitate toward a more active function in the State, the squire extended his rôle as leader of village life—this not merely as justice of the peace, as chief landowner, as uncle of the vicar, but also in many cases as the recipient of tithes and advowsons formerly in monastic hands. As for advowsons, though they gave many a family a closer hold over its village church and clergy, they did not come every squire's way, since the Crown granted so many to the bishops and kept so many others in its own hands. The increased devolution of the greater tithes to the gentry constitutes a result of profounder importance. The so-called 'spiritual' income of the former abbeys had comprised about a quarter of their total receipts, and tithes formed by far its major part. Tithes thus represented a large field of investment for laymen. The transfer of the greater tithes into their hands was eased by the fact that the monks themselves had normally entrusted their collection not to vicars, who had no personal interest in exacting them, but to lay bailiffs or special receivers. In many cases the monks had actually leased them for long periods of years to laymen. In the popular mind tithe was hence already assimilated to temporal revenue and no outcry of sacrilege arose when it was bought by the 'new monastics' of the squirearchy.

The social and cultural effects of this transformation of a feudal and ecclesiastical society to one dominated by gentry, yeomanry and traders are obviously complex and far-reaching, and here again the pressures exerted by the Dissolution merge inextricably with a bewildering range of forces, many of them international and totally unconnected with the ecclesiastical policy of the Crown. Yet about this same time the English ceased being a nation of church-builders, or even of castle-builders; they poured their material resources into manor-houses, farm-houses and town-houses; also, let it be recognised, into education and other practical charities. They abandoned the last shreds of their former veneration for the celibate devotee and produced a large narcissistic literature, both religious and secular, devoted to the needs and praises of lay family-men of the middle and gentle classes. During these decades too, the same classes tended increasingly to abandon the image for the printed word; they continued to narrow the gap in matters of literacy which had separated them from the clergy. Amid this profound and many-sided change in the spirit of the age we feel tempted to place the Dissolution of the monasteries in the category of effects as well as in that of causes.

What pressures did the Dissolution exert upon subsequent religious settlements and opinions in England? However freely religious conservatives bought monastic lands, did not the reception of abbey lands induce many families to desire, in the longer run, a 'forward policy' in religion? That such a tendency developed seems possible enough, but the notion must nevertheless be stated with cautious reserves, since the known anecdotes hardly warrant generalisation. Here at least is one of them. Writing to Thomas Cromwell during the actual Dissolution from his home in Cornwall, Sir Richard Grenville, high marshal of Calais, sued for the purchase or gift of some monastic land. Otherwise, he said, he would stand in a different position from that of most men of worship in the realm. He was glad to see overthrown 'these orgulous persons and devourers of God's word and takers away of the glory of Christ'. The monks had been also 'takers away of the wealth of the realm and sprys to the devilish bishop of Rome'. In order that his heirs may be of the same mind for their own profit, Grenville would gladly buy some of the suppressed lands in these parts, even if this meant selling part of his inheritance.[56] We see here an important family becoming not only bound more closely to the Crown but committed to suspect any reversal of ecclesiastical policy which might betoken the revival of monasticism and the restoration of its former estates. This naïve admixture of cupidity and genuine conviction cannot have been uncommon in the minds of the first generation which purchased dissolution properties. On the other hand, this fact did not tie every future government to a Protestant doctrinal policy. Henry's persecution under the Six Articles was still to come; later on Queen Mary's more ambitious Catholicism had its turn; but neither ruler was dissuaded from doctrinal reaction by any resistance from apprehensive land-grantees. Nevertheless, at least the worldly scope of future Catholic reactions remained very limited. Certainly Henry and Mary might maintain or restore Catholic liturgies, but they could not rebuild the material fabric of the medieval church. Given another decade of life and a much more liberal supply of English commonsense, the Spanish Tudor might just conceivably have preserved the soul of English Catholicism, yet from the beginning she had no chance whatever of re-endowing it with its former body. And many a landowner, even among the Catholic-minded, must have breathed a sigh of relief when Mary passed, sorrowing but unlamented, from a scene well and truly set by her own father.

8 A Balance of Forces

The Henrician Parties

DURING THE REVOLUTIONARY YEARS 1532–40 two pressure-groups contended for the ear of the King. The radical group, headed by Cromwell and Cranmer, stood for the policy of the open Bible and for the further diminution of ecclesiastical wealth and privilege. Increasingly it felt the attraction of Lutheran teachings and envisaged an alliance with the German princes of that faith. It enlisted some of the ablest writers in the kingdom, but only a handful of its adherents ascended to the bishops' bench—Nicholas Shaxton to Salisbury, Hugh Latimer to Worcester and Edward Fox to Hereford. During Cromwell's vicegerency the new Archbishop took a very modest part in the formulation of policy, and no one can have foreseen the great influence he was destined to exercise upon the history of English religion.[1] The second son of the squire of Aslockton in Nottinghamshire, Thomas Cranmer had spent a quarter of a century in residence at Cambridge without attaining any fame beyond his fellowship at Jesus College. About 1515–16 he had married obscurely but had lost his wife in childbed very shortly afterwards. By 1520 he had been ordained priest; six years later he became a doctor of Divinity and as a university examiner was demanding from ordinands a high standard of scriptural knowledge. Already he stood amongst those theologians who, in the tradition of Colet, exalted the authority of the Bible above that of the medieval schoolmen. Nevertheless, we lack evidence that he either attended the White Horse meetings or entertained especially hostile views concerning the Papacy. He must during his Cambridge days have been laying the foundations of that admirable knowledge of Christian liturgies from which was to spring the main achievement of his life.

In 1529 Cranmer had engaged the King's personal interest by his suggestion that the divorce was a problem to be settled by theologians and not by canon lawyers in the courts. Entering the royal service, he accompanied the

Earl of Wiltshire to Italy and took part in eliciting the opinions of the Italian universities. After his return to England in 1530 he continued in intimate association with the Boleyn family, probably living in their household and serving as chaplain to Anne. Sent in 1532 on an embassy to the Emperor, he quietly married a niece of the prominent Lutheran divine Andreas Osiander, but this idyll was soon disturbed when Henry recalled him—no doubt at the instigation of the Boleyns—and made him Archbishop of Canterbury in succession to Warham. Later on he was tacitly allowed to bring over his wife, but had to keep her so far in the background as to give rise to the fable that he carried her about in a chest.[2]

From this point, leaving the most arduous public tasks to Cromwell, Cranmer set about a more intimate enterprise which enabled him to survive the minister and hence to preside over the second stage of the English Reformation. Armed with modesty, sound scholarship and pleasant manners he gained a unique place in the trust and affections of the King. 'You were born in a happy hour', Cromwell told him, 'for do or say what you will, the King will always well take it at your hand.' From the first he was ready to purchase this privileged relationship by his subservience to Henry's demands. Without awkward questions he managed the successive annulments of the King's ill-fated marriages. That of Anne Boleyn herself he appears to have annulled on the delicate grounds of Henry's own earlier association with her sister Mary.

Despite his merciful temperament Cranmer took part in the condemnation of several sacramentarian heretics, some of whose views he was destined in later years to approach. His apparent lack of sympathy toward these unfortunates contrasted with his extreme mildness toward conservative opponents, whom he thought to win over by gradualism and persuasion. It should nevertheless be observed that during the thirties Cranmer did not even approach the eucharistic heresies of men like John Lambert; his opinions shifted but slowly, and his acceptance of Henry's doctrinal conservatism cannot reasonably be diagnosed as that of a plotter biding his opportunity until the King's death. Again, his subservience cannot be attributed to mere cowardice. On the contrary, he took many risks on humanitarian grounds; he alone interceded for Fisher and More, for Anne Boleyn and the Princess Mary, for Thomas Cromwell and for Bishop Tunstall. In later life his courage rose in fits and starts, yet he gave more evidence of that virtue than did the majority of men in high office. The integrating principle of Cranmer's career has rightly been found in his belief that a divine sanction underlay the royal authority. Like his adversary Gardiner—and most responsible Englishmen—he saw in the strong hand of monarchy the nation's one hope of vanquishing false doctrine, aristocratic faction, popular rebellion and foreign invasion. With his eyes wide open he accepted for the English Church a new bondage in place of the old bondage to Rome. Along with most of the senior clergy—but by virtue of his position more conspicuously than any—he accepted any command of the Sovereign which did not involve gross and manifest sin.

Cranmer excepted, the more prominent of Cromwell's partisans tended to prove embarrassing in prosperity or unreliable in adversity. Amongst the laymen Cromwell was bound to attract climbers like Audley and Rich, both of whom betrayed him the moment treachery promised a certain reward. Again, Protestants as indiscreet as Latimer and Shaxton made matters difficult for a government attempting to hold the bishops together and to coax conservatives like John Stokesley of London into moderate reforms. In particular, Cromwell's surviving correspondence with Shaxton exemplifies the shortcomings of an academic Reformer who failed to realise that even ecclesiastical politics represent the art of the possible. This former Cambridge theologian and *habitué* of the White Horse attained the See of Salisbury through the patronage of Anne Boleyn, to whom he owed £200 at the time of her execution. Once in his bishopric, Shaxton justified Cromwell's taunt that he had 'a stomach more meet for an emperor than for a bishop'. He tried hard to revive the former supremacy of the prelates of Salisbury over the local mayor and aldermen, who appealed to Cromwell against his claims. In 1538 a more serious difference arose when Shaxton attempted to expel a Catholic reader from Reading Abbey and to replace him by a Reformer. As vicegerent, Cromwell took this contentious matter into his own hands, and in the course of an unusually frank correspondence plain words came from both sides. A modern reader with the conventional view of Thomas Cromwell would hardly recognise as his that strangely heartfelt, even emotional letter sent to Shaxton in March 1538.[3] In the calling of a statesman the minister claims to be doing God's work as well as any priest. 'I do not cease to give thanks that it hath pleased his goodness to use me as an instrument and to work somewhat by me. . . . My prayer is that God give me no longer life than I shall be glad to use mine office in edification and not in destruction.'

Somewhat apart, yet also among the clients of Thomas Cromwell, stood the ex-Carmelite John Bale, one of the stranger human creations of early academic Protestantism.[4] Having a large family and small means his parents had consigned him at the tender age of twelve to the Norwich Carmelites, who seem to have taken good care of his education. In 1529 he took his B.D. at Cambridge and about this time was converted to Protestantism by Thomas, first Lord Wentworth, a soldier and later a privy councillor to Edward VI, who must have been among the earliest English laymen to disseminate the new doctrines. Bale soon became immersed in varied literary activities and the list of his works includes some ninety separate items, including those lost or as yet unprinted.[5] He laid the foundations of English literary biography,[6] made extensive collections of Carmelite antiquities[7] and set a pattern for his younger friend Foxe by writing biographies of Protestant heroes like Sir John Oldcastle, Anne Askew[8] and Martin Luther. His plays occupy a striking position between the old 'morality' and the Elizabethan drama. Writing under the patronage of Cromwell he did much to initiate the strong blast of Protestant propaganda which came from our nascent national theatre. His best-known drama *King John* (the first version of which seems to have been performed in Cranmer's household at Christmas 1538[9]) featured that monarch as England's heroic defender against the tyranny of Rome.[10] Even in an age of bitter pamphleteering, Bale's controversial works handsomely outshone the rest, though they are sometimes relieved by a real literary flair and by touches of biographical interest. His life has all the ingredients for a novel. His two periods of continental exile were separated under Edward VI by a short (and sensationally-terminated) career as Bishop of Ossory in Ireland. When at last the accession of Elizabeth brought him into calmer waters, Bale wisely refrained from rejoining his Irish friends and enemies, but finished his days in a Canterbury prebend. Through all these adventures he had the solace of his faithful wife Dorothy and, if his private demeanour was half so rancorous as his public one, she must be placed among the unsung heroines of the English Reformation.

Among the more effective elements in the Cromwellian group were other publicists and printers, who within six years emitted nearly fifty books defending the new settlement. Perhaps for the first time in history a government monopolised the presses in order to commend its policies to a people by something approaching mass propaganda. Of Cromwell's writers the most thoughtful was Thomas Starkey, the most prolific Richard Morison. Both these men were Italianate humanists who had enjoyed the patronage of Reginald Pole in Italy; they wielded their pens in Cromwell's service from 1535 and were patriotic Henricians rather than Protestants. Both were far more than mere topical pamphleteers. While thundering against the sin of rebellion they did not hesitate to criticise the existent social structure, understanding well that the roots of popular unrest were economic rather than religious. Another member of the group was the printer and translator William Marshall, who, aided by a £20 loan from Cromwell, published in 1535 the first English version of Marsiglio's *Defensor Pacis*. Yet another was Richard Taverner, a convinced Lutheran who is mentioned as Cromwell's client in 1533 and who translated not only the Bible but Melanchthon and other Protestant authors.[11] These men wrote in English for the people, not in Latin for the rulers and scholars of Europe. They were by origin poor scholars, not great officials in Church or State. Like Cranmer they believed in a greater measure of educational opportunity, and they thought that the peace of the commonwealth depended upon a progressive improvement in the harsh lot of the poor. Alongside its insensitivity to suffering the sixteenth century displayed a passionate interest in the problems of social amelioration; as a true child of the age, the English Reformation could scarcely help translating some of this idealism into religious terms.

The difficult situation of the Cromwell–Cranmer group can be illustrated by reference to its part in the tragic story of the heretic John Lambert.[12] This former fellow of Queens' College, Cambridge, had been one of Bilney's converts; he later became a chaplain at the notorious English House of the Merchant Adventurers in Antwerp and an associate of Tyndale and Frith. On Sir Thomas More's insistence he had been sent back to England and confronted by Warham with forty-five charges of heresy, to which he composed able and learned answers. Kept in protective custody at the Archbishop's manor-house at Otford, Lambert obtained his release on Warham's death and thereafter ran a school in London. In 1536 the Duke of Norfolk and other noble traditionalists complained about attacks made by him upon the worship of the saints. He thus appeared before Cranmer, Shaxton and Latimer, who, while personally in agreement with the accused, were desperately anxious to avoid a frontal clash with his influential accusers. Deeply embarrassed, they offered to release him if he would state that prayers to saints were unnecessary yet not sinful. This compromise the scrupulous Lambert rejected and he further exasperated the prelates by declining to accept even a secret release from confinement. They hence remitted him to Lord Chancellor Audley, who kept him in prison for a time.

In the autumn of 1538, now again at liberty, Lambert decided to tread much more dangerous ground. He attended a sermon on the eucharist by John Taylor, himself a sympathiser with Lutheran doctrine and in later days deprived by Queen Mary of the bishopric of Lincoln. After the sermon Lambert sought out the preacher for disputation, but Dr. Taylor unwisely told him to set down his opinions on paper. Having received these opinions, Taylor consulted Robert Barnes, who had now become a member of a commission to extirpate Anabaptist sectaries. Seeing himself as guardian of a Lutheran orthodoxy, Barnes advised Taylor to forward Lambert's paper to the Archbishop. The last and most curious link of this upward chain was then forged by Cranmer himself.

It so happened that at this moment the King, disappointed in the Lutheran princes, desired not merely to placate Catholic opinion but to gain the friendship of the great Catholic powers. Cranmer can hardly have been unaware of his master's eagerness to impress Europe with a spectacle of orthodoxy when he now allowed and even advised Lambert to appeal to the King in person. One can only hope that he did not consciously offer the heretic as a sacrifice to Henry's diplomatic needs.

Lambert's doctrinal position appears in a *Treatise upon the Sacrament* addressed at this stage to the King. It was based upon the far from novel contention that since Christ had bodily ascended into heaven, he could not in a corporeal sense be in the sacrament. 'Thus, O most gracious and godly prince, do I confess and acknowledge that the bread of the sacrament is truly Christ's body, and the wine to be truly his blood, according to the words of the institution of the same sacrament; but in a certain wise, that is to wit, figuratively, sacramentally or significatively.' And in support of a non-corporeal presence he cites Tertullian, Augustine and Jerome. It may be inaccurate to dismiss Lambert as a straightforward sacramentarian; some of his phraseology does not differ markedly from that which we shall see Cranmer himself adopting under Ridley's influence some eight years later.

John Foxe describes the trial scene with his usual vividness and not without evident touches of malice. It was splendidly staged for the benefit of its Europe-wide audience. Symbolising an awful doctrinal purity, the King appeared clad in white from head to foot. With the accused he soon showed himself in his most brutal and peremptory mood. Cranmer tried in contrast to reason quietly with 'brother Lambert', but being no great disputant made little headway against this able opponent. The other bishops intervened in relay; the King bullied, the audience was violent in its hostility toward Lambert, who nevertheless acquitted himself well until exhausted by five hours of continuous bombardment. As torches were brought in at five o'clock that winter afternoon, the voice of the defendant died into a stupefied silence; he submitted himself to the King's mercy, and the King, unmoved, ordered the hitherto silent Cromwell to read out the sentence. On the morning of the execution, if Foxe is to be believed, Cromwell held an interview with the doomed man in his private room, after which Lambert was allowed to breakfast with the gentlemen in Cromwell's hall. This much the minister may indeed have ventured, but the rumour that he asked Lambert's forgiveness sounds like the wishful thinking of Protestants. What we know for certain is that Cromwell sent off a report of the trial to Sir Thomas Wyatt in Paris, lauding in Byzantine phrases the King's inestimable gravity, wisdom and benignity. 'I wished the princes and potentates of Christendom to have had a meet place for them there to have seen it.' Behind the minister's sardonic sense of humour and Italianate sophistication there doubtless lurked a certain conviction of duty done. He was no doubt more sorry for Lambert than for most of the King's victims, but he had to disseminate the propaganda. Like his friend the Archbishop, he held an uncomfortable and insecure position, but he had no intention of risking it over a pertinacious enthusiast who had gone so busily about the world in search of trouble.

The conservative group of courtiers and officials which stood in opposition to Cromwell and Cranmer was led by the Duke of Norfolk and by his son's former tutor, Stephen Gardiner, Bishop of Winchester. On its fringes stood the majority of the bishops, headed by the virtuous Catholic humanist Cuthbert Tunstall of Durham. It lacked ideas on religion or on government, but it had a priceless asset in the King's deep suspicion of doctrinal change, and its leaders did not lack talents appropriate to their opportunities. We have already remarked upon the Duke's blind loyalty, his lack of scruple and his talent for court-intrigue. In this field Gardiner proved himself an even subtler schemer; the memory of his humble origins certainly failed to soften a proud and ambitious spirit. Unlike Cranmer he was every inch a man of affairs—a committee-leader and negotiator who never achieved the rank of a creative statesman. His fine legal training and diplomatic experience were accompanied by little political originality, his sincere hatred of heresy by no marked spiritual endowments. Yet he and his associates were as good Henricians as their opponents, and intellectually they stood even closer to the King's conventional mind. In the practical matters of the divorce, the Papacy, the Royal Supremacy, they took (but with some misgivings in Tunstall's case) a diametrically opposite line from that of Fisher and More.

Gardiner's famous book *De Vera Obedientia* (1535) leans as strongly toward the uncompromising doctrines of Marsiglio as any of the works arising from the circle of Thomas Cromwell.[13] The true Christian, it argues, must obey those whom God has appointed his representatives on earth; their authority resembles that of masters over servants, fathers over children. Set above all such god-given rulers, the Princes stand at the very apex of human society. When Parliament recently proposed that King Henry should proclaim himself Head of the Church, it was guiltless of innovation; it was disburdening the nation of the privileges falsely assumed by the bishop of Rome. To Gardiner as to Marsiglio the individuals who composed the kingdom were the same as those who composed the Church within the kingdom, and the ruler who was head of the former must logically be head of the latter. 'Is John', he asks, 'the King's subject only as an inhabitant of England, and the same John not the King's subject as a Christian?' The Church in England is not, of course, the whole Church, but it is another aspect of the kingdom of England. There can be only one sovereign power in a kingdom. To the *imperium* of a King Scripture sets no limit, and it is sinful to prescribe any limits to the obedience due from a subject. Illustrating the legitimacy of Henry's claims Gardiner cites a series of precedents from the Old Testament down to Justinian, who legislated not only upon the clergy but upon Christian doctrine itself. Despite some acknowledgments wrung from them under duress, Christian princes have never really believed the bishop of Rome to be rightful head of the Church. Had they believed this, how could they so frequently have defied popes? Had the popes really believed their own claims, how could they have consented to such legislation as the English statutes of Provisors and *Praemunire*? And how could Our Lord have given an authority to the popes which he declined to exercise himself? Of the primacy as defined by Rome no trace appears in the pages of Scripture, and such headship as that historically conceded to the popes has arisen merely from human tradition. They can claim no rightful jurisdiction over churches other than that of Rome and, if they attempt to exceed their rights, they must suffer the consequences. They should seek to manifest a primacy in virtue, not in political power. And in his conclusion Gardiner reveals a nationalism as blunt as that of any popular writer. The English government has now agreed that its people shall have no further dealings with Rome; hence it remains the plain duty of every English subject to obey without question.

In Queen Mary's time Gardiner alleged he had written *De Vera Obedientia* out of fear, lest he should suffer the same death as Fisher and More. This excuse he may by then have persuaded himself to accept but it fails to carry conviction. Unjust as were some of the punishments meted out during the crisis, the King could scarcely have procured the execution of a bishop merely on account of his failure to compose a really outstanding and powerful defence of the Royal Supremacy. The modern apologists who have accepted his plea should surely reflect that in 1535 the credit of the Papacy had not yet begun to rise from its nadir, even among such doctrinally conservative bishops. Not satisfied with enunciating erastian theory Gardiner even wrote a tract to justify the execution of Fisher. This Janelle seeks to explain by the phrase, 'he was quite simply abject'. But it remains far easier to suppose that in 1535 Gardiner accepted the whole royalist position and really believed what he wrote. If Cranmer's biography and opinions cannot be made wholly consistent, neither can Gardiner's. Amid the enormous psychological pressures of the period who save men of heroic simplicity could occupy high office and yet emerge with a record of consistent belief and profession?

The Fall of Cromwell

DESPITE the responsible spirit in which Cromwell exercised the functions of vicegerent, his overthrow by Norfolk and Gardiner resulted from an unwonted act of imprudence as well as from a measure of ill-luck. He failed to check a dangerous trend which involved the English Reformation in the unpredictable turmoil of continental Europe. More perilously still, he assumed responsibility for one of Henry's matrimonial adventures. Though in most English minds France remained the traditional foe, the King's schismatic policy and his humiliation of Katherine had now alienated the other 'great power' of Europe in the person of the Emperor. From the English viewpoint Charles V was first and foremost ruler of the Netherlands, with which brilliant and prosperous region so much of our trade and our civilisation had long been intimately related. To Cromwell, as to any man who had worked for years in Antwerp, a war with Charles V seemed a heavy penalty to pay for the divorce and the Royal Supremacy.[14] Yet a bleak threat now appeared that King Francis would bury his feud with Charles, uniting both great powers in a crusade against England. Given that a *rapprochement* with Charles could not immediately be achieved, it seemed prudent at least to keep him occupied in Germany by supporting the Lutheran princes who, led by the Elector of Saxony and the Landgrave of Hesse, had formed the Schmalkaldic League. After long preliminary investigations Cromwell sent Edward Fox in 1535 to ask under what conditions these princes would accept Henry as a member of their League. They demanded not merely financial backing but an acceptance of the Confession of Augsburg as the basis for a Lutheran Reformation in England. This price Henry found too high. He replied that he had every intention of setting forth true doctrine according to the Scriptures, that he was reckoned 'somewhat learned' and that, with the assistance of other learned men in his realm, he could manage the sacred task without foreign help. Thenceforward he maintained this posture during years of negotiations with the Lutherans. It was an attitude based upon something more than religious conservatism, upon more than a natural desire to manage his own Reformation. England had not at this date the resources to become—as she became in the prosperous Hanoverian age—the paymaster of German princes. Moreover, Henry never felt himself in extreme danger. He stood prepared to gamble on the unlikelihood of an offensive alliance between Francis and Charles. Even if the worst should happen, he trusted in his strengthened navy to cripple any attempt at invasion.

Armed with this assessment of the facts Henry felt no strong impulse to toe the Lutheran party-line. The Ten Articles which he caused Convocation to adopt in 1536 have often been taken as a conciliatory approach toward the recent Wittenberg Articles, but they might rather be used to exemplify our English talent for concocting ambiguous and flexible documents. They mention, it is true, only three sacraments (baptism, penance and the eucharist), but they define these in an orthodox sense and do not deny the validity of the other four accepted by Catholics. Their phraseology concerning the eucharist could be interpreted in a Lutheran sense, yet it likewise admits of transubstantiation, in which doctrine the King maintained a steadfast personal belief. They contradict the Lutherans by retaining auricular confession and penance. They also defend prayers for the dead, while yet avoiding a definition of purgatory and acknowledging that Scripture does not tell us exactly where the dead are, the name of that place or the pains there imposed. On the vital topic of Justification a definition by Melanchthon is cited, but then the solifidian position is carefully avoided by the phrase 'sinners attain this justification by contrition and faith joined with charity'.[15]

Whatever his personal beliefs and diplomatic ambitions, Cromwell cannot seriously have hoped to coerce the King in doctrinal matters and his continuance in office by no means guaranteed that further favours would be shown to the Protestants. In actual fact the next year saw a fresh compromise between the two parties along lines even more conservative than those of the Ten Articles. This was embodied in the *Institution of a Christian Man*, usually called *The Bishops' Book*, which took the form of an elaborate exposition of the Creed, the Seven Sacraments, the Ten Commandments, the Lord's Prayer and the Ave Maria.[16] After much consultation, argument and answering of questionnaires, it was completed in July 1537 by a large committee of bishops and divines. It gratified the conservatives by restoring the four sacraments (matrimony, confirmation, holy orders and extreme unction) omitted from the Ten Articles. Taken as a whole it looked a Catholic rather than a Lutheran document. Yet it refrained from imposing transubstantiation, acknowledged the lower status of these non-scriptural sacraments and placed emphasis on scriptural authority and on current problems like that of Justification. It constituted more than a mere reiteration of medieval doctrine. Perhaps the most remarkable passage is that in the exposition of the Creed which sets forth the theory of a Church Universal, composed of free and equal national churches. In almost every detail this passage might still be accepted as a classic statement of the Anglican position. Both groups of bishops—including Gardiner, who was in France—signed the Book. Yet the King carefully refrained from giving it his authority and used it instead to test the theological appetite of the nation. Early in 1538 he suggested many revisions with a view to another edition, and these were criticised with great frankness by Cranmer, who even went so far as to correct the royal grammar. The King at no time sent the book to Parliament or to Convocation; he merely commended it for study by clerics having the cure of souls. Knowing the parish clergy, one may doubt whether *The Bishops' Book* made much impact upon them; its length, expense and sophistication must likewise have placed it above the heads of most literate laymen.

While the desultory exchanges with the Lutheran princes dragged through the year 1538 and into the spring of 1539, the plans of Cromwell began to diverge ominously from those of the King. While the former strove to keep open the channels and even to widen them by a marriage-alliance with the ducal house of Cleves, the King—no doubt encouraged by the Duke of Norfolk and the conservative bishops—resolved upon 'a devise for the unity in religion' couched in conservative, not to say reactionary terms. The new Parliament assembled on 28 April and at Henry's request a committee was set up in the Lords consisting of Cromwell as vicegerent and of four

Reformers (Cranmer, Latimer, Goodrich of Ely and Salcot *alias* Capon of Bangor) and four Catholics (Lee of York, Tunstall, Clerk of Bath and Wells and Aldrich of Carlisle). When, as the king doubtless anticipated, holy deadlock ensued, he took personal command and authorised Norfolk on 16 May to offer six articles to Parliament for discussion. These were politely framed as questions, but Henry already knew the right answers; he in fact revised with his own hand the earliest extant draft of the Six Articles Act. Its enactment was virtually decided in the predominantly Catholic House of Lords and through the intervention of the King, who came down in person to the debate and, in the words of one approving peer, 'confounded them all with God's learning'. It is certain that Cranmer opposed some of the Act's provisions in the Lords and that, even after the King's pronouncement, he spoke against it in Convocation. It is not thought that he ventured to oppose transubstantiation, but it seems probable enough that he defended the marriage of priests, opposed the necessity of the confessional and advocated the communion of the laity in both kinds. Ceasing this resistance only just short of the danger-point he then surrendered responsibility to the King and agreed, though with reluctance, to join in enforcing the Act during the rest of the reign. It proposed a persecution more ferocious than that of the church courts and marked a mood of determination on the King's part to stamp out nonconformity in his realm. It upheld transubstantiation, the sufficiency for laymen of communion in one kind, clerical celibacy, the obligation to keep vows of chastity, the orthodoxy of private masses and of auricular confession. Should a man deny transubstantiation, he would incur death by burning and total forfeiture of property—even abjuration would not save him. Obstinate denial of any other of the articles rendered an offender liable to the same penalties, except that in the event of abjuration he would merely suffer imprisonment at the King's pleasure, while sentence of death would only be passed on a man twice convicted of such felony. Even to Henry and the Lords the Act seemed on second thoughts a trifle heavy-handed; by an amendment of 1540 priests and women twice convicted of concubinage were exempted from the death-penalty. In the event, the persecution proved intermittent and the total number of victims small. From the first, however, the Protestant minority among the clergy saw the Act as a disastrous defeat at the hands of Gardiner and Norfolk. Shaxton and Latimer resigned their sees, while Cranmer himself was compelled to return his wife to her people in Germany. Thomas Cromwell, momentarily shaken, strove to regain his hold upon the King, and for a few months it seemed as if his pertinacity would be rewarded.

At this moment threatening continental developments seemed to be aiding his endeavours. In the summer of 1538 the Emperor Charles had met King Francis at Aigues-Mortes, and in January 1539 they came together again at Toledo, where they agreed to make no alliance with Henry except by mutual consent. While these overtures did not presage any immediate anti-English crusade, they added some weight to Cromwell's demand for alliances, and Henry agreed to allow further negotiations with the Lutheran princes. This time Cromwell resolved to abandon theological debates and to concentrate upon marriage-alliances. Two of these were proposed, one between the Princess Mary and the young Duke William of Cleves, the other between Henry himself and Anne, the elder of Duke William's unmarried sisters. The Cleves dukedom, though modest in extent and resources, lay at a focal point between Emperor Charles in the Netherlands, and the lands of the rebellious Lutherans. Again, the ducal family had recently inherited Gelderland, a province also claimed by Charles. While not yet formal Protestants themselves, William and Anne had a sister married to the Lutheran Elector of Saxony, who thereby became their chief protector against the Emperor.

The outcome of the Cleves negotiation displayed Henry in his most petulant and irresponsible moods. With ill grace he married the unattractive Anne in January 1540. Finding himself unable to consummate the match, rendered increasingly irascible by the decline of his health, irritated by the continual pressure of the Lutherans for a doctrinal agreement, he soon afterwards listened to the criticisms directed against his minister by Gardiner and Norfolk. Cromwell was destroyed without trial by an Act of Attainder based upon fabricated charges of heresy and treason. Of the judicial murders sanctioned by Henry this was perhaps the least intelligible, and in later years he certainly realised the pointlessness of killing the most loyal and industrious minister ever to serve a King of England. Cromwell did not die gloriously for a cause, as did his one-time friend Thomas More, but Protestant propagandists made what capital they could of the event. At least he made an edifying speech on the scaffold and this, duly written up by Grafton, was later on embellished in the accepted tradition of Renaissance historiography by John Foxe, who paraded the deceased minister as a 'valiant soldier and captain of Christ'.

Two days after this execution Smithfield saw a more spectacular and fundamentally more meaningful event—the hanging of three Catholic traitors and the burning of three Protestant heretics.[17] The latter were the more eminent of their species, for they included those pillars of early English Lutheranism, Thomas Garret and Robert Barnes. Despite their theology both these men had become staunch Henricians, and Barnes had for a time controlled his naturally impulsive disposition and made a praiseworthy ambassador to the Lutherans. But the significance of this *auto-da-fé* lay not in its individual victims but in its studied impartiality, in the perceptiveness with which the monarch fostered his new and unique creation. Under the stern eye of their own godly prince Englishmen already found themselves marching along a *via media*.

The Origins of Anglicanism

AMPLE evidence suggests that Cromwell's leanings toward Lutheranism should be taken quite seriously; they were not invented by Foxe. Throughout his ministry he stood deeply involved with the radical group, which was Protestant or turning Protestant as fast as it dared. His efforts to establish the English Bible reflect not merely a long-standing personal interest but a characteristic determination to imprint something indelibly on the English mind. The content of the years 1532–40 proves on examination religious as much as legal; it also involves a process passing beyond the mere absorption of Lutheran theology. At a time when so many modern ideas were coming to birth, there arose the concept of an independent national Church, the basis of which was stated in prophetically Anglican terms in *The Bishops' Book*. The plea that the English nation should pursue a middle path between Romish superstition and licentious heresy was seldom made more clearly than by Cromwell in his speech at the reopening of Parliament on 12 April 1540.[18] Five years earlier it had been stated with equal fluency and greater elaboration by his publicist Thomas Starkey in *An Exhortation to the People*.[19] This not unworthy forerunner of Hooker points with true English complacency to the dreadful disorder in Germany, which has arisen concerning 'things in no point necessary to man's salvation, but about ceremonies and traditions'. Both in Germany and in England, the right path, argues Starkey, lies somewhere between those who 'stiffly stick in the old ceremonies and rites of the Church, wherein they have been of youth brought up', and, on the other side, the arrogance of those who indiscriminately deny all pious customs, and will accept nothing but Scripture—and Scripture interpreted after their own fancy. 'For these men, under the pretence of liberty, covertly purpose to destroy all Christian policy, and so in conclusion bring all to manifest ruin and utter confusion.' This attitude of disapproval combined with the ingrained xenophobia of Henrician Englishmen to demand a highly cautious approach to the continental Reformation, a less than semi-detached relationship with foreign churches and a periodic resort to ambiguities and doctrinal compromises worked out in committee.

The nascent Church did not, however, lack a positive basis, even though this could be stated only in broad terms. In the view of Cranmer and Cromwell 'a pure and sincere doctrine of the Christian faith' should be formulated closely upon Scriptural authority, should be set forth by a Christian King in Parliament and accepted by the people without opinionated haggling over details. Such a notion appealed more readily to laymen than to the clergy, whose professional training made them more conscious of impending intellectual difficulties and whose traditions tended to fetter them to the notion of an orthodoxy based on precise scholastic definition. On the other hand, the very concept of a Scriptural religion encouraged, and almost entailed, a neglect of Aquinas and Scotus in favour of the humanist and educational ideals of the new age. Against an Erasmian background it stressed a sound learning in the sacred text and in the early Fathers of the Church. Its ideal human type was no longer the disputant of the schools, but the patristic scholar in the deanery or the Bible-reading priest in the vicarage. These latter figures the Anglican Church has never ceased to produce, yet as we shall later observe, impending cultural changes were about to create many interesting mutations and variants.

Whatever their political limitations, the Reformers comprised many of the best scholars then living in England. Men like Tyndale, Cranmer, Ridley, Coverdale, Cheke, Parker and Jewel were proving, or were soon to prove, more than a match for the English conservatives of their generation. The latter, so often trained in the laws and occupied by official duties, lacked both the time and the intellectual background to become worthy exponents or regenerators of Catholic theology. As for the liberal elements in later Anglican thought, these too had their Henrician forerunners, not merely in Frith but in Starkey himself, for it was he who introduced Melanchthon's doctrine of *adiaphora*, or 'things indifferent', to a permanent place in the Anglican scheme. The whole plan of the Ten Articles is also adiaphorist. In Latimer the Henricians had their Evangelical, in Gardiner their High Churchman, whose uneasily maintained place in Queen Mary's establishment has often been allowed to obscure this more accurate image. From the first, the coherence of Anglicanism depended upon the State. Confronted by this motley scene of the thirties one must detest the King's fitful acts of terror, yet one cannot avoid admiring that strength of character which combined into one organism men and opinions so exceedingly diverse.

If this curious situation tended to inhibit constructive theology, it did not prevent the promulgation of a series of commonsense, practical reforms. The first and clearest examples of Anglican reform may be seen in the two sets of ecclesiastical injunctions imposed by Cromwell in 1536 and in 1538.[20] Of the former series those with educational aspects may perhaps be accorded most significance. The clergy are ordered to teach the Paternoster, the Articles of Faith and the Ten Commandments both to their congregations and to the young. They must urge parents to educate their children or apprentice them to honest occupations, since crime and social disorder will result from their failure. Rich clerics must support scholars at the universities and grammar schools; if non-resident, they must distribute a fortieth part of their incomes to the poor and a fifth to repairing the chancels of their churches. The injunctions of 1538 are those which we have already observed as providing for parish registers. They demand in addition the examination of parishioners in the articles of the faith, quarterly sermons by licensed preachers based upon Scriptural religion, the removal of such images as are abused and the provision by non-resident incumbents of curates able to do their work.

The immediate effectiveness of many of these rules may be doubted, yet at least they began that unduly slow process whereby a good many of the hoary anomalies of the late medieval church were mitigated and ecclesiastical practice brought nearer toward the rising expectations of the period. Such modest and mundane reforms sprang naturally from our Tudor age, with its deep aspirations to good order in Church, commonwealth and society at large. And though parallel reforms were ere long to spring from the continental Counter-Reformation, these of the thirties are typically English in spirit as well as earlier in date. Both before and after the Reformation the religious life of England was not outstandingly productive of saints, mystics and ascetics, of those extraordinary beings who are best fostered and best kept in order by the Church of Rome. As a people we have scarcely grasped the deepest implications of either Catholicism or Protestantism; we have tended to avoid the peaks and the abysses of both, and our greatest men have seldom found it easy to operate within the framework of either. If we have in any respect excelled, it has been in the provision of conditions enabling average Christians to practise a devotion heartfelt enough, yet not so deeply committed as to demand a severance from secular activities and values. If such sober aims and methods are deemed especially characteristic of the Anglican Church, then the thirties can boast one more claim to have laid the foundations of that Church.

Nevertheless, at this primitive stage certain features prominent in later Anglicanism lay as yet undeveloped. Though Cranmer and others were privately questioning transubstantiation, this doctrine was still enforced by the courts and presumably held by the majority of those clerics and laymen who reflected on matters of doctrine. Though Calvinism was coming to birth in Geneva, no one could yet have predicted its immense influence over the next generation of Anglicans. Again, at the time of Cromwell's fall only the first tentative steps had been taken toward a vernacular liturgy. By 1538 Cranmer was devising the first of his schemes for an English Prayer Book.[21] He is unlikely to have embarked upon such plans, however tentatively, without the sanction of the King, who was at this moment still seeking an accord with the Lutheran princes. While the preface to his scheme derived from the revised Breviary produced in 1535 by the Spanish Franciscan Cardinal Quignon, his drafts for matins and evensong were inspired by the work of Luther's intimate friend, Johann Bugenhagen, a copy of which had just been presented to the King. Again, various unofficial and semi-official prymers, printed in English during the thirties, were now habituating the laity to the notion of vernacular prayers and offices.[22] Of these publications the best known are by William Marshall, whose blunt attacks on the veneration of saints soon caused his prymer to be banned, and by the talented ex-Dominican John Hilsey, Bishop of Rochester. The latter naturally dedicated his work to his patron Cromwell, who published a second edition in 1539 after the author's death. This prymer forms another characteristic manifesto of the Henrician *via media*, denouncing various superstitions, yet condemning Zwinglian disbelief in a real and corporeal presence. Altogether, movement had at least begun on the liturgical front, and even the reaction of 1539–40 by no means brought it to a standstill.

Thomas Cromwell's eight-year ministry is now widely recognised as a period when the formation of the modern English State underwent a marked acceleration. In the history of religion we have traditionally regarded it as a period of clearance, as the period when the government swept away the papal connection and the monasteries, while legally subordinating the national Church to the control of the Crown in Parliament. The foregoing paragraphs are intended to suggest that this traditional view is an incomplete view, that the inner significance of this astonishing fourth decade of the sixteenth century should be seen in relation to the Anglican future as much as to the medieval past. Already the government and the intellectuals were groping their way toward a Reformation of compromise and detachment, partly because these attitudes come naturally to the English temperament, partly in consequence of a patriotic distrust for foreign models, partly since both Catholic and Lutheran powers failed to comprehend our situation, most of all because the divisions between Englishmen made it safer to attempt a settlement based on balance and comprehension rather than upon a narrow orthodoxy. However one measures these forces, it remains imperceptive to date the genesis of Anglicanism from the accession of Elizabeth, or even from the publication of Cranmer's First Prayer Book.

Cranmer's Position during Henry's Last Years

If in 1539–40 the King tilted the balance, he never unhinged it. From the fall of Wolsey to the time of his death his situation resembled that of his daughter Elizabeth, in that he took constant pains to avoid becoming the instrument of any one group or any one idea. Tudor monarchs were essentially lonely figures; they knew that the courtly pomp of their entourage masked self-seeking and faction, as well as a fund of genuine devotion. It was their ceaseless and highly personal task to disentangle these warring elements, a task which over the years might have made the gentlest character moody and suspicious. Yet even as the King's health and temper declined, only for short periods did his intellect lose control of his emotions. He soon showed he had every intention of maintaining a two-party system in his executive and in the Church, so long as he could be sure both parties were wholeheartedly Henrician. Events soon conspired to restore a better equilibrium. A little over a year after Cromwell's fall the misconduct of Katherine Howard abased the prestige of her uncle Norfolk, who had contrived that Henry should marry her on the rebound from Anne of Cleves. From July 1543, when the King married Katherine Parr, Protestant opinions once more began to make progress at Court. They were cautiously favoured by the Queen and several noble ladies, again by Sir William Butts, the King's personal physician and a friend of Cranmer. Increasingly identified with the cause of further moderate Reform were the two ablest of the younger men of action, the men destined successively to dominate the reign of Edward VI—Edward Seymour, Earl of Hertford, and John Dudley, Lord Lisle. Despite the efforts of its advocates, the Six Articles persecution was never allowed to reach these high quarters. Yet at the time of the Parr marriage four humble men about the Court at Windsor were condemned, two of them being singers of the Chapel Royal. John Marbeck, interestingly enough, had made extracts from the writings of Calvin, but he had powerful friends, received a pardon and so lived to become one of the fathers of English music. The others, who went with constancy to the flames, included Marbeck's colleague Robert Testwood, who with more ingenuity than taste had altered the wording of an anthem so as to protest against the worship of the Virgin Mary.[23] After this trial accusations were directed against some of the King's gentlemen, but their imprudences were hushed up by a whole series of royal pardons, while the condemnation of the obnoxious Dr. London for perjury also helped to enjoin prudence upon the heresy-hunters.

The King's steady reluctance to allow his personal favourites to be brought within the net does much to account for the survival of his chaplain Cranmer during these difficult years. Admittedly, the Archbishop's situation remained uncomfortable. In Convocation his enemy Gardiner commanded an easy majority, while the resignations of Latimer and Shaxton limited his episcopal backers to Goodrich of Ely and Barlow of St. David's, neither of them being a figure of weight. The true source of strength for the Reformers lay in the maintenance of Cranmer's personal bond with the King, who not only defended him against several concerted attacks but allowed him to continue planning advanced liturgical reforms. When a group of malevolent Canterbury canons, perhaps backed by Gardiner, made charges of heresy against their Archbishop, Henry called at Lambeth, took Cranmer for an outing on his barge and menacingly remarked, 'Ah, my chaplain, I have news for you.

I know now who is the greatest heretic in Kent.' But he ended by placing Cranmer in charge of the enquiry against himself.[24] On another occasion, when Sir John Gostwick raised the question of Cranmer's orthodoxy in the House of Commons, Henry sent a messenger to warn him off. 'Tell that varlet Gostwick that if he do not acknowledge his fault unto my lord of Canterbury . . . I will sure both make him a poor Gostwick, and otherwise punish him, to the example of others.' Even after these rebuffs Norfolk and other members of the Council attempted to procure Cranmer's overthrow, only to be snubbed by the royal command, 'I pray you, use not my friends so.'

The Bishops' Book

MEANWHILE the conservative bishops were having by far the better of the argument when it came to the long-anticipated revision of *The Bishops' Book*. After a long period of gestation, this was first presented to Convocation early in 1543 under the title *The Necessary Doctrine and Erudition of a Christian Man*.[25] The modifications appear to have been negotiated and written chiefly by Cranmer and three other bishops: Thomas Thirlby of Westminster, Nicholas Heath of Rochester and John Salcot of Salisbury. Yet had Stephen Gardiner written the whole work himself it could scarcely have been more to his taste. The Book clearly upheld transubstantiation, made no distinction between the scriptural and the non-scriptural sacraments and frankly described the lay demand for communion in both kinds as 'pestiferous and devilish'. While sanctioning prayers and masses for the dead, it nevertheless acknowledged that every mass was offered for the whole congregation of Christian people and that its benefits could not be limited to private persons or purposes. In general terms it also denounced the financial abuses of purgatory, blaming them upon the Papacy. By implication correcting Tyndale, it said that the 'word *ecclesia* is in English called *Church*', but it naturally distinguished between the Church Universal and its components the national churches, with their diversity of traditions and ceremonies. Again, Scripture itself commits ministration to bishops and priests, whereas the grouping of dioceses under patriarchs, primates, archbishops or metropolitans springs merely from man-made law. In particular, the Bishop of Rome's claim to sovereignty over the rest cannot be maintained by reference to the Scriptures, to the ancient General Councils or even to the general consent of the Catholic Church. The unity of the latter is not conserved by his authority and the Church of Rome has no unique claim to be called

Catholic. The only universal governor of the whole Christian Church is Jesus Christ, whom all Christians are bound to obey. But next to him they must obey Christian kings and princes, 'which be the heads governing under him of the particular churches'.

The 'new' developments in *The Necessary Doctrine* are few, but important. Luther's solifidianism is more clearly rejected than hitherto. Men are not justified by faith alone and the righteousness of Christ is not 'imputed' to them, as Luther supposed. They win justification by faith coupled together with hope, charity, fear of God and repentance. Justification means 'the making of us righteous afore God' and is based on life-long effort; at any time a man may lose it by sin and no man is entitled to any comfortable 'assurance' of his own salvation. Again in opposition to Luther, the freedom of the human will is asserted; the will remains free to choose good by the assistance of divine grace, free to choose evil by rejecting that assistance. In this scheme of justification and salvation good works have a necessary rôle. But by good works we mean, say the authors, neither the superstitious observances of monks and nuns, nor works done to earn human respect, nor merely corporal works, but rather 'all inward and spiritual works . . . as the love and fear of God, joy in God, godly meditations and thoughts, patience, humility and such like'. On a lower level the penitence of the converted sinner and the penances he performs may also be admitted as good works.

It remains impossible to do justice in a few sentences to this outstanding example of committee-theology which happens also to be a neglected masterpiece of Tudor prose, combining the grand writing of its predecessor *The Bishops' Book* with a greater conciseness and an improved arrangement. Fully authorised by the King and furnished with a preface by him, it inevitably became known as *The King's Book*. The title still seems most appropriate, for the work forms the handsomest monument of Henry's experiment in Anglo-Catholicism. And after standing for little more than three years it collapsed for ever at the moment of the monarch's death. Though no doubt owing some of its literary merit to Thomas Cranmer, it might also be described as a monument to the defeat of the Archbishop in committee. In later years he was to accuse Gardiner of 'seducing' Henry into accepting the book, but his rival was able to retort with justice that it had also been accepted by Parliament and that Cranmer himself had made no complaint while the King lived but had sanctioned its use in his diocese. From every logical viewpoint save that of extreme erastianism Cranmer stood in an unenviable position during the King's declining years. Any Archbishop of Canterbury was a great servant of the State; he could neither live a retired life nor avoid direct participation in the actions of his Sovereign. Cranmer was compelled to sit on the Privy Council and there suffer himself to be pushed along by Gardiner, for in that setting the decisive official had every advantage over the tentative scholar. A man fully aware of the pros and cons of every doctrine, a man wholly prepared in his open-mindedness to allow his studies to lead him to fresh conclusions, such a man could scarcely be at home in the ruthless ecclesiastical politics of that intolerant century.

Cranmer's Eucharistic Beliefs and Liturgical Plans

CRANMER'S private beliefs concerning the central problem of the eucharist developed but slowly and were much influenced by a mind with a keener cutting edge—that of his former chaplain Nicholas Ridley, trained in the schools of Cambridge, Louvain and Paris. The evidence for Cranmer's own doctrinal development contains exasperating difficulties and seeming contradictions. Since at present eminent scholars differ on some important issues,[26] it would ill befit a non-specialist to declare for any one hypothesis. A letter of Cranmer to Cromwell concerning the sacramentarian Adam Damplip strongly suggests that the Archbishop had already in 1538 abandoned his belief in transubstantiation, yet that he continued to attach importance to a real presence in the sacrament, possibly in general consonance with the Lutheran doctrine. In that same year he was doubtless sincere enough in expressing disagreement with John Lambert. At his trial in 1555 Cranmer told his judges he had been converted to his later view of the eucharist by Nicholas Ridley and that this change had taken place shortly before 1548. A preface to one of his works, published at Emden in 1557 and attributed to his close friend Sir John Cheke, gives the exact date as 1546. We also have Ridley's own assurance that in 1545 he, Ridley, had been convinced by a 'new' doctrine through reading the work *De Corpore et Sanguine Domini* of the ninth-century Benedictine Ratramnus of Corbie.

At this date the revival of Ratramnus did not represent any very profound research, for the book had been printed at Cologne in 1531 and at Geneva in 1541 and its author's name—often in the form 'Bertram'—was often bandied between Tudor controversialists. The doctrine itself involved a dual and simultaneous operation. On the one hand, the recipient's body received and fed upon the symbolic bread and wine; on the other, his soul received and fed upon the body and blood of Christ, their presence being spiritual only and not corporeal. Ridley was to enunciate this doctrine in his disputation with Queen Mary's Catholic theologians in April 1554, while Cranmer himself maintained it during a similar disputation in April 1555. 'The soul', he claimed, 'is fed with the body of Christ, the body with the sacrament . . . so one thing is done outwardly, another inwardly: like as in baptism, the external element, whereby the body is washed, is one; so the internal element, whereby the soul is cleansed, is another . . . Outwardly we eat the sacrament; inwardly we eat the body of Christ.'

These ostensibly simple phrases concealed a multitude of metaphysical and historical problems; some modern theologians think them not far from Zwinglian symbolism while others regard them as closely related to pre-medieval Catholic tradition and as presenting a genuine *via media*, quite distinct from transubstantiation or consubstantiation or the radical teaching of Zwingli and the other Swiss Reformers. Cranmer's own indecisions of the year 1548 provide further complications. He then published a translation of the catechism by the Lutheran Justus Jonas, which taught the real presence in a manner wholly unacceptable to the Zwinglians and which Cranmer toned down but did not completely revise. On the other hand, in December 1548 Cranmer's speech in the House of Lords debate on the eucharist suggests that his view had now been strongly affected by his recent discussions with the Zwinglian immigrant John à Lasco. It has, however, been forcibly argued that this last phase was brief and that Cranmer thereafter maintained the Ratramnian compromise until his trial. He then claimed that he had held only two beliefs, presumably regarding his 'real presence' belief of *c.* 1538–46 as still Catholic and meaning by his second position the Ratramnian view to which Ridley had converted him.

This was a simplification but it need not be taken as deliberately disingenuous. Two points seem now generally agreed. Both Ridley and Cranmer were revolted by the crudely irreverent attacks made against the sacrament of the altar by the proletarian extremists of the reign of Edward VI. Again, neither of them can be regarded as at any stage a mere shadow of the continental theologians. Those Marian judges (and modern critics) who depicted Cranmer as first orthodox, then a Lutheran, then a Zwinglian, did not merely simplify his development; they also ignored the massive evidence concerning his independent study of the early Fathers and of later theologians. In particular, his acceptance of Ridley's viewpoint occurred three years before the arrival in England of the eminent Martin Bucer, who had come by a different route to a similar doctrine of the eucharist but whose influence upon Cranmer lay in other directions. Everyone who has studied the growth of Cranmer's convictions must sometimes have shared the feeling of Cardinal Gasquet, who found it 'difficult to determine with precision, at any given time, the exact phase of a mind so shifting'. Yet if we go on to imply that a man was a fool or a knave to move from one position to another, especially in relation to this particular doctrine, we misunderstand the enquiring spirit of these years, the doctrinal maelstrom which caused even the unimaginative Gardiner to show uncertainties and Tunstall, the most conservative of Henry's bishops, to regret Innocent III's rigid definition of transubstantiation, while accepting it as a loyal son of the Church.

Meanwhile, during the years 1540–47 Cranmer busied himself far less with speculations on the mass than with projects for an English Prayer Book. He was not alone in his desire to simplify and to rationalise the divine offices, which as collected in the Breviary had reached an elaboration and a complexity quite out of touch with the needs of secular clerics and laymen. This demand had already been recognised by reforming Catholics. It was under commission from Clement VII and with the final approval of Paul III that Quignon had revised the Breviary; and this revision continued to form a basis for Cranmer's studies during the forties and for his Prayer Book of 1549. He did not enjoy a complete monopoly of the liturgical field. In 1543 a committee of bishops produced a *Rationale of Ceremonial* which proved to be a competent but most conservative anthology of medieval usages.[27] Cranmer, who doubtless bore not a little of the responsibility for its quiet suppression, soon hastened to produce a first instalment of his own work. This was the English Litany, printed in May 1544 and thereafter used by royal command in the churches. Here he displayed not only a splendid gift of English phrase but a marked flair for selecting ideas from different sources—the Sarum and York Uses, Quignon, Luther and others—and fusing them into a devotional unity able to commend itself to successive generations of English churchmen. Its quality may still be assessed in the Prayer Book version, though the invocations to the Virgin and the saints, retained in 1549, were omitted altogether in 1552 and subsequently. To take a point of detail, Cranmer's skill in this *genre* may be seen in his grouping of the petitions. The Latin litany had the frequent congregational responses: 'Ab omni malo: *libera nos Domine*. Ab insidiis diaboli: *libera nos Domine*. A ventura ira: *libera nos Domine*', and so forth. But Cranmer's version has, 'From all evil and mischief; from sin, from all crafts and assaults of the devil; from thy wrath, and from everlasting damnation, *Good Lord, deliver us*.'[28]

Henry did not envisage doctrinal change when he permitted Cranmer to plan a modification of the mass by the insertion of devotional passages in English. This project nevertheless went far beyond mere translation. It entailed a radical change of purpose, whereby the infrequent lay communion and the many private masses of medieval custom would be replaced by a regular congregational service. Though this *Order of Communion* was not published until almost a year after Henry's death, the work had been almost completed during his reign: being again in a forward state of mind, he would probably have sanctioned its use had he lived a little longer. This was not the only one of Cranmer's schemes which bore fruit in the subsequent reign. To deal with the problem of disaffected, extravagant and illiterate preaching, he had taken the initiative in compiling a *Book of Homilies*, twelve in number, four or five of which he wrote personally, while assigning two others to the conservatives Harpsfield and Bonner.[29] In 1543 he laid these sermons before Convocation, but for reasons now obscure no immediate progress ensued. A more successful enterprise was the *King's Prymer*, published in 1545 with a royal preface ordaining that all schoolmasters must use it to instruct their pupils 'next after their A.B.C.' and that no other prymer should henceforth be read, printed or sold. The literary and liturgical superiority of this work to its predecessors has been taken to show the hand of the Archbishop, though the King's marked complacency over its merits suggests that he may also have taken a personal share in its revision.

The Bible and Public Opinion

DURING these years many preparations for a future Protestant advance were taking place behind the façade of reaction. Amongst Cranmer's partial successes we may count his ability to contain the violent attacks made by his adversaries against the English Bible. From the outset the Gardiner faction found it easy to prey upon Henry's fears concerning the policy of the open Bible; the more easy since even the Great Bible could scarcely be regarded as other than a Protestant document. Cranmer must have been acting under pressure when in the Convocation of 1542 he asked the bishops whether the English Bible could be retained without 'scandal, error and open offence to Christ's faithful people'. The majority of the bishops replied that it could not, unless it were first corrected by the Vulgate. Upon this, the New Testament was divided into fifteen portions and assigned to as many bishops for summary examination, while the Lower House of Convocation was encouraged to produce a list of errors from the Old Testament. Committees of bishops were then appointed to accomplish the actual revision, and at this point Gardiner produced his exotic list of Latinisms from the Vulgate, which he desired to embody in a revised version. On 10 March 1542, however, the Archbishop suddenly reported that the King had decided to have the Bible examined by the two universities. This, as he doubtless foresaw, procured a useful delay, but the conservatives were not slow to follow another line of attack. In the spring of 1543 they induced the King to let them bring into Parliament an 'Act for the Advancement of True Religion'. It condemned 'crafty false and untrue' translations, including that of Tyndale, while limiting the reading of the licensed Bibles on a class-basis not unlike that of the medieval sumptuary laws. Noblemen and gentlemen might read to their families at home, substantial merchants and gentlewomen were trusted to read by themselves, while the common people must not read the Scriptures at all.[30]

Amongst our somewhat meagre evidence concerning popular Bible-reading at this stage is the vivid narrative by William Malden,[31] describing his experiences as a youth at Chelmsford. When Henry VIII set forth the Scriptures to be read in churches, he recalls, 'Immediately after, divers poor men in the town of Chelmsford in the county of Essex, where my father dwelled and I [was] born and with him brought up, the said poor men brought the New Testament of Jesus Christ, and on Sundays did sit reading in [the] lower end of the church, and many would flock about them to hear their reading.' Finding his son among this study-group, Malden senior pulled him out and made him say the Latin matins. 'Then I saw I could not be in rest. Then, thought I, I will learn to read English, and then I will have the New Testament and read thereon myself; and then had I learned of an English prymer as far as *Patris sapientia*, and then on Sundays I plied my English prymer. The May-tide following, I and my father's prentice Thomas Jeffrey laid our money together and bought the New Testament in English, and hid it in our bed straw and so exercised it at convenient times.' Soon afterwards young Malden was sent to keep a shop some distance away, thus gaining a better chance to pursue his forbidden studies. One day he remonstrated with his mother for worshipping the crucifix: 'Then I went and hid Frith's book on the Sacrament, and then I went to bed.' In response to these actions his distraught father beat him, put a halter round his neck and might have strangled him but for his mother's intervention. No doubt the Reformation occasioned many such emotional clashes between the generations, each well-intentioned by its own lights. And as for the elder Malden, he may perhaps have thought some calculated violence at this stage preferable to seeing his son involved in dangerous charges of heresy.

The text of the prohibitory Act of 1543 suggests how widespread Bible-reading had now become by listing amongst the unprivileged classes 'women, artificers, apprentices, journeymen, servingmen under the degree of yeomen, husbandmen and labourers'. The King perhaps exaggerated the situation when in his famous last speech to Parliament (24 December 1545) he complained that the 'most precious jewel, the Word of God, is disputed, rhymed, sung and jangled in every alehouse and tavern'. Naturally, the more literate members of the working classes read aloud to the illiterate, and inability to read did not exclude a man from Biblical study and from the convictions it entailed. In the pages of Foxe we encounter offenders with little or no knowledge of reading and writing, who yet argued over texts with their prosecutors and disputed the more familiar points of doctrinal controversy. That the prohibition of 1543 caused distress among such people is suggested by the chance survival of a copy of Thomas Langley's *Abridgement of Polydore Vergil* (published in April 1546) containing a bucolic inscription by a Gloucestershire shepherd named Robert Williams. This man apparently kept the flock of William Latimer, the humanist parson of Saintbury and Weston-sub-Edge, who had in fact died the previous year. 'At Oxforde, the yere 1546, browt down to Seynbury by John Darbye, pryse 14d, when I kepe Mr. Letymer's shype. I bout thys boke when the Testament was obberagatyd [abrogated], that shepeherdys myght not red hit. I prey God amende that blyndnes. Wryt by Robert Wyllyams keppynge shepe uppon Seynbury Hill, 1546.'[32]

This quiet and dignified protest forms a contrast with more sensational acts of defiance like that of the young London tailor John Porter.[33] At St. Paul's Bishop Bonner had set up six public Bibles, forbidding readers to gather crowds, to expound the Scriptures or to disturb the services. Foxe admits that Porter gathered a multitude and read in a 'very audible' voice. He was also charged with expounding the text and thrown into prison where, alleges the martyrologist, he was loaded with chains and found dead by the morning. In all likelihood, Porter's death in prison (perhaps from starvation) took place two years later in 1542, when the bishop's chancellor kept him there on an unconfirmed charge of sacramentarian heresy. Whatever the precise details, we can believe that cruel punishments were sometimes imposed; yet Porter may well have been one of those brave but impatient enthusiasts who brought trouble upon themselves without substantially advancing the cause. As the story of the Reformation unfolds, it suggests with increasing emphasis that by no means all the arrogance lay on the side of the bishops.

Eagerly as we sift the scattered evidence concerning the early impact of the English Bible upon the common people, we should not assume that at every stage this development was the most vital factor in the progress of the Reformation. At this moment the future of the movement did not lie so much with Gloucestershire shepherds and London tailors as with their economic and social superiors. The fact that the gentry and the middle classes continued to read the Bible mattered far more than the fact that poor men suffered a temporary restraint. At the moment of his greatest power Henry VIII dared not attempt to wrest the Bible from the hands of the political classes, and amongst them a New Learning, compounded of biblicism, Erasmian reformism and Protestant beliefs, seems to have continued steadily developing throughout the Cromwellian years and the years of ostensible reaction which followed. With a view to discerning trends of religious opinion the present writer made a study of the religious phraseology of wills—mainly those of gentry, substantial yeomen and clergy—in Yorkshire and Nottinghamshire throughout the middle decades of the century.[34] The traditional Catholic form involved bequeathing one's soul not only to Christ, or to

Almighty God, but also to the Blessed Virgin and the glorious company of the saints. Though in individual cases testamentary forms may have been influenced by some person other than the testator, anything like a mass movement to omit mention of the Virgin and the saints must reflect a decline of these cults. This seems especially probable in the later years of Henry VIII, when no legal or social pressures induced testators to abandon the traditional forms. And even in these conservative and slow-moving parts of England such a trend begins in the late thirties, becoming steadily more marked in the reign of Edward VI. The following table should be viewed with less reverence than we accord to modern statistics, yet it does not fail to tell a story.

Years	*Traditional Wills*	*Non-traditional Wills*
1538–40	70	9
1541–44	82	33
1545–46	99	32
1547	24	15
1548	24	19
1549	23	24
1550	18	31
1551	21	35

Moreover, from 1537–8 small but steadily growing minorities of these testators do not merely omit the saints, but also use positively Protestant terms, stressing salvation through the merits of Christ alone. Such, for example, were William Holmes and Robert Thomson of Halifax, a great parish comprising many weaving communities with an early (and thereafter continuous) Protestant tradition. These men in 1538 specifically reject the intercession of the saints, commending their souls 'unto Christ Jesu, my maker and redeemer, in whom, and by the merits of whose blessed passion, is all my whole trust of clean remission of all my sins'.[35]

In this same year Robert Ferrar, prior of Nostell yet a fervent Protestant, graphically described to Cromwell the ardent desire of men in the clothing towns of the West Riding to hear the Gospel preached; he even suggested a plan to turn his own priory into a school and a centre for evangelism.[36] Similar hints occur in other sources. Wilfrid Holme of Huntington near York, who wrote in 1537 his long denunciation of the Pilgrimage of Grace, gives us a deeper insight into the minds of these provincial squires who were at once hero-worshippers of Henry VIII, believers in Justification by Faith, enemies of saint-worship and exponents of critical attitudes which can be traced back to Reuchlin and Erasmus.[37] In Holme's view a Golden Age was already at hand. Scholastic philosophy, ungodly medieval science, the mumbo-jumbo of saints, relics and pilgrimages, the lusts of hypocritical monks and nuns would all be swept away, and the godly monarch would lead forth the nation in the light of the Gospel. Some of these are modern phrases, but that they summarise Holme's attitude with entire fairness will, I think, be admitted by any reader who can stomach his high-flown diction. Even in these remoter provinces a fair proportion of the gentry had been educated at the Inns of Court; very many leaders of local opinion were frequent visitors to London, where they had every opportunity to encounter new religious opinions. Amongst the substantial classes, and even amongst the populace of London, the Home Counties and East Anglia, these opinions were making still more rapid progress during the last decade of Henry VIII. On the passage of the Six Articles Act more than 500 Londoners were immediately indicted (and many arrested) as notorious disbelievers in its provisions,[38] and no doubt this number, though hitherto unknown in such a context, could have been multiplied, given more official energy and more commodious gaols. In the same year the heretical preaching of the Scots Reformer George Wishart gained many converts among the citizens of Bristol, where feeling between the rival parties apparently ran as high as it had done six years earlier under the stimulus of Latimer's preaching.[39] If under the threat of the Six Articles most Protestants used discretion, their numbers continued to grow.

Opinion in Tudor England was not created by Acts of Parliament, and its development cannot be gauged by reading the Statute Book. Whatever the King might say, the Protestants do not seem to have believed that at any stage he had abandoned Reformation principles. Religious opinion never became stabilised. Protestantism was emphatically never limited to the clerical group which acknowledged the leadership of Cranmer or to the knot of 'advanced' courtiers under Edward Seymour, Earl of Hertford, who in January 1547 awaited the impending death of their master with a strange mixture of grief and impatience. Yet these latter were the men upon whom the next phase of the Reformation depended, and by some remarkable strokes of fortune the key to the new reign had just been pressed into their hands.

Signs of Change

FROM the age of six Prince Edward had been taught by Dr. Richard Cox, whose subsequent dramatic part in the furtherance of the Reformation we shall have ample opportunity to witness.[40] In July 1544 Sir John Cheke, the greatest English classicist of his day, was summoned from Cambridge 'as a supplement to Mr. Cox', and soon became one of the very few to gain the affections of the reserved boy. Cheke was already in trouble with Gardiner, who even forced him to desist from teaching the revised pronunciation of Greek, and he ultimately fell victim to the Marian persecution. The third among Edward's tutors was the celebrated Sir Anthony Cooke, who had qualified for the post by making his own daughters the most learned women in England. His religious opinions matched those of Cox and Cheke; in 1559 he was to become one of the two leaders of that radical party in the House of Commons which forced through the Elizabethan Settlement. These men were not the only Protestants in the Prince's entourage. It is impossible to believe that the King had no inkling of their proclivities, and even tempting to suppose that he had divined the future to the extent of training his successor for a course of action which he himself hesitated to adopt. Few of his earlier decisions had been more momentous in regard to the English Reformation. Edward's precocity and strongly Protestant views are well attested from the time of his accession; they played a real part in subsequent events, since he was called upon to take a quasi-adult part in public events and would not have been easy to manipulate by any save Protestant politicians.

During the summer months of the year 1546 the outcome of the party-struggle was far from being a foregone conclusion. At this time the Catholic party remained energetic in the Privy Council and still in good hopes of stamping out heresy. The well-known London preacher Dr. Crome had been forced into public recantation, Latimer closely examined, Shaxton driven into preaching against his former friends. An energetic drive against notorious heretics in London found its main victims in Anne Askew and John Lascells, who on 16 July were burned with two others for refusing transubstantiation.[41] Only a year later, attracted by Anne's extraordinary fortitude, John Bale published in her honour the remarkably vivid collection of original materials subsequently utilised by Foxe.[42] If the documents present anything like an accurate picture, this daughter of a Lincolnshire knight proved herself an educated, pert and formidable disputant, quite unabashed by Gardiner and Bonner, who both attempted to re-convert and save her. The villains of the story are not churchmen, but Lord Chancellor Wriothesley and Sir Richard Rich, who wracked Anne in the Tower with their own hands in an unsuccessful attempt to make her implicate her alleged patrons, Queen Katherine Parr, the Duchess of Suffolk and the Countesses of Sussex and Hertford. Her friend John Lascells, though a somewhat obscure figure, was in all likelihood the real intellectual leader of the group. He was a gentleman of good Nottinghamshire family, a member of Furnivall's Inn, a sewer of the King's Chamber, and almost certainly that same John Lascells who in 1541 had given important evidence concerning the misconduct of Katherine Howard.

From this last point he may well have become a target for revenge. On examination he left no doubts regarding his defiance of the Six Articles, and the polemical letter which he wrote in prison was recognised in later years by the Jesuit Robert Parsons as a most persuasive document. In the course of an elaborate attack upon its sacramental teaching Parsons asserted that Lascells had passed beyond Luther, Zwingli and Calvin, and claimed that his doctrine derived from Andreas Carlstadt, the extremist who had been denounced by Luther himself. Equally well, Lascells and his friends might be regarded as disciples of John Frith. These two martyrs and their plebeian fellow-sufferers also appear to exemplify the democratic tendencies inevitable within a persecuted minority. In London there had developed heretical groups compounded of people with varied social and educational backgrounds and it became increasingly easy for working-class Protestants to gain indoctrination from educated leaders.

By the time of these martyrdoms the Seymours had become predominant at Court, while during a banquet given in August to Admiral d'Annebault the King himself suggested that England and France should act in concert to extirpate popery and establish a communion service in place of the mass. Cranmer, who related this story to his secretary and biographer Morice, also claimed that the King had ordered him to prepare such a plan for submission to the French court. On 26 December the failing ruler nominated a Council of Regency for his son. Virtually all its sixteen members belonged to the 'new' families, and its strong personalities leaned toward Protestantism. Noting the omission of Bishop Gardiner's name, Henry's close friend Sir Anthony Browne knelt at the royal bedside and asked whether it might be due to negligence. 'Hold your peace', growled the King, 'I remembered him well enough, and of good purpose have left him out. . . . I could myself use him, and rule him to all manner of purposes, as seemed good unto me, but so will you never do.'

It now remained for the Seymour faction to overthrow that last political bulwark of Catholicism, the Howard family. Thanks to its internal quarrels and to the recklessness of Norfolk's brilliant son the Earl of Surrey, the task proved unexpectedly simple.[43] This 'foolish proud boy' had begun seriously to overplay his hand, for he could boast no services to match Hertford's two ably-managed expeditions into Scotland. Indeed, not long before, Surrey's defeat at the hands of the French near Boulogne had been retrieved by Hertford in person. He was now loudly demanding the future regency for his father and announcing his intentions of settling faithfully with friend and foe when the Howards should come into their own. Within a few months Surrey threw away all the advantages built up by his father's long years of subservience, and his conduct ensured that the Catholic party would enter the new reign without its traditional lay leadership. Yet he was not a Catholic martyr and could not be presented as such; he could not even build up a party, for the new nobility and the King's servants had no intention of quarrelling and dividing along religious lines at the behest of an arrogant young man who overstressed the claims of ancient ancestry. Sir Richard Southwell, who denounced Surrey for treasonably using the arms of Edward the Confessor, was a pious Catholic and in later years a pillar of Queen Mary's government. Wriothesley, who took a large part in investigating the charges against Surrey, had achieved notoriety as a persecutor of Protestants. The accusations themselves sprang in part from internal family quarrels and particularly from the fratricidal hatred of Surrey's own sister, the Duchess of Richmond. They were flimsy enough, but the jury, apparently encouraged by Henry's minister Paget, found the accused guilty. He went to the block on 19 January 1547, while the old Duke was being condemned by the more deliberate process of attainder for concealing these offences. Norfolk would in fact have followed his son on 28 January, had he not at the last moment been reprieved by the death of the sovereign whom he had served both fairly and foully throughout a long and momentous reign. About two o'clock on the morning of that same day Henry died, assured and rational to the end. And speech having at last failed him, he had firmly gripped Cranmer's hand when urged so to display his confidence in the mercy of the Lord. In that confidence had ever lain his greatness and his peril.

9 The Reformation under Somerset

Calvin and Calvinism

BEFORE HENRY'S DEATH there began a gradual infiltration into England of Protestant concepts more advanced than those of Luther. Having at first engaged the interest of university theologians, they presently extended to a new generation of Bible-reading lay people. Deriving mainly from Zürich, Strassburg and Geneva these ideas became increasingly dominated by the intellect of John Calvin.[1] Amid the Protestant refugees from Mary's persecution, and subsequently among the more religious of Elizabeth's subjects, Calvinism became the weightiest of the many foreign influences brought to bear upon the English Reformation. At this moment of its first incursion we must therefore pause to reflect, however inadequately, upon its origins and character.

When Henry died, Calvin had already held sway in Geneva for nearly six years. As a religious and social leader he possessed immense qualifications: a natural intensity of moral feeling; an acute and systematic mind, nourished by a long humanist, legal and theological training under the best teachers of France; a splendid lucidity of expression both in Latin and in French; a temperament which could combine tireless concentration upon essentials with an ability to compromise over details. Though he had no use for traditional mysticism, Calvin experienced toward the end of 1533 a conversion which left him, as he supposed, utterly subdued to the power of God and no more (but no less) than an instrument of the divine purpose. Henceforth he stood in the most parlous of all spiritual situations, for he never doubted his own special mission to reform the Church or the peculiar validity of the theological system revealed by God to his intellect as the basis for that great Reform. Religious history supplies other examples of such terrifying convictions, but seldom if ever have they been allied with gifts more capable of devising and implementing a practical programme. He spoke as one having authority and, when men had heard him, they tended to feel that his rivals were scribes and pharisees.

For nearly three years after his conversion Calvin wandered about France, talking, writing, narrowly skirting the nets of persecution and ripening his mind in contact with the many Protestants and reforming humanists who still contrived to flourish under Francis I. In March 1536 he published anonymously, and dedicated to that King, the first edition of his *Christianae Religionis Institutio*, which underwent so many expansions and rearrangements before reaching its definitive form in 1559. Without doubt the ablest of all Protestant essays in systematic theology, its basis is biblical and its resemblance to a *summa theologica* no more than superficial.

In this same year, while avoiding the forces of Francis and Charles on a journey from Italy to Paris, he made a fortuitous visit to Geneva. There he found himself detained by the appeal of the local Protestant firebrand Guillaume Farel, who two months earlier had gained a precarious local ascendancy. Their first attempts to establish a new order ran into powerful opposition on the city council and led to their expulsion. Withdrawing in 1538 to Strassburg, Calvin ministered to the French colony in that great city of refuge, married Idelette de Bure and wrote a fine French translation of his own book. He also gained a wider vision of international religious politics, concerning which he learned most from Martin Bucer, the Strassburg reformer then attempting to mediate between the Lutherans and the Zwinglians. From Bucer and from Melanchthon—he became friendly with the latter at the Diet of Ratisbon—Calvin accepted only what they could contribute toward his own system. Meanwhile in faction-ridden Geneva his party had regained the upper hand, and from the time of his recall in 1541 he trampled down one opponent after another in his steady march toward the triumphant theocracy of his later years.

By the mid-century the growing success of the Genevan experiment had already brought him a special authority throughout the Protestant world. When Englishmen first came under his spell, he was already becoming a Hildebrand among the Reformed, one seated in a state better ordered—or so it seemed to many who looked beyond the plastic arts—than the rival establishment which bestrode Renaissance Italy. If a man enjoyed theological instruction, could live a moral life and avoid criticising the government, Geneva offered him unequalled advantages in public order, social justice and educational opportunity. If he fully accepted this interpretation of Christianity, Geneva became, in the words of John Knox, 'the maist perfyt schoole of Chryst that ever was in the erth since the dayis of the Apostillis'. By an unsurpassed feat of committee-government, psychological tyranny and social engineering Calvin and his successors turned this confused and demoralised town into one of the proud centres of European culture.

Then, and for long afterwards, such a regeneration could only be accomplished on the basis of theological concepts, yet any attempt to summarise those of Calvin runs in danger of caricaturing some deep and subtle passages of thought. His predestinarian doctrine was the culmination of a long revival operative at least since the fourteenth century. He did not pursue it so far as some of his successors, and alongside it he composed some noble reflections on the lovingkindness of God and the work of Christ the Redeemer. Nevertheless his development of this doctrine has always been taken as Calvin's chief legacy. He took over Luther's basic doctrines of the total sovereignty of God, the total corruption of man, Justification by Faith Alone, together with their corollary of each man's predestination to bliss or damnation by the sovereign will of God. This last teaching Calvin drove to that conclusion which St. Paul himself had hesitated to elaborate. By any standards he must be ranked among the greatest of biblical theologians, yet here he made some bold deductions falling well outside any direct statement in the Scriptures. Before the universe began, God had by his terrible purpose (*decretum horribile*) chosen some men for eternal salvation and others for eternal reprobation. In both cases God made the choice quite irrespective of their personal merits and demerits, which he could perfectly foresee. How satisfactorily Calvin reconciled this crushing omnipotence of God with the total responsibility of man for evil may be left to professional theologians to assess. He himself faces the task and frankly admits it cannot be accomplished by mere human intelligence. Yet once a devotee had learned to live with this baffling central antinomy, the rest of the system might well seem more intelligible, more consistent and more adult than those offered by timid thinkers unwilling (as most Christians are) to face the disturbing implications of divine omnipotence. Here was a coherent system which seemed to fill the aching void left when men abandoned the Catholic Church, a system which assuaged that dread of chaos ever besetting our sixteenth-century ancestors. Alongside it the Anglicanism of Cranmer tended to appear little more than a *moyen de vivre*, that of Elizabeth at best a staging-post on the way to the City of God once and for all exemplified in Geneva. And if some lightly built minds despaired to find themselves caught up in God's machine, robuster ones developed an invincible certainty that they would pass perfected through its wheels.

So far from inducing fatalism, Calvinist doctrine instilled a burning desire to prove to oneself and others that one's name stood upon the roll of the elect. And how otherwise than by an alacrity to fight the good fight? Calvin did not personally advocate revolt, resistance and tyrannicide. His mission was not only to restore a spiritual dynamic to the Reformation but also to bring order into a world where Luther's message seemed in process of degenerating into subjectivism, individualism and licence. But ere long the chief danger was seen to come not from the Anabaptist sectaries but from the original enemy. The Roman Church had already begun to recover its inspiration and its influence. Protestants soon needed doctrines of resistance against political Catholicism and whatever Calvin had said, they were swiftly guided to the necessary biblical texts. The time was not far distant when an equally political Calvinism would strengthen the arms of French Huguenots, Dutch Sea-beggars, Scots Covenanters and English Puritans. This muscular Calvinism saved the Reformation. In a sense it even served the cause of liberty, since so often it promoted national or regional self-determination. And much of its effectiveness sprang from something Geneva had given it—an essentially cellular organisation under which large numbers of men could retain a substantial unity of belief, while yet being trained to worship and fight in the small group. This in turn sprang from the success of the Genevan model in integrating a body of highly-trained pastors, teachers and deacons with committees of lay elders nominated by the city magistrates and exercising moral supervision over congregations. However intolerable to modern eyes, this control was based chiefly upon persuasion; excommunication and other forcible sanctions were used only as last resorts. The operative word in John Knox's description was 'school'. The system was less narrowly juridical, more personal, more pedagogic, than that of medieval discipline. It also allowed far greater scope for lay initiative. With one stroke Calvin solved the old problem of anticlericalism. At last the essence of the social revolution behind the Reformation was understood and a place found for the solid, pious, educated layman, who demanded a share in matters hitherto monopolised by bishops and kings. Whatever his doctrinal arrogance, Calvin showed himself more perceptive than Elizabeth and her successors in thus canalising and controlling that aspect of the Reformation which might be called the lay demand. In Elizabeth's England the retention of an old-style clerical hierarchy tended to limit the legal expression of this demand to the House of Commons and, by neglecting it at the lower levels, to produce a series of tensions which later almost destroyed the monarchy and the Anglican Church themselves.

Our glance at Calvinism has taken us far beyond the year 1547, and we are already in danger of antedating its importance. It is true that in the reign we are about to describe Calvin's influence already became manifest in England. He sent advice several times to Edward VI and to Protector Somerset, who both held him in high esteem. Sir John Cheke and Edward's French tutor Jean Bellemain were also among Calvin's correspondents, as were many of the foreign Protestant visitors, from the eminent Martin Bucer downward. The M.P. Bartholomew Traheron, keeper of Edward VI's library and tutor to the Duke of Suffolk, had been with Calvin in Geneva in 1546 and accepted his system. Again, in the writings of several leading English divines ample evidence of Calvinist doctrinal emphases can be observed, for example in those of the two future martyrs, John Bradford, chaplain to the King and canon of St. Paul's, and John Philpot, archdeacon of Winchester.[2] Yet for many years to come most Englishmen saw Calvin merely as one of the greater stars among the Protestant galaxy. English divines still paid much regard to Johann Brenz, who had established Lutheranism in Württemberg, to Bucer of Strassburg, who was soon to end his days in England, and to Heinrich Bullinger, Zwingli's successor as chief pastor at Zürich, who in 1549 concluded with Calvin a treaty on the eucharist called the Zürich Agreement (*Consensus Tigurinus*). In so far as they depended on foreign inspiration, the popular pamphlets attacking the mass—and these became legion in 1547–49—mostly adopted a Zwinglian standpoint. But at least the new English trends were non-Lutheran and increasingly directed toward Switzerland, where after due inspection connoisseurs of religious landscapes tended to find that of Geneva especially fascinating. Yet Geneva was a city-state and England a national monarchy. It needed no genius to perceive that, for Englishmen, Calvinist ideas on church government and church-state relations would afford difficulties far greater than those attaching to predestinarian theology. Calvin had abolished the Lutheran pattern of erastianism and had related his church with his little state by links impossible to reproduce in the kingdom of England, impossible even when the Crown lay in the hands of a Protector or a clique of noblemen.

Protector Somerset

THE subsequent phase of the English Reformation depended in large part upon the outcome of Hertford's plot to take charge of the nine-years-old King and to establish himself as Protector. The will of Henry VIII had given the Council no presiding officer and had intended its decisions to be made by a majority vote of equals. The speed and audacity of the action whereby Hertford seized regal powers stands in strange contrast with his fumbling approach to the later crises of his career. All was made possible through the compliance of the two men who had been standing at Henry's elbow—Sir William Paget, since 1543 one of the Secretaries of State, and Sir Anthony Browne, Master of the Horse. The former was the son of a sergeant-at-mace of the City of London; later on he not only discovered blue blood in his veins but obtained a patent of nobility. He also discovered, when it became safe so to do, that he had been a keen Protestant in the early days at Cambridge. Yet his religion seems never to have been very fervent; rather may he be regarded as *par excellence* the lay civil servant and ambassador. On the other hand, Sir Anthony Browne favoured the old religion, even though he soon showed himself ready to subordinate its claims to those of the State. As recipient of Battle Abbey he stood prominent among the 'new monastics', and as an intimate friend of the King he had recently been appointed guardian to Edward and Mary. To him had just fallen the unenviable task of breaking the news to his master that the hour of death was at hand.

Immediately before the end, and again an hour after it, Hertford and Paget paced the gallery outside the King's room in the Palace of Westminster. Their conversations ended with Paget's agreement to support the ambitions of the Earl, to keep the King's death secret for a few days and to publish only so much of the will as favoured their aims. Hertford then hastened to get possession of the young King at Hatfield. During his return journey on 30 January he met Browne at Enfield and persuaded him to back the plan of a Protectorate as most likely to ensure stable government. On the same day Hertford adopted the style 'we'; on 31 January he arrived with Edward at the Tower, published the news of Henry's death and assembled the Council. When Paget proposed that Hertford should be made Protector, the rest of the members seemed evenly divided on the essential matter of future religious policy. Cranmer, Hertford and Lisle backed Reformation; Tunstall, Wriothesley and Browne were Henrician Catholics. But with Gardiner excluded, Browne adhering to Hertford, Tunstall an elderly and never very forceful servant of the Crown, the only strong opposition came from Wriothesley. It was easily overborne, and by 5 March the Chancellor found himself removed from the Council. Throughout the month of February offices were showered upon the Earl, while on 12 March his patent as Protector gave him an authority only just short of royal. The official form of prayer spoke of him as 'caused by Providence to rule', and he soon ventured to address the King of France as 'brother'.[3]

This sudden restoration of quasi-monarchical government in the person of a mature, able and opinionated nobleman undoubtedly hastened the advance of the Reformation in England. Hertford was the first Protestant to enjoy independent control of the State. If he was not, as some historians have alleged, a 'rank Calvinist' at his accession, he soon established cordial contact with Calvin, who urged him to undertake forthwith a Reformation along Genevan lines. Yet he intended no Calvinist theocracy, and in accepting his leadership Archbishop Cranmer found himself manipulated by an erastianism at least as thoroughgoing as that which had dominated the previous reign. This situation became plain in the first of Hertford's ecclesiastical measures —the issue of fresh commissions to the bishops, making their offices tenable only at the pleasure of the Crown, and subject to their good conduct. When on 20 February Cranmer addressed Edward at the coronation, he too was not backward in asserting the divine right of kings or in denying theories of popular election and papal claims to deprive monarchs.[4] During the summer a visitation of the Church by royal commissioners temporarily inhibited the powers of the bishops; Thomas Cromwell's injunctions were reissued and enforced by the commissioners, who placed in the churches copies of Nicholas Udall's edition of the *Paraphrases* of Erasmus, and of the *Book of Homilies*, at last issued from the press.[5] While the latter taught Justification by Faith in terms much nearer to those of Luther than Anglican commentators have been willing to acknowledge, the former also advanced the cause of the Reformation, since Erasmus had made the gospel-story a vehicle for countless pointed allusions to the pride, pomp and contentiousness of the early sixteenth-century Church. The availability of the *Paraphrases* in the churches continued to be enforced under Elizabeth, and over the years its impact upon humble readers must have become significant. Alongside these official actions a certain amount of lawless image-breaking occurred in various towns, while a spate of unofficial publications, including irreverent attacks upon the mass, showed that Protestant extremism had fully realised the opportunities offered by the change of government. Gardiner and Bonner resisted the royal visitation, the former on the grounds that the injunctions lacked parliamentary sanction and that the King should not be heavily committed during his minority. Both bishops were sent to the Fleet prison, where Bonner made a rapid submission but Gardiner maintained his defiance until released under a general pardon in January 1548. Meanwhile in the late August of 1547 Hertford, now Duke of Somerset, went north for his Scottish campaign, an episode made notable not merely by his victory at Pinkie but by his attempt to convert the Lowlands through the distribution of cartloads of Bibles. He returned in October amid a blaze of glory, and in the following two months he passed an important group of government measures through the first Parliament of the reign.

Of these measures the most striking was the Act removing Henry's harsh additions to the old treason laws of Edward III, together with the Statute *De Haeretico Comburendo*, the Six Articles Act, all restrictions on printing, reading, teaching or expounding the Scriptures, and even the Act giving royal proclamations the force of law. Some attempt was made to placate Catholic and moderate Protestant opinion by a measure threatening irreverent speakers against the sacrament of the altar with fines and imprisonment, but the same Act ordered that communion should henceforth be administered to the laity under both kinds and should be denied to no one without lawful cause. The elaborate Henrician procedure of *congé d'élire* and letters missive for the election of bishops was swept away. Henceforth they were to be appointed by mere letters patent, their courts held in the King's name, and by implication their character as State officials displayed beyond all argument. This change, though destined to be short-lived, represented a resounding triumph for Marsilian and Cromwellian theory. The important Act confiscating chantries and other religious endowments also dates from the same revolutionary session of Parliament, and we shall shortly examine its effects.

This spate of legislation has not undeservedly been called a self-denying orgy on the part of Somerset's government.[6] It tended not merely to move faster than public opinion, but to ignore the hard facts of sixteenth-century political life. As events were to prove, the government was not yet strong enough to deprive itself of so many powers. The merits of liberalism are relative to a nation's social and political maturity, and Englishmen remained as yet incapable of the self-discipline demanded by so rapid a withdrawal of the late King's heavy hand. Yet at this stage Parliament, Convocation and public opinion made themselves Somerset's accomplices; everywhere an unmistakable mood of relaxation became apparent and the Duke proceeded to further enterprises in a spirit of overweening confidence.

The new ruler of England could boast many qualifications for his office.[7] Amongst his fellow noblemen he could claim the closest blood-relationship with King Edward. As a soldier he had succeeded in every operation to which he had been called. His presence was handsome, his manner affable, his moral reputation good, his adherence to Reformation principles sincere. He desired to win friends and to govern by consent; he had a genuine sympathy for the hardships of the lower orders, and amongst them he enjoyed to the end a tenacious popularity. Above all he disliked religious persecution, and the period of his rule saw less of it than any part of the Tudor age, possibly less than any comparable period before the Revolution of 1688. Yet in the event, he soon came to display an equally impressive array of handicaps, shortcomings and misconceptions. While he could claim political incentives to build up a private fortune, he grasped at money and spent it with unnecessary ostentation. Having inherited estates worth £2,400 a year, he had acquired since 1540 an additional income of over £2,000, while under Edward VI he was soon to achieve the splendid total of £7,400 in landed income, besides other official emoluments. Soon after his accession he began to build Somerset House, removing various episcopal buildings to clear the site and gathering his materials not merely from the former Clerkenwell Priory but also by demolishing the cloister of St. Paul's Cathedral and other ecclesiastical fabrics. He took a warm personal interest in the work, and John Knox lamented the fact that he preferred watching his masons to hearing sermons. This episode perhaps did as much as any to tarnish the image of the Reformation; for the first time, the scale of the operation and the prominence of its author enabled men to say that the greed of Protestant magnates exceeded even that of their conservative compeers.

Along with Somerset many noblemen and gentry more acquisitive and less idealistic had also mounted the chariot of the Reformation, and of these men two would have brought great hazards to a statesman far wiser than Somerset. One was that resolute intriguer John Dudley, formerly Lord Lisle and now become Earl of Warwick. The other was Somerset's own brother Thomas Seymour, whose harsh but not undeserved condemnation in March 1549 looked like a case of fratricide to those ignorant of his treacherous folly. To this quarrel a major contribution had already been made by Somerset's wife Anne Stanhope, who disputed with furious pride the precedence allowed to Thomas Seymour's wife, the former Queen Katherine Parr. Yet even had he been spared these family trials, Somerset could scarcely have survived, for he lacked the instinct, the wariness, the patience, the sense of timing which marks the true politician. There yawned a fatal gap between his admirable theories and their implementation in a difficult world. His own adherent Paget warned him concerning the folly of 'having so many irons in the fire'. Against a background of falling revenue he faced two major problems—agrarian unrest and the divergence of Scotland—either of which would have tested the resources of any statesman. But during the years 1547–9 he attempted not only to solve them together and in haste but to accompany the feat by new programmes of secularisation and liturgical reform. Even then he might have managed to survive, had he not in the summer of 1549 allowed Dudley control of the military forces to put down Kett's Revolt in Norfolk. This elementary blunder serves to illustrate the true weaknesses of his position and his equipment. In a society where overmighty subjects and their 'affinities' of lesser men were still threatening to restore the chaos of the fifteenth century, Somerset lacked that healing magic which lay only in the touch of a crowned king. He should have faced the fact squarely and picked up some cruder weapon. Might this not have been an enlarged version of that force of foreign mercenaries which fought so effectively against the rebels? Had such a force been kept under his personal command, it might have compensated for the want of an inherited authority; it could at least have enabled the Duke to overawe his rivals on the Council, for they in their turn could boast no securer hold upon the loyalties of the nation at large. At all events, faced by the instructive story of Protector Somerset, no historian can avoid the temptation to be wise after the event.

The Edwardian Dissolutions

So far as ordinary Englishmen were concerned, the most important measure of Edward's first Parliament was the one which assigned to the Crown all chantries, free chapels, colleges, hospitals, fraternities, guilds and similar institutions throughout England and Wales.[8] This return to the policy of secularisation can have surprised no one, since by an Act of 1545 Parliament had already allowed King Henry to appropriate these foundations during his lifetime.[9] This earlier Chantries Act had not denounced them on doctrinal grounds but had boldly stated that the money forthcoming from their dissolution was needed for the war against France and Scotland. The old King had already caused his commissioners to make a survey of the extensive properties involved and had actually seized a number of them.[10]

The new Chantries Act was legally necessitated by Henry's death, yet it also adopted a different and openly Protestant standpoint. According to its preamble, superstitious errors and ignorance of salvation through the death of Christ had been caused 'by devising and phantasying vain opinions of purgatory and masses satisfactory, to be done for them which be departed'. These false beliefs had been chiefly maintained by the abuse of chantries, but now these superstitious institutions could be put to good and godly uses 'as in erecting of grammar schools to the education of youth in virtue and godliness, the further augmenting of the universities, and better provision for the poor and needy'. The Act ostensibly gives the King not only religious institutions, but *all* guilds and fraternities, since the government was well aware that many of the more secular ones supported observances of a 'superstitious' nature. It may well be that some of the civilian lawyers actually envisaged a wholesale attack on corporations, which they detested as impugning the sovereignty of the State. But the government dared not touch the general funds of secular guilds and it merely levied a charge on such guilds, covering the funds they had hitherto devoted to 'superstitious' usages. Until its spokesmen explained this limited aim, severe opposition threatened to develop in the House of Commons. In pursuance of the Act new surveys were completed by the summer of 1548; they supplemented the Henrician surveys in that they paid less attention to the lands and properties but more to the characters of the incumbents and to the degree of usefulness claimed for the various foundations.

In the August of the same year Somerset appointed two special commissioners, Robert Kelway and Sir Walter Mildmay, to assign pensions to the dispossessed priests and to sanction the continuance of certain 'necessary' institutions. Mainly speaking, these last were the grammar schools attached to chantries and collegiate churches, and the endowments of chaplains in the outlying chapels of large parishes, which could not be dissolved without grave local inconvenience. Though many of the Henrician Surveys have been lost, most of the Edwardian materials can still be studied at the Public Record Office. Considerable selections from this mass of documents have already been published,[11] and their voluminous character can be gathered from the fact that the Henrician and Edwardian Surveys for Yorkshire alone occupy over 550 pages of print.[12] The evaluation of all this material in terms of social and religious history represents a complex and often tedious task, which in many areas has been neglected or considered merely from the viewpoint of the local antiquarian. Hence our verdicts concerning the effects of this dissolution must remain somewhat provisional in character.

The traditional figures concerning the various foundations have not yet been checked by modern research. Camden and other early historians reckon 2,374 chantries and chapels, 90 colleges and 110 hospitals, estimates probably not far wide of the mark.[13] The total value of their endowments may prove difficult to calculate with exactitude, but the great majority of chantries yielded very small incomes and the aggregate figure cannot have represented more than a small fraction of that arising from the monastic lands. Thanks to the financial straits of Edward's government, a high proportion of these properties were rapidly sold off, thus helping to maintain the fluid market in land with all its economic and social consequences. The social effects of the Edwardian dissolution cannot, however, be adequately measured in financial terms. Chantries, endowed chapels, religious guilds and stipendiary priests bore a far closer relation to the daily life of the people than did the majority of the monasteries. Unlike the latter they had in most cases been founded during the fourteenth and fifteenth centuries by merchants and gentry, whose descendants often took an active interest in their management. Despite the marked decline of the impulse to found chantries, a few had originated quite recently. Whereas the monastic estates had been overwhelmingly rural, a large part of the chantry properties lay in the towns. The multiplication of chantries may be regarded as an aspect of the rise of a middle class; here the hard-headed and unsentimental businessmen of the later Middle Ages had given their most impressive witness to the Faith.

A chantry was essentially an endowment—usually in real estate—to provide masses for the souls of the founder and of others nominated by him. The incumbent who drew the stipend commonly said these masses at a particular altar in a cathedral, collegiate or parish church, but a separate chapel or other physical structure did not necessarily form part of the foundation. In regard to the underlying doctrines, we cannot accurately guess the extent to which Englishmen in the year 1547 continued to believe in purgatory, in 'satisfactory' masses and in other beliefs criticised by the Edwardian Act. If a man really believed that the ministrations of a chantry priest shortened the bitter years of purgatory for himself and his dearest departed relatives, then the Dissolution gave him great spiritual offence and became a matter for his passionate concern. That such ardent believers existed we can prove;[14] that by this time they were very numerous we may well doubt. The evidence suggests that a marked decline of interest, a more secular and sceptical attitude, was beginning to manifest itself even before the rise of Protestant beliefs. However brutal its intrusion, the State discovered here a world already in decay, a world sadly in need of control, reform and revitalising influences.

The Surveys prove beyond all doubt that the conversion of endowments to secular purposes, their 'resumption' by patrons, their outright embezzlement or forcible seizure, had become exceedingly common during the previous two decades. Yet it is fair to add that, throughout these years, rumours of impending confiscation by the government had encouraged such actions. One may even sympathise with the emotions of a squire who felt he had a better title than any government to the lands his grandfather had devoted to the support of a chantry. In the Suffolk Surveys,[15] for example, one Richard Sawyer had encroached on land belonging to a chantry at Mildenhall; the free chapels of Palgrave, Cowlinge, Lindsey and Ufford all had lay 'incumbents', who left the chaplaincies vacant and drew the stipends themselves; the Duchess of Norfolk's officials had removed the bell belonging to the free chapel in Long Melford parish, while the Duke had ten years ago seized certain copyhold lands hitherto devoted to maintaining a guild priest at Framlingham. Likewise in the Somerset Surveys[16] we read that at Ailston Sutton the chapel was utterly decayed; in Babcary parish, Foddington Chapel had fallen down and (not unnaturally) was noted to be 'clearly decayed'; at Congresbury, St. Michael's Chapel served for storing lime and the parishioners were offering to buy it; at Wiveliscombe the chapel was also used as a store, no mass having been said there for eight years. At Winford the chapel had actually been purchased by the parishioners nine years earlier, while at Yatton the people wanted to buy the old chapel 'to make therewith a sluice against the rage of the sea'. At Aller, Ashbrittle, Long Ashton, North Cadbury, Long Load, Pawlett, North Petherton and Wraxall, the rents of chantries, chapels and other foundations had been withheld from their true purposes upon one pretext or another. A free chapel in Clevedon parish had lacked any incumbent since about 1535; at Charlton Adam the chantry priest had drawn his stipend regularly but had said no masses for twenty or thirty years. And the foregoing Somerset instances of decay and expropriation are by no means all those revealed by the commissioners in this moderate-sized county. The supposed conservatism and simple piety of the Henrician North Country had imposed little more restraint, for the Yorkshire commissioners gave a formidable list of 'resumptions' and embezzlements both by laymen and by clerics, a list too long to be recited here.[17]

Apart from personal greed, and from a desire to forestall the government, the prevalent spirit of utilitarianism also played its part. At Henbury, the Gloucestershire village lying between Bristol and the Severn, the rents and profits which had formerly supported a priest had been for some years devoted to repairing the riverside embankments, and the parishioners explained that sixty years earlier the river had here broken its banks, flooding the marsh and drowning no less than 220 of their predecessors.[18] When the Edwardian Chantries Act was being debated, a stern opposition arose—but on economic grounds—from the burgesses of Coventry and of Lynn, who were finally placated by Somerset's promises to restore the lands of their religious guilds. But the representatives of Lynn demonstrated that the income had already long been used to maintain the pier and sea-banks and to prevent inundation of the neighbouring countryside.[19] For a variety of economic reasons trade and manufacture had declined in several old cities like York and Coventry, which strove to secure the gift or cheap purchase of the extensive chantry properties within their walls. As early as 1536, over ten years before the Edwardian dissolution, the city council of York had staged a little dissolution of its own by special Act of Parliament empowering it to abolish nine chantries and various lesser endowments and so to relieve its embarrassed municipal finances.[20] Nevertheless, deliberate acts of secularisation had probably wrought less havoc than the common tendency of urban property to lose its value. In the two neighbouring Oxford parishes of St. Mary Magdalen and St. Michael's the chantry priests had been maintained by the rents of two breweries, one of which, said the commissioners, was *in magna ruina pro defectu reparacionis*, while the other had 'fallen in far decay', yielding only £2 6s. 8d. instead of its former £6 per annum.[21] Some minor endowments were even more insecurely based. At Nettlebed in Oxfordshire a widow named Ann Eaton had given a cow worth ten shillings to maintain a lamp before the altar, but when the Reformers abolished such lamps the old lady—no doubt in high dudgeon—withdrew the cow and died shortly afterwards. The unsympathetic commissioners nevertheless debited the parishioners of Nettlebed with the sum of ten shillings![22]

Quite apart from such minor anecdotes, we should flatter our medieval ancestors if we supposed that they had carefully and lovingly maintained all their religious and charitable institutions until these fell into greedy hands at the Reformation. The situation was in fact less simple. In Yorkshire at least ninety-four hospitals or almshouses are known to have existed at some time or other during the Middle Ages. But of these no less than fifty-five had vanished altogether before the year 1500, while a further seventeen had become in effect the property of a master or chaplain and no longer maintained any paupers. Of the remainder four had their surviving inmates pensioned off by the Edwardian commissioners, three disappeared about this time, possibly by actual dissolution, while fifteen continued intact, in some cases being strengthened by private re-endowment soon afterwards.[23]

In relation to the popular religion the functions of all these numerous and disparate foundations varied so greatly as to defy any simple generalisation. While chantry priests did not officially have cure of souls, they were often more than singers of masses for the dead. They had commonly been placed by their founders under the direction of the parish incumbent, and helped him with some of the parochial duties. At Doncaster, for example, there were no less than seven chantry priests, and together, so the commissioners were told, they could scarcely hear the confessions of the 2,000 communicants during Lent and then administer the sacraments in Holy Week, together with all the other business of the parish church.[24] Even so, the same number of parishioners at Sheffield had the services of only three stipendiary priests,[25] while in Crosthwaite parish, Cumberland, also with about 2,000 communicants, only one such priest had been provided.[26] Some at least of the masses said by chantry priests were attended by congregations. At Wakefield, Doncaster and Newark they were combined with the *missa pro itinerantibus*—the mass at four or five o'clock, frequented for example in these three places by the early-rising wool-traders on their way to Boston from the sheep-farms of Yorkshire. The chantry of St. Agnes in the parish of St. Denis, York, had been founded in 1424 by an alderman to provide a mass between eleven o'clock and noon, but subsequently the parishioners had brought it forward by seven hours, both for their own convenience and for that of travellers, who heard mass here on their way out of the city.[27] Needless to say, the spectacle often proves less inspiring. A considerable proportion of chantry priests belonged to the cathedrals; they swelled the already enormous contingent of cathedral clergy, had too little to do and had usually been organised in colleges in order to curb their former indiscipline. Often enough the uneven incidence of private charity had endowed small parishes while neglecting large ones. At Oxford, for example, the parish of St. Giles with only eighty communicants had an assistant priest; St. Michael's another for 200, St. Ebbe's none for 363, while not many miles away the town of Thame had only one for 1,200.[28]

In terms of mid-Tudor prices most chantries were wretchedly endowed; their very existence helped to perpetuate and enlarge the self-selected, ill-educated lower strata of the clerical profession. Yet we need scarcely observe that such imperfections supplied arguments for reorganising and not for confiscating these useful or potentially useful endowments. The ministers of Edward VI committed at least two offences against the principles of logic and integrity. In their Chantries Act they spoke of converting the endowments to the needs of education and of the poor, yet they failed to found genuinely new grammar-schools and almshouses. Moreover, even if it be granted that a Protestant religion needed a far smaller clerical body, a large parish still demanded proper provision for one or more assistant priests. In some pressing cases such provision was made; in others it was not. The best that can be said of this unedifying transaction is that the government lay in desperate financial straits and that the merchants and gentry (whose reluctance to pay taxation had done much to produce the crisis) did in course of time accept their responsibilities, did found new schools and almshouses, did endow curacies in the parishes. In view of these complex circumstances, how far can we safely generalise concerning the religious and social results of the Edwardian dissolutions? While remembering that many individual institutions were hybrids, we need to take a careful glance at each basic type in turn.

The disappearance of the chantries must chiefly be viewed alongside the changes imposed by official religious policy. In so far as people ceased to believe in the doctrine of intercessory masses for souls in purgatory, chantries lost their main reason for existence. In so far as a minority persisted in this belief, the dissolution occasioned spiritual offence, yet there is not much evidence for any resistance movement in the form of private masses. The chantry priests themselves suffered no great hardship; in accordance with the Act of 1547 they were awarded pensions payable like those of ex-monks by the Court of Augmentations. Certain chantry foundations had also comprised grammar schools, and the dissolution hence takes a place in the history of English education. Teaching was not indeed the normal duty of a chantry priest; in Shropshire about six out of fifty such priests conducted schools, in Yorkshire about thirty out of 400.[29] With extremely few exceptions the chantry grammar schools were refounded as Edward VI grammar schools, and their masters were assigned salaries at the current rate and paid by the Augmentations. The real problem concerns the longer-term effects of this arrangement, since these salaries, tied to fixed amounts, declined in real value during an age of steady inflation. It has been argued that the pre-Reformation endowment in real property would, amid the general rise in rents, have provided a steadier basis. This contention would nevertheless seem arguable, since one has only to examine the Chantry Surveys themselves to see how often an endowment in urban rents could slump disastrously. When critics of the Edwardian dissolutions go beyond this point to speak of the whole Reformation period as one of decline for English schools, their mistake can be indicated with some precision.[30] In any area it is sufficient to compile a careful census of schools with their dates of foundation or first appearance in records. This has recently been done in the case of Yorkshire, then not an exceptionally rich or progressive area. In that county about forty-six grammar schools existed during the first half of the sixteenth century. Scarcely any of these collapsed as a result of the Chantries Act, and no fewer than sixty-eight new schools appear for the first time between 1545 and 1603.[31]

Tudor Englishmen, Catholics and Protestants alike, were highly aware of the importance of education. Even the odious Sir Richard Rich ended in 1564 by founding Felsted School near his splendid Essex mansion. The educational idealism and practical beneficence of Reformers like Cranmer, Latimer, Archbishop Holgate, Thomas Lever, Walter Mildmay and Thomas Becon cannot be questioned. The last of these, though among the more tasteless Protestant bigots, was nevertheless the first Englishman to campaign for the establishment of girls' schools. 'It is expedient', he wrote, 'that by public authority schools for women children be erected and set up in every Christian commonwealth, and honest, safe, wise, discreet, sober, grave and learned matrons made rulers and mistresses of the same, and that honest and liberal stipends be appointed for the said schoolmistresses, which shall travail in the bringing up of young maids.'[32] These particular proposals went ahead of public opinion, yet no Protestant, no Elizabethan Anglican could claim to be logical if he failed to support the idea of universal education. This spate of new foundations and re-foundations came from men whose religion demanded at least an ability to read the Scriptures and the Prayer Book. The hapless ministers of Edward VI may well have done more harm than good to English schools, but the short period of their rule formed only a parenthesis in a very different story.

Of the other foundations threatened by the Chantries Acts the most essential to public worship were those chapels of ease and free chapels which did service for outlying portions of large parishes. They were especially important in the hill-country running from Derbyshire up to Cumberland. Here there were parishes ten or twenty miles across, and each containing a dozen or more villages and hamlets. In many parts of England seasonal flooding separated communities from their main parish church. Of Wombwell chapel in Darfield parish the commissioners wrote, 'The necessity is that there is a water between the said church and the chapel, that the inhabitants there can by no means come to the said church at divers times.'[33] Again, some chapelries were held to their inferior status by legal anomalies, even though in all physical respects they resembled important parishes. Woodstock in Oxfordshire, a mere chapelry of Bladon, had some 360 communicants, over half the population of the parish, and enjoyed the services of three priests.[34] In a very different setting the port of Hull boasted in its church of the Holy Trinity the largest parish church in all England, yet this still remained a chapel of the rural parish of Hessle, some five miles outside the walls of the town. Thanks to stupid drafting the Chantries Acts imperilled all endowed chapels, but even the ministers of Edward VI did not expect parishioners to swim torrents in order to escape excommunication, or the people of a leading port to manage without a church. Though the records of the commissioners for continuance are scattered and incomplete, they appear to have preserved nearly all the more essential chapels. In Lancashire, for example, there were no less than ninety-four chapels, none of which is known to have been sold at this time.[35] In Oxfordshire, however, some undesirable dissolutions sprang from the surprising discretion allowed to the over-zealous deputy surveyor, John Maynard.[36] Here and there affronts to local pride as well as to convenience may have aroused anger against the emissaries of the government. In the summer of 1549, while Kett's Revolt and the Western Rising were in full swing, a much smaller rising occurred around Ayton near Scarborough, during which the prominent chantry commissioner Matthew White and some of his associates were killed. These rebels seem to have had several grievances, yet it is noticeable that Ayton chapel had been dissolved in the previous year and the lead removed from its roof. Moreover, after the trouble had died down, the villagers combined to thatch the building and were still maintaining it by a self-imposed rate in the early seventeenth century.[37]

With regard to the hospitals or almshouses we have already seen that many medieval foundations had vanished long before the Reformation owing to neglect, declining revenues or perversion of the founders' intentions. The great majority of those still active in 1547 survived the Chantries Act, but often through the action of municipalities which, having bought or begged them from the Crown, thenceforward administered them on a municipal basis. Once again, the total was in due course augmented by a large number of Elizabethan and later almshouses. On the other hand, it can only have damaged the reputation of Protestantism whenever a Protestant government allowed any functioning almshouse to disappear, or to survive merely through local initiative, because it was in no sense a controversial institution. Against the religious guilds more convincing reproaches could be brought, since so many of them encouraged saint-worship, for example by maintaining candles at the altars of cathedrals and parish churches in honour of specified saints. Perhaps about half the religious guilds helped their members in time of undeserved poverty, paid burial expenses or afforded some other rudimentary form of social insurance. In general, however, such guilds were joined by solid people; they cannot be regarded as the democratic guardians of the poor. Rather did they resemble modern clubs in their varying subscriptions and degrees of exclusiveness. Their masters held positions of great social distinction, but did not always conduct their affairs in an atmosphere of old-world piety. About 1533 numerous witnesses testified in the Star Chamber that two prominent aldermen of York, the former masters of the united guilds of St. Christopher and St. George, had not only been unconstitutionally elected but had embezzled substantial amounts of the funds. Amid further charges and counter-charges the quarrel was dragged into Chancery, into the Council in the North and even into the ecclesiastical court. An astonishing amount of foul linen was washed in public and the honour of another alderman's wife besmirched during a consequential suit for slander.[38] Such prominent guilds were often closely involved with municipal corporations. These York guilds had in fact helped to rebuild the magnificent Guildhall of York and possessed a share in its use. And when their end came in 1548–9, the city council, after protracted negotiations, managed to purchase their properties.[39]

The incidental activities of these associations were most varied. The remarkable York guild of Corpus Christi managed the famous Mystery Plays and also supervised a hospital. At Banbury that of Our Lady kept four priests, who were regarded as necessary to minister to the 1,400 communicants.[40] At Ludlow the wealthy Palmers' guild, with a net annual income of £87, maintained a school; so did the Trinity guild at Chipping Norton, that of Our Lady at Burford, the three North Riding guilds at Pickering, Middleton and Northallerton.[41] Such schools survived under conditions similar to those of the chantry-schools. Perhaps the best-known of all our former guild-schools is that of Stratford-on-Avon, conducted until the dissolution by the guild of the Holy Cross, but in 1552 repurchased from the Crown and managed by the corporation. This recovery took place in good time—some dozen years before the birth of its most famous pupil.

Of the colleges and collegiate churches at least eighteen had already surrendered their properties to Henry VIII between 1541 and 1547, in the manner of the monasteries before them.[42] The wealth, organisation and social importance of such foundations varied immensely.[43] At one end of the scale were modest parish churches, administered by a corporate body of four or five priests; at the other end were the superb minsters of Ripon, Beverley and Southwell, having the prestige and some of the functions of regional sub-cathedrals in the immense diocese of York. In general, however, two types predominated. The first consisted of old foundations, many of them royal, each with a dean and a number of prebends financed from specified estates. Such, for example, were the churches of Westbury-on-Trym near Bristol, St. Mary's-in-the-Fields at Norwich, St. Mary's at Shrewsbury, St. Martin's-le-Grand in London, Wimborne Minster in Dorset and St. Mary Magdalene at Bridgnorth. Their prebends were very commonly regarded as the perquisites of successful administrators. All the prebends at St. Martin's-le-Grand and Bridgnorth were at the disposal of the Crown and went almost entirely to the King's clerks, especially to those of the Wardrobe. The other main type comprised the colleges of chantry priests founded by wealthy clerics and magnates during the fourteenth and fifteenth centuries. In many cases, like Cotterstock in Northamptonshire and Sibthorpe in Nottinghamshire, ordinary parish churches had been elevated to this status, with a master or provost and a body of chaplains exercising the parochial functions. Elsewhere, as at Wappenham, Northamptonshire, a collegiate chantry of several chaplains might be founded in a parish church, yet without legally appropriating the church itself to the new body. There were also colleges for cathedral chantry priests, as at York and Wells, and yet others in which educational purposes bulked large. Of the latter class a good example appears at Rotherham, where in 1480 Archbishop Thomas Rotherham had included in his establishment three schoolmasters—one for grammar, one for writing and a third for music. But of such foundations by far the most magnificent were the colleges of Eton and of St. Mary at Winchester, where the fame of the schools soon overshadowed that of the colleges themselves. In general, it may be said that the Edwardian changes did not interfere catastrophically with the educational and parochial work of these institutions. In such instances where the colleges suffered dissolution, the commissioners for continuance took action to secure the survival of the attached grammar schools. Likewise collegiate churches with pastoral functions did not cease to operate but merely reverted to the status (and the reduced staffing) of ordinary parish churches.

What effect did the Edwardian dissolutions exert upon the course of the English Reformation? If the fall of the monasteries may be thought to have occupied too much space in our Tudor histories, this second phase of destruction has certainly been permitted too little, for it impinged far more obviously and directly upon the spiritual and social life of the English people. The fall of religious houses hurt few people outside their walls, but now the ministers of Edward VI were operating upon a more sensitive area of the nation's anatomy. That some loss of social amenities did in fact occur may be proved from the cases of the more beneficent guilds, or from those instances where functioning schools and hospitals disappeared in the rush or were refounded after delays and difficulties. Thanks, however, to the policy of continuance and to energetic local action, such grievous cases of loss were far from numerous, while the claim that appreciable damage was done, even temporarily, to education seems dubious. Yet while the institutional and material losses should not be over-dramatised, they do not constitute the whole of the adverse balance. We have nowadays begun to take more interest in the psychological and religious aspects of Tudor social history, and with some confidence we may maintain that this revival of secularisation tended to lower the cohesion and morale of the nation. From the outset of the new reign gloomy prophets had quoted the text 'Woe be to thee, O land, whose King is a boy'. Now there had duly appeared factions among the rulers, inflation, plague and widespread agrarian unrest. Against this ominous background the sordid competition of all classes for a share in ecclesiastical spoils impugned the credit both of the government and of the religious principles which that government was claiming to promote by destroying 'superstitious' institutions.

Within two years of its apparent triumph the Reformation had begun to pay a heavy price for its involvement with coarse-grained and bankrupt politicians. It had indeed much to lose at this moment. We ignore much evidence if we suppose that in 1549 the nation was divided into two parties, one of ardent Catholics, another of ardent Protestants. On the contrary, there existed a large uncommitted element, cautious, waiting for a lead, but all too ready to be offended and disillusioned by the errors of profiteers and extremists. Tudor opinion was quick to detect the upstart and the self-seeker. Protestants who laid claim to a spiritual religion were vulnerable from many sides; they had perhaps less to fear from frontal attacks by their Catholic opponents than from the undermining influences of distaste and cynicism. Michael Sherbrook, who was rector of Wickersley near Rotherham throughout almost the whole of Elizabeth's reign, has left us certain memories from his youth which preserve something of this atmosphere.[44] His father had bought some properties of Roche Abbey and in later days told Michael he saw no reason to entertain grudges against the monks themselves. Yet the old man had added significantly, 'Might I not, as well as others, have some profit of the spoil of the Abbey? For I did see all would away; and therefore I did as others did.' Turning to the Edwardian dissolutions Sherbrook himself recalls seeing churchwardens selling off church goods at bargain prices, while a clandestine trade developed in old brasses and gravestones. The story even circulated that Thomas Bosvill, a Duchy of Lancaster official, had stolen the great bell from the steeple of Laughton and carried it away in the night. Sherbrook also comments in scandalised terms on the dissolution of the College of Rotherham.

> The foundation whereof was not to make a malt-house, as it is now used: but it was to this end and purpose, that the master thereof should be a preacher, and to have three fellows within it; of the which fellows, one should freely teach a grammar school within the town for all that came to it: the second should teach freely a writing school, and the third a song school . . . but so soon as the said house was dissolved, neither preacher nor schoolmaster was provided, but the town hired the schoolmaster for the school many years after, until they made unto the Queen's Majesty, and obtained £10 yearly toward the finding of the schoolmaster for the grammar school; which cost the town not a little before they could get it.[45]

These complaints Sherbrook accompanies by sarcastic comment on the insatiable demands of the politicians; and as an example of poetic justice he points to the impoverishment of the State at the very time when it was behaving most rapaciously toward the Church.

These comments, it is true, were made long after the event, and made by a stubborn believer in a mythical golden age before the Reformation, yet they help to recover the atmosphere of disillusion which beset the later years of Edward VI. Meanwhile people who persisted in Catholic doctrine reflected upon the work of destruction in more strictly religious terms. In the reign of Mary a petition was addressed to Cardinal Pole pleading for the restoration of the Trinity Hospital at Pontefract. The petitioner was John Hamerton, sub-controller of the Household to Henry VIII and Queen Mary, and a member of a West Riding family notable over a long period for its Catholic sympathies.

> My Lord [he pleads] we had in that town one abbey, two colleges, a house of friars preachers, one ancress, one hermit, four chantry priests, one guild priest. Of all these, the inhabitants of the town of Pomfret are neither relieved bodily nor ghostly. We have there left an unlearned vicar, which hireth two priests, for indeed he is not able to discharge the cure other ways, and I dare say the vicar's living is under forty marks. . . . My suit to your noble Grace at this present is, most humbly to desire your Grace that you will have compassion of the great misery that this said town of Pomfret is fallen into, both bodily and ghostly since the godly foundations aforesaid hath been so amiss ordered and misused, and the holy sanctuaries of God so pitifully defiled and spoiled.[46]

Queen Elizabeth subsequently revived the almshouse, and an analysis of the situation at Pontefract might well suggest that Hamerton's petition gives the blackest view, at the most cheerless moment, of an unusually unfortunate town. Nevertheless, such a document doubtless represents the viewpoint of the large conservative element in English society during the years before people made physical and mental readjustments to the new order. To Catholic opinion the problem set by these legal confiscations did not seem primarily social and economic. Alongside the destruction of chantries, guilds and chapels, they witnessed the disappearance of a large clerical society from their midst, the silencing of masses, the rupture of both visible and spiritual ties, which over so many centuries had linked rude provincial men with the great world of the Faith. In taking an essentially religious view of these events, these Englishmen seem to the present writer to have had every justification. Whatever its interest for the social historian, the Edwardian dissolution exerted its profounder effects in the field of religion. In large part it proved destructive, for while it helped to debar a revival of Catholic devotion it clearly contained elements which injured the reputation of Protestantism. Nevertheless, it was in no small degree bound up with the constructive doctrinal and liturgical changes which we must now describe.

The First Prayer Book and the Rebellions

THE triumph of Somerset freed Cranmer from conservative shackles, but the Archbishop, as cautious in his relative freedom as he had been compliant under Henry's tutelage, refrained from sponsoring any swift doctrinal and liturgical revolution. About January 1548 he circulated a questionnaire to the bishops, inviting their views on the nature of the mass and on the desirability of celebrating it in the English language. Concerning the latter problem the episcopate displayed a number of divergent opinions. Holgate of York showed himself strongly in favour of a vernacular service, while at the other extreme Bonner and Tunstall would allow of no more than a few English prayers 'for the instruction and stirring of the devotion of the people'.[47] The immediate sequel to this enquiry was the *Order of Communion*, a brief pamphlet issued by royal proclamation on 8 March 1548 and appointed for use from the subsequent Easter. It paved the way toward an English prayer book by inserting into the Latin mass English prayers of preparation for communion. While continuing communion in both kinds for the laity, it said nothing clearly repugnant to Catholic sacramental doctrine.[48] It nevertheless encountered opposition among the clergy, who soon discovered that more radical experiments were following upon its heels. By May 1548 mass, matins and evensong, wholly in English, were being allowed in St. Paul's and in certain London churches. Here too, masses at which the priest alone communicated no longer appeared in the daily routine. Meanwhile, during the early months of the year, the Privy Council abolished the ceremonies of candles at Candlemas, ashes on Ash Wednesday, palms on Palm Sunday, creeping to the cross on Good Friday and the use of holy bread and water. The Council also decreed the abolition not merely of 'abused' images but of 'all the images remaining in any church or chapel'.

During the month of September a number of bishops and other divines of both parties assembled at Chertsey and at Windsor to decide upon 'a uniform order of prayer'.[49] Though mystery still surrounds their deliberations, they were evidently confronted with a draft of Cranmer's First Prayer Book and accorded it some sort of general assent. The Book was probably never submitted to a formal session of Convocation, though later official statements attempted to suggest the contrary.[50] When at last in mid-December it came to be openly debated in Parliament, the deep divisions among the bishops became manifest. The doctrine of the eucharist remained the central issue. Tunstall of Durham, Rugg of Norwich, Bonner of London, Heath of Worcester, Day of Chichester, Skip of Hereford and Thirlby of Westminster all continued to uphold transubstantiation, while Ridley of Rochester, Holbeach of Lincoln and Goodrich of Ely maintained in substance the teaching to which Ridley had recently converted Cranmer. The Primate's early interventions in the debate seem to have been marked by some confused thinking. Though he continued to agree substantially with Ridley's group, he was anxious to avoid a final breach with the conservatives. In addition, his views had been complicated for the moment by the arguments of the foreign theologians recently arrived in England.[51] Despite these polemics the new liturgy had passed through both houses of Parliament by 21 January 1549; it received the royal assent on 14 March and came into operation as the sole legal form of worship by Whit Sunday 9 June.

Though wholly in the English language, this Prayer Book remained a masterpiece of compromise, even of studied ambiguity. While it did not specifically deny Catholic doctrine, its ambiguous phrases were understood by its author in a Protestant sense and intended to enable Protestants to use it with a good conscience. In essentials it was a revision of the old Sarum Use, chiefly influenced by Quignon's Breviary, by the Lutheran Church Orders and by the *Consultatio* of Hermann von Wied, Archbishop of Cologne, the last work being itself a conservative attempt to combine medieval and Lutheran usages. For the first time in England all the rites required by clergy and people were now comprehended in one volume, while no formula was left in Latin, so that the people could understand the whole of the priest's rôle as well as their own. To a large extent the order of the Latin mass was retained, but with some changes carefully designed to remove the notions that each mass was a sacrifice supplementing the sacrifice of the Cross and that any change in the substance of the bread and wine took place at consecration. Cranmer and his associates made direct and independent reference to patristic opinions and were no longer reverent disciples of Wittenberg; they had in fact rejected the basic Lutheran concepts of consubstantiation and the ubiquity of Christ's glorified body. Again, apart from the words of Christ's institution, the Lutheran rite abolished the Canon—the long prayer containing the consecration of the bread and wine. In the Prayer Book, however, the Canon was kept in modified form, substituting for the idea of a placatory sacrifice what the Reformers considered the older emphasis upon a thanksgiving and a memorial-service. Here only one sacrifice is pleaded—that of Christ on the Cross, 'who made there (by his oblation once offered) a full, perfect, and sufficient sacrifice, oblation and satisfaction, for the sins of the whole world'. The moderate character of the Book had one outcome most annoying to its author. From his apartment in the Tower Bishop Gardiner announced himself prepared to use it and claimed that its phraseology implied, if it did not specifically affirm, the doctrine of transubstantiation. This degree of latitude had certainly never been intended by the Primate.

To the common man the use of the English language must have seemed by far the strongest element of novelty. Taken merely as a spectacle the mass underwent little significant alteration; even the medieval vestments, alb and cope, survived. There also lingered various old-fashioned pieties frowned upon by all Protestants save the most conservative. The Canon still included a prayer for the dead, a commemoration of the Virgin Mary and other saints. Auricular confession was still sanctioned, though its use became a matter for the individual conscience. Anointing was omitted at confirmation but retained at baptism, while extreme unction could still be found in the service for the visitation of the sick. There is no evidence that contemporaries were overawed by the literary excellence of the First Prayer Book. Yet as we now see it, Cranmer here attains a mature mastery of language, selection and arrangement. Whatever further changes the future might bring, the new Church was henceforth furnished with a devotional asset ranking second after the English Bible. One Anglican at least is prepared to admit that for him the Prayer Book sometimes seems a shade over-felicitous. Intoxicated by verbal beauty, the feeble spirit can find a barrier—or invent a sub-Christian cult—as readily as when confronted by images and incense. Idolatry is a term with wider connotations than the early Reformers supposed!

The first Edwardian Act of Uniformity, with its interestingly graduated penalties, was to form the model for its better-known Elizabethan successor. It begins with the plea that the variations between the medieval uses had caused offence and confusion—a mistaken or even disingenuous plea, since they had done so to an infinitely less extent than had the recent Protestant experiments. For refusal to use the new Prayer Book, for using other forms of worship or for 'depraving' it, a cleric became liable to lose the profit of one of his benefices for a year and to suffer six months' imprisonment. For a second such offence he would permanently lose all benefices and go to prison for a year. For a third offence life imprisonment would follow. Again, any person openly attacking the Book or procuring a cleric to use other forms of service would incur fines—£10 for the first offence, £20 for the second and loss of all goods for the third. On the other hand, no penal clause was directed against laymen absenting themselves from church, cognizance of this offence being still left to the church courts.

Though this Act was less harsh than that of the Six Articles, it proved in general severe enough to ensure compliance by the clergy, and the Prayer Book was utilised even by those priests who (like Robert Parkyn in Yorkshire) are known to have disliked its innovations. By far the most striking exception arose in the so-called Prayer Book Rebellion which raged in Devon and Cornwall from the June to August 1549.[52] Secular motives, personal enmities, economic grievances all played a large part in this affair, yet one cannot doubt the presence of an authentic if indiscriminate religious conservatism, which was sedulously fostered by the numerous parish priests among the leadership. Richard Carew, the famous Elizabethan antiquary of Cornwall, relates how even the boys of Bodmin School divided themselves into two fighting factions, the Old Religion and the New, each under its captain. Their exploits (which included blowing up a calf by gunpowder) were ended by a general thrashing at the hands of the schoolmaster. Some of their elders were not noticeably more adult. In particular, the leaders of the revolt produced one of the least discriminating documents of the period.

They demanded the restoration of the Six Articles; the Latin mass with communion in merely one kind for the laity, and this only at Easter; a ban on the English Bible, for otherwise the clergy could not confound the heretics; the restoration of ashes and palms; the use every Sunday of holy bread and water. The sacrament should be reserved and worshipped as before; those refusing should die as heretics. The rebels described the new Prayer Book as 'but like a Christmas game . . . and so we Cornish men (whereof certain of us understand no English) utterly refuse this new English'. In his reply Cranmer could not resist the temptation to ask whether any more of them understood Latin.

This manifesto has too often been accepted as typifying the attitude of simple Englishmen toward the Edwardian Reformation. Public opinion, even among the peasantry, proved in fact far from homogeneous throughout the several risings in the summer of 1549. Kett's revolt in Norfolk,[53] significantly from the first in the hands of laymen, produced a strongly anticlerical manifesto and, though essentially a revolt against enclosures, had a Protestant flavour in so far as it took notice of religious issues. The manifesto urges that priests should not be permitted to buy any more lands and that their present properties should be let to laymen; that priests unable to preach should be replaced; that all incumbents should reside in their benefices and none be gentlemen's chaplains; that all clergy with benefices worth ten pounds a year or more should teach poor children the catechism and prymer; that tithes should be commuted for cash. Taking their cue from the quasi-Lutheran article of the German peasant-rebels of 1524–5, the Norfolk leaders propounded their famous demand, 'We pray that all bondmen may be made free, for God made all free with his precious blood-shedding.' Moreover, a Norwich incumbent daily used the new Prayer Book in the great public services held by the rebels on Mousehold Heath, while Matthew Parker, the local man with a distinguished future, preached to large congregations under the 'Oak of Reformation'. In short, this was not a revolt against the Protestant government, the policies of which it approved, but against the Norfolk gentry. It did not march on London but concentrated upon rectifying the regional situation.

Peasant opinion was usually malleable on non-agrarian issues. At this same time in Oxfordshire the local clergy were angered by the opinions enunciated at Oxford by the foreign Reformer Peter Martyr. They managed to call out a force of insurgents and several of them ended their lives dangling on ropes from their church-steeples at Deddington, Chipping Norton, Bloxham and other places. Even, however, within the conservative areas other groups diverged from the priest-peasant alliance. In Devon and Cornwall the seafaring population supported the new religion and a group of sailors saved Sir Walter Raleigh's father from the countrymen. The people of the towns also strongly tended to oppose the latter, Exeter independently withstanding a pertinacious siege of six weeks. The Yorkshire rioters of 1549, though encouraged by foolish prophecies, certainly opposed the Edwardian Reformation. Yet by far the most significant feature of this northern tumult was its utter inability to spread beyond a very small area along the boundaries of the North and East Ridings.[54] After the Pilgrimage of Grace prudential considerations outweighed doctrinal misgivings in the North Country.

Protestant Propaganda

THE staunch but unreasoning conservatism of the Cornish peasantry was no more and no less typical of England than its direct antithesis—the torrent of Protestant writings which marked the rule of Somerset and in particular the year 1548. John Bale, who had fled to the Netherlands on the fall of his patron Cromwell, returned and wrote with undiminished vigour. Not a few of the humbler controversialists did their best to match him in bitterness of spirit and in the pungency with which they attacked the mass. A characteristic example appears in the verse-dialogue on the sacrament of the altar between the ploughman John Bon and a parson,[55] the former a sarcastic rationalist, the latter a reactionary clerical with a perverted idea of transubstantiation,

And after that we consecrate very God and man,
And turn the bread to flesh with five words we can.

Though operating for the most part through the London presses, the Reforming publicists were active in some other towns, notably in Ipswich.[56] The founder of this local group may have been the schoolmaster and physician Richard Argentine, an enthusiastic Reformer under Edward VI, a strong Catholic under Mary and a remorseful Anglican under Elizabeth. The printers connected with him were Anthony Scoloker, whose seven or eight Ipswich books include three translations made by Argentine from continental Protestant writings, and John Oswen, who produced at Ipswich in 1548 no fewer than ten books by Calvin, Oecolampadius, Melanchthon and other Reformers. Oswen then moved on to Worcester and there continued his propaganda. Two other Ipswich writers, Peter Moone and John Ramsey, composed for Oswen coarse attacks upon the Catholic clergy and upon transubstantiation. Ramsey's *Plaster for a Galled Horse* does not scruple to conjure up the picture of a 'godmaker' (his term for a priest) intimately fondling a whore before going to the altar to celebrate mass. Peter Moone headed a local company of players and like Bale represents that interesting connection between the infant national theatre and the Reformation. His rhymed *Treatise of Certain Things Abused* recalls the old proletarian anticlericalism as much as the more constructive emphases of the new theology:[57]

This mass, as they [the priesthood] supposed, was alone sufficient
To pacify God's wrath for our wretched misery.
Free forgiveness of sins, being never so unpenitent,
Might be received at the mass: this was their doctrine daily.
No small time were we blinded with such popish peltry,
Making us pay for the holy consecration.
Like thieves that were insatiate, they robbed soul and body,
Without the fear of God's Word, the light of our salvation.

. . . . .

Let us forsake all ceremonies that to Scripture be not consonant,
Traditions of forefathers wherein we have been led,
And with the lively Word of God let us now be conversant,
For therein shall we see with what baggage we were fed,
Wandering in the Pope's laws, forsaking Christ our head,
Heaping upon ourselves the more greater damnation.
Thus were traditions and ceremonies maintained in the stead
Of God's true and sincere Word, the light of our salvation.

That these raucous proto-puritans had their more persuasive aspects can scarcely be questioned. John Ramsey's other publication, *A Corosive*, is an earnest little evangelical tract which resists the temptation to turn aside and abuse the Catholics. In fact, by no means all the propaganda of these years consists of crude invective and intolerant satire. In this year, for example, Richard Tracy (son of the William Tracy associated with Tyndale and Frith) published two treatises soberly opposing transubstantiation by reference to pre-medieval traditions and taking a position nearer to Frith than to Luther.[58] Again, during the last years of Henry VIII and throughout the reign of Edward VI, Henry Brinklow, William Turner, dean of Wells, and several other Protestant publicists deplored the whole concept of juridical persecution; some of these men were liberal adiaphorists, while others took the view that spiritual error should be opposed only by spiritual weapons.[59]

The pamphleteers do not, of course, adequately represent the whole range of Protestant literature during the reign of Edward VI. In 1547 there appeared a first edition of nineteen metrical Psalms by Thomas Sternhold, a gentleman of the royal household who in 1543 had been under suspicion for Protestant views. In 1549, the year of Sternhold's death, the Suffolk clergyman John Hopkins published a larger selection of Psalms by Sternhold, along with some of his own versions. A third edition containing some forty-four Psalms appeared in 1557, by which time the English exiles in Geneva were publishing in their metrical Psalter some of these versions, supplemented by others of their own. The long-continued popularity of such trite and heavy verses has been attributed to the fact that Sternhold largely used the popular ballad-metre of *Chevy Chase*. At least for scrupulous bibliolaters, the metrical Psalms solved the problem of finding something easy to sing, which—unlike the *Te Deum* and Luther's hymns—could also pass as fully scriptural.[60]

Though the state of English poetry afforded a poor weapon to the Reformers, it was quite otherwise with English prose. Apart from Cranmer's work a host of Edwardian writings illustrates this important advantage. Nowhere may it be observed more clearly than in Hugh Latimer's famous *Sermon of the Plough*, preached at St. Paul's on 18 January 1548. Medieval sermons, even those of John Fisher in the previous generation, cannot show anything to match this fusion of flexible language with deep feeling, both religious and humane. As we re-read these warm-hearted paragraphs, the early Tudor clerical tradition seems suddenly remote from us; we seem to have crossed a watershed into a new territory of the spirit. Latimer has little importance as a theologian, and if his message was primarily religious it concerned itself scarcely less with social morality. In his mind and in that of his friend and fellow-martyr John Bradford the notion of the Commonwealth has a deep religious connotation; it almost involves a species of Christian socialism. From the prison to which Queen Mary's advent consigned him Bradford cried, 'O this is a sin, dear Father, that I always have been a private man more than a commonweal man; always I seek for mine own commodity, contemning that which maketh to the commodity of others.'

Latimer became the chief inspirer and mouthpiece of the 'Commonwealth Men', the Protestant group which denounced covetous landlords and demanded a more equitable deal for the common man. It included an enclosures commissioner and M.P., John Hales; a Secretary of State, Sir Thomas Smith; and Latimer's fellow-preachers, Thomas Lever, Robert Crowley and Bishop John Scory. Such men found sympathetic hearers not only in Protector Somerset and Thomas Cranmer but in those humane and learned spirits who lend no little lustre to the reign of Edward VI, men like Mildmay, Cecil, Cheke and Matthew Parker. And while they owed something to the spirit of Erasmus and to More's and Starkey's social criticism, they were most pointedly the disciples of Thomas Cromwell, who had conceived a new social, educational and administrative system arising on the ruins of the old Church and the old aristocracy.[61] Unfortunately for their hopes as for those of Cromwell in earlier days, the forces of social and economic conservatism, enlisting backers among Protestants, Catholics and materialists alike, proved too strong both for Somerset and for themselves.

Perhaps the most characteristic of all Edwardian religious writers was

Thomas Becon,[62] who while yet a boy had learned his Protestant zeal at Cambridge from Latimer and George Stafford. His writings reflect not a little of the former's engaging vitality. It was indeed the fortune of Protestantism during the years following More's death to recruit not only the hacks but most of the real literary talent in the religious field. Between 1541 and his death in 1567, Becon published some seventy devotional and controversial works, certain of which ran into so many editions as to claim places among the Tudor best-sellers. Deliberately he strained every nerve to reach the common man or at least the swiftly-growing class of *bourgeois* readers. 'In all my sermons and writings', he remarks, 'I have not attempted matters of high knowledge and far removed from the common sense and capacity of the people.... To teach the people to know themselves and their salvation in the blood of Christ through faith, and to walk worthy of the kindness of God, leading a life agreeable to the same, hath only been the stop and work whereunto I have directed all my studies and travails both in preaching and in writing.' Yet Becon has in fair measure the weakness as well as the strength of his tribe. 'I have sought', he continues, 'in all my doings to offend none but to please the godly. And therefore have I ever used a temperate, moderate and quiet kind, both of preaching and of writing.' Here at least he deceived himself, for alongside the sweetness and the light are at least a few passages of invective which Bale himself might have envied. It exceeded the bounds of Christian quietness to call the Marian clergy who put away their wives 'filthy dogs', to construct elaborate parallels between Queen Mary and Jezebel, to compare Catholic priests with those of Baal, or to call Gardiner—

> that great wolf, whose face is like unto the face of a she-bear that is robbed of her young ones, whose eyes continually burn with the unquenchable flames of the deadly cockatrice, whose teeth are like to the venomous toshes of the ramping lion, whose mouth is full of cursed speaking and bitterness, whose tongue speaketh extreme blasphemies against thee and thy holy Anointed, whose lips are full of deadly poison, whose throat is an open sepulchre, whose breath foameth and bloweth out threatening and slaughter against the disciples of the Lord, whose heart without ceasing imagineth wickedness, whose hands have a delight to be imbrued with the blood of the saints, whose feet are swift to shed blood, whose whole man, both body and soul, go always up and down musing of mischief.

And if such diatribes may be explained by the cruelty of the Marian persecution, the same plea will not cover those crudely offensive, almost obscene, passages in *The Displaying of the Popish Mass*, which Becon wrote in exile toward the end of Mary's reign. In the spirit as in the flesh, 'total' war can lead good men into ugly courses.

It could scarcely have been expected that Somerset's optimistic liberalism would impose charity upon the controversialists. Even less did it avail to prevent private acts of iconoclasm and truculent outbursts by wandering preachers. In London people referred to the reserved sacrament as 'Jack in the Box', 'Round Robin' or in other opprobrious terms.[63] Under the year 1548 Robert Parkyn relates how on Rogation Day 'no procession was made about the fields, but cruel tyrants did cast down all crosses standing in open ways despitefully . . . yea, and also the pixes hanging over the altars (wherein was remaining Christ's blessed body under form of bread) was despitefully cast away as things most abominable; and [heretics] did not pass of the blessed hosts therein contained, but vilainously despised them, uttering such words as it did abhor true Christian ears for to hear: but only that Christ's mercy is so much, it was marvel that the earth did not open and swallow up such vilainous persons, as it did Dathan and Abiron.'

Showing equal sincerity in the opposite cause, one of the gospellers has left us a vivid account of his exploits during the reign of Edward VI.[64] His incidental information on the religious factions in various towns of southern England is perhaps of greater interest than his personal biography. Thomas Hancock graduated B.A. at Oxford in 1532 and subsequently became curate of Amport in Hampshire. In 1546 he was suspended from sacerdotal functions for casting doubt on the sacrificial character of the mass, and in the following year preached at Christchurch, his native place, citing *John*, xvi, to prove that the host elevated by the priest could not be God, because God was invisible. 'Then you that do kneel unto it, pray to it, and honour it as God, do make an idol of it, and yourselves do commit most horrible idolatry.' The vicar, who was sitting opposite the pulpit, then interposed, 'Mr. Hancock, you have done well until now, and now have you played an ill cow's part, which, when she hath given a good mess of milk, overthroweth all with her foot, and so all is lost.' Having said this the vicar stumped out of church in a rage. Hancock afterwards went on to Salisbury and, in a sermon before the diocesan chancellors of Winchester and Salisbury, not only inveighed against superstitious ceremonies but also 'against the idol of the altar, proving it to be an idol and no God by the first of St. John's Gospel' (i.e. *John*, i, 18: 'No man hath seen God at any time'). The mayor, Thomas Chafyn, with the recent legislation in mind, charged him with giving a nickname to the sacrament and would have jailed him instantly had not six honest men offered to stand surety for his appearance at the forthcoming assizes. Hancock obviously enjoyed much support from the substantial men of Salisbury. At the assizes a woollen-draper named Harry Dymoke assured the Lord Chief Justice 'that a hundred of them would be bound in an hundred pound for me; another said that a thousand of them would be bound in 1,000 pound for me'. At this the Lord Chief Justice taxed Hancock with causing an uproar and compelled him to find ten sureties of £10 each and also to sign a recognizance of £90 for his future conformity to the law. Undefeated, he rode immediately to interview the Protector himself at Syon, obtained an order to cancel the sureties, tracked the Lord Chief Justice to Southampton and flourished a letter to this effect. The Lord Chief Justice remarked that Southampton 'was a haven town, and that if I should teach such doctrine as I taught at Salisbury, the town would be divided, and so should it be a way or a gap for the enemy to enter in'. When Hancock nevertheless pressed for permission to enter the pulpit, the mayor of Southampton persuaded him to allow another preacher, one Griffith, to take his place. But this substitute, much to Hancock's joy, improved upon his original by openly reproaching the Lord Chief Justice for suffering images to remain in churches and the 'idol' to hang above the altars.

In the same year Hancock was called to minister at Poole in Dorset, at that time a wealthy town in favour with the government and ready to embrace God's Word: 'They were the first that in that part of England were called Protestants.' Nevertheless a Catholic faction remained, being led by Thomas White, a very rich and elderly merchant who had repeatedly served as mayor. When on All Saints Day Hancock refused to say the *dirige*, White and two other former mayors of Poole threatened to disembowel him in the church itself. Again he went up to interview Somerset and his secretary William Cecil, returning with 'another letter for my quietness in preaching of God's Word in the town of Poole'. Under this powerful protection he continued to minister there, until the advent of Mary forced him to flee the country with his wife and children. In Geneva they awaited better days. 'In the which city, I praise God, I did see my Lord God most purely and truly honoured, and sin most straitly punished: so it may be well called a holy city, a City of God.' In such minds was English Puritanism coming to birth.

The Fall of Somerset

THIS atmosphere of political, social and religious confusion did much to discredit Somerset and to bring about his fall in the autumn of 1549. By this stage he could number few friends among the governing classes. Every convinced Protestant was demanding a liturgy more radical than that of the First Prayer Book. The Catholics resented a continuing series of affronts. In September they saw Bishop Bonner tried and deprived by means of a commission erected by the Council and headed by Cranmer and Ridley. The charge followed upon Bonner's refusal to proclaim in a sermon the unfettered authority of an infant King, the implications being obvious enough. Yet the bishop skilfully strove to make it appear that his offence lay in his championship of transubstantiation.[65] Meanwhile, irrespective of their religious views, the gentry and the wealthier citizens of London detested Somerset's sympathy with the unprivileged orders of society and with such social liberals as Latimer and Hales. Landlords found concrete reasons for their distaste when they surveyed the damage inflicted upon their property during the revolts of the summer. Nevertheless, to achieve political change these malcontents needed a highly-placed leader, and in the last resort the fall of Somerset sprang in large part from the personal ambitions of the magnate to whom the Protector had with such consummate folly entrusted a large part of the armed forces. John Dudley, Earl of Warwick, permitted himself no sentimental loyalties, and by October every circumstance conspired to favour his intrigues with the other lords of the Council.

The crucial moment arrived when the Catholic politicians (the former Chancellor, Thomas Wriothesley, Earl of Southampton, the Earl of Arundel and Sir Richard Southwell) proved gullible enough to believe that Warwick would co-operate with them to reverse Somerset's Protestant policy. Even more surprisingly, Cranmer in effect took part with the plotters by first persuading the Protector to surrender and then by presiding at the Council meeting (14 October) which sent him to the Tower. These questionable steps cannot be justified by the plea that Cranmer foresaw Warwick's future championship of the Reformation, since people were at this moment anticipating the contrary. One must suppose that Cranmer took the obvious way to preserve political unity by backing the stronger group; perhaps he took it with real conviction when Somerset unwisely attempted to raise the common people.[66] An indulgent observer of his conduct might add that he had no means of preventing the coup, that he and Somerset could not have waged a successful civil war and that he did all in his power to obtain kindly treatment for the fallen Protector. At all events, for the time being Cranmer's luck held. At the end of the month it became evident that Warwick had decided to continue the Reformation and to oust his conservative backers. By February 1550 Wriothesley had been expelled from the Council, Southwell imprisoned in the Fleet and Arundel placed under house-arrest, while Gardiner and Bonner remained in the Tower. Somerset himself was liberated on 6 February. Having resumed his office of Lord Admiral, Warwick became President of the Council and proceeded to distribute the spoils to his adherents. Lord Russell obtained the earldom of Bedford, William Paulet, Lord St. John, that of Wiltshire, and Paget a barony. Meanwhile the Protestants in their joyous relief were proving themselves even poorer judges of character than Warwick's Catholic dupes.[67] The political theorist John Ponet, later Bishop of Rochester and of Winchester, compared the Earl with Alcibiades. More conventionally, Bale selected Moses for that honour. John Hooper, soon to receive the See of Gloucester, hailed the new ruler as a 'faithful and intrepid soldier of Christ', 'a most holy and fearless instrument of the word of God'. The succeeding years were indeed to be marked by a strange and rather ridiculous alliance between Hooper, 'the father of English Nonconformity', and one of the least scrupulous politicians ever to govern England.

10 The Reformation under Northumberland

Northumberland's Position

DURING THE UNEASY YEARS of his power Warwick (who made himself Duke of Northumberland in October 1551) faced a series of interlocking problems which could not be solved by mere ruthlessness.[1] Financial embarrassment has been a common fate of English governments but few if any have experienced it more acutely than his. He could reject continental ambitions, allowing the prestige of England to reach an abysmal level. He could not, however, avoid making handsome grants to his greedy supporters or expensively underpinning his rule by what amounted to a standing army under the newly-invented lords lieutenants. Any recourse to heavier direct taxation threatened special difficulties, since the less legitimate and popular a governor, the less dare he face Parliament with demands for subsidies. In 1551 the Duke resorted to a further debasement of the coinage and followed this by a device of remarkable crudity. Having met some of its liabilities with the debased shillings the government then depreciated their value to ninepence, later to sixpence, demanding payment from its own unfortunate debtors in the deflated currency.

Upon a problem of this magnitude such church property as could still be seized made little impression. Even the hitherto buoyant Court of Augmentations defaulted for a time on its payments; many monks and chantry priests faced arrears of six to eighteen months on their pensions. The chantry lands continued to be sold off, and Cranmer offended Northumberland by suggesting that the remainder should henceforth be kept until the King's coming of age. From the viewpoint of the politicians this idealism was no more helpful than Latimer's magnificent denunciations of human covetousness, or the conviction amongst Catholics that death and plague sprang from divine wrath against an apostate nation.

Not long after Somerset's release from the Tower it became evident that he might recover a big following in Parliament. His agent Richard Whalley busily canvassed support for a plan to denounce the inefficiency of the government during the next session and thereafter to restore Somerset to his protectorate. These activities formed the basis for the charges of treason levelled against the former Protector during the autumn of 1551 and, though Somerset had not advanced his ambitions with any ardour, his fate was sealed by the demonstrations of popularity accompanying his trial in the December. He was pronounced guilty of felony (though not of treason) and Northumberland needed to act quickly in order to dispose of him before the meeting of Parliament called for 23 January 1552. The method employed was effective rather than subtle. By altering the phraseology of an instruction by the young King to the Council, Northumberland converted an order for the trial of Somerset's confederates into an order for Somerset's execution. When this event was staged the very day before Parliament met, the fallen statesman behaved with great resignation and dignity. By now he had wearied of the long contention. It so happened that a panic beset the crowd, but he disdained to take what witnesses thought an easy chance of escape.

Foreign Influences and Sectarian Groups

IN this atmosphere, darkening still further as the sweating-sickness succeeded the plague, the advances of the Reformation were bound to prove insecure and ambivalent, yet the self-centred intrigues of Northumberland did not exclude certain positive developments. Among the more interesting of these was the rising influence of foreign theologians and continental religious movements. For some time Archbishop Cranmer had been attempting to link England with international Protestantism by consulting with governments and scholars abroad.[2] His friendship with Osiander, his marriage, his many contacts with foreign Reformers, all disposed him to this end. The men he befriended display in their life-stories almost the whole range of European religious politics, yet amongst them one grievous omission remained. Cranmer failed to persuade Melanchthon or any other representative leader of the Lutherans to visit England. Though henceforth foreign influences upon the English Reformation steadily increased, they came not from Wittenberg but from Strassburg, Zürich and Geneva. The Saxon Reformers, having gained their local objectives, left the leadership of international Protestantism to others, and their renunciation has an especial importance in the history of English religion.

Even before the end of 1547 the two Italians Pietro Martire Vermigli (Peter Martyr) and Bernardino Ochino had come to England after spending a period in Strassburg, now a major focus of Reformation thought. Having first received a government pension Martyr became in 1548 Regius Professor at Oxford, where a Protestant party soon developed but where people could still be startled when he took his wife, a former nun, to live with him in Christ Church. Ochino, once a Capuchin and a favourite preacher of Charles V, had been led into the new beliefs by Martyr and had ministered to the Italian Protestants in Augsburg. For him Cranmer secured a prebend at Canterbury, where he wrote busily against Rome and even against Calvin. Meanwhile the Emperor had begun more actively to encourage an exodus from those territories where his writ ran. Following up his victory at Mühlberg he imposed from May 1548 the Interim of Augsburg, an alleged compromise which could not in fact be accepted by any convinced Protestant since, while it granted clerical marriage and communion for the laity in both kinds, it retained transubstantiation, saint-worship, the seven sacraments and Catholic ceremonial in general. Over 400 Protestant clergy are said to have left southern Germany at this time. Yet the more eminent of the newcomers were not passive refugees; they soon showed themselves curious to observe and eager to influence the situation in this hitherto little-known island. In 1548 Cranmer also received Francisco de Encinas (Dryander), a Spanish nobleman who had for some time occupied a position to the left of centre among the Lutherans. In the autumn of the same year there appeared John à Lasco, the son of a Polish squire, an old friend of Erasmus, a former archdeacon of Warsaw and latterly living at Emden as superintendent of the Reformed churches of Friesland. This divine held advanced Zwinglian and Calvinist views; he had contacted Cranmer and influenced Hooper even before his first brief visit to England in 1548. Returning in 1550 he was named as superintendent over the four other ministers in the charter which granted the foreign Protestants in London the use of the Austin Friars,[3] on which site their successors of the 'Dutch Church' still worship.

By far the most distinguished of the newcomers was Martin Bucer,[4] who already stood among the acknowledged patriarchs of the continental Reformation. Beginning his career as a Dominican and an admirer of Erasmus he had in 1518 been won over by Luther, had secured a papal dispensation from his monastic vows, had married in 1522, and the following year had come to Strassburg. Here Matthew Zell and Wolfgang Capito had already initiated a Reformation, but ere long they accepted the newcomer as their leader. Under his guidance Strassburg became not only an eminent school of biblical studies but the great haven of the needy, the oppressed and the religious refugees from Calvin downwards. In sacramental and other doctrines Bucer developed independently of Luther, yet he was among the least arrogant of Reformers, believing that outside the primary beliefs there were many points on which differences of view remained inevitable and perfectly tolerable. It was he who wrote those rare and refreshing words: 'Flee formulae, bear with the weak. While all faith is placed in Christ, the thing is safe. It is not given for all to see the same thing at the same time.'[5] He was also a bold, but a thoughtful and creative liturgist.

After Zwingli's death Bucer became pre-eminent among the leaders of the Reformed churches in Switzerland and south Germany, placing Strassburg alongside Wittenberg and Geneva as the third centre of the international movement. During the three years of Calvin's exclusion from Geneva, he had used his opportunities to form a close friendship with the great Frenchman, and his influence became noticeable in the 1539 edition of Calvin's *Institutes*. When Charles V imposed his Interim upon Strassburg, it was time for Bucer to go; despite his failing health he adventurously accepted the most arduous of many invitations and accompanied by his friend the Hebraist Paul Fagius he slowly made his way toward England. This was the man whom Cranmer received with great honour at Lambeth in April 1549 and who by the end of the year occupied the Regius chair at Cambridge. There he completed his treatise *De Regno Christi*, at once a retrospect and a forerunner of Puritan idealism. Though his conservatism disappointed the most radical Reformers at Cambridge, his presence sealed the triumph of Protestantism in that important focus of theological ideas. Cranmer, finding his view of the eucharist especially congenial, consulted him often and allowed him an important share in drafting the Ordinal of March 1550. As will appear, Bucer's part in the framing of the Second Edwardian Prayer Book also proved appreciable, and but for his death in February 1551 this verbose, earnest but singularly charitable German divine might well have prompted a more effective *rapprochement* toward the continental schools. In the very last months of his life Bucer was apparently brought by Peter Martyr to the Zwinglian standpoint on the eucharist, yet his influence upon Cranmer did not belong to this phase. Interred with every mark of honour in Great St. Mary's his body lay there for six years until the Marian authorities exhumed and burned it—along with that of Fagius and a cart-load of books—upon Market Hill. But in 1560 the university restored the pair to honour in a solemn ceremony, the public orator remarking that 'whereas in every singular place was executed a singular kind of cruelty, . . . this was proper or peculiar to Cambridge, to exercise the cruelty upon the dead, which in other places was extended but to the quick'.

Paul Fagius, a former professor of Hebrew at Strassburg and Heidelberg, had died soon after his arrival and appointment as reader in that subject at Cambridge. There he was succeeded in office by John Immanuel Tremellius, by birth a Jew of Lucca but converted by Reginald Pole. Already a protégé of Cranmer at Lambeth in 1547, he was styled 'King's reader of Hebrew' in 1549; he also derived emoluments from a Carlisle prebend before the accession of Mary brought about his return to the continent. As a Calvinist he was to fall foul more than once of Lutheran rulers, but he managed to revisit England early in Elizabeth's reign. The Calvinist element among the refugees was also represented by Valérand Poullain, who had followed Calvin as minister to the French congregation at Strassburg. After a brief visit Poullain returned to superintend a colony of Flemish weavers planted by Protector Somerset amid the ruins of Glastonbury Abbey, and in Mary's reign he became closely involved in the affairs of English Protestant refugees at Frankfurt. Another foreigner of some importance between 1548 and 1553 was the Fleming John Utenhove, who took a prominent part in the Glastonbury colony, co-operated with à Lasco in organising the congregations of foreign refugees and became 'first elder' of the Foreigners' Church at the Austin Friars.[6]

Within the category of immigrant divines we may also place John Knox,[7] since both in Edwardian England and amongst the exiles from Mary's persecution he influenced the course of the English Reformation years before he began to dominate its Scottish counterpart. The circumstances which preceded his appearance have a melodramatic character. Though he had studied at either St. Andrews or Glasgow and had accepted orders, Knox does not appear to have exercised clerical functions or to have begun his intensive study of the Scriptures until about the time of his association with his forerunner George Wishart. The latter is often classed as a Lutheran, but he imported into his country some of the advanced ideas of the Swiss Reformers and translated the *First Helvetic Confession* into Scots. He also preceded Knox in setting the tenor of uncompromising zeal and measureless invective which came to mark the Scottish Reformers. Pursued as a heretic by Cardinal Beaton, Wishart received shelter in 1545 from certain Lothian gentlemen who were then employing Knox as tutor to their sons. Shortly before Wishart's arrest Knox had accompanied him on a preaching visit to Haddington, bearing a 'twa-handed sweard, which commonly was caryed with the said Maister George'. The burning of Wishart on 1 March 1546 was followed on 29 May by the murder of Beaton at the hands of Wishart's admirers, who took refuge in the castle of St. Andrews. Knox's patrons induced him to join the besieged party, now headed by the ex-Dominican John Rough, the deprived Secretary of State Henry Balnaves and the poet Sir David Lyndsay. These leaders soon perceived the magnetic character of Knox's preaching and formally urged him to assume the ministry. Demurring at first, he succumbed to an emotional appeal made by John Rough in a sermon. The congregation expressed its approval and for the first time in Scotland asserted the claim of a congregation to select its own spiritual leader. This was the significant pattern deriving from the Reformed religion of democratic Switzerland, not from its Evangelical rival in prince-ridden Germany.

At the end of July 1547 the French Queen Regent of Scotland captured St. Andrews with the aid of a fleet of French galleys. In breach of the surrender terms the defenders were not only transported to France but indefinitely detained. Knox himself remained on his galley, which presently returned to Scotland, but he did not recover his liberty until early in 1549, when the English government interceded on his behalf and gained his services. In April the Privy Council started paying him a regular salary as preacher at Berwick, where he lived for nearly two years and attracted large congregations. Cited by Bishop Tunstall before the Council in the North for his attacks on the mass, Knox replied in the form of a syllogism: 'All service invented by the brain of man in the religion of God, without his express command, is idolatry. The mass is invented by the brain of man without the command of God; therefore it is idolatry.' Tunstall soon became powerless and no further steps were taken to silence the Scot. At the end of 1550 he removed to Newcastle to serve as preacher at the church of St. Nicholas. Though with his usual boldness he denounced the execution of Somerset, Northumberland saw his value and retained his services.

John Knox was not in fact the only Scottish Reformer to transfer his activities to England. At these same northern places he had been preceded by his friend John Rough, who had earlier been receiving a large annual pension from Henry VIII for promoting English interests in Scotland. While escaping Knox's harsh experiences, Rough had been constrained to take refuge in England soon after the battle of Pinkie. After an interview Somerset had continued his pension and sent him to preach at Carlisle, Berwick and Newcastle. In due course Rough met Archbishop Holgate, who found him a stipend at Hull, where he seems to have founded the strongly Protestant tradition which later marked that port. The popular success of these preachers in northern England, where Scotsmen in general remained so unpopular, gives a striking example of the hunger for religious instruction which existed in that sermon-starved society. Late in Edward's reign the future martyrs John Bradford and George Marsh were preaching with success in the populous towns of south Lancashire. Robert Ferrar had found this hunger in earlier years, while the careers of Bernard Gilpin and Edmund Bunney, the northern apostles of the subsequent decades, were to prove its continued intensity. In 1551 the government planned to exploit this fluid situation in the conservative provinces by appointing six itinerant ministers to tour in rotation Lancashire, Yorkshire, the Borders, Wales, Devon and Hampshire. Yet this scheme had little time to bear fruit, while the Elizabethan government was to revive it belatedly and half-heartedly.[8]

The lesser foreign immigrants were mainly poor fugitives from persecution in France and the Netherlands. With their advent arose the longstanding and honourable tradition whereby England, to her great mental enrichment, has admitted so many refugees from foreign oppression. At this time over 5,000 of them are said to have settled in London alone. To their congregations Cranmer assigned a high degree of autonomy, despite the less liberal views of Ridley, who doubted the wisdom of licensing wholesale contraventions of the Act of Uniformity. It was also Cranmer who planned to call an international congress of Protestants and in March 1552 sounded Calvin, Bullinger and Melanchthon. More dogmatic and less naïve than the English Primate, these eminent leaders sensed the depth of Protestant differences, especially on the important matter of the eucharist, and they soon displayed a lack of enthusiasm fatal to the project.

A far less attractive side of Cranmer's outlook may be observed in his asperity toward a very different movement of foreign origin—that of the Anabaptist sects,[9] which during the last three decades had spread so portentously through Switzerland, central and eastern Europe and the Netherlands. Today many aspects of this movement are receiving far more sympathetic treatment than in the past. The Anabaptists may be placed among the pioneers of the liberalising process in western history, while the abominable severity with which thousands of their harmless members were hounded to death forms one of the darker chapters in the history of continental persecution. On the other hand, it might with equal reason be contended that the early excesses of Anabaptism retarded the growth of religious liberty. The most infuriating aspect of the movement lay in its inclusion of so many disparate and inconsistent groups, incapable of formulating any common policy. So-called Anabaptists can be found to represent Arianism, Socinianism, Pelagianism, Manichaeism, Docetism, Millenarianism, mysticism and communism. Their varied programmes embrace almost every imaginable reform from pacifism to polygamy. Undoubtedly a few of them entertained the antinomian perversion of the text 'To the pure all things are pure'. They almost all rejected the baptism of infants, believing that the rite should be administered only on profession of faith. Even more offensively to contemporaries, some of them denied the Incarnation on the ground that if Christ had derived flesh from the Virgin he would have shared the sinfulness of human nature. Neither the prophetic demand for spiritual liberty made by the continental Anabaptist 'prophets' and writers, nor the heartfelt piety discoverable among their followers should blind us to the fearsome problems which they presented to the more moderate protagonists of Reformation.

Since the origins of Lollardy, the progress of Reforming beliefs had always been hampered by the suspicion that they might also involve anarchy or social revolution. Medieval and Tudor men were social pessimists with little trust in the resilience of human organisation. Especially since its alarming excesses under the mad John of Leyden at Münster in 1533–5, Anabaptism had confirmed the fear of many cautious people, especially those of the landed, *bourgeois* and clerical classes, that all changes in belief threatened the dislocation of ordered secular society. The English rebellions of the thirties and forties had owed nothing to extremist religions, yet they had heightened this general obsession with the problem of social order, and by 1549 it needed only Anabaptism to supply Catholics and uncommitted people with some formidable arguments against Protestantism in general. Faced by this menace even the gentle Cranmer was anxious to prove his respectability by denouncing Anabaptism more fiercely than he denounced Romanism. Today we find it logical that the moderate Protestants should have granted that same measure of toleration to the radical sects which they demanded for themselves. Yet with a few exceptions they lacked this logic, and they failed to discard the concept of punishable heresy. They also overestimated the strength of sectarianism and feared that by sparing it they would risk a repetition of the horrors which had attended the Kingdom of the Saints in Münster, when King John took sixteen wives and beheaded one of them in the presence of the others for saucily criticising his rule.[10]

In May–June 1535 some twenty-five Dutch Anabaptists were tried at St. Paul's and fourteen of them burned in London and other towns. The King excepted such foreign offenders from his general pardons and a few more went to the stake in 1538 and 1540. In the early stages these heretics seem all, or almost all, to have been Netherlandish or German immigrants, keeping in close touch with their continental brethren. By the reign of Edward VI a number of native converts were joining their ranks in Kent and Essex. In June 1549 Hooper writes to Bullinger that the Anabaptists are flocking to his London lectures, 'and give me much trouble with their opinions respecting the Incarnation of our Lord; for they deny altogether that Christ was born of the Virgin Mary according to the flesh. They contend that a man who is reconciled to God is without sin, and free from all stain of concupiscence, and that nothing of the old Adam remains in his nature; and a man, they say, who is thus regenerate cannot sin.' After retailing further heresies he concludes that, what with these people and the 'great proportion of the kingdom' which 'adheres to the popish faction', he greatly fears rebellion and civil discord. In the course of that year Hooper even wrote a treatise to disprove Anabaptist doctrines of the Incarnation,[11] while with similar objects works by Calvin and Bullinger were published in English translation.[12] In the April of that year Joan Bocher, alias Joan of Kent, underwent condemnation for denying that Christ was incarnate of the Virgin Mary. This remarkable woman was perhaps the wife of the London butcher Thombe, who abjured the same Melchiorite Anabaptist heresy.[13] A former seller of Tyndale's Testament, Joan had also known and venerated the martyr Anne Askew, who was not an Anabaptist. While her associates recanted, she remained defiant and after many delays suffered burning in May 1550. The story that Cranmer persuaded the distressed young King to sign her death-warrant is probably untrue, but there seems no reason to doubt the Primate's acquiescence. The only other extremist to suffer death was the Dutch surgeon George van Parris, a Unitarian who was tried before Cranmer (with Coverdale assisting as judge and interpreter) for denying the divinity of Christ.[14]

In 1552 the Council urged the Archbishop to repress a new sect in Kent; this may have been that branch of Anabaptism called the Family of Love, a pantheistic and antinomian sect founded by Hendrik Niclaes in the Netherlands but destined to survive chiefly in Elizabethan England.[15] During the fifties the Anabaptist Robert Cooche, though duly denounced by William Turner and John Knox, contrived to get his writings widely circulated.[16] But perhaps the most influential English sectary of these years was Henry Hart of Kent, who ventured in 1548–9 to publish two tracts on his beliefs. He was a member of a group meeting in 1549 at various places in Kent, especially at Faversham.[17] Sometime in the second half of 1550 its members fled from impending persecution to Bocking in Essex, where they continued to hold assemblies of about sixty persons. They are known to have discussed the Scriptures, to have dismissed outward observances as unimportant and to have repudiated with violence the predestinatory doctrines of Calvin. Some of them were heard to declare that learned men were the cause of all errors, that children were not born in original sin, that no man was irrevocably damned or saved, that gambling was wicked, that sinners and men unknown to their congregation should be shunned. What little we know of these Pelagian dissenters suggests a subdued and anglicised type of Anabaptism, while the names taken by the Privy Council give no hint of a foreign background. Even so, this group cannot be claimed with confidence to represent a purely native congregationalism. Of the named members Humphrey Middleton and Nicholas Shetterden died as martyrs in the Marian persecution.[18] And at that time, when the Anglican martyr John Bradford lay in the King's prison, he engaged in lively disputes with Henry Hart and others of these 'Freewillers', whom he desired to convert to orthodox Protestant views.[19] Though Anabaptists and Familists survived under Elizabeth, the outcome showed that their potential had been greatly overestimated at the mid-century.

The impact of foreign scholars, refugees and sects upon the English Reformation cannot be assessed with much precision. Apart from the significant results of Bucer's association with Cranmer and the later stimulus exerted by Knox on the English Calvinists, their influence upon doctrinal and liturgical policy may not claim much importance. And while à Lasco exercised a firm hold upon John Hooper, the positions they adopted were too austere to command a large following in this country. Nevertheless the foreigners, so many of whom were not merely non-Lutherans but anti-Lutherans, helped to prevent Protestant thought from consolidating in its earlier forms. Especially did their presence generate new theological ideas in both universities. Cambridge in particular stood on the eve of its most dominant period in English intellectual life; Bucer and his associates undoubtedly furthered the process whereby the Cambridge of Robert Barnes grew up into that of William Perkins.[20]

As in that narrow world, so in the larger world of London, the foreigners enhanced the ferment of ideas. In à Lasco's congregation London saw for the first time a church of full-fledged Puritan type, one organised no longer upon episcopal or even sacerdotal principles but based upon a powerful group of ordained and elected 'elders' or 'presbyters'. Some of these supervised discipline; others (who were salaried) preached and taught. To produce an informed laity, there were two hours of expository sermons every Sunday and instructional classes called 'prophesyings' during the week. On the first Sunday of each month communions were celebrated, but they were preceded by compulsory services of preparation, in which the elders examined the lives of intending communicants and drew up lists of those fit to receive the sacrament. Foreign refugees did not automatically gain admittance to the church; if of mature age, they had to show a knowledge of the Reformed faith and undertake to lead a Christian life. Excommunication was employed only when interviews and disputations with the offender had failed; moreover, it excluded only from the sacrament, not from attendance in church or from civil rights. Thus the laity were disciplined, yet for action, not for submission—disciplined in order to fit them to select ministers and to manage the Church in a fashion unknown since the early Christian era. The clergy themselves were closely regimented by their colleagues, while at a meeting held every three months complaints could be brought against them by any member of the congregation.[21] No wonder Bishop Ridley became uneasy when he saw these modes of church government licensed in his diocese. In the last two years of the reign three congregations, French, German and Italian, existed at the Austin Friars. They co-operated harmoniously in one church under a single constitution, and they afforded an exhibition of religious internationalism with some strange undertones for the founders of a national, State-controlled Church. During the Marian persecution, when the more radical English exiles on the continent were ostensibly imitating this former London model, the rival concepts of nationalist Anglicanism and internationalist Puritanism stood starkly opposed.

The extent to which these early contacts leavened the insular chauvinism of Tudor Englishmen remains a matter for debate. Medieval Londoners had been anything but internationalists, and those who—in the manner of their forefathers—ran amok against foreigners on Evil May Day 1517 had learned depressingly little on this practical matter from the Church Universal. But in 1553, when their sons discussed foreigners, they at least had the opportunity of setting the image of a Protestant refugee alongside that of a rascally foreign merchant. Very soon some influential Londoners would themselves be refugees, dependent on foreign goodwill. The pressures of the Reformation were internationalist as well as insular and we should treat with caution the reproach that it divided England from Europe. That this censure contains only a half-truth will become more apparent when we turn to the second phase of continental influence, that which developed through the Marian Exiles.

The Edwardian Bishops

AFTER the change of government Cranmer's first ecclesiastical scheme was the completion and publication in March 1550 of the Ordinal, the alleged imperfections of which have since formed the main basis for the rejection of Anglican orders by the Church of Rome.[22] This first Ordinal was a fairly conservative document, modelled on the Sarum Pontifical but restricting the orders to those of bishop, priest and deacon. It preserved the historic rites of prayer, the laying-on of hands and the delivery of 'instruments', including the paten and chalice given to priests and the pastoral staff to bishops. But in the case of priests Cranmer added a Bible, to indicate their preaching function. And whereas the priest had formerly been charged: 'Receive authority to offer sacrifice and celebrate mass both for the living and the dead', now the charge ran: 'Take thou authority to preach the word of God and to minister the holy sacraments in this congregation.' When a revised Ordinal came to be incorporated with the Prayer Book of 1552, Cranmer significantly made the Bible the only 'instrument' delivered to bishops and priests alike. In the case of deacons a New Testament figures as the 'instrument' in both versions, but this represented no real innovation, since a book of the Gospels had been handed to deacons in the medieval rite. Martin Bucer wrote his work *De Ordinatione Legitima* especially to guide Cranmer, and in numerous places the Primate's debt to the Strassburg Reformer patently appears. Even so, Cranmer's decisions often proved more conservative, and in both versions he displayed his customary skill in blending medieval with Reformation ideas. The new Ordinal was first used at St. Paul's in June 1550, when John Foxe appeared among those ordained deacon by Bishop Ridley.

Amongst the few who refused to subscribe to the Ordinal was Nicholas Heath, Bishop of Worcester, who went to the Fleet Prison and in October 1551 suffered deprivation. In June 1550 the government also decided to prosecute the imprisoned Gardiner under the Act of Uniformity, while during the subsequent months it began legal proceedings against Bishop George Day of Chichester and several other ecclesiastics of known conservative views. At this moment Somerset still lingered in the political arena, and he attempted to extricate Gardiner from the Tower on condition he should undertake to obey the Act of Uniformity. Yet this suggestion, made during Northumberland's absence in the North, was quashed on his return and in February 1551 Gardiner was duly deprived of the See of Winchester. Meanwhile during the summer of 1550 Cuthbert Tunstall, who had remained a consistent Henrician Catholic, had to face false charges of encouraging a conspiracy in the North and was placed under arrest in his own house in London. Defended against Northumberland by Cranmer, Tunstall was not brought to trial until October 1552, after which he suffered imprisonment and virtual deprivation of his See of Durham. In March 1553 an Act of Parliament divided this wealthy bishopric into two portions under two salaried bishops, one of whom would have been Ridley had not the government collapsed that summer.[23] These were far from being the only significant changes on the bench. In April 1550, six months after Bonner's deprivation, Ridley was nominated to London, into which Henry VIII's new See of Westminster was incorporated. John Ponet succeeded Ridley at Rochester and then in March 1551 progressed to Winchester. John Scory, the one-time Dominican who had become Cranmer's chaplain, replaced Ponet at Rochester but in May 1552 was nominated to succeed Day at Chichester. A further complicated manoeuvre affected the See of Gloucester, which until 1541 had been part of Worcester diocese and to which in July 1550 Hooper was nominated. When, however, Worcester fell vacant by Heath's deprivation, Hooper resigned Gloucester in order to be named (May 1552) as bishop of both sees, which were now amalgamated. By all these measures the government secured an episcopate of strongly Protestant flavour; moreover, it took such opportunities to diminish the wealth of various bishoprics by 'exchanges' even less equitable than those made by Henry VIII.

Amid these developments the quarrels surrounding Hooper's accession foreshadowed the great rift within the Elizabethan Church.[24] His earlier life abroad had placed the new bishop far nearer to the foreign visitors than to those of his fellow-countrymen who had contrived to live alongside Henry VIII. Beginning his career as a Cistercian of Cleeve in Somerset he had fallen under the spells of Zwingli and of Bullinger. Having fled to Strassburg in order to avoid prosecution under the Six Articles, he there met and married a Flemish noblewoman. Subsequently he lived at Zürich with Bullinger (who baptised his daughter Rachel) and was deeply affected by the advanced views of John à Lasco. His belated return in 1549 brought a dynamic figure into English Protestant circles. Hooper's single-minded zeal became apparent to friends and enemies alike; even Dr. Richard Smith, who in earlier days had helped to drive him out of Oxford, admitted that 'he was so admired by the people that they held him for a prophet; nay, they looked upon him as some deity'. Becoming Somerset's chaplain he took a prominent part in the deprivation of Bonner and was offered the Gloucester bishopric as early as April 1550. Then difficulties began to arise, for Hooper had lost what little he ever possessed of the English capacity for compromise. He believed that if the Bible should be taken as final on any issue, it should be so taken on all issues. Consequently he could accept no ceremonial as lawful unless it were enjoined in the Scriptures. Moreover, the demands now made upon him seemed in themselves intolerable and he refused the proffered bishopric on two grounds. The oath of Supremacy had still to be sworn by God, the saints and holy evangelists, while the vestments seemed 'Aaronic' in that they conveyed the idea of a sacrificing priest. Northumberland stood prepared to oblige him. The letters patent nominating Hooper to the See of Gloucester are dated 3 July 1550 and on 5 August the Council issued a dispensation to empower the Archbishop to consecrate Hooper without the obnoxious vestments. But Cranmer and Ridley, braving the Duke's wrath, refused to consecrate Hooper on his own terms; this line they took not so much because they felt any enthusiasm for the oath or the vestments but rather because they did not desire to see so stiff-necked a radical upon the bench. In October Hooper presented a series of Latin 'notes' to the Council on his position and to these Ridley replied point by point in English. At last, after the saints had been removed from the oath and after his truculence had earned him a short spell of imprisonment, Hooper agreed in March 1551 to undergo consecration in vestments. Nevertheless, he gave no undertaking to wear them regularly, except 'that sometimes he should in his sermon show himself apparelled as the other bishops were'. By any standards his position was that of an extremist, since none of the foreign divines in England, apart from John à Lasco, is known to have pronounced vestments positively sinful.

Intelligibly enough, one so fanatical as John Hooper has found little favour in the eyes of English ecclesiastical historians, yet recent research upon his short but intensive career as a diocesan bishop has tended to enlarge his stature.[25] Finding his clergy and officials lethargic and ineffective, Hooper went to work amongst them with almost superhuman energy. He presided in person over his diocesan court and made frequent tours of the diocese on the spur of the moment. His charity and concern for the poor were daily manifest and he made it clear that his social sympathies lay not with the landlords but with the unprivileged; his views squared in fact with those of the 'Commonwealth Party'. Basing the picture not upon Foxe but upon the court records of Gloucester, Mr. Price has written that 'the personal touch of the bishop regularly shines through the dull formal records of the diocesan administration, bringing together unhappy husbands and wives, restoring concord among families divided against themselves over disputed wills, pointing out their follies to gossiping and quarrelling women, and giving good advice to all and sundry.'[26] Without fear or favour toward the eminent he continued to impose penances upon offenders, yet in place of the old ritual actions he substituted definite statements of the offences committed and straightforward appeals for forgiveness.

Hooper's most difficult problem lay, however, in the ignorance and individualism of his clergy. In turn these faults sprang from the fact that pluralism and poor endowments encouraged only men of mediocre quality to seek livings in the diocese. In 1551 he found that, of the 311 clergy he examined, 168 could not repeat the Ten Commandments, thirty-nine did not know where the Lord's Prayer appeared in the Bible, while thirty-four could not say who was its author. He also lacked knowledgeable senior clerics to act as rural deans and hold other responsible offices. On the other hand, like so many dedicated Reformers, he was full of enthusiasm for the potentialities of the common people and felt himself to be teaching the Christian religion anew to those who had hitherto lacked opportunity to hear its claims. In a letter to William Cecil he writes, 'You and I, if we should kneel all the days of our life, could not give condign thanks to God for that he hath mercifully inclined the hearts of the people to wish and hunger for the word of God as they do. Doubtless it is a great flock that Christ will save in England . . . there lacketh nothing among the people but sober, learned and wise men.'[27] If he did not transform his clergy this was chiefly because good ordinands proved hard to find in the brief time at his disposal. Hooper's struggle was not waged against Catholic resistance, for such little resistance as may be observed in the Gloucester diocese sprang from the immobility of custom rather than from an informed Catholicism. Rather did he need to fight the evils which sprang from that long spoliation of livings, that neglect of churches and congregations, for which so many agencies stood responsible—the Crown, the religious houses, the colleges and cathedral chapters, the lay patrons and speculators, even the parish clergy themselves. Hooper might do his utmost to play the part of a primitive apostolic bishop, but without tangible support from the government and from society at large he could scarcely hope to rebuild the material foundations of a teaching Church.

In his doctrinal beliefs, in the decisive character of his continental influences, even in his attempt to discipline clergy and laity, Hooper was a true forerunner of that large body of Elizabethan Puritans who remained despite misgivings within the fold of the national Church. Some of the other

Edwardian bishops showed themselves as forerunners of a strongly Protestant, yet nevertheless more central Anglican position. A fair example appears in Robert Holgate, sometime Gilbertine prior and master of Sempringham, who became Bishop of Llandaff in 1537, Lord President of the Council in the North in 1538 and finally Archbishop of York in 1545.[28] In many respects he followed the old traditions of the prelatical civil-servant and educational benefactor, yet within his limits Holgate also showed himself a sincere Reformer. The year following his accession to the See of York he founded by letters patent three grammar schools, respectively at York, at Old Malton (where he had been prior) and at his birthplace, Hemsworth. For these he drew up detailed and thoughtful statutes, while showing his zeal for education by protecting and helping other northern schools during this difficult period. By his will, made after he had been deprived by Mary and was living quietly in London, he founded an almshouse at Hemsworth. This and two of his schools are still in existence.

Robert Holgate's ideals as a Protestant bishop may best be studied in the thirty injunctions which he issued in August 1552 for York Minster,[29] yet here again his chief emphasis lay on education, especially on that of the vicars choral and other junior members. They must, he orders, attend regular lectures in divinity, undergo a monthly examination, memorise weekly a chapter of St. Paul's Epistles in the Latin translation of Erasmus, possess a New Testament, reading a chapter after dinner and another after supper. In the Minster the tablernacles over the high altar must be replaced by sentences of Scripture. The Minster Library must be modernised to include the Fathers up to 600 years after the Ascension, and also scriptural commentaries by Erasmus, by the Lutherans Musculus and Brenz, and by Calvin and Bullinger. While Holgate's views on the nature of the eucharist were somewhat more conservative than those of Ridley and Cranmer, he saw at least as clearly as they that the future of reformed Christianity in England must depend upon an educational programme centred around the vernacular Scriptures. In such sober documents, just as surely as in Cranmer's Prayer Books, we see a truly creative stage in the evolution of Anglicanism. Such a programme typifies the best of the tradition which the Edwardian Anglicans handed on to their Elizabethan successors.

Clerical Marriage

ARCHBISHOP Holgate was one of those prelates who married in late middle age in order to demonstrate their Protestant principles. When taken to task for this offence under Mary, he claimed ungallantly that the step had been compelled by the Duke of Northumberland, who had taunted him with lingering papistry.[30] It so happened that his young wife Barbara Wentworth was a parishioner of our south Yorkshire commentator Robert Parkyn, who refers in deeply scandalised terms to the 'lewd example' set by his Archbishop. Parkyn's sense of justice was nevertheless to be gratified when presently the marriage turned to 'trouble and business'. Barbara was claimed as lawful wife by an impecunious local gentleman named Anthony Norman, to whom she had been contracted in church under the absurd system of child-marriages tolerated by ecclesiastical law. Both Norman and Barbara had since proved mutually unresponsive, and on reaching the age of consent —this was fourteen—had not cohabited as the law demanded for the completion of a binding marriage. But whereas in the end Holgate successfully resisted Norman's claim, his fellow-Reformer Bishop Ponet of Winchester had the misfortune to blunder into a genuinely illegal marriage. In July 1551 the London diarists noted with relish that Ponet had been divorced from the wife of a butcher of Nottingham 'with shame enough' and that henceforth he paid 'a certain money a year during his life' to her rightful spouse.[31]

Throughout the remainder of this reign, and much of the next, this matter of clerical marriage bulked large. Though bills to sanction it had passed Convocation and the Commons in 1547, they had failed to pass the Lords, and the clergy did not receive permission to marry until the enactment of a statute to that effect in February 1549.[32] Then, despite a widespread popular taboo, many priests availed themselves of the new privilege during the four years which remained before the Marian reaction. Of the 319 priests beneficed in Essex about eighty-eight were to be deprived by Mary's government for marriage. In the diocese of Norwich about one in four was removed, while in London nearly a third underwent deprivation for marriage. The record for Lincolnshire remains less complete, but a very conservative estimate suggests over seventy deprivations in 616 parishes.[33] Even in the more conservative North the urge to matrimony proved far from rare, and in the York diocese about 100 incumbents (out of over 1,000) ventured upon this course.[34] These clerics were not necessarily keen Protestants. It has been shown that the Essex married clergy formed a very mixed group, learned and ignorant, godly and disreputable. Few of them left any clear evidence of special devotion to Protestant principles.[35] Though ardent Reformers attacked the celibate ideal as leading to vice and gloried in the estate of matrimony, many a mundane glebe-farmer in a country vicarage must have seen marriage in terms of worldly convenience and natural impulse. From the social and economic standpoints the change had much to commend it, especially in a rural background. If in his earlier years the married parson had many mouths to fill, later on he had hefty sons to till his glebe, besides a wife to order his household, tend his poultry and organise his relations with female parishioners. In the cases of incumbents who were small farmers, the transition to family life does not seem on balance to have produced impoverishment. A detailed comparison of probate inventories in the diocese of Lincoln has shown that there the rural clergy had bigger and far better-furnished houses at the end of the sixteenth century than on the eve of the Reformation. In comparison with tradesmen and other comparable laymen they also seem here to have progressed favourably.[36]

Despite such evidence, the broader question regarding clerical living-standards has no simple answer; as with the gentry in the century 1540–1640, some clerics prospered while other battled hard with poverty. Rectors, including lay impropriators, enjoyed the great tithes and in a period of rising prices they had every chance to forge ahead. The income of vicarages, based on the small tithes, can be shown to have increased much less steeply than that of rectories, and many vicars can barely have maintained standards as the inflation advanced. Mere curates with fixed or but slightly increased stipends became even poorer than in the past. Even in 1650 some fifty-one Lancashire and Cheshire curates averaged less than £9 per annum, while twenty-three of them, with £5 or less, were worse off than many agricultural labourers.[37] In general, the processes which followed the Reformation, while diminishing the number of pluralists and very rich clergy, may have tended to increase inequalities among parish priests. And while it can be demonstrated that clerical households in 1600 were far more comfortable than those of 1500, this was also the case with all other classes of society above the pauper level. Taken as a whole the parish clergy may be thought to have obtained less than their fair share of the nation's increasing wealth, yet they were entering upon a new phase of social influence. As they enlarged their houses and bred their big families, they began to make a new contribution to English life. Their wives, sons and daughters extended the scope of the middle classes, subtly changed the ethos of organised religion and played a notable part in the historic achievements of Britain both at home and abroad. Nevertheless, the innovation of 1549 had to encounter many decades of opposition. While conservative old women in the North called the children of the vicarage 'priests' calves', Queen Elizabeth herself snubbed the wives of her bishops and would have had them expelled from the precincts of cathedrals. Her smart modernity had some limitations and it did not conceal the oddity of her complexes about marriage.

The Second Prayer Book

THE Ordinal represented but the first stage of a movement far more decisive than that hitherto undertaken by Somerset. In May 1550, less than a month after his installation as Bishop of London, Ridley officially enjoined his clergy and churchwardens to turn from 'the old superstitious opinions' by removing altars and replacing them with 'the Lord's board after the form of an honest table decently covered in such place of the choir or chancel as shall be thought most meet by their discretion and agreement'. He also forbade celebrants to counterfeit the mass by kissing the board, elevating the sacrament or by other traditional gestures. Elsewhere Ridley expressed the view of the Reformers on this matter with blunt simplicity. 'Now, when we come unto the Lord's board, what do we come for? To sacrifice Christ again, and to crucify him again, or to feed upon him that was once only crucified and offered up for us? If we come to feed upon him, spiritually to eat his body, and spiritually to drink his blood (which is the true use of the Lord's Supper) then no man can deny but the form of a table is more meet for the Lord's board, than the form of an altar.' Accordingly, in June 1550 he made this change in St. Paul's and the London parish churches. In November the Council ordered all the bishops to follow his example. As they complied, further arguments arose concerning the position of the table in the chancel and the direction in which it should face. Ridley and others then took steps to prevent the attendance of people who did not intend to communicate, since they felt it necessary to discountenance the old notion of the mass as a good work in itself.[38] As usual, Hooper would have gone still further. In a Lent sermon of 1550 he had expressed the wish that the government would put preacher, minister and people together in one part of the church and close off the chancel, 'that separateth the congregation of Christ one from the other'. By this change all would understand what was read, while the communicant would hear and see plainly what was done, 'as it was used in the primitive Church'. Cranmer and Ridley nevertheless continued to resist Hooper and à Lasco in refusing either to abolish vestments or to seal off the chancels of churches. And much as they wished to see moderate advances upon the conservative Prayer Book of 1549, they now realised the danger of reopening the doors to this radical pressure. As they hesitated, Northumberland decided the matter by urging them to proceed.[39]

Concerning the genesis of the Second Prayer Book[40] we know little, apart from the fact that a draft was being discussed by the bishops as early as January 1551. The Book of 1549 had previously been submitted to Bucer, whose *Censura*, a critical appraisal in twenty-eight chapters, exercised marked effects upon the thinking of Cranmer and his fellow-revisers. The new Prayer Book acknowledged about two-thirds of the objections raised by Bucer against the old one, though it did not always meet them in quite the manner advocated by the Strassburg theologian. It made few changes in matins or evensong but significantly modified the structure of the mass, the very title of which now disappeared. To banish the suggestion of a solemn, sacrificial approach, the Canon was split into three separated portions. The prayers relating to the communion of the people now came before the consecration of the elements, thus implying that consecration took place for the purpose of a congregational communion. The medieval vestments were expressly forbidden and only the use of the surplice required. The communion table was now specifically placed with its ends east and west instead of altar-wise, the priest standing on the north side. No longer did it remain possible for the most determined traditionalist to counterfeit the spectacle of the mass. The words of administration were changed from the form of 1549—'The Body of our Lord Jesus Christ which was given for thee preserve thy body and soul unto everlasting life'—to a form with which Zwingli himself could scarcely have quarrelled—'Take and eat this in remembrance that Christ died for thee, and feed on him in thy heart by faith with thanksgiving.'

This second Prayer Book cannot rightly be judged by the normal criterion of liturgists, that of fidelity to old models.[41] Particularly in its communion service, the Book makes some deliberate breaks with the past. It is based on the notion that everything without scriptural warrant should be omitted and a form of worship evolved which the Apostles themselves could have sanctioned. Today this objective is no longer regarded by scholars as literally attainable, yet we should misunderstand the intention if we thought it any less ambitious. In this aim the communion service is doubtless an attempt at the impossible, but it is a gallant and a skilful attempt. While its literary excellence derives from Cranmer's Book of 1549, it may liturgically speaking be regarded as an original rather than an imitative work, and one which displays logical principles within its restricted terms of reference. Of the eucharistic doctrine alleged or implied, it has been said that the service primarily sought to express the command, 'Do this in remembrance of me.' The words of administration could indeed be taken to imply no more than a commemorative rite, and a receptionist view of the Presence. On the other hand, they do not directly contradict Ridley's 'Ratramnian' view, which Cranmer had accepted in 1546 and later claimed never to have discarded. In general, it seems certain that Cranmer and his associates were not aiming to write a Zwinglian or a Calvinist Prayer Book. Had they so intended, they would have paid some regard to the services devised by à Lasco for use at the Austin Friars and by Valérand Poullain for his refugee congregation. Demonstrably the Book of 1552 follows neither of these, both being far more revolutionary in their departure from the original shape of the mass.[42]

On Cranmer's own intentions and on the degree of his personal responsibility for the more 'advanced' features of the Book, leading scholars have differed, and the paucity of direct evidence does not encourage dogmatism. Certainly the Archbishop lay under heavy pressure from the Hooper-Knox-à Lasco group at the time of the Book's completion. It is also certain that this group had the ear of the Privy Council. The new liturgy was due to come into use on 1 November 1552, but in September Knox protested in a sermon before the King against the rubric directing that the people should communicate in a kneeling posture. When pressed by the Council to modify this rubric, Cranmer refused. Even though copies were already in the press, the Council then inserted (apparently on its own authority) the so-called 'Black Rubric', denying any intention to adore the elements by kneeling, or any presence of Christ's natural body therein. The evidence arising from this quarrel throws little fresh light on Cranmer's doctrinal position in the year 1552. And whether or not he remained dissatisfied on points of detail, he had incurred official responsibility for the Prayer Book which, despite the important amendments of 1559, forms substantially the present Prayer Book of the Church of England.

The Parliament which assembled the day after Somerset's execution passed in April 1552 the second Act of Uniformity, but not without protests from three lay peers and from the conservative bishops Thirlby of Norwich and Aldrich of Carlisle. This Act states that 'a great number of people in divers parts of this realm, following their own sensuality, and living either without knowledge or due fear of God, do wilfully and damnably . . . abstain and refuse to come to their parish churches'. It then exhorts the bishops to use ecclesiastical censures to remedy this situation. Commanding that the new Book be used from 1 November next, it reasserts the authority of the former Act of Uniformity and in addition threatens those attending any other form of worship with six months' imprisonment for the first offence, a year for the second and life imprisonment for the third.[43] During the short period of their operation these penalties did not need significantly to be evoked. Once again, even the conservative element among the parish clergy operated the new services without overt signs of disapproval. They were organised neither outwardly nor inwardly to resist, but one cannot doubt that they made even stronger mental reservations than those they had entertained in 1549.

The Canon Law and the Articles of Religion

ALONGSIDE the Second Prayer Book Cranmer optimistically undertook two other great schemes—to reform the canon law and to codify the beliefs of his Church in a document widely acceptable among Protestants. It is hard to say which of these was the more arduous task. No aspect of ecclesiastical affairs stood in greater need of revision than the law administered in the church courts. In particular the field of matrimony afforded a confused prospect of irrational and sub-Christian principles. Here as usual, the government of Somerset had shown itself full of good intentions. By virtue of an Act of 1549 a reform-commission of eight had been appointed, but when this Act expired neither Northumberland nor his successors caused it to be renewed. Indeed, until the passage of the canons of 1603–4, there was a notable lack of practical enthusiasm.[44] The canon law had many foes, especially among the common lawyers and the civilians, who had no wish to reinvigorate their rival by means of reforms. Again, an interesting passage in the *Journal* of Edward VI seems to reflect the view instilled into the boy by his mentor Northumberland. It is to the simple effect that the execution of discipline could not be entrusted to the bishops, some of whom were papists, some ignorant, some aged, some of bad repute.

In the last resort the laymen deserve the main blame for this lost opportunity, and a nation which would neither abolish nor reform the jurisdiction of the Church ended by obtaining its just deserts. That the study of ecclesiastical law survived the threats of the Reformation was largely due to the college called Doctors' Commons, which had been formed in 1511 for advocates practising in the church courts, and which survived until 1857. Usually trained at the university in the civil law, these advocates received their canon law education both by working in the church courts and by studying in the great library built up by the gifts of bishops at Doctors' Commons. English ecclesiastical law therefore became ever more strongly influenced by the civil law. As for the courts, they survived the Reformation almost intact, and the enormous deposit of Tudor books and papers in our diocesan registries affords an uncanny sense of continuity across the period of cataclysm. Through the reign of Elizabeth and far beyond, the church courts continued to grind through their cumbrous and irritating routines, attracting the abuse of the Puritans and the dislike of the laity, still undertaking the tutelage of the nation, yet remote from the spiritual aspirations and sensitive consciences of the age.

Of this missed opportunity Cranmer's *Reformatio Legum Ecclesiasticarum* forms a striking memorial, though it remained unpublished until Foxe undertook the task in 1571. While deriving all ecclesiastical jurisdiction from the Crown, it proposed to retain the traditional control of the church courts over marriage, tithes, testaments, perjury, slander and benefices. Again, had this code been adopted, the church would have continued to try heresy and to hand defiant offenders, 'all other remedies having been exhausted', to the secular arm for punishment. On the other hand, the *Reformatio* proposed some 'advanced' reforms of the divorce-law, recognising adultery, desertion and ill-treatment as sufficient reasons for the divorce of either partner. Equally forward-looking was its plan for annual diocesan conferences attended by laymen as well as by clergy. Had this one provision been enacted, an immense amount of tension between the two classes might have been saved in years to come. If the bishops had been compelled to consult regularly with their parish priests and with representatives of the laity, they might well have been spared some of the appalling attacks made upon them by the malcontent outsiders of subsequent generations. Despite the curtailment of episcopal estates, it may reasonably be argued that the Reformation failed to break with the feudal character of the bishop or to bring him out of his isolation into regular exchanges with his flock. It may well be the case that the best chance to accomplish such a reform without sacrificing the proper dignity of the office was missed at this early stage of Anglican history.

The parallel task met with more success. Cranmer had long ago been concerned with the compilation of articles of religion. In 1538 he and some of his colleagues had agreed with a group of Lutheran divines upon a series of thirteen articles based upon the Confession of Augsburg, and these he certainly had in mind when he reverted to the task under Edward VI. As early as 1549 he drew up a code to be signed by clerics desiring a licence to preach. From May 1552 some version of these articles came under discussion by the bishops; in the October it was referred by order of the Council to a committee of six, including John Knox. Discussions seem to have continued in a desultory fashion until at last a final series of articles, now numbering forty-two, received the royal assent on 12 June 1553.[45] The King had then less than a month to live, and consequently the importance of these articles lies in the fact that they were destined to become, after several excisions and additions, the familiar Thirty-nine Articles of Elizabeth. In both these recensions they form a decisively Protestant interpretation of the Faith. The saying that the Church of England has Calvinist Articles alongside a Catholic liturgy simplifies the facts, yet it has a rough and ready justice in relation to articles xii (xiii in the Thirty-nine), xvii and xviii. Here we are assured (xii) that good works done without the inspiration of Christ are not pleasant to God and 'have the nature of sin'. In case we are in any doubt about the unpleasant prospects of Socrates in the next world, article xviii denies that a man could be saved by diligently following any other law save that of Christ. And while this article was perhaps no more than an incautious attack upon the Anabaptists, article xvii cannot be glossed over by the phrase 'moderately Calvinistic'.[46] The text of 1553 says that 'predestination to life is the everlasting purpose of God, whereby (before the foundations of the world were laid) he hath constantly decreed by his own judgement secret to us, to deliver from curse and damnation those whom he hath chosen out of mankind, and to bring them to everlasting salvation by Christ, as vessels made to honour.'

This is not the position of the moderate or 'sublapsarian' Calvinists, who at least conceded that the Fall was not predestined and that the election of the redeemed took place only thereafter. Article xvii still appears to contain the most rigorous 'supralapsarian' position—that the salvation of some men and (by implication) the damnation of others was from the first built into the very order of the universe. True, the phraseology is urbane, perhaps not wishing to invite comparisons with articles ii and xxx (xxxi in the 1571 version of the Thirty-nine), which imply that Christ died for all men, not merely for the elect. But the purely verbal nature of this restraint is stressed rather than concealed by the fact that article xvii hastens on to rather irrelevant considerations on the subject of human despair.

While Anglican writers have been reluctant to take this immoderate Calvinism at its face-value, they have seldom acknowledged an even more striking characteristic of the Articles—that they are in very large part directed against the Anabaptists, the fashionable menace of 1552. Over a century ago this fact was nevertheless remarked in detail by Archdeacon Charles Hardwick, who was far from inclined to minimise the general validity of the Articles but who rightly showed that the attack on Anabaptism can be traced in no fewer than eighteen of them (ii–iv, vi, viii–x, xv, xviii, xix, xxiv and xxxvi–xlii).[47] Some of these, one must hasten to add, could also stand in their own right as statements of central Christian traditions. On the other hand, by no means all of those with a more ephemeral interest were omitted when the Thirty-nine Articles came to be compiled. In these and in some of the anti-Roman Catholic articles the Anglican Church has thus been left with a rather heavy clutter of anachronisms. Like the Calvinist article xvii, these outmoded items have been retained in recent times because of the internal disharmonies which might follow any attempt to modernise the Articles. There also remains a lingering, superstitious reverence, from which a frank recognition of the historical and impermanent factors of 1552 might well help to wean the Church of England four centuries later. At least we are no longer terrified by Anabaptism!

The Forty-two Articles leave no doubt as to the medial position of the 'new' Church, yet it is chiefly medial between Rome and the Anabaptists, rather than between Rome and the Calvinists or between Rome and the Lutherans. As we have already seen, there are adiaphorist elements which recall Melanchthon and his English followers of the thirties. Several articles are directly borrowed from, or are very close to the Augsburg Confession, for example article xi, asserting justification 'by only faith in Jesus Christ'. Purgatory and the cults were denounced in a crushing article (xxiii, becoming xxii in the Thirty-nine) which has ever since been solidly maintained by the Church of England: 'The doctrine of School authors concerning purgatory, pardons, worshipping and adoration, as well of images as of relics, and also invocation of saints, is a fond thing vainly feigned, and grounded upon no warrant of Scripture, but rather repugnant to the word of God.'

Many of the remaining items, and portions of some already mentioned, are directed against medieval Catholicism: the Roman primacy and the infallibility of General Councils (xx, xxii, becoming xix, xxi); the scholastic accretions of recent centuries (xii, xiii, xxii); the doctrine of transubstantiation (xxix, becoming xxviii), and the concept of the mass as a sacrifice (xxx). As for the actual teaching on the eucharist in article xxix (much modified as xxviii of the Thirty-nine), its lack of precision must be accepted as deliberate. Its first clause suggests receptionism, limiting effective communion to worthy receivers; its second regards transubstantiation as 'repugnant to the plain words of Scripture'; its third (omitted from the Thirty-nine) echoes the Lollard and Zwinglian argument that the faithful should not believe in 'the real and bodily presence', on the ground that Christ's body cannot be present in many places at once; its fourth declares that the sacrament was not commanded by Christ to be 'kept, carried about, lifted up, nor worshipped'. The total effect of this article has been most variously regarded by theologians.[48] Few cautious readers would agree either with Hardwick, that it repudiates the errors of the Zwinglians, or the precisely contrary view of Dix, that it forms 'the perfect summary of the Zwinglian belief in the Real Absence'. It savours more of compromise between Cranmer and his committee-rivals than of a real consensus of minds. It cannot be taken to prove that Cranmer had whole-heartedly embraced Zwinglianism, yet in both its omissions and its inclusions it could well indicate heavy pressure by the Hooper-Knox group upon the Primate. On the other hand, we have no direct evidence that Cranmer disagreed with the Articles, and in 1555 he appears to have accepted a general responsibility for them. He did, however, immediately reject the Privy Council's unscrupulous claim that they had been agreed on by Convocation. This claim was certainly untrue, but his protest was brushed aside by the astonishing reply 'that the Book was so entitled because it was set forth in the time of Convocation'.

So much must be said, yet the present writer must confess whenever he re-reads the Articles, he finds admiration becoming preponderant over other emotions. This, no doubt, is in part a literary admiration, yet it has some more solid ingredients. However strongly one may reject the Articles as a statement of twentieth-century thinking in the Anglican Church, one must admit that they wore remarkably well until the later nineteenth. However much they may now savour of long-dead ecclesiastical politics, they remain among the most striking formularies of an age when theology still lacked most of the weapons of textual criticism. They still deserve serious study as a historical monument, and even as a point of departure for any new codes which may be attempted. Despite the bargaining which seems to underlie them, the Articles cannot justly be dismissed as mere timid compromise; their flexibility represents at least the dawning of the notion that honest doubt, alternative solutions and agreements to differ have their places in the doctrinal sphere. In very large part they represent what was most sensible and maturely-considered in the Reforming thought of the mid-century, and their authors cannot be blamed if in later times misguided people took them as something which Protestantism of its very nature cannot and must not suppose itself capable—an immutable, obligatory and comprehensive code of beliefs. The most important function of the Articles was a pragmatic one. They were in due course to bring a much-needed element of stability to the intellectual and social scene. In their conscious attempt at a shrewd balance between the extremes of an unbalanced age, they are intensely English, and a student of English history unfamiliar with their text suffers from a grievous gap in his documentary knowledge.

The Fall of Northumberland

Also among the last acts of Northumberland's régime was the confiscation of plate, vestments and other valuables regarded by the government as unnecessary for the revised form of divine service. A Council order as early as 3 March 1551 frankly states 'that for as much as the King's Majesty had need presently of a mass of money, therefore commissions should be addressed unto all shires of England to take into the King's hands such church plate as remaineth, to be employed unto his Highness' use'.[49] Various inventories were ordered both before and after this decision, but the final seizure came in consequence of a new commission directed in January 1553 to Sir Richard Cotton, comptroller of the Household, and others.[50] This body was subsequently assisted by separate commissions for each shire. Having delivered a chalice to the incumbent (two chalices, if necessary, in cathedrals and large churches) and left a sufficient stock of surplices, the commissioners handed over the rest of the goods to the master of the Jewel House. Even ready money could be taken, if any were found, and handed to the treasurer of the Mint. This process was still in full swing at the accession of Queen Mary, who restored what little plate remained intact but kept plate already melted down and the money raised from sales.

While the second Act of Uniformity had rendered most of these objects liturgically inappropriate or superfluous,[51] the action remains difficult to defend even on these grounds. It did not, for example, take into account the need for new and larger cups demanded by a congregational communion in both kinds. To many contemporaries it seemed the most sordid of all governmental appropriations. Christopher Trychay, vicar of Morebath in Devon from 1520 to 1574, wrote in his parish book that the sale of church goods had been proceeding unofficially since 1545 'and no gifts were given to the Church, but all from the Church . . . by the time of King Edward VI the Church ever decayed'.[52] Seeing everything threatened, and their incomes gravely diminished, some clerics and chapters joined in the scramble. In February 1553 the dean and two canons of Chester were imprisoned in the Fleet for stripping the cathedral of its lead.[53] Reckless in their financial desperation the politicians did not pause to reflect on the alarming degree to which they were fostering corruption and discouraging the interest of the people in their parish churches. And some degree of responsibility must also fall upon enthusiasts like Hooper, who would make no concessions toward gradualism and who seemed to suppose that the new forms of devotion could be implanted overnight in the minds of simple people. Yet in attempting to assess the state of opinion during these disillusioning years we should probably be mistaken on a point of fact if we supposed that the rapacious politicians and the tactless Puritans were driving many of the English people back into the Catholic fold. Such evidence as we can adduce suggests that Protestantism continued steadily to expand amongst the upper and middle orders, while able preachers could still make many converts among the working people of the towns. The Spanish resident Guaras thought that Somerset and Northumberland backed Protestantism 'both because they were themselves of this opinion and from seeing the people inclined to it',[54] while in 1551 the Venetian ambassador Barbaro reported that 'the detestation of the Pope was now so confirmed that no one, either of the old or new religion, can bear to hear him mentioned'.[55]

These judgements may be based on no evidence outside the London area. There are also hints of a popular mood little related to either creed—cautious, unspiritual, perhaps a little stunned by the events of the last twenty years. The failings of the party in power did not necessarily involve any sort of religious response. In 1553 the greater part of the nation was neither ardently Protestant nor ardently Catholic. Lord Paget had recently written to Somerset that both religions were sadly wanting in England. 'I fear at home is neither. The use of the old religion is forbidden, the use of the new is not yet printed in the stomachs of eleven of twelve parts of the realm.'[56] A related and no doubt common viewpoint is represented by Capper, one of the speakers in the *Discourse of the Common Weal*; he roundly denounces all the theologians for bringing strife and division among the people and thinks that education should be limited to useful modern languages and to literacy in English, so that 'we might read the holy Scriptures in our mother tongue'.[57]

This indeterminacy is of the utmost importance in relation to the origins and the results of the Marian reaction. Mary was soon to be wafted in by the wind of legitimism, but not by the gale of a Catholic revival. If she wanted such a revival, she would have to foster it herself, and her opportunity was now at hand.

Northumberland's policy had one clear objective—the maintenance of his personal ascendancy, with which was bound up his personal survival.[58] On this second issue he can have had few illusions by the early months of 1553, when his general unpopularity was accompanied by a mounting spirit of distrust even among his Protestant adherents. Latimer, Knox and Bartholomew Traheron (the Calvinist layman who briefly held the deanery of Chichester) spoke pointedly of covetousness and pride in high places. For his part Northumberland threatened punishment to preachers guilty of attacks upon his friends, and he became extremely brusque in the House of Lords when Cranmer continued mildly to press for the reform of the canon law. Amongst the 'new' laymen like Paget and William Cecil he had contrived to give almost as much offence as among the established nobles like the Earls of Arundel and Westmorland. His most faithful supporters were notorious adventurers like Sir Thomas Palmer and Sir John Gates. Among the magnates he could boast only one devoted adherent, Henry Grey, Marquis of Dorset, whom he had created Duke of Suffolk after the death in 1551 of Charles Brandon's sons. This unintelligent nobleman had married King Henry's niece Frances Brandon and his main political asset was hence his daughter, Lady Jane Grey. When on 21 May 1553 Jane married Northumberland's son Guildford Dudley, the attempt to bring the crown itself into the Duke's family became completely transparent.

Already in August 1551 the Duke had brought the young King to sit in person on the Council and since then he had redoubled his efforts to maintain a complete control over his puppet. The task would have become increasingly difficult had the boy survived, since already he gave ample indications of unusual intelligence. On Edward's death observers of various shades of opinion suspected that Northumberland had poisoned the King in order to promote a less independent figure to the throne. Yet no real evidence supports this improbable notion. Desperately indeed should Northumberland have prayed for Edward's recovery from the decline which beset him early in the year 1553. The figure of the Princess Mary loomed ever larger as the months passed. She had gallantly maintained her personal right to practise the Catholic religion and no one felt any doubt regarding the results of her succession to the throne. Faced by this menace Northumberland naturally worked upon the pious Edward with the plea that only a change in the succession could ensure the survival of Protestantism. The King consequently agreed to a 'devise' whereby the princesses Mary and Elizabeth should both be excluded in favour of the children of Frances Brandon. The further intrigues and self-contradictory arguments whereby the Duke tried to consummate this design have little direct connection with our present subject. The squalid affair is relieved only by the noble spirit of Jane, who was still in her mid-teens when she won her small but secure place in the story of the Reformation. She won it not through the futile usurpation into which she was led but through those personal virtues which exemplified the educative power of Protestant humanism. Had such influences been widely brought to bear on pupils less exalted, the history of English spirituality might have been directed into serener courses than those which lay ahead.

When Edward died on 6 July, Northumberland made a surprising mistake—he failed to get Mary under lock and key. Unhindered she escaped from Hunsdon into East Anglia, where the gentry and people, though more inclined to Protestantism than those of most regions, embraced her cause with a singular unanimity. Their action showed that Tudor Englishmen placed peace, unity and lawful succession to the throne before any of the religious causes for which enthusiasts would have had them wage civil wars. Amongst Mary's earliest backers was the Protestant Sir Nicholas Throckmorton, whose contemporary biographer makes him say:[59]

And though I liked not the religion
Which all her life Queen Mary had professed,
Yet in my mind that wicked notion
Right heirs for to displace, I did detest.

Northumberland's appeal to the fear of Spanish domination fell on deaf ears. Though here he spoke truth, his notorious self-seeking and the rumour that he had poisoned Edward caused his outcry to seem merely that of a criminal at bay. He then made his second obvious error by leaving his fellow magnates behind and setting off in person to stifle the revolt against his authority. Swift intrigues developed both upon the Council and among the gentry of the southern counties. Even Protestant London was shocked when Ridley with wild courage declared both Mary and Elizabeth bastard children of Henry VIII and as such incapable of the succession. The hopelessness of the plan to enthrone Jane became most apparent to the Secretary of State, Sir William Cecil, who had been the fly-wheel of Northumberland's daily administration and who was a Protestant and a trusted friend of Cranmer. Cecil joined the rush of councillors to meet Mary at Ipswich, and if self-preservation was his chief motive it is likely enough to have been accompanied by more patriotic considerations. By 19 July Jane's father Suffolk had abandoned the game. All the church bells were ringing for the lawful Queen; a *Te Deum* was sung in St. Paul's and the night blazed with bonfires. Meanwhile Northumberland received no ostensible aid as a result of the devout prayers submitted on his behalf by the trembling Protestant dons of Cambridge. On 20 July he pathetically threw up his own cap for Queen Mary, and four days later he was brought up Bishopsgate to the Tower of London, 'all the streets as he passed by standing with men in harness afore every man's door till he came to Tower Wharf, all the streets full of people, which cursed him, and calling him traitor without measure'.[60] And as the gates of the fortress closed behind him, the most dubious episode in the political history of the English Reformation came to an end.

11 Queen Mary's Contribution

The Reaction and Public Opinion

ON MARY'S ARRIVAL in the capital the population of the prisons rapidly changed. As Suffolk, Jane and the Dudleys left the scene, there reappeared the old Duke of Norfolk and Bishops Gardiner, Bonner, Tunstall, Heath and Day. And as Northumberland had injured the cause of the Reformation by his policies, so at his execution he continued the work by recanting and by exhorting the spectators to eschew all heresy. In the words of an eye-witness, 'He edified the people more than if all the Catholics in the land had preached for ten years.' Those who knew him were equally confident that he apostatised in the hope of a last-minute reprieve.[1] His sons, together with Jane and Cranmer, were duly convicted of treason but for the time being left in prison. Latimer, Ridley, Hooper, Coverdale, Becon, Rogers and other Protestant divines soon found themselves in captivity, though in their cases treason did not figure alongside heresy. The married, ex-monastic bishops, Ferrar of St. David's, Bird of Chester, Bush of Bristol and Holgate of York, were also deprived of their sees, though of these four Ferrar alone continued in his resistance and perished at the stake. Ochino, Martyr, à Lasco and Poullain, together with numerous other foreigners, received permission to leave for the continent; indeed, during the first months of the reign, the less prominent of the English Reformers also found little difficulty in escaping abroad, and hundreds wisely availed themselves of the chance.

To the Catholics who had comforted her in adversity and led the East Anglian movement—Sir Robert Rochester, Sir Francis Englefield, Sir Henry Jerningham, Sir Edward Waldegrave—Mary added *politiques* like Paget, Arundel, Pembroke and Petre, thus constructing a Council of great numbers and notorious disunity. Its bulk was enlivened by little wisdom; it lacked antennae, breadth of view and authority to enjoin prudence upon the Queen. A striking example of its impotence appears in its failure to get rid of the large non-Catholic group in the Commons, even though circular letters to this effect were despatched before every election to the sheriffs. Mary's parliaments varied in their degrees of compliance with her wishes but they all included a considerable group of members whose Protestant leanings were thinly veiled by a show of conformity.[2] Both these men and their secular-minded colleagues stood prepared as typical Tudor parliamentarians to march with the government of the day but they had every intention of preventing the route from becoming too arduous. In the Parliament of the autumn they consented, after 'marvellous dispute', to repeal the Acts of Uniformity and the other ecclesiastical legislation of Edward VI. A large minority of the Commons—the two estimates vary from a quarter to a third—had the courage to vote against this repeal. And once the first rejoicings had subsided, Mary began to receive some sharp reminders from this sober political world. Parliament would accept a return to the last years of Henry VIII but not a return to the Middle Ages. It refused to rescind the Royal Supremacy, and the scrupulous Queen often placed a non-committal '&c' after her secular titles. Likewise, the problems of papal power were left for future debate, no punishments attached to absence from the mass and heavy hints dropped that any attempt to restore ecclesiastical lands would be resisted. More pointedly still, when the Commons heard that Mary proposed to negotiate a marriage with her cousin Philip of Spain, they sent a deputation begging her to marry an Englishman.

Early in the reign there arose a popular agitation in Kent and Essex for the restoration of Protestant worship,[3] while it was not long before iconoclasm and insults to Catholic clergy began to occur in London. Yet the dangerous factor lay not in religion but in the growing fear of foreign domination. Quite apart from the touchy nationalism which always marked Tudor public opinion, certain changing patterns had begun to work against Mary's plans for a close alliance with the Habsburgs. As native manufactures had developed, England had become less dependent upon the traditional ties with the rulers of the Netherlands, while the collapse of the Antwerp market in 1550 encouraged the search for new markets. Especially since Henry VIII had defied the Emperor, patriotic Englishmen had felt little attraction toward the Habsburgs or Spain, while Philip, though conscious of the need for caution, did nothing to revive in English minds the historic Anglo-Burgundian ties to which he was the lineal but not the spiritual heir. He was not alone in seeming too Spanish. In her pitiful honesty Mary took no pains to hide the loyalties derived from her Spanish forebears and from her violent partisanship of her mother. No doubt the very ease of her initial success helped to blind her to the constant necessity for wooing English opinion. The causes of her failure lay less in her religious intolerance than in her inability to be, like her successor on the throne, 'mere English'. Even the

Emperor urged her to be *une bonne Anglaise*, but she lacked the temperamental and histrionic gifts demanded by the rôle. The Venetian ambassador Girolamo Soranzo wrote that she scorned to be English and boasted her descent from Spain.[4]

There can be no question regarding the intense unpopularity of the Spanish match arranged in January 1554 and celebrated in the subsequent July. Granted her desperate need for an heir to prevent the accession of Elizabeth, who lay under constant suspicion of heresy, this still remained an imprudent means and one which she adopted not only against the will of Parliament but against the advice of Gardiner and at least a third of her Privy Council. Recent research has modified the view that the mood of the nation was merely one of sullen acquiescence. Active unrest proved as characteristic of this reign as of its predecessor; the Marian state papers are saturated with reports of sedition and discontent. Mary had been on the throne but a few months when a fourfold series of risings occurred. Sir Peter Carew, backed by the Earl of Devon, tried to raise Devonshire. Sir James Croft worked similarly in Wales and the Marches, while the Duke of Suffolk, along with his brothers Lords John and Thomas Grey, attempted with great ineptitude to stir the Midlands. The collapse of these three movements owed more to poor leadership, to respect for legitimate government and to the discouraging memory of recent fiascos than to the Queen's popularity, which had already entered upon a steep decline.[5] Yet neither these, nor Wyatt's more dangerous rising in Kent at the end of January 1554, should be regarded as Protestant crusades.

Sir Thomas Wyatt,[6] a son of one celebrated poet, had also been a drinking-companion of another, the unfortunate Earl of Surrey. He could not pose convincingly as a Protestant zealot. For the benefit of the pious he talked about the restoration of God's Word, while Bishop Ponet, who had escaped abroad, ventured back to participate in his rebellion. It is also true that the heresies of Kent were both widespread and complicated and that the county was soon to provide fifty-eight Protestant martyrs. Nevertheless, the records show conclusively that it was hatred of the Spaniard which induced over 4,000 men to march with Wyatt. When the London militia in their white coats confronted him at Strood on 29 January, they shouted 'We are all Englishmen' and spontaneously deserted to the rebel forces. It was a moment of dire peril, since Wyatt, unlike the rebels of earlier years, had struck at the heart of the State from very close quarters. Impeded by stupid counsellors and commanders Mary was saved by her personal courage and by the fortunate but rather unpredictable support of magnates like William Herbert, Earl of Pembroke, and John Russell, Earl of Bedford, who not many months earlier had sat on Northumberland's Council. Again, Wyatt's friends in London did not succeed in overcoming the caution of the citizens, to whom his name meant very little. The gamble ended as he rode up to Temple Bar, shouting 'I have kept touch',[7] only to be greeted by an ominous silence from within the city.

The retribution was handled without much acumen or equity. While Suffolk earned his fate by his folly, the beheading of his daughter added nothing to Mary's reputation. Overcome by Jane's fine bearing historians have often forgotten to add that this execution was an offence against decency, fit to be placed alongside the worst of those perpetrated by Henry VIII. A month later the already popular Princess Elizabeth was also sent to the Tower, and the Habsburg agent Simon Renard persistently intrigued to bring about her execution, in order to enhance Philip's prospects of succession to the English throne. On the scaffold Wyatt exonerated Elizabeth of any share in his revolt and no convincing evidence could be discovered against her. Despite a vehement desire to ensure a successor likely to preserve Catholicism, Mary shrank from a crime of this magnitude, and she presently placed her sister under the surveillance of Sir Henry Bedingfield at Woodstock.

Numerically speaking, Wyatt's followers did not suffer a harsh fate, and of the 480 convicted only about ninety suffered death. These were almost all poor people. The wealthier and more responsible offenders escaped with fines assessed not in accordance with their guilt but with the influence of their friends on the Council. In later years it became easy to misrepresent the obscure victims as martyrs for religion. Nevertheless, the Spanish match itself was the main reason why Mary became unpopular long before she began to persecute for religion. Quite apart from its intrinsic shortcomings, Marian Catholicism was stifled in its infancy through becoming linked in the minds of Englishmen with the idea of Spanish overlordship. Confirmed by Alva's ferocity in the Netherlands and by Elizabeth's long struggle with Spain, this impression fatally weakened the chances of any Catholic revival in England. Spain had become what she was long to remain—the curse as well as the mainstay of the Counter-Reformation, and scarcely did she cease to menace the northern peoples when her spiritual heir, Louis XIV, rebuilt her image—for Englishmen an image which associated autocracy, aggression and persecuting Catholicism. And meanwhile *émigré* Catholicism inevitably developed its own blend of foreign idioms. But of all these handicaps imposed upon the old Faith the original, the profoundest and the most avoidable was that imposed by Mary Tudor's nexus with Spain.

After Wyatt's failure Mary's second Parliament (April–May 1554) inevitably consented to the Spanish marriage, while circumscribing Philip's powers with every possible paper-safeguard. When Gardiner suggested that Mary should be permitted to disinherit Elizabeth and bequeath the crown by will, the ugly prospect of a Spanish King immediately prevented either house from giving the plan serious consideration. By a strange irony the Spanish marriage thus helped to make inevitable the succession of Elizabeth and the consequent overthrow of Catholicism. This Parliament also saw the defeat of various ecclesiastical laws introduced by Gardiner, including measures to revive the anti-Lollard statutes and the Act of Six Articles. This result sprang, however, not from crypto-Protestant opposition in the Commons but from the bitter quarrel between the lay peers, headed by Lord Paget, and the bishops, headed by Gardiner. These two factions on Mary's Council did not merely revive the old Henrician quarrel between Catholic erastians and Catholic clericals; they even transferred it to the public forum of Parliament in a manner quite alien to the spirit of Tudor conciliar government. While the clericals were soon to get their way over the heresy laws, Paget's faction duly defeated their attempts to recover the lands lost to the Church. This matter involved something more than the possible confiscation of property purchased by laymen. The idea of wholesale monastic revival was also anathema to the lay peers, because it might have entailed the revival of a clerical majority in the House of Lords. A true disciple of Henry VIII, Paget had no intention of allowing his master's work to be undone. Rather than see this he would have allied with the Protestants; given his way on this point he was prepared to let the clericals have their persecution.

The reunion with Rome aroused less contentious issues than the Spanish match or the former church lands. When Henry VIII abolished the Roman jurisdiction there had been few enthusiasts for papalism in England, and since then twenty years of savage anti-papal propaganda had taken effect, even among those who leaned to the old religion. The foreign residents in England, for what their views are worth, agree that no Catholic revival was taking place about this time. Soranzo thought in 1554 that a majority of the population felt dissatisfied with the restoration of Catholicism.[8] His successor Michiele believed in 1557 that the restoration of Catholicism was being accomplished out of fear, or by people wishing to ingratiate themselves with the Queen, while everyone, except a few pious Catholics over the age of thirty-five, wanted to return to an unrestricted life by abandoning the Faith.[9] A third Venetian Suriano, observed that the people 'appeared to be Christians [i.e. Catholics] from fear rather than from will'.[10] Simon Renard took the view that the realm was only pretending to be converted and stood prepared to deny Catholicism if the Princess Elizabeth should succeed.[11] While, however, there is little reason to suppose that Englishmen were being converted to a more favourable view of the Papacy, the majority may not have been stirred by passionate feelings in either direction when, in November 1554, they at last witnessed the arrival of Reginald Pole as Papal Legate. By this time even elderly Englishmen could no longer argue from personal experience concerning the advantages and disadvantages of papal jurisdiction in their country, for if the Roman yoke had pressed but lightly in the reign of Henry VII, it had scarcely existed in England since the time of Wolsey's greatness. By now the issue belonged in large part to the field of ideas, and in London it paled into insignificance beside the presence of Philip and his great retinue of tactless Spaniards.

A few days after Pole's arrival both houses of Parliament petitioned for reunion with Rome, and after formal intercession by Philip and Mary the Legate absolved the realm from schism. It remains notable that this third Parliament, the most compliant of the reign, had only consented to the admission of Pole on the clear understanding that no restoration of the monastic lands was being contemplated.[12] Thus satisfied on the crucial point Parliament repealed all statutes passed against papal authority since 1529; it even agreed to revive the anti-Lollard laws, though few of its members can have foreseen the scale upon which the Queen was soon to employ them. Mary's fourth Parliament (October–December 1555) contained a far stronger opposition, headed by Sir Anthony Kingston. This group, to which Sir William Cecil certainly belonged,[13] forcibly prevented members leaving the chamber until they had voted down a government bill seeking to confiscate the revenues of Protestants who had fled abroad. Many members had friends among the exiles; all tended to bristle, for obvious reasons, when they saw religious policy tampering with the property of laymen, heretical or orthodox.

The Martyrs

The burnings for heresy began on 4 February 1555 with that of the biblical translator John Rogers. Within a week there followed him to the stake Bishop Hooper, the prominent London cleric Laurence Saunders, and the patriarchal rector of Hadleigh, Dr. Rowland Taylor. The persecution which followed has been blamed upon many individuals.[14] Foxe suggests that it was initiated by Gardiner and soon passed on to Bonner for execution. Yet here his familiar prejudices seem to distort and over-simplify the facts. With the arrival of Pole, and before the lighting of the fires at Smithfield, Gardiner had lost most of his influence over policy. He died in November 1555, his appearances at heresy-trials being limited to the commission (on which he sat as Lord Chancellor) which condemned Hooper, Rogers and others in the previous January. Bonner was far more deeply and personally involved, yet as Bishop of London he was bound to examine a large proportion of the accused, many of whom were sent on to him by the Privy Council, by other bishops, by justices of the peace and commissioners appointed by the State. Short of resigning, Bonner could scarcely refuse to try, or abstain from condemning, a heretic who pertinaciously opposed transubstantiation. This situation he himself outlined in conversation with the martyr Archdeacon John Philpot, and he ended by regretting that in London he was under the eyes of the Court and could not evade the task of persecution. His zestful, coarse-grained personality and bullying demeanour did much to earn his unenviable reputation, but the actions presented by Foxe as sadistic could, even if accurately reported, be interpreted as rough but well-meaning attempts to frighten the less resolute offenders and so to save them from the flames. Sir John Harrington records an anecdote to the effect that, when someone reproached Bonner for allowing an elderly man to be whipped, he replied, 'If thou hadst been in his case, thou wouldst have thought it a good commutation of penance to have thy bum beaten to save thy body from burning.'[15]

The sources give me a distinct impression that the urge to severity came from the Queen herself. There are many official minutes and letters showing how constantly she incited both civil and ecclesiastical authorities to greater zeal in their unwelcome tasks. Even Bonner received an official reproof for his slackness in allowing heretics to go unpunished. She was neurotic, increasingly assailed by illness, and in the later stages embittered both by Philip's neglect and by the wounding attacks of Knox, Goodman, Ponet and other Reforming writers. The personal influences which lay behind her religious ardour remain a matter for argument. Even when due allowance has been made for our tendency to blame foreigners for what now seems the least English episode in our history, it remains more than probable that Mary received active encouragement from her Spanish confessors, some of whom were distinguished Dominicans closely involved with the work of the Inquisition. Bartolomé Carranza certainly took part in dealing with several heretics, including Cranmer himself, and subsequently boasted with a fine scorn for statistics that while in England he had caused 30,000 heretics to submit, be burned or go into exile.[16] Two other chaplains, Juan de Villagarcia and Pedro de Soto, had much to do with Cranmer's recantations. But the chief Spanish agent is likely to have been the Observant Alfonso y Castro, who before coming over with Philip in 1554 had written two methodical books concerning the theory and practice of persecuting heretics. Both these he republished in 1556, with a preface urging Philip to continue the good work in England. For two years Alfonso belonged to the inner circle of Mary's court. Though in February 1555 he engaged in disputation with the imprisoned John Bradford, he avoided notoriety, and on one occasion he preached against haste and severity, urging that heretics should live and be converted. Here only a simpleton could avoid suspecting a device to divert English attention from the Spanish share in the persecution. Philip's own caution in England should not be allowed to obscure his later addiction to *autos-da-fé* or the fact that his own historians were to claim for him the glory for the English persecution. Yet while in England, the Spaniards had every reason to conceal their influence.[17]

As for Reginald Pole, he stood far closer to Mary than any other adviser during the period in question, and he is not known to have attempted any mitigation of her policy. While Foxe's impression tends in some measure to exonerate Pole, his successor Matthew Parker, who was not uncharitable and may have known more than Foxe, described Pole in the terrible phrase, *carnifex et flagellum Ecclesiae Anglicanae.*[18] In his diocese of Canterbury Archdeacon Harpsfield and Pole's other deputies were exceptionally zealous in burning and imprisoning heretics, while the Cardinal's own communications with the fallen Cranmer never departed from that cold, official ferocity which he had long used against his enemies. Whatever the truth regarding Pole's active participation, he must bear much of the moral responsibility. From a merely pragmatic viewpoint it was unfortunate, both for herself and for her victims, that Mary chose as her *alter ego* a man who had abandoned his former conciliatory ideals, a rhetorical humanist deficient in that sort of humanity which raises a statesman to the first rank of his calling.

The best contemporary list of the burnings, found among Cecil's papers and printed by Strype,[19] includes 282 persons. Of these Foxe records 275, and in addition there were a few other victims included in neither list. The executions were heavily concentrated in south-eastern England, a feature which roughly reflects the actual distribution of Protestantism, though it could well be accentuated by the closer control exercised by the government over reluctant officialdom in areas near the capital. In London sixty-seven were burned, in Middlesex eleven and in Essex thirty-nine. The Kent victims number no less than fifty-eight, all except six of them executed at Canterbury. The other larger county totals are Sussex with twenty-three, Suffolk with eighteen and Norfolk with fourteen. Apart from Gloucestershire with its ten martyrs, very few offenders paid the ultimate penalty in western England and Wales. While a number of northerners suffered in the South, only one burning actually took place in the whole of the northern counties.

The vast majority of the victims belonged to the working classes. Foxe records the status of some 135, comprising five bishops, sixteen priests, nine gentlemen and ladies, four tradesmen, twenty-six weavers and clothworkers, seventy-five labourers for the most part directly concerned with agriculture. Apart from these 135 the remainder is likely to have consisted almost wholly of obscure people. Yet while these figures are among the many facts which forbid us to dismiss Protestantism as a *bourgeois* movement, they need not seriously disturb our impression that early Protestantism found a considerable proportion of its adherents among the upper and middle orders of

English society. Before the Marian persecution had reached its height, 800 or more notorious Protestants mainly from the gentry, the priesthood, the professional and merchant classes had emigrated—a step easier for them than for their plebeian co-religionists. If these exiles were mostly unheroic people, they doubtless included a certain number capable of embracing martyrdom had they been confined to England and subjected to the test. In this event the social complexion of the Marian martyrdoms would have been changed. The whole martyr-group contains some further striking features. It includes the surprisingly high total of more than fifty women, mostly poor widows, and a very large proportion of persons in their twenties or late teens. There are signs both in Foxe and elsewhere that the new doctrines had developed a strong appeal for apprentices and young journeymen.

For what precise creed did all these people die a painful death? A learned Anglican historian held the view that 'at least two-thirds of the martyrs who were burnt by Queen Mary would almost undoubtedly, had Edward VI survived, have been burnt in the normal course by the Church of England'.[20] The remark has been duly adopted by certain apologists for Mary Tudor, yet it would seem invalid. After all, the Edwardian government in fact burned only two extremists during more than six years. Again, the evidence for Anabaptist heresies among the working-class martyrs is far too limited to warrant this conclusion. It cannot be denied that the body of Protestantism was widely permeated by a radical spirit derived from a variety of sources—neo-Lollard, Zwinglian, Calvinist, Anabaptist and others. Within the new national Church sectarian trends can already be perceived, and in this developing situation all its members could not possibly have maintained a precise harmony with the beliefs of Archbishop Cranmer or of whatever figure we may care to select as indicating a hypothetical Anglican norm. Men and women who went to the stake must obviously have been strong Protestants, yet there is no evidence inside or outside the pages of Foxe to indicate that the vast majority of them worshipped otherwise than from the Prayer Book of 1552, that they were classed by anyone as Anabaptists or even that their eucharistic beliefs stood to the left of Cranmer's or Hooper's. All save a handful can still be claimed as Anglican martyrs provided we admit that the infant Church of England already exhibited a fairly wide spectrum of emphases and bore singularly little resemblance to the Church as later envisaged either by Archbishop Laud or by Dr. Pusey.

To assess the immediate effects of these martyrdoms upon English public opinion is not a simple task. Very few people of that period denied in principle the justice of capital punishment for religious opinions; of the Marian martyrs Philpot, Rogers and others had specifically permitted the burning of Anabaptists, while several of the latter persuasion were again to be executed during the reign of Elizabeth. The mode of punishment itself remained in the normal repertoire of secular justice, especially for women convicted of capital crimes, until the later eighteenth century. Moreover, by current continental standards, the Marian burnings formed no great holocaust.[21] These facts agreed, the adverse and lasting effects upon the public mind should not be underestimated. By 1554 few Englishmen regarded a heretic with the horrified eyes of the thirteenth century, while when men judged the process quantitatively they are more likely to have judged it by the precedents of their own national history, which had seen no combustion on this scale. There is no reason to suppose that the majority of English Catholics relished the spectacle of a persecution along these lines. Some of the recorded instances of distaste and distress derive from people who did not share the religious views of the victims, while ample evidence remains that sheriffs, justices and gentry were reluctant to carry out these acts or grace them with their presence. Magistrates like Edmund Tyrrel, who hunted down so many heretics in Essex, appear to have been exceptional and unpopular figures. In the later stages demonstrations of sympathy by the crowds toward the sufferers became so frequent that a proclamation forbade them under pain of death. Its ineffectiveness in one instance appears in a letter from Thomas Bentham, minister to the secret Anglican congregation in London and in Elizabethan times Bishop of Lichfield. He describes the scene at the burning of seven heretics caught at a prayer-meeting in a field near London. As the people crowded round the stake with consoling expressions, Bentham himself cried out, 'We know that they are the people of God, and therefore we cannot but wish well to them and say, God strengthen them. God Almighty, for Christ's sake strengthen them.' The crowd shouted in reply, 'Amen, Amen', and amid the confusion Bentham was able to withdraw unmolested.[22]

Mary lacked the ingredients for a popular and successful policy of repression—a general mood of orthodox religious exaltation or a sense of national peril. The Tudor public felt more pity for a politically inoffensive neighbour than, say, for a foreign-trained seminary priest thirty years later, since the latter could easily be depicted by authority as a murderous traitor in the pay of Spain and the Pope. A burning could be a very horrific affair, and in the wet English climate it was apt to be inordinately prolonged. It was often accompanied by touching family circumstances likely to excite pity even in that inscrutable creature, the Tudor bystander. Moreover, the great majority of the executions took place in those areas of England where positive sympathisers were most numerous. In London, Essex and Kent—crucial areas for any Tudor government—the persecution must have seemed more dramatic and more severe than the national total of victims might suggest to a modern observer. All in all, we cannot reasonably doubt that the response to Mary's policy in south-eastern England was both hostile and immediate. Foxe did not create anti-Marian sentiment, even if he did much to perpetuate it as anti-Catholic sentiment. In this longer perspective, there can be no question of Mary's folly in relation to her own aims and ideals. She did more than anyone, more even than Foxe himself, to create that unreasoning Protestant bigotry which for a century and a half after her death was to prove England's most evil inheritance from the Reformation. As usual, one extremism enhanced its opposite extremism; the noisome smoke inevitably followed the horrors of the fire.

While the great majority of the martyrs were obscure men and women, a small number of Reformers eminent by reputation and character also summoned the fortitude to suffer for their beliefs. The leading clerical martyrs, Latimer, Ridley, Hooper, Ferrar, Philpot and Bradford, had hitherto been compromised by the self-seeking of their political associates; the fact that they showed themselves able to die with such aplomb changed at a stroke the moral status of Protestantism, the future of which depended in large degree upon its capacity to inspire a few Englishmen of prominent position and cast in a heroic mould. This was a period when opinion judged a man's spiritual situation by his conduct in the face of impending death, and when the example of a great spirit could prove immensely contagious. The course embarked upon by the government may largely be explained by its anticipation of weakness in its leading opponents. 'Thou wilt not burn in this gear, when it cometh to the purpose', said Sir Richard Southwell to the proto-martyr John Rogers.[23] At the outset there was indeed little reason to suppose that the new doctrines had attracted heroes.

The story of the Oxford martyrs has been too often retold to need further repetition. Equally impressive is that of Dr. Rowland Taylor, rector of Hadleigh in Suffolk, who may be taken as most characteristic of the new type of national hero.[24] Gigantic in physical stature, learned in the laws, unsparing in his zeal to bring Gospel Christianity to all sorts and conditions of men, endlessly active in practical charities to the poor, forward-looking in his valuation of marriage and family life, Taylor had also the obverse characteristics of the fighter. He could see nothing in the viewpoint of an opponent. A hard controversialist, he wounded without hesitation and stood always eager to exchange stroke for stroke in the cause. In earlier years Hadleigh had responded to the teaching of Bilney, and under Taylor it became famous throughout that region. According to Foxe a great number of its parishioners 'became exceedingly well learned in the holy Scriptures, as well women as men, so that a man might have found among them many that had often read the whole Bible through, and that could have said a great sort of St. Paul's epistles by heart, and very well and readily have given a godly learned sentence in any matter of controversy. Their children and servants were also brought up and trained so diligently in the right knowledge of God's word, that the whole town seemed rather a university of the learned, than a town of cloth-making or labouring people.'[25] Allowing for the enthusiasm of the martyrologist there can be no reasonable doubt that communities with something of this flavour had come into existence by the middle of the century. Being near the base of the social pyramid they represented one of the most solid achievements of the English Reformation and stood among the guarantees of its survival.

When the persecution set in, Taylor's fame and defiance placed him among the first of those to be prosecuted and condemned. In February 1555, a day or two before the burning, Bonner came to degrade him and by custom should have struck him on the breast with a crozier. Faced by Taylor's bulk and formidable demeanour the frightened chaplain of the bishop cried, 'My lord, strike him not, for he will sure strike again.' 'Yea, by St. Peter will I', replied Taylor, 'the cause is Christ's, and I were no good Christian, if I would not fight in my Master's quarrel.' So Bonner omitted this feature of the grim ceremonial, and once back in his cell with John Bradford, Taylor mirthfully recounted the story to his companion. 'And by my troth,' said he, rubbing his hands, 'I made him believe I would do so indeed!' To traverse the last intimate scenes with his wife, his children and his disciples might well seem to savour of Protestant propaganda. Yet they should be read by anyone genuinely interested to understand the spiritual dynamic now being achieved by the English Reformation. This was the choice of a man who had not, like Prior Houghton or Edmund Campion, taken his leave of mere human affections. While no more nobly met than theirs, the fate of a family man who had rubbed shoulders with all and sundry must have had a more obvious appeal to ordinary men and women in the world.

Very different from this, different from the equally unswerving witness of Ridley, Latimer and Hooper, was the conduct of Mary's most famous victim. Thomas Cranmer lacked the massive simplicity of his friend Taylor. Nature had scarcely fashioned him for a heroic rôle, and in the strictest sense he cannot be claimed as a martyr.[26] Though in terms of spiritual agony he suffered more than his colleagues, his courage failed him more than once throughout the prolonged processes. His defiance at the stake, magnificent though it was, came only after he realised that his former recantations had failed to save his body from the flames. Yet as so often, he managed to outwit more consistent adversaries, and the last surprising scene not only recalls its counterpart in *Samson Agonistes* but bears a curious harmony with a life which had always drawn strength from seeming weakness. Shortly before the execution the government decided to make capital out of Cranmer's recantations by printing them, together with the final one which he was due to pronounce at the stake. But this he failed to deliver. Instead, he managed before he was pulled down to repudiate all his recantations, to denounce the Pope as Antichrist and to repeat his Protestant doctrine of the eucharist. Then, as the faggots blazed around him, he received some extraordinary access of strength and held his guilty right hand in the fire, once withdrawing it to wipe his face, but only to replace it until the end came. Hundreds of people saw these events, and within a few days the government admitted them in terms which led people to doubt even the authenticity of the actual recantations. Hence, with their usual blend of bad luck and blundering, the Marians had failed to exploit the supreme opportunity they had so assiduously sought. To gain Cranmer's discrediting surrender rather than risk this appalling rebuff it would have been a thousand times preferable to have spared his life.

The madness of a system which would burn a virtuous human being for his inability to accept a metaphysical theory of the eucharist must stagger even a generation well accustomed to institutional and doctrinaire crimes. Moreover, many a modern observer would hesitate to attribute mental balance to a man who suffered himself to be burned over such an uncertainty. Yet the Marian reaction did at least reveal a wealth of human fortitude, of 'civil courage', of adherence to mere principle which the English have seldom in their history found a comparable chance to display. For both good and ill it became an integral part of the memory of a people; it took its place alongside King Alfred, the Black Prince and Agincourt as a factor in the evolution of our national self-consciousness. By every right it was a story which belonged to the common man, and slowly, indirectly, deviously, it helped to supply some of the elements of constitutional and social libertarianism. Though the contestants of the seventeenth century understood the nature of liberty better than those of the sixteenth, the later stage could scarcely have arrived save on the basis of the former. Though the memory of the Marian martyrs provoked Protestant bigotry, it also helped to provoke more worthy and creative attitudes—an independence of outlook, a confidence that the future belongs to God, a contempt for fashions and establishments; all those attitudes we find fully developed amid the contemporaries of Oliver Cromwell, John Milton and John Bunyan.

In our reaction against Protestant bigotry we have tended overmuch to neglect the martyrs and to forget that aspect of their message which is still relevant to our need. It is the reverse of our craving for security. It is the simple and perennial message of unconquerable spirit, bereft of material weapons, yet prepared to take its stand in passive opposition to the might of principalities, powers and mob-instinct.

> Therefore [wrote Latimer to Ridley], there is no remedy (namely now, when they have the master-bowl in their hand, and rule the roast) but patience. Better it is to suffer what cruelly they will put upon us, than to incur God's high indignation. Wherefore, good my lord, be of good cheer in the Lord, with due consideration what he requireth of you, and what he doth promise you. Our common enemy shall do no more than God will permit him. God is

> faithful, which will not suffer us to be tempted above our strength. Be at a point what ye will stand unto; stick unto that, and let them both say and do what they list. They can but kill the body, which otherwise is of itself mortal. . . . The number of criers under the altar must needs be fulfilled: if we be segregated thereunto, happy be we.[27]

The Protestant Underground

DURING the Marian persecution a few well-known Protestants managed to live in obscurity without being compelled either to recant or to emigrate. The most notable among them was Matthew Parker, whom we last saw preaching to the Norfolk rebels of 1549. The future Primate was deeply compromised on the accession of Mary. An old patron of the White Horse, a friend of Bilney and Latimer, he had also been chaplain to Anne Boleyn, who confided to him the care of her daughter Elizabeth. Having tutored this very rewarding pupil, Parker had become master of Corpus Christi College, Cambridge, and latterly dean of Lincoln. Fortunate to avoid a charge of treason for his interest in the claims of Lady Jane Grey, he lost all his preferments and went to live in the house of a friend near Norwich. A great collector of manuscripts, an assiduous antiquary and editor of medieval chronicles, he rejoiced in his new leisure for study, even though it had to be passed in poor circumstances and in hourly fear of arrest. He also writes with great affection concerning his partners in poverty: 'my godly and most chaste wife, with my two most dear little sons'.[28] Here was a new type of ecclesiastic evolved by the Reformation.

The Protestant content of the many movements of sedition and protest during the later stages of the reign is not easy to unravel from the surrounding political and economic turmoil. The London printers were widely involved in both political and religious pamphleteering, and several of them, including John Day and Hugh Singleton, had to flee abroad.[29] Likewise the justices were ordered in 1557 to prohibit all stage plays, many having attacked the government.[30] In London the molestation of Catholic clergy involved at least two cases of attempted murder, while even the venerable Observants of Greenwich, Elstow and Peto, were stoned as they re-entered their old house.[31] During the spring and summer of 1555 there were disturbances in Sussex, one of the leaders being Thomas Reed, later burned for heresy at Lewes.[32] The following year a Suffolk schoolmaster named Cleobury and a local parish priest concerted a plot to proclaim the death of Mary and the accession of

Elizabeth.[33] Suffolk in general and Ipswich in particular became notorious for their conspiracies, which were certainly Protestant-inspired.[34] Essex and East Anglia saw the labours of the wandering preacher George Eagles *alias* Trudgeover, whom Foxe depicts as a romantic innocent living close to nature in the woods and hedgerows. On the other hand, the Privy Council Register shows that he was pursued from July 1556 as an agent of sedition and was hanged for treason a year later.[35] This same official source proves beyond doubt the extreme restiveness of south-eastern England in Mary's later years. Even in quiet Lincolnshire agitators were in July 1558 attempting to create a rebellion.[36] When Paget thought optimistically of Mary's prospects, Cecil replied with reason, 'My Lord, you are therein so far deceived, that I fear rather an inundation of the contrary part, so universal a boiling and a bubbling I see.'[37]

Concerning the underground Protestant congregations, we know by far the most about that in London, which was formed early in the reign and had an attendance fluctuating between 40 and 200.[38] It boasted a brave and distinguished succession of ministers: Edmund Scambler, later Bishop of Norwich; Thomas Fowle, fellow of St. John's, Cambridge; John Rough, the old associate of Knox, who returned from abroad and suffered martyrdom; Augustine Bernher, Latimer's Swiss follower; and Thomas Bentham, the deprived fellow of Magdalen, who led the bold demonstration at the stake. The last-named, who relinquished his comfortable exile to face these perils, did even more than Matthew Parker to earn his Elizabethan bishopric. The London church maintained close contact with the Reformed churches and English Protestant exiles; like the latter it seems to have used the recent model of the Foreigners' church at the Austin Friars when planning its organisation. It had deacons who kept membership lists, collected and distributed large relief funds and succoured prisoners for religion. One of these deacons, the martyr Cuthbert Simpson, was described by an informer as 'paymaster to the prisoners in the Marshalsea, Ludgate, Lollards' Tower and other places of prison as the Compter, etc., and executor to the prisoners that die, and collector of the assembly when the reading is done'. Occasionally the minister excommunicated members, as in the case of Margaret Mearing, whom John Rough so punished for bringing strangers into the meeting and for talking too openly. When, however, he was thrown into prison, this valiant woman took him clean linen, courted arrest and ended by burning at the stake alongside him.[39]

Despite its congregational form there can be no doubt that the London church was an Anglican body and used the Prayer Book services. The informer Roger Sergeant reported: 'Commonly the usage is to have all the English service without any diminishing, wholly as it was in the time of King Edward the Sixth.' With these leaders it is most unlikely to have shown any leanings toward Anabaptism; one of the members was in fact accused of reading an anti-Anabaptist book,[40] very possibly William Turner's *Preservative against the Poison of Pelagius.* The meetings of the congregation took place at seven, eight or nine in the morning, 'and then, soon after, they dine and tarry till two of the clock, and amongst other things they talk and make officers'. Spies and renegades called for elaborate security measures. We hear of meetings at an astonishing number of places, mostly along the Thames, which afforded special opportunities for escape. They met 'at one Church's house, hard by the water-side'; at the King's Head, Ratcliff, where the widow Alice Warner was hostess; at the Swan at Limehouse; at St. Katherine's (east of the Tower) in the house of a Dutch shoemaker named Frogg; 'at Horsleydown (in Bermondsey) beyond Battle Bridge, at a dyer's house betwixt two butchers there'; 'about Aldgate'; at Blackfriars, 'where they should have resorted to Sir Thomas Carden's house'; 'at the Saracen's Head at Islington... under colour of hearing a play'; 'between Ratcliff and Rotherhithe in a ship called Jesus Ship'; 'in a cooper's house in Pudding Lane'. Once a party was besieged by government agents while in a house on Thames Street, but a resourceful seaman among them swam out from the back of the house, got a boat and using his shoes for oars painfully rowed his friends out of peril.

Foxe speaks of John Rough as 'chief pastor of the congregation', but his evidence does not entirely prove Strype's statement that there were several organised subsidiary congregations.[41] Certainly a number of other clergy were active in London, one being Thomas Rose, the deprived vicar of West Ham, who escaped martyrdom by making a partial recantation, obtained permission to visit friends and so fled abroad.[42] The London priest and informer Stephen Morris mentions 'three preachers of King Edward's days', who 'lived mostly at the King's Head at Colchester', but when in London could be traced through the ale-house in Cornhill, 'for there is much resort [i.e. of Protestants] to that house'.[43] These three clerics obviously formed the connecting link between the London Protestants and the congregation in Colchester. One was John Pulleyne, a Yorkshireman and Oxford graduate, who had forfeited the rectory of St. Peter's Cornhill. He subsequently celebrated communion 'at two Eastertides' (1555–6) at his own house in the parish of St. Michael's Cornhill.[44] Among those associated with him was Christopher Goodman, Lady Margaret professor of divinity at Oxford, and an important political theorist. In Colchester Pulleyne 'preached privately to the brethren' and he may already have been (as he certainly later became) a disseminator of anti-Marian pamphlets. He was not denounced to Bonner until 1557, when he fled to Geneva and contributed to the Genevan versification of the Psalms. He is said, however, to have made previous secret journeys overseas to contact his patroness, the exiled Dowager Duchess of

Suffolk. Another of the Colchester–London clerics was 'William, a Scot' so far unidentified; the third was Simon Harlestone, brother of Matthew Parker's wife. Foxe claims that Harlestone had been driven with his family from his home at Mendlesham in Suffolk and, according to Stephen Morris, he lived not only at Colchester but at Dedham nearby, being 'a great persuader of the people, and they do mightily build upon his doctrine'.

This Colchester congregation appears to have centred around twenty-two Protestants who went up to London, submitted, and then renewed their activities on returning home.[45] Thomas Tye, a priest of the town, complained that some were 'mocking also those that frequent the church, and calling them church-owls, and blasphemously calling the blessed sacrament of the altar a blind god'. In a subsequent report to Bonner placed by Foxe in 1557, Tye wrote that the heretics 'assemble upon the Sabbath Day in the time of divine service, sometimes in one house, sometimes in another, and keep their privy conventicles and schools of heresy'. The local officials, including Bonner's, had refused to take further action against them. Meanwhile Catholic priests were 'hemmed at in the open streets and called knaves', the sacrament of the altar was blasphemed and railed upon in every house and tavern in Colchester, prayer and fasting were disregarded and seditious talk had become rife. The outcome showed that this report did not lack substance. Prominent among the group were William Mount of Much Bentley, his wife Alice and her daughter Rose Allin, who were all burned, along with seven others, in April 1557 at Colchester. Some of the offenders seemed to bear a charmed life; along with the Mounts the priest mentions John Love of Colchester Heath, 'a perverse place', who had been twice convicted of heresy but had somehow managed to return home in triumph. It is evident that a persistent and organised underground congregation existed in Colchester. These were the 'brethren' to whom John Pulleyne preached and who were visited by other clerics intermittently concealing themselves in London.

Other groups can scarcely be called congregations, since they do not seem to have enjoyed the regular ministrations of Protestant clergy. One of these was at Stoke by Nayland in Suffolk,[46] where even in 1558 many parishioners, 'especially the women', continued to absent themselves from the Catholic services. At Easter 1558 the authorities, reluctant to arrest so large a number, gave them a final respite of sixteen days in which to receive the sacrament. The group met and made a solemn compact with one another not to receive. They then approached their parish priest, one Cotes, with the suggestion that the communion should be ministered 'according to King Edward's Book'; it seems evident that they already knew he was secretly inclined to Protestantism, otherwise such a request would have been absurd. If Foxe is accurate, Cotes made the significant reply that 'to such as he favoured . . . he would give it after the right sort; the rest should have it after the papistical fashion'. He was presumably not deceiving them, since they remained unmolested a further six months and then avoided the apparitors of the Bishop of Norwich by a temporary disappearance. Having been duly excommunicated some of them left the town, but by this time the reign had drawn to its close. This and others of Foxe's anecdotes concerning Stoke illustrate the important part played by women (now Protestant but later Catholic) in resisting the religious policies of Tudor governments.

Particulars concerning an Anglican congregation in Lancashire also came to the ears of Foxe, who reports them with a convincing wealth of circumstance, though with the one or two minor errors one would expect in the case of a district so unfamiliar to him.[47] At Shakerley near Bolton lived a nail-maker named Jeffrey Hurst, who married a sister of the martyr George Marsh. The latter, whose birthplace at Dean was also close by, taught Hurst a good deal of the doctrine which he himself had acquired at Cambridge and as curate to Laurence Saunders. Having absented himself from mass since Mary's accession Hurst had to flee into Yorkshire, where he was not known, but from time to time he returned by night to visit his family, 'bringing with him some preacher or other, who used to preach to them so long as the time would serve'. Foxe names four of these clerics, and says that whenever one of them came to Shakerley there assembled 'about twenty or twenty-four sometimes, but sixteen at least, who had there also sometimes communion'.

Elsewhere, both in Foxe and in diocesan records of heresy, it is indicated that Protestant meetings and resistance groups were by no means uncommon during these years. The Lincoln records afford several examples. In St. Martin's parish, Leicester, twenty-eight persons were indicted for displaying scorn toward the sacrament of the altar, while at Gaddesby in the same county the parishioners were charged with refusal to attend mass and to rebuild the altars.[48] At Ipswich in 1556 a large number of people went into hiding or fled to avoid participation in Catholic rites.[49] There may indeed have existed unrecorded congregations, but in most parts of England they cannot have been easy to organise. They demanded frequent visits from a minister, and the parish clergy were in general conservatives, or else unadventurous men, unwilling to become involved in such dangerous activities. As the Catholics were to discover in the next reign, the problem of concealing a priest in the normal English rural background afforded great difficulties, except through the efforts of a network of favourable squires. Had the Marian reaction lasted much longer, the Protestant exiles on the continent would almost certainly have conducted their English underground on lines not dissimilar to those followed by the Seminarists and Jesuits thirty years later. Over and above their personal fears and internal disputes the exiles had a clear common ambition—the preservation of Protestantism in England, and even within their brief period on the continent they were training over a hundred young men for the ministry. The most significant advances in the organisation of English Protestantism were in fact now being made, not by secret congregations and conventicles in England but by English Protestants in Frankfurt, Zürich, Geneva and other centres of exile activity.

The Marian North

THOSE few men and women who climbed the higher peaks of fortitude show us only one aspect of this strange but important episode of the English Reformation. They have tended to focus our attention too narrowly upon the dramatic events of south-eastern England, and as we now learn more of the situation in the quieter regions, the shortcomings of the reaction continue to emerge with at least equal clarity. What was happening in these parts of Marian England? In reading, for example, the manuscript act books of the diocese of York, we sense the colourless character of the régime in relation to a conservative society wherein a lively Catholicism might in time have been re-engendered. The North cannot be described as ardently Catholic but it still stood at the parting of the ways. It also displayed its share of cautious secularism, its own marked relics of the old proletarian heresy, together with a considerable dissemination of the new teachings among the gentry, the clothiers and the town populations. Cases of contempt shown toward Catholic clergy and the restored Catholic ritual were far less common in Yorkshire than in London, yet several clear examples have recently been discovered. In 1554 offences against the reserved sacrament were committed at Halifax and Hull, two places later celebrated for their solid Protestantism as well as for their summary methods of punishing criminals. At Beverley another group of oppositionists were found in possession of books by such notorious Protestant authors as Thomas Becon, Roger Hutchinson and Ridley's chaplain, Nicholas Grimald.[50]

In reply to these and many similar offenders the Marian authorities had neither a programme for reconversion nor even up-to-date ideas on persecution. Heresy cases in the church courts were conducted not only in medieval forms but in a leisurely, archaic spirit before Dr. Rokeby, vicar-general of the diocese, and Dr. Dakyn, archdeacon of the East Riding. These elderly ecclesiastics represented Nicholas Heath, the newly-appointed yet merciful Archbishop of York, and they typify the agents upon whom Mary had to rely in the provinces.[51] Dakyn was a Henrician Catholic who had lacked enthusiasm for Rome, yet embraced the cause of Mary to the extent of composing

Catholic school-statutes and sending a heretic to be burned at Richmond. His colleague Rokeby was an eminent canonist and civil servant, always at the disposal of the government in power. From 1548 to 1573 he dutifully served every régime as a leading member of the Council in the North. While men of this stamp lacked the ardour of Archdeacon Harpsfield at Canterbury, their heretical opponents showed few traces of courage. Compared with the lurid scenes in south-eastern England, the picture in the North—and in general throughout the remoter provinces—is painted in pastel shades. Yet here, where the government had genuine conservative traditions upon which to build, it did not even begin to lay its foundations. Mary's experiences in East Anglia had not greatly interested her in the provinces, and the tether binding her to London was no longer than that which bound the rest of her family. Elizabeth also showed little curiosity concerning the more distant parts of her realm, but in her case it mattered less, since her popularity was far more firmly grounded in the dominant South-east.

In a multitude of ways the unusually informative records at York serve to stress the arid character of the Marian years. Apart from cases of heresy they are dominated by numerous processes brought against the married clergy.[52] As elsewhere, the Marian deprivations resulted from the fact of marriage, not from heretical doctrine, not even from ordination under the Edwardian rite. As we have seen, marriage was a poor index to Protestant convictions. The married clergy soon showed themselves anxious to please authority and so to recover their positions in clerical life. Their individual trials often lasted intermittently over several weeks. The Archbishop's Court of Audience, having established the fact of matrimony, first ordered the offender to abstain from sacerdotal functions. Later on he suffered formal deprivation of his benefice—a severer punishment than clerics had hitherto suffered for adultery—even though marriage had recently been legalised by statute law and by Convocation. The secular priests then undertook to live chastely apart from their 'pretensed' wives, and several introduced the latter into court, in order that they too should register express consent to the separation. Often the guilty pair were ordered to refrain from meeting, except in church or market, and to avoid referring to each other as husband and wife. The court, of course, took no further interest in the plight of the women and their children. In the cases of ex-monks a formal sentence of divorce was read, accompanied by even more solemn adjurations against renewed contacts. This stage concluded, the cleric performed in his church an act of penance similar to that associated with ordinary sexual lapses. When its completion had been duly certified, he was restored to sacredotal functions and hence made free to seek a benefice, so long as it was not the one he had recently lost. Foxe sardonically writes that such submissive clerics had in fact found marriage less agreeable than they had anticipated, and were 'contented, of their own unconstant accord, to be separated from their wives'.[53] Nevertheless, a few of them were later in trouble for revisiting their spouses, while a good many are known to have re-established their family lives under Elizabeth. As already noticed, the Marian courts also punished certain former nuns who had committed matrimony under Edward VI. These were formally divorced and put to penance, in some cases being ordered to resume monastic apparel but licensed to live elsewhere than in the now disused buildings of their former houses. The whole trivial business remained irrelevant to the real needs of the Marian reaction.

Beyond all this arid legalism the Marian government accomplished singularly little in the North. The gentry showed not the slightest inclination to countenance the restoration of religious houses, and betrayed no hint of superstitious misgivings about their ownership of monastic lands. Mary's own restorations in the North were necessarily few. She gave several manors back to Archbishop Heath and reinstated Manchester College and the chapter at Southwell Minster. At the request of the Earl of Shrewsbury she intervened at Sheffield to return to the burgesses the lands of the parish church, which by a flagrant abuse of the Chantries Act had been deemed appropriated to superstitious uses. But even the Edwardian politicians had made similar small-scale restitutions, and the little Mary could afford to restore cannot have reconverted many waverers to the Catholic Faith.[54] In these distant provinces, which did not directly feel the weight of the persecutions, all too little is known concerning the reactions of the man in the street when he heard of the martyrdoms. Yet in that world of localised sympathies the wave of hatred which radiated from Smithfield is unlikely to have been impressive by the time it reached Lancashire. That the North had not become actively disloyal is indicated by the complete failure of Thomas Stafford to find a following, when in April 1557 he invaded by sea and seized Scarborough. Even this minor and short-lived exploit was due to the staggering incompetence of the Privy Council, which had been forewarned in detail.[55]

Failure and End of the Reaction

If Mary had little trouble with the North and the West, there is no evidence that she began to inspire them with any positive Catholic enthusiasm. And if she failed here, she could scarcely succeed elsewhere. In the last resort, the chief weakness of her rule was the same as that of Edwardian Anglicanism—it lacked a real missionary-organisation. Such an organisation the English

Catholics only achieved in the mid-Elizabethan period, when in the face of governmental repression it came too late to achieve more than a very limited success. Reginald Pole in exile had failed to anticipate the great work of William Allen, and Mary had no band of seminary priests to do her work. As the mediocrity of the parish clergy had hampered Cranmer, so now it hampered Mary, for they were the same clergy; they were in essence late-medieval clergy, little touched by the new spirit of reform, Catholic or Protestant.

Mary's restoration of certain religious houses also links with the medieval past rather than with the seminarist future. The Catholic cause needed training colleges, not retreats from the world. It is, of course, imaginable that in time the Benedictines at Westminster, the Carthusians at Sheen, the Bridgettines at Syon and the three other smaller restored houses might have become power-houses of an English Counter-Reformation, yet their membership and short history under Mary gives little reason for such a belief. Though some estimable characters emerged from the past to resume their places in the cloister, the number of surviving monks with strong vocation and professional competence had become very small. By 1557 the six restored houses contained just over 100 religious persons out of some 1,500 still alive.[56] Certainly the monastic movement needed to be fostered for many years in a favourable setting, if it were to generate energy and begin to feed it back into the spiritual life of England. Even had Mary lived longer, she could have enjoyed little success as a result of these methods. The parlous situation of English Catholicism demanded measures more direct, more didactic, more swift in operation among the people. Axiomatically, a religious *policy* was concerned with the minds of men outside the cloister. In January 1555 St. Ignatius Loyola invited Pole to send young men from England to the Roman and German colleges for training as Jesuits. Characteristically Pole's reply covers Loyola's other points but maintains a frigid silence concerning this ardently-phrased offer, which was repeated in vain by Loyola during the subsequent July.[57]

It should have been engraven on Mary's heart, not that she lost Calais but that she failed to discover the Counter-Reformation. Her government was haunted by the ghost of her father; intent upon the legal undoing of his legalism it forgot that in the last resort religious teaching mattered infinitely more than ecclesiastical legislation. The exceptional religious and cultural sterility of these years has often been observed. For creative instruction the ceaseless processions made by government order round the streets and churches of London provided a poor substitute. The man who raised a laugh by handing a pudding to one of the peripatetic prebendaries[58] was no doubt a ribald Protestant, but his action would have been still more fitting had it come from a percipient Catholic.

The devotion of Mary and Pole to Rome and to Spain received some strange rewards when Paul IV, a Neapolitan who detested Spanish rule over his country, proceeded to extremities against Philip. In 1557 Mary found herself without financial resources but committed to war with France; Pole found his legatine commission revoked and himself summoned to Rome to be tried for heresy. Philip's neglect of English interests now justified everything which had been said against the Spanish marriage. Even Mary's ministers took little pains to hide their hatred, yet they could not justly blame him for their own surpassing blunders in relation to the defence of Calais. After 211 years in English hands the town fell in January 1558, and the Spanish ambassador wrote, 'I am told that, since the loss of Calais, not a third of the people who usually go to church are now attending.'[59] No doubt adolescent chauvinism and doctrinal uncertainties often went together, and this terrible affront to national pride cannot have been without its effect on religious opinion at this moment of climax.

The last months of the ill-starred reign were marked by a season of exceptional storms and floods and by fevers with a heavy mortality. Men drew the same conclusion as they had drawn five years earlier at the expense of Northumberland. 'God did so punish the realm with quartan agues', wrote Sir Thomas Smith, 'and with other long and new sicknesses, that in the last two years of the reign of Queen Mary, so many of her subjects was made away, what with the execution of sword and fire, what by sicknesses, that the third part of the men of England were consumed.'[60] About the time of Mary's departure her personal physicians Hughes and Owen both died, together with many leading ecclesiastics like William Peto, whom the Pope had wanted to set in Pole's place, and William Peryn, the Dominican devotional writer, one of the few of Mary's subjects conversant with the new Jesuit techniques of meditation. Yet of far greater historical significance were the deaths within the year of thirteen diocesan bishops. Nature seemed determined to complete at least one side of Mary's work by removing what remained of the original cast from the drama of the English Reformation.

The Queen's last official acts continued in keeping with her previous policy. She transferred an extraordinary number of Crown livings to the bishops, appointed more Catholics to judicial and administrative offices; she even began to fill the vacant sees. For her failure to complete this important undertaking the Spanish ambassador blamed 'that accursed cardinal', Pole. At her death there were five vacant sees, a figure which had increased to ten by the end of the year. Hence when Elizabeth undertook the reversal of her religious policy, only a depleted group of Catholic bishops stood in the way. Mary died on 17 November, Reginald Pole a few hours later, both displaying to the end of their sufferings an admirable piety and an unflinching sense of rectitude. Faithful to duty as they saw it, they had undergone great trials in the defence of an idea they were personally ill qualified to defend. Both displayed the tragedy of the doctrinaire called to practical leadership, yet lacking that instinct toward human beings, that sense of the possible in a real world, which have always proved more useful in English affairs than high principles and strict logic based on narrow premises. But shortcomings of this sort could never be alleged against the young Queen in whose honour the relieved Londoners feasted in the streets and lit bonfires on the night of Mary's death.

12 The Foundations of Elizabethan England

The Exiles

WHILE THE MARTYRS helped to ensure a reversal of Mary's policy, the radicalism and the swiftness of that reversal may largely be ascribed to another group of the Queen's opponents, the so-called Marian exiles.[1] In these people abroad we see a microcosm of mid-century English Protestant opinion, free for once from the inhibiting influences of an English government. Foxe states that some 800 English men and women fled abroad, and modern research has located at least 788 specific persons.[2] Though it cannot be assumed that the surviving records mention all the obscurer people, the movement certainly consisted in large part of noble, gentle, moneyed and clerical refugees. Of 472 men whose status is known, 166 were gentry, sixty-seven clergy, forty merchants and 119 young men classed as students and mainly intended for the ministry. The known working-class element consists only of thirty-two artisans and thirteen servants. The lawyers and physicians are not heavily represented among these names, but there appear at least seven printers, who helped to send back a steady stream of anti-Marian propaganda and who exemplified the tendency of English printers to embrace the Reformation as eagerly as continental printers had embraced humanism.

More important, the exiled clergy, so far from being ordinary parish priests, included the leading figures among the Protestant scholars of both universities, many of whom were to achieve bishoprics and other high offices in the Elizabethan Church. From Oxford came King Edward's tutor, Dr. Richard Cox,[3] dean of Christ Church and vice-chancellor of the University from 1547 to 1552. A man of strong, not to say overbearing personality, he had also been a prominent member of both Prayer Book commissions, while his zeal for uprooting 'Romish' practices at Oxford had caused him to be known there as 'the Cancellor'. Other notable exiles from Oxford were

Laurence Humphrey and Thomas Bentham of Magdalen, William Cole of Corpus, the Lady Margaret professor, Christopher Goodman, and William Whittingham of Christ Church, who had studied abroad for three years, but had not yet been ordained at the time of his exploits in Frankfurt. From Cambridge came an equally varied group—Thomas Lever, master of St. John's, James Pilkington, a later master and ultimately Bishop of Durham, and young Perceval Wiburn, then already a fellow of the same college but destined to a stormy career as an Anglo-Genevan Puritan extending into the seventeenth century. Edwin Sandys, one of Queen Elizabeth's Archbishops of York, was vice-chancellor of Cambridge at Mary's accession and as one of those implicated in Northumberland's conspiracy he was well advised to leave for the continent.

One of the sadder stories is that of Sir John Cheke, provost of King's College, whose influence over Edward VI we have already observed. As a close associate of Cranmer he was in 1556 kidnapped in violation of a safe-conduct, sent back to England and placed in the Tower. After a long resistance he accepted a humiliating recantation and soon afterwards died broken-hearted at the age of forty-three. Yet another of Edward's tutors had gone abroad with Cheke—Sir Anthony Cooke, whose four intellectual daughters married those eminent Elizabethans, Sir William Cecil, Sir Nicholas Bacon, Sir Thomas Hoby and Sir Henry Killigrew, the last two of whom were also exiles. Another destined for an important rôle was Sir Francis Knollys, whose wife was first cousin to the Princess Elizabeth and whose mysterious first journey to the continent in 1553 may have been a mission from the Protestant opposition to Calvin. Alongside these men went a host of well-known preachers, pamphleteers and writers like John Knox, Anthony Gilby, Bishop Ponet and John Jewel. The last, since famous as a defender of the Elizabethan Settlement, had been a close friend of Peter Martyr at Oxford and had acted as notary to Cranmer and Ridley at their trials. He had then been forced to abjure before contriving to flee to Frankfurt. Altogether, it would be hard to find in European history such a concentration of intellectual and social distinction within an emigrant body of such modest numbers. And the great volume of clandestine support enjoyed by these people illustrates in itself the hold now gained by Protestantism upon the leadership of England.

It has been suggested that the exile was in the main a voluntary movement, not so much enforced as astutely planned in order to ensure a future religious revolution.[4] Able Protestants like Cecil came to regard it in this light, while others looked well to the future by educating young English clerics abroad, far from the lures of Papistry. Again, the stream began long before the persecution directly threatened ordinary Protestants. London businessmen helped to promote and finance it; advance agents went ahead to some of the centres of settlement, while strenuous efforts were made to organise and link the various communities abroad. On the other hand, much of the evidence does not square with this picture of an easy, orderly, confident emigration. The ideas of Cecil and his like scarcely disturb the fact that many of the refugees fled because of justified fear, and many others after the persecution had set in. And one proves nothing about the majority by recalling the exceptional case of Katherine, Dowager Duchess of Suffolk, who departed in great state, accompanied by her major-domo, gentlewoman, joiner, brewer, kitchen-maid, laundress and fool, 'a Greek rider of horses' and her own recently-acquired little husband, Mr. Richard Bertie.[5]

Most of the emigrants went under very different circumstances. Their uncertain movements, their acute divergences of view and purpose, their open quarrels, afford anything but the impression of a co-ordinated political manœuvre directed by a group of master-minds, dreaming of the spacious Elizabethan days ahead. If many had access to large sums, others soon depended on charity, though perhaps their main hardship arose from the overcrowding of the walled cities of Germany and Switzerland. There they lived five families to a house, insecure, restive and intermittently troubled by the plague. The truth doubtless lies somewhere between the excessive optimism of the modern picture, and the old legend of hapless fugitives, weeping by the waters of Babylon. Wherever educated Englishmen were involved, no movement could be wholly unplanned or without a shrewd eye to the future. However intolerant and irascible, they had a flair for organisation unsurpassed in the world of their day and their situation obviously demanded political foresight. A cancellation of Mary's religious policy could not be brought about save by her death or by political revolution, yet in 1554–5 neither of these eventualities could be expected at any near date. The organisation of Protestant communities with long-term plans was hence bound to become the major aim of the clerical leadership and of their more responsible lay colleagues.

Men of this outlook normally passed into Germany and Switzerland, since neither the Netherlands government of Philip nor France under the orthodox Henry II welcomed Protestants. Nevertheless, a number of politically-minded gentry lingered in France, where the government also had ample reason to encourage anti-Spanish plotters and would-be invaders of England. In this category were Henry Dudley, Thomas Stafford, Bryan Fitzwilliam and Wyatt's fellow-conspirator Sir Peter Carew, though the last two later made their peace with Mary. The most colourful of all the romantics was Peter Killigrew of Arwennack in Cornwall, who lived in luxury on the proceeds of piracy against both Spanish and English shipping in the Channel. Such figures among the exiles foreshadowed certain aspects of Elizabethan character and enterprise, but it was not given to them to lay the solid foundations of the Elizabethan Settlement in Church and State. At this moment ideas mattered far more than muscles and the ideas were primarily theological even if at one remove they tended to become political.

During the years of exile eight English congregations were established in the continent. The original five were Emden, Wesel, Frankfurt, Strassburg and Zürich, while Basel, Geneva and Aarau were their subsequent offshoots. Despite the pleas of Melanchthon the Lutheran states proved most inhospitable, partly because they believed English Protestants held the wrong sacramental beliefs, partly because they feared political complications. Whatever the justification for this attitude it should be numbered among the many opportunities missed by the ultra-cautious Lutherans, and it killed any remaining possibility that the English Church might gravitate into a Lutheran orbit. At Wesel Melanchthon's recommendation carried weight with the city authorities, but in 1556 the latter managed to rid themselves of their visitors. Shepherded, like Puritan emigrants of the next century, by their pastor (Thomas Lever), the whole congregation migrated thence to the pleasant town of Aarau, west of Zürich.[6]

Each of these communities developed its distinctive character. Emden, where some of John à Lasco's London congregation were worshipping by May 1554, became the chief centre of propaganda—it already had presses and was a port in easy contact with England. Hence flowed many of the pamphlets which drove Queen Mary to distraction and which came from the pens of John Knox, William Turner and John Scory. The last-named, having been deprived of his bishopric of Chichester, had at first recanted, but then taken his opportunity to escape to Emden, where he became minister to the congregation.[7] At Zürich, where both Peter Martyr and Heinrich Bullinger exercised much influence over the Englishmen, the latter nevertheless remained a distinctively Anglican body under their leaders Jewel, Parkhurst and Pilkington. This happy setting they had good reason to recall even in more prosperous times. 'O Zürich,' wrote Jewel after his return, 'how much oftener do I now think of thee than ever I thought of England when I was at Zürich.'[8] When Whittingham left Frankfurt under the dramatic circumstances we shall describe, John Foxe accompanied him, but instead of following most of Whittingham's group to Geneva he was attracted to Basel, perhaps on account of its pre-eminence in the world of printing and publishing. Here he soon set to work on his martyrological collections, and he found a helper in the future Primate Edmund Grindal, who not only polished Foxe's Latin but supplied much material for the lives of Cranmer and Bradford. At Basel Foxe joined a growing community of English students, who lived *in collegio* at the buildings of the former Clarakloster. Among his fellow-exiles there were two men due to attain fame in Elizabethan public life. Sir Francis Knollys was already forty years of age and a Protestant of many years standing, while Francis Walsingham was still a student fresh from Cambridge and Gray's Inn.

At Strassburg Peter Martyr prepared the way for the establishment of another peaceful and moderate community, basing its worship upon the Prayer Book. Here Bishop Ponet wrote his *Short Treatise of Politic Power* which, published in 1556, was the first book by an English Reformer embracing the doctrine of tyrannicide.[9] It is based on the contention that God has conferred authority upon the community, which may establish any form of government it thinks best. No wise community would establish autocratic kingship—a man's allegiance is due first to God, then to his country, and only last to the king. Commonwealths can exist without kings, who are often in fact tyrants and brigands. It is merely a law of nature that bad kings should be deposed and tyrants punished with death. Under certain circumstances (which Ponet does not clearly define) even the killing of a tyrant by some private individual might be justified. While some parallels can be detected in medieval political thought, Ponet's treatise comes first in a new wave of anti-monarchical writings. It was written strangely enough by an anti-Calvinist Anglican, the highest-ranking ecclesiastic among the exiles. It has never been assessed at its true importance, for it antedates by several years those more brilliantly expressed but less radical Huguenot writings which have usually been taken to represent the tyrannicide-theories of the Reformation. Significantly again, Ponet's work was to be republished in 1639 and in 1642; it was still being studied on the eve of that new conflict to which its message seemed equally applicable.

Just as Ponet parted company from his cautious master Melanchthon, so the exiled Calvinist writers abandoned the circumspect attitudes of Calvin. In 1558 there appeared at Geneva Christopher Goodman's *How Superior Powers ought to be obeyed of their Subjects* and John Knox's *Appellation.*[10] These are closely related and say almost the same thing—that rebellion against ungodly and idolatrous sovereigns is a duty. They both go so far as to impose this duty not merely upon the nobles and the higher magistrates of a kingdom but upon the common people themselves. Such works show a striking abandonment of the godly prince and of that hatred for rebellion which had marked English Protestant thought during the previous reign. As usual, political thinking had adapted itself to the hard facts of the situation. There can be little doubt that these intellectuals stood prepared to applaud the assassination of Mary Tudor, while by 1558 Knox also felt the time ripe for an appeal to the nobility and estates of Scotland in order to overthrow the Catholic Regent, Mary of Guise.

The Geneva community was founded in October 1555 by forty-eight of the followers of Knox and Whittingham, after these leaders had left Frankfurt. At one time or another thereafter, over 200 Englishmen became members,[11] yet the common statement that only a quarter of the exiles were exposed to Genevan influence has no great significance. To be influenced, one was not compelled to visit Geneva any more than a good Marxist must necessarily visit Moscow or the British Museum! The original ministers at Geneva were Goodman and Anthony Gilby; they were soon reinforced by other ecclesiastics of remarkable character, among them Scory, Bentham, Thomas Cole and Perceval Wiburn. Such men found a congenial home in the city of Calvin and if, when they became Elizabethan dignitaries, they could not seek to reproduce it, they nevertheless like Knox regarded it in retrospect as the model of a perfected Christian community. Already in 1555 many of them had become highly impatient with the non-biblical elements remaining in the Prayer Book of 1552. They resolved forthwith to lay the foundation of a truly scriptural religion, not only by improving on Cranmer's work but by re-translating the Bible itself and presenting it in a Reformed edition.

The first-fruits of this movement appeared in June 1557, when William Whittingham published a version of the New Testament with a prefatory epistle by Calvin and containing many revisions based on the work of Beza. Meanwhile, headed by Whittingham and Gilby and with some assistance from the veteran Coverdale, the exiles produced the Geneva Bible, often called the 'Breeches Bible' from its odd translation of *Genesis*, iii, 7. It was ultimately published there in April 1560 by the English printer Rowland Hall.[12] This Bible possessed many technical advantages over its predecessors. It had a convenient quarto format, and following Whittingham's Testament of 1557 it abandoned the old black-letter type for clear Italian characters. It also divided the chapters into numbered verses. The text was more revolutionary than any since Tyndale and many of its innovations were to be followed by the Authorised Version of 1611. The critical notes, though embodying the best Reformed scholarship of the day, bore in some cases a bitter partisan flavour. Under Elizabeth this Geneva Bible was to find no close rival. Some sixty editions appeared before the publication of the Authorised Version, whereas its competitor the Bishops' Bible (produced in 1568 to counteract its Puritan tendencies) attained only a quarter of that number. Even the Authorised Version did not immediately oust the Geneva Bible, since between 1611 and 1640 ten more editions of the latter came from the press. The exiles thus produced the version on which Shakespeare and the great majority of our Elizabethans and Jacobeans were reared, and it takes its place among the factors which explain the Calvinist flavour of Elizabethan Anglicanism.

At Geneva also, Whittingham, William Kethe and others began to compile a new edition of the Psalms in English verse.[13] Beginning with only fifty-one Psalms in 1556, the Anglo-Genevan Psalter underwent—like the Sternhold version to which it was partly indebted—a gradual expansion throughout successive editions. It was Kethe who wrote that spirited version of the hundredth Psalm so familiar in English hymn-books, and at Geneva in all likelihood it was first sung to the Old Hundredth, then a new tune. Like the Geneva Bible this compilation achieved great popularity in Elizabethan England; it also became parent to the *Scots Psalter* of 1564 and so attained a special influence among the Covenanters. All in all, had there been no exile-community save that in Geneva, the emigration must still have exerted conspicuous effects upon British history.

The Troubles at Frankfurt

THE most controversial and best-documented of the settlements abroad we have left to the last. The *Brief Discourse of the Troubles Begun at Frankfurt*, first published by a group of English Puritans in 1574–5, was traditionally ascribed to William Whittingham in person, but is now thought to have been compiled by his inseparable companion Thomas Wood.[14] The story which it tells in such vivid detail has been so often retold as to leave an overpowering (though in fact untypical) impression of Protestant life in exile. At first blush these endless quarrels seem to form one of the more arid and even ridiculous episodes in Tudor history. Yet on closer examination the troubles are seen to involve broad and vital issues, for Frankfurt became the battleground of those controversies left unsolved by the reign of Edward VI and soon to be revived under Elizabeth. The little group of English refugees amid the seething population of the great free city on the Main may have mystified their kindly and tolerant hosts, but to historians they display a preview of the tensions and divisions which have ever since that day beset Protestant society in the English-speaking world.

When in June 1554 Whittingham and a few of his friends arrived in Frankfurt, they were welcomed by the pastor of the French church, Valérand Poullain, formerly so prominent among the foreign Protestants in England. On his suggestion that the newcomers should join his own congregation, the city authorities permitted both to share the church of the White Ladies, but the English soon gained virtual freedom to order their own devotional lives. Whittingham, who knew Geneva well before he came to Frankfurt, then remodelled the Prayer Book of 1552 along Calvinist lines, abolishing vestments, the Litany, the oral responses and other features which savoured of the unreformed religion. The congregation made no strong objection and by the end of July had become an independent Church with elected ministers and deacons. Yet instead of working out their own experiment the Frankfurt leaders soon issued letters to the English in Strassburg and Zürich, inviting them to come and join in their enlightened proceedings at Frankfurt. The response from these more conservative groups lacked warmth. The men at Zürich replied politely but evasively, while those at Strassburg hinted that things had gone too far; indeed, they urged their compatriots at Frankfurt to appoint more competent ministers, suggesting the names of Cox, Ponet, Bale and Scory. So far from accepting this gratuitous advice, the Frankfurt congregation summoned John Knox from Geneva, allowed him to become their real leader and to oppose an iron front against any restoration of Cranmer's Prayer Book. Meanwhile, however, a group of Prayer Book adherents, led by Lever, began to emerge in Frankfurt, and in order to silence them Knox and Whittingham resolved upon a personal appeal to Calvin. They therefore drew up a Latin synopsis of the Prayer Book, apologising 'with a certain kind of pity' for shortcomings inevitable at the time of its composition.[15] This they submitted to Calvin, who replied in urbane and moderate terms. In his view the Book contained ineptitudes tolerable for a time but now due to be replaced by 'something more filed from rust, and purer'. He also counselled Knox and Whittingham not to be too fierce with those 'whose infirmity will not suffer them to ascend a higher step'.[16] On this wise sentence the recipients are not likely to have dwelt for long. We do not know the precise terms of the agreement which they made with their opponents in February 1555, but it seems to have represented their almost complete victory and to have allowed most of the Calvinist forms adopted by Whittingham.

Scarcely had a return to brotherly concord been celebrated when on 13 March 1555 the new and formidable figure of Dr. Richard Cox erupted upon the Frankfurt scene. Soon after Mary's accession the former 'Cancellor' had been imprisoned in the Marshalsea on a charge of treason and then placed under house-arrest. In May 1554 he had escaped to Antwerp. Since then he had consulted with various English groups on the continent, though it is uncertain whether he now came to Frankfurt as a commissioned agent of the Prayer Book parties at Strassburg and elsewhere. At all events, he came with John Jewel and other followers, and as befitted a former Prayer Book commissioner he had but one thought—to smash the Knox–Whittingham ascendancy at Frankfurt. At the first Sunday service after his arrival Cox created a disturbance by interjecting responses to the officiating minister. When the elders remonstrated, he and his followers made their Anglican and patriotic position very clear, saying that 'they would do as they had done in England, and that they would have the face of an English church'. Knox replied, 'The Lord grant it to have the face of Christ's Church', but he now found himself in a difficult situation; he wanted to appeal to English nationalism against Spanish Mary and yet to convert Englishmen to an international creed.[17]

On the second Sunday Cox put one of his backers into the pulpit to read the Litany, while he and his faction made the responses from the body of the church. Tempers rose to a point not far short of physical violence. Knox denounced the Prayer Book of 1552 as superstitious, impure and imperfect. Amid recriminations and fiery debates the Frankfurt congregation divided itself into 'Coxians' and 'Knoxians'. All this had happened, however, before the newcomers had obtained formal admission to the congregation, and the Knoxians confidently expected that their opponents would henceforth be excluded, so long as they refused to subscribe to the recent agreement. Then, with a moderation unexplained by our sources and utterly out of keeping with his normal fanaticism, Knox himself surprised everyone by urging their admission. Yet so far from being mollified by this strange generosity, Cox redoubled his efforts to undermine the position of his chief antagonist. During the first days of doctrinal debating he failed, and even agreed to abandon private baptism, confirmation, saints' days, kneeling at communion, surplices, crosses and other features which he admitted to be 'not papistical, but by their nature indifferent'. Unsatisfied the Knoxians demanded also the abolition of the Litany, the responses, the *Te Deum* and other parts of the Prayer Book. At this point Cox refused further concessions, and Whittingham, who had the ear of the Frankfurt magistrates, now induced them to threaten the Coxians with expulsion if they would not conform. When Cox had already begun to acknowledge defeat, one of his party, Edward Isaac of Patrixbourne in Kent, also devised a political weapon. It was an unclean one, even though it was used against a man whose own methods lacked delicacy. Isaac observed that Knox in his *Faithful Admonition* had heavily libelled Mary, Philip and the Emperor Charles. He had called Mary 'false, dissembling, inconstant, proud and a breaker of promises', averring that 'if she had been sent to hell before these days, her cruelty would not have so manifestly appeared to the world'. Her father-in-law Charles he had called 'no less an enemy to Christ than was Nero', while Philip he regarded as fully implicated in the deeds of both. When Isaac, abetted by Henry Parry, later chancellor of Salisbury Cathedral, reported these opinions of Knox to the Frankfurt authorities, they could not turn the blind eye. They were most anxious not to offend the Emperor, who had recently held their city in his power and had treated it with clemency. They therefore decided to expel Knox, who on 26 March duly left for Geneva. Thanks to this stratagem Cox had thus been carried to outright victory inside a fortnight. For a time he strove to avoid the secession of Knox's followers, but in the summer Whittingham, Gilby, Goodman, Kethe, Foxe, Sir Francis Knollys and others, having failed in renewed attempts to enlist the support of the magistrates of Frankfurt, also left the city. Most of them migrated to Geneva with the interesting results we have already described.

The triumph of Cox contributed much to the survival of Cranmer's Prayer Book, but many of his own ideas on doctrine and church government would seem to modern eyes nearer to Geneva than to Canterbury. During the struggle he too had appealed to Calvin,[18] while the new *Book of Discipline* resulting from his success derived more from the Swiss Reformers and from the foreign refugees in Edwardian London than from anything which could be discovered in the previous practice of the English Church. It envisaged not only a pastor but a powerful group of elders, who acted as censors of manners, and a number of deacons responsible for assisting the poor and visiting the sick. The conflict at Frankfurt was not a conflict between erastian prelatists and Calvinists, but between Prayer Book Puritans and Genevan Puritans. Yet in this it did but foreshadow the dichotomy within the Anglican Church during the coming half-century.

Having made plans for an English university to promote the study of theology, Cox departed for Zürich, feeling that his great work had been accomplished. Many of his supporters returned to Strassburg or Zürich, whence they had recently come to his aid. Yet Frankfurt had still to witness a second round of the contest not unrelated to the first. As soon as Cox had gone, an anti-sacerdotal party raised its head and, under circumstances somewhat obscure, forced the resignation of David Whitehead, the pastor left by Cox. In March 1556 they elected Robert Horne, the former dean of Durham, but he too became embroiled with the laymen, who were now led by John Hales, the civil servant and member of Parliament who had been so important in the party of social reform during Edward's reign. On the other side, among Horne's supporters was the rich merchant Richard Chambers, who had supported poor refugees from his own pocket and from a stream of secret subscriptions obtained from his business friends in London. Now he came under fire for his handling of the funds. But apart from such side issues the chief dispute raged over the pastor's authority over his congregation, and by February 1557 it resulted in the complete collapse of Horne's position and in the formulation of a fresh *Book of Discipline* by a committee.[19] This involved some startling principles. It made the Frankfurt congregation 'a particular visible Church',[20] in fact a self-governing body politic, owning no allegiance to monarchs or bishops and fully subordinating the authority of the minister to that of the congregation, the sole source of law. And as if to add the democratic to the congregational principle, certain of the humbler laymen, including two of Hales's servants, were now permitted to vote upon the adoption of the *Book of Discipline*.[21] With some reason it has been contended that the history of English Congregationalism and Independency begins here, rather than with Browne and Barrow. Though few of the group can have expected to impose such ideas at home, in this free context they emerged naturally enough.[22] As we have seen, they were also emerging in the surreptitious

Protestant congregations at home. At Frankfurt they even scored an initial success. Having for some time waged a running battle with his critics Horne at last withdrew to the calmer atmosphere of Strassburg, while at Frankfurt a period of relative quiet occupied the remaining months to the death of Mary.

The full importance of these events was soon to become manifest in England. Radical groups had come to birth, this time not among poor Anabaptists or neo-Lollards but among educated and opinionated men of good social standing. They had become well versed in the arts of politico-religious intrigue; they stood prepared to entertain new modes of church government and to propound relationships between Church and State inconceivable to the subjects of Henry VIII. Weaned of uncritical royalism by the actions of Queen Mary, they had begun to derive nourishment both from Presbyterian and congregationalist principles. The political thinking of men like Ponet, Knox, Goodman and Hales showed a new attitude of irreverence toward monarchy in general. The spirit we have seen in the martyrs becomes even more explicit and conscious in the exiles; it is the spirit of the self-reliant oppositionist, the man with the hard core to his mind, the man with 'civil courage', proof against even the claims of the Tudor dynasty. Though these men could not foresee the day when their descendants would crush the monarchy itself, they were determined to win every possible concession to their own viewpoint as soon as Mary should pass from the scene. Even the more conservative of the exiles looked with respect to Genevan and other Reformed ideals; for them also there could be no return at Mary's death to the world of Henry VIII, or even to that of Protector Somerset.

In stressing the immense and often neglected importance of these exiles in the history of the English Reformation we should not fail to conclude on a note of caution. While on the continent, the exiles never became a single and united party, and some Anglican historians have too neatly labelled them as a Calvinist faction. Since 1540 English Protestantism had admittedly made a massive shift from its original Lutheran inspiration, yet while the pundit of Geneva may be regarded as the strongest single influence at work in the English exile-communities, he still represented only one influence among several.[23] The appeal of the Coxians to Calvin's authority did not mean that they had enrolled in his church. Pilkington and Nowell, who were in charge of the Frankfurt congregation just before the return from the exile, rejected a proposal made by Knox, Whittingham and others at Geneva that the Prayer Book should be Calvinised and a Genevan order established as soon as possible in England. At Strassburg Grindal and Horne made a similar reply; so did Jewel and Peter Martyr at Zürich, where Martyr, the foreigner most trusted by the English, had joined forces with Bullinger. These moderates were at no stage submerged by Genevan influences. Their theology, it is true, differed little from that of Calvin. Nevertheless, they shrank from the full rigours of Genevan church government and social organisation. They were prepared to accept not only episcopacy but a considerable measure of state-control. They were loyal to Cranmer's memory and did not want a Prayer Book much more Protestant than that of 1552; indeed, they were soon to accept, provisionally at least, one less Protestant. In the last resort the importance of the Marian exiles lies in the fact that most of them were patriots who preserved Anglicanism rather than in the fact that some of them experimented with foreign and more radical ideas. When the exiles returned in 1558–9, a crucial stage in the combat had still to be fought, but neither the Catholic nor the pure Calvinist was a contender deserving to attract heavy wagers.

The Revolution of 1559[24]

As the daughter of Anne Boleyn, as a child of the Protestant humanism which had nourished Edward and Lady Jane, above all as the idol of the anti-Marian Londoners, the new Queen was deeply committed to reverse the religious settlement of her predecessor. At the moment of her accession the domestic situation was largely favourable to such a design. The Catholic bishops formed a depleted group; their strongest character, Bonner, had attracted general execration, while their moderates, like Heath and Tunstall, felt personally amicable toward Elizabeth and far from anxious to disrupt the kingdom. In the country the Catholic faction had no obvious nucleus; even in the North there existed as yet no camarilla of Catholic neo-feudalists prepared for a resort to arms. Philip's ambassador Feria estimated that the Catholic party was 'two-thirds larger than the other'.[25] Such estimates—and many were to be attempted by wishful thinkers—can only be regarded as impressionist guesses, and they presupposed in the individual a degree of clarity most untypical of this period. Elizabethan writers are for ever alleging that a high proportion of their compatriots lacked any keen sense of religion. Whatever the accuracy of Feria's conjecture, the majority of the people cannot possibly have been ardent or even convinced Catholics. Few religious revolutions have been more dramatic than that of 1558–9, yet none has encountered more feeble opposition.

The foreign situation seemed at first to demand a most cautious approach to religion. The financial and military weaknesses of the country were notorious, yet it was still at war with France and dependent upon the Spanish alliance. For some months Philip toyed with the idea of holding England by marrying Elizabeth, and it seemed most unwise to disillusion him too rapidly by taking irrevocable steps toward Protestantism. Likewise, to attract outright denunciation by Rome might do harm. The Pope soon hinted at Elizabeth's illegitimate origins and the French pressed him in this direction, since in the Dauphine Mary Stuart they controlled a rival candidate to the English throne. Again, the Lutheran states still appeared potential allies; their political and theological beliefs attracted Elizabeth and they would only be repelled by the Swiss-type Reformation advocated by the exiles now returning to England. For such reasons, secular wisdom suggested the avoidance of radical religious changes during the early months of the reign. Of the several extant papers of advice submitted to Elizabeth all save one agree on this principle of caution.[26] Sir Nicholas Throckmorton, a keen Reformer who had helped John Jewel to escape from England, urged the Queen to 'have a good eye that there be no innovations'. The prominent lawyer and official Richard Goodrich likewise hated Rome, but showed himself prepared to retain awhile the Papal Supremacy and a Catholic order of service. He and others urged that no important changes should be undertaken during the first Parliament. The exceptional paper, the *Device for the Alteration of Religion*, was written by an unknown Protestant enthusiast. It advocates the immediate establishment of a national Church with a Protestant liturgy and, since this in fact occurred, the *Device* was formerly accepted by historians as a governmental programme. On the contrary, it now seems certain that Elizabeth and her Council had decided upon caution and that they were jockeyed into a change of plan by fresh developments, especially by the unforeseen activism of the House of Commons.

That the character and personal views of the new monarch exerted a restraining force cannot be doubted. Elizabeth was an admirer but not a mental replica of her father. Theological tastes and learning were not hereditary in the family, and her education had been chiefly linguistic. Though she admired 'advanced' intellectuals like Ochino and Jacobus Acontius,[27] and though she lacked religious fervour, we have no reason to credit those who depicted her as an Italianate atheist. Such unbelievers were then very rare, even in Italy. Yet a cool humanism matched her cool temperament, and she had already seen enough of the opposing fanaticisms to inspire her with distaste for both. She leaned strongly toward external seemliness in church, liked vestments and hankered ineffectively after a celibate priesthood. She appears to have believed in a real presence in the sacrament. She cannot be credited with a prophetic latitudinarian policy which foresaw the rich diversity of Anglicanism. Her preferences of 1558–9 nevertheless made this diversity possible; perhaps no young woman of twenty-five has ever taken personal decisions having consequences so momentous. While intelligent and cautious to the point of indecision, she exuded an air of authority. 'She seems to me', wrote Feria, 'incomparably more feared than her sister, and gives her orders and has her way absolutely, as her father did.'[28] Her religion was deeply permeated by a secular idealism which related to her office, to England, to the well-being of the subjects committed to her charge by a very English Deity. She was a consummate actress who looked convincing, even to zealots, when she kissed the Bible in public. She had the inestimable advantage of understanding Englishmen far better than Calvin, or Philip, or Mary Stuart; more clearly than the other Tudors she perceived their hunger for romance without expense.

This range of ideas had nothing in common with the internationalism of Geneva. Its religious content related to the kingdom of England, to some sort of Royal Supremacy and to the accepted medieval and Renaissance concepts of a society based, like the world of Nature itself, on order, degree and hierarchy. The old clerical pyramid extending from archbishops down to deacons and parish clerks may seem to modern observers little more than a mirrored image of feudal society, but to a national ruler of Elizabeth's day it continued to correspond in considerable measure with the facts of life and the needs of monarchy. Elizabeth was called to rule not a city-state, but a still half-feudal and largely rural nation. To preserve sovereignty and the chain of command it was safer to retain the clerical hierarchy and somehow to reconcile it with the aspirations of the squires and merchants, who had grown rich and numerous within the secular hierarchy and had substituted themselves for its former baronial pillars.

Inevitably, after the disorders and humiliations of the last decade, the figure of Henry VIII looked more commanding than any other which sprang to Elizabeth's imagination. The fact that she 'gloried' in her father might form a more valuable clue to her psychology than has yet been realised. But when she suggested to Feria that she would restore the religious position of Henry VIII,[29] she must have been impressing him with her conservatism rather than announcing a serious intention. At this stage one could not plan to deprive the Marian bishops and yet go back to the Six Articles. Even the most conservative of her immediate plans involved communion for the laity in both kinds, and other proposals which Henry had never sanctioned. When, however, she praised to Feria the Confession of Augsburg and professed her belief in a real presence, she probably voiced her actual opinions. Other evidence suggests that she may have considered taking the conservative Prayer Book of 1549 as a basis of reconciliation between those two important groups,[30] the Prayer Book Protestants and the many Catholics who lacked much enthusiasm for papalism. But even the former, the Coxians, would not accept this starting-point—no group of the returning exiles wanted a basis more conservative than that contained in the Book of 1552. 'Now is the time for the walls of Jerusalem to be built again in that kingdom, that the blood of so many martyrs, so largely shed, may not be in vain.' Men who had just been writing in this strain had no intention of returning to the Augsburg Confession or to a Prayer Book almost accepted by the late Bishop Gardiner.

During the early weeks of the reign Elizabeth does not appear to have been under heavy pressures from her Privy Council; like herself they were cautious people, waiting for a wind. As yet they included no divines in a position to carry weight. She excluded fifteen of Mary's Council while keeping eleven of the more pliant characters.[31] The seven newcomers were lay politicians inclined to a moderate Protestantism, chief among them Sir William Cecil, whom she immediately summoned to the office of Secretary and so to that wonderful partnership of forty years. Nevertheless, the settlement agreed upon by Parliament did not spring from the brains of Elizabeth and Cecil; it was a compromise made by them with the militant group of Protestants in the Commons. In no sense did it arise from a Catholic-versus-Protestant tension. By a whole series of actions before Parliament met Elizabeth showed her personal and independent desire for a non-Catholic settlement. Pending parliamentary recognition she kept open her claim to the Royal Supremacy by adding '&c' after her royal titles. She chose William Bill, a noted Protestant, to be the first preacher at Paul's Cross, and she imprisoned a Catholic who answered him too fiercely. On Christmas Day she commanded Bishop Oglethorpe to omit the elevation of the host at mass, and on his refusal she left the chapel. On 15 January 1559 at the coronation service, Oglethorpe repeated his action and the Queen her withdrawal. A few days later, at the state opening of Parliament, she rudely ordered the abbot and monks of Westminster to extinguish their ceremonial tapers. 'Away with those torches, we can see well enough!' On the first day of its meeting the chosen preacher was none other than Dr. Richard Cox, who thundered at quite inordinate length. Already on 31 January Feria was writing to Philip that 'the Catholics are very fearful of the measures to be taken in this Parliament'.[32] All these hints were deliberately given by Elizabeth before she began to come under parliamentary pressure. However remote from Geneva, she intended from the first to figure in the character of a Protestant monarch. Whatever her pretences, one finds it almost impossible to believe that at any stage she seriously contemplated a concordat with Rome or even a return to her father's brand of conservative orthodoxy.

That the Parliament which began on 25 January 1559 was not packed, Mr. Bayne proved many years ago,[33] and the fact is now accepted by all serious students of parliamentary history. The elections were not even preceded by circular letters attempting to influence the composition of the Commons, about a third of whom had sat in Mary's last Parliament. No Catholic group emerged to oppose the Protestant activists, who from the first days showed themselves vigorous, vocal and well organised. In the Lords a different situation obtained. The lay peers included very few enthusiastic Protestants, yet the whole body was small, most of the peers being office-holders or otherwise closely connected with the court, men traditionally reluctant to stand in opposition to the monarchy. Only one lay peer, Lord Montague, steadily voted along Romanist lines. In contrast, the Marian bishops voted consistently against all Reforming legislation. Some attended very seldom, but all behaved with dignity and courage, knowing they would be overwhelmed, uncertain that they would be handled with mercy. They also desired to be patriotic Englishmen; they were concerned to obey their consciences rather than to provoke unrest. When Bishop Scott of Chester, one of the most convinced papalists, opposed the new Act of Supremacy, he confessed he felt restrained from forceful speaking through respect to the Queen, 'unto whom I do acknowledge that I owe obedience, not only for wrath and displeasure's sake, but for conscience sake, and that by the Scriptures of God'.[34] The real problems concerning the revolution hence relate to events in the Commons, the records of which are regrettably laconic and sometimes difficult to harmonise. With great ingenuity Sir John Neale has resolved nearly all the difficulties; other historians have suggested some amendments of detail,[35] but it seems improbable that any more satisfying general hypothesis will appear.

On 9 February the government introduced into the Commons 'a bill to restore the supremacy of the Church of England to the Crown of the realm'. It is assumed that, like the final Statute, this bill contained a section allowing the laity communion in both kinds. Yet such a provision would have been redundant if the government had intended during this first session to produce an Act of Uniformity imposing a fully Protestant Prayer Book. Therefore it appears that the government had accepted the pleas for caution and planned a piecemeal Reformation. Had this slow pace been maintained, a Catholic service, tempered for Protestants by lay communion in both kinds, would have been permitted at least until the next Parliament. The government had still no ecclesiastical advisers and it does not appear to have worked out interim liturgical plans in any detail. Having dissolved this Parliament it presumably intended to deprive the Marian bishops and other potential leaders of reaction by enforcing the oath of Supremacy. Then, alongside the next Parliament, it could easily have passed a Protestant Prayer Book through a Convocation purged of Catholics.

The Protestant group which sought to alter this leisurely plan was certainly headed by a group of Marian exiles, though not by those from Geneva, who had been among the last to hear of Mary's death and whose distrustful leaders did not arrive in time to influence the proceedings. John Knox, having so deeply offended the Queen by his writings, was not permitted to re-enter

England; Goodman, who had given almost equal offence, speedily went to Scotland and did not see England again until 1565. Whittingham returned only in the summer of 1560 and Coverdale in the autumn of 1559. On the other hand, the Coxian or Prayer Book exiles were well represented in the Commons. Our list of members is far from complete, but of the actual exiles we have twelve names for certain and another four probables. There may have been still more. They were led by Sir Anthony Cooke and Sir Francis Knollys, whose influential connections we have already mentioned. Knollys in particular was to figure for many years among the most ardent Puritan laymen of the reign. If these members faltered, they had around them their spiritual directors, Cox, Jewel, Sandys, Grindal, Scory and others, who are likely to have been in London during the sessions.[36] These men were very able, very determined and fully conscious that the decisive moment had arrived. In addition to this spearhead of exiles the crypto-Protestant members of Mary's obstreperous Parliament of 1555 were still present in some force. At the most cautious estimate, a quarter of the 404 members are likely to have felt disappointed at the slow tempo proposed by the government.[37] Unopposed by any comparable nucleus of Catholics, undistracted by the Genevans, the Protestant group swept the uncommitted majority along the path of Reformation. Feria suggested that Cecil himself abetted them, all unknown to the Queen.[38] If so, one may be sure that he did it with enormous discretion.

Led by Cooke the Commons seized upon the government's Supremacy bill, and when by 21 February it emerged from the committee stage, it was found to have been drastically re-written. It had been greatly extended to cover a Protestant form of service, becoming in effect a measure both of Supremacy and of Uniformity. The actual text of this amendment has not been preserved, but it appears to have revived Edward's second Act of Uniformity, the Prayer Book of 1552 and the Act permitting the marriage of the clergy. It also aimed to stiffen the penalties for refusing the oath of Supremacy. Having sent up the transformed bill to the Lords, the Commons on 27 February embarked on a new scheme—the revival of Cranmer's old committee to reform the canon law. Here they may well have designed to give authority to the abortive *Reformatio Legum*, the document which had seemed too radical even for the Duke of Northumberland. The Queen regarded such notions with distaste, and this bill cannot have been conceived by the government.

When on 13–18 March the Supremacy bill was debated by the Lords, a committee of that House, no doubt acting in concert with the government, restored it to its previous tepid form, in which it received support by all save the bishops and a couple of Catholic peers. To this damping manœuvre the reaction of the Commons proved vigorous. Without waiting for the emasculated bill to return to them they swiftly produced a counter-measure to legalise immediate Protestant worship: 'that no persons shall be punished for using the religion used in King Edward's last year'. This they cannot seriously have expected to impose upon the Lords, and their intention must rather have been to assure the Court of their defiant determination. They remained nevertheless astute enough to avoid running risks and giving gross offence by voting down the Lords' Supremacy bill; when it returned, they let it through, and by 22 March it awaited the royal assent. Pending its publication, the Queen issued on that day a proclamation allowing communion in both kinds, and she was still preparing to dissolve or prorogue Parliament before Easter. Perhaps she intended to summon another to continue the work in the autumn, when the balance of public opinion and of the political forces at home and abroad might be better assessed. During the interval, armed with the Supremacy, she would no doubt have sanctioned on her own initiative some form of English service, since she attended an English communion in her own chapel at Easter. Whatever the case, between 23 and 24 March—literally overnight—she altered her mind and instead of dissolving Parliament merely adjourned it to 3 April. The actual arguments which prompted this dramatic change of front are not recorded, but some powerful ones can easily be deduced.

The foreign situation had hitherto supplied weighty reasons for gradualism, but it had now markedly improved. On 19 March had arrived the reassuring news that France had concluded the Peace of Cateau-Cambrésis with Spain and England. The domestic position had also altered since the meeting of Parliament, and the aggressive unity of the Commons probably emboldened their sympathisers on the Council to speak more freely with the hesitant Queen. Cecil, Bacon, Parry, Knollys and the Earl of Bedford all belonged to this category, and the first three stood among her closest associates. The business of a Tudor government was to supply confident leadership, and none of these shrewd men can now have felt entirely happy to dismiss Parliament with the crucial problem of public worship still undecided. Perhaps at this stage they made Elizabeth see more clearly her dependence upon the Protestant divines for her Church. With what other human materials could she build it? By now everyone knew that the Marian prelates would refuse all co-operation, and their removal left the rest of the clergy a compliant but lukewarm, leaderless and intellectually undistinguished body, an army of private soldiers incapable, except under new officers, of commanding respect at home or abroad.

Elizabeth's dependence on the former exiles found at this moment a plain illustration. On 20 March she agreed to a conference or disputation between representative Catholic and Protestant divines, and she chose all except one of the latter from among the exiles. These men, Scory, Cox, Sandys, Grindal, Horne, Aylmer, Jewel and Whitehead, were soon, with the single exception of the last, to be her new bishops. The eighth disputant was Edmund Guest, who had emulated Matthew Parker by lying low during Mary's reign.[39] The Queen and her advisers did not love exiles as such; the fact remained that the moderates among these men had become indispensable because of their exceptional opportunities to acquire a viable Protestant theology and because their seniors had perished in the Marian persecution.

The actual conference held in the choir of Westminster Abbey on 31 March and 3 April proved a fiasco. It was not intended to afford the Catholics a fair opportunity to put their case before the nation but simply to deprive them of the plea that they had been suppressed without a hearing. The Protestants drew up the articles for debate, and they were listed by Jewel in a letter:

> Our first proposition is, that it is contrary to the word of God, and the practice of the primitive church, to use in the public prayers and administration of the sacraments any other language than what is understood by the people. The second is, that every provincial church, even without the bidding of a general council, has power either to establish, or change, or abrogate ceremonies and ecclesiastical rites, wherever it may seem to make for edification. The third is, that the propitiatory sacrifice, which the papists pretend to be in the mass, cannot be proved by the holy Scriptures.[40]

These points do not lack a general significance as bases of the Anglican position, but the second was also designed to force the Catholics into the open. They could not accept it without renouncing Rome, yet if they opposed it they would risk becoming involved in treason. It is hence not surprising that they created procedural difficulties and brought the conference to an abortive end on its second day. Here, however, they may have served their cause less effectively than by disputation, since their refusal enabled the government to depict them both as contumacious and as incompetent to defend their standpoint. In any case, two of their abler spokesmen, Bishops White of Winchester and Watson of Lincoln, soon found themselves in the Tower.

On reassembling after the adjournment the Commons again showed their spirit when they tried on their own initiative to restore the clergy dispossessed by Mary. This bill the Lords rejected, no doubt with the Queen's approval. The Commons then drafted a bill to abolish the restored monasteries, their violent anti-Catholic phraseology contrasting with the restraint of government-sponsored legislation. Meanwhile the government was introducing into the Lords a measure of its own, enabling the Crown during vacancies of episcopal sees to subtract estates from them and assign them, in exchange, tenths, tithes and impropriated benefices of equal value—equal as estimated by royal commissioners. For obvious reasons, a large element among the laity was still prepared to allow further profiteering exploits against the bishops. In Cecil's case something more than a financial motive was involved, for this worthy successor of Thomas Cromwell once said that the way to reduce the political power of the Church was to diminish its wealth. Nevertheless, many zealous Protestants no longer shared this view, and the ninety members who opposed the bill appear to have represented that Reformed element which protested throughout the reign against impoverishing the Church. And once they were appointed, the new Protestant bishops also protested, though in vain.[41]

The remaining important events of the session after Easter revolved around the two central measures of Supremacy and Uniformity. In the matter of the Supremacy Elizabeth had again changed her mind and had decided—it was said on the representations of Thomas Lever[42]—to drop the title of Supreme Head and accept that of Supreme Governor. The former seemed inappropriate to an age better attuned to the anti-feminist views of St. Paul than to the advantages of female sovereigns. A third Supremacy bill embodying this change was drafted, and after some minor conservative amendments in the Lords and some Protestant ones in the Commons it duly passed before the end of April.

This prophetic measure[43] repealed the Marian Statutes which had reinstated Roman jurisdiction and the heresy laws. It revived ten statutes of Henry VIII, including those of Annates and Appeals; by consequence it restored the Henrician mode of electing bishops by *congé d'élire* and not the Edwardian method of appointment by letters patent. It abolished all 'usurped and foreign' jurisdictions; it authorised the Queen to visit and correct the Church through her commissioners. This last section formed the basis of Elizabeth's various ecclesiastical commissions, especially the High Commission and its now better-documented equivalent for the Province of York. The Act showed its lay origins by the careful limitations which it placed upon the powers of such ecclesiastical commissioners. They were to adjudge no matter to be heresy except upon the authority of the canonical Scriptures, of the first four General Councils of the Church or of the English High Court of Parliament, with the assent of the clergy in Convocation. The Act imposed an oath of Supremacy upon all ecclesiastical persons and upon all judges, justices, mayors and other officers of the State. Loss of benefice or office would follow refusal. The oath was also to be tendered to those about to enter into office, and even to men taking holy orders or university degrees. Again, persons maintaining any foreign authority would lose all their properties or benefices for a first offence. For a second they would fall under the penalties of *Praemunire*. For a third the penalties of high treason would follow.

What sort of Supremacy emerged from this Act? The Queen later took pains to depict it as identical with that wielded by her father, but under James I the great jurist John Selden rightly thought otherwise. 'There's a great difference between head of the Church and supreme governor, as our canons call the King . . . Conceive it thus, there is in the Kingdom of England a college of physicians: the King is supreme governor of those, but not head of them, nor president of the college, nor the best physician.'[44] If this description fitted Elizabeth and James, it would not have fitted Henry VIII, who saw himself as the functioning head of his Church and chief physician to the souls of his subjects. Over matters of dogma and ritual Elizabeth did not exercise this same personal and quasi-papal control. Moreover, she had a partner. Parliament, having enhanced its status during the minority of her brother, was becoming a co-ordinate power rather than an agent. Parliament now defined certain aspects of the Queen's legal authority over the Church. In effect, it told her to act through ecclesiastical commissioners and it defined rather narrowly their powers. Never again could England see a vicegerent like Thomas Cromwell, a personal deputy of the King, lording it over the episcopate in Convocation. And while Elizabeth took no small part in controlling the policies of the Anglican Church, she exercised her influence indirectly, often covertly and with an infuriating reluctance to appear responsible for contentious rulings. No longer was the throne occupied by a crowned theologian, confounding Parliaments and bishops with God's learning; its occupant was an adroit and devious politician, operating through the interstices of Statute Law.

Meanwhile, as the government reviewed the vital matter of public worship, it became ever more apparent that the Prayer Book of 1552 must inevitably form the basis for negotiation with the Protestant divines, who were all serious Reformers, as deeply committed by their past conduct as the Marian bishops themselves. Admittedly the Queen had bishoprics to offer them, but they would have faced ignominy among their friends as well as pangs of conscience had they even agreed to discuss the Prayer Book of 1549. Almost nothing is known about the deliberations of the committee which took instead the Book of 1552 and agreed to certain changes in its text. These changes were few in number but considerable in significance; they were all designed to meet the Queen's political needs and her conservative tastes. Offensive references to the Pope disappeared. A remarkable latitude of eucharistic belief was allowed by prefixing the 1549 words of administration: 'The body of our Lord Jesus Christ, which was given for thee . . .', to the words of 1552: 'Take and eat this in remembrance . . .' Likewise the new Book omitted the Knoxian 'Black Rubric', which had explained away the practice of kneeling at the reception of communion. These two provisions retained commemorative phraseology, yet reopened the way for belief in a real presence falling short of transubstantiation. Thanks in part to a shift of interest among Protestants this bold solution was to raise surprisingly little contention in Elizabethan times.

A very different future awaited the other important change made in the Book of 1552—the notorious Ornaments Rubric inserted before Morning and Evening Prayer. Instead of preserving the rubric of 1552 (that the minister should never wear alb, vestment or cope) it ordered that the ornaments of the church and the ministers should be those in use 'by authority of Parliament, in the second year of the reign of King Edward VI'. Here was an odd inaccuracy, since the Book of 1549 had been authorised in the third year of King Edward. Moreover, the Act of Uniformity which accompanied Elizabeth's new Book added that these ornaments should continue in use 'until other order shall be therein taken by the authority of the Queen's majesty, with the advice of her commissioners . . . for causes ecclesiastical, or of the Metropolitan of this realm'. The Reformers leapt to the mistaken conclusion that the Queen did not intend to press upon them the obnoxious vestments of 1549. 'Our gloss upon this text', wrote Edwin Sandys, 'is that we shall not be forced to use them.'[45] On the contrary, the Queen, no doubt nettled by their thrustful tactics, proceeded to hold them to their bargain. This misunderstanding soon led to a renewal of the hostilities first provoked by the scruples of John Hooper. Cox, Sandys and Jewel were also to quarrel with the Queen over the ornaments of her chapel, the last two almost to the point of losing their bishoprics. The Vestiarian Controversy formed merely the first of a series of intermittent clashes over vestments lasting until our own times. Blundering attempts to obtain a legal decision succeeded only in creating more complex and irrational situations, while in recent times uniformity would have involved violence toward one or more of the major schools of thought within the Anglican communion.

The penalties under the Act of Uniformity were graduated similarly to those of the Edwardian Acts, but made in some particulars rather more severe. Forms of service other than those in the new Prayer Book were forbidden and clerics attempting to use them became liable to deprivation of all benefices for a year and to imprisonment for six months. For a second offence the penalties were permanent deprivation and a year's imprisonment; for a third, life imprisonment. Those openly attacking the Book were liable to fines of 100 marks (£66 13s. 4d.) in the first instance, 400 marks in the second, total forfeiture of goods and life imprisonment in the third. Absentees from church must now forfeit the sum of one shilling per Sunday, to be levied by the churchwardens and used to help the poor. The Act also empowered the judges of assize and municipal officers to seek out and punish all these offences. The bishops were authorised to co-operate with the justices, while retaining in addition their ecclesiastical jurisdiction.[46]

Despite the opposition of the Marian bishops this Act of Uniformity enjoyed as rapid a passage through the Lords as through the Commons. Nine lay peers voted against it; with one or two exceptions they were not Romanists but conservatives who probably thought to please the Queen by demonstrating against a measure forced upon her by radical opinion in the Commons. In thus interpreting her view they may well have been correct, but on the whole she had little reason to complain. She had gained as much as possible from a difficult situation, and probably far more than would have been possible at any later stage of her reign. This legislation cannot be called a victory for either side actually engaged in the tussle, yet it was certainly a defeat for a third force—that of the Genevans, who had not been able to deploy their strength in the parliamentary arena. Their day had yet to come. Under their guidance English Puritanism had before it a long period of steady advance. It soon became fashionable to regard the Elizabethan Settlement as running a middle course between Rome and Geneva, but so far as concerns the very decisive contest of 1559 both these great powers were non-starters. It would be vastly more accurate to call the Settlement a middle way between the personal prejudices of Queen Elizabeth and those entertained by Dr. Richard Cox and his ebullient friends in the House of Commons.

The four years following the parliamentary decision saw the Queen, under the patient diplomatic protection of Philip II, carefully completing the foundations of the Elizabethan Church. As her first Primate she could have made no cleverer choice than her former tutor Matthew Parker, modest and retiring in his reluctance to assume office, judicious and tolerant in its exercise; as a non-exile free from rigid continental allegiances, as a historian and antiquarian not overmuch entangled in bitter doctrinal controversy. His chief colleague John Jewel proved not only a model bishop of Salisbury but a most able defender of the national Church in his *Apologia Ecclesiae Anglicanae* (1562). There followed a literary event of still more momentous consequences—the publication in 1563 of the first English edition of John Foxe's *Acts and Monuments*, which lay for many generations alongside the Bible and the Prayer Book in countless gentle, clerical and middle-class houses, even in those where other books seldom intruded. In the same year the Edwardian Articles of Religion were revised and reissued as the Thirty-nine, though without modification of their essentials. Yet only one early Elizabethan event can compare in broad historical importance with the parliamentary actions of 1559. This event was Elizabeth's well-timed intervention in Scotland. In July 1560 her expedition culminated in the Treaty of Edinburgh, driving French influence from the northern kingdom and placing control in the hands of John Knox, William Maitland of Lethington and the Protestant Lords of the Congregation. Thereafter Mary Stuart failed to prevent the steady convergence of the two countries, which continued its triumphal march through history past the milestones of 1603, 1643 and 1707. The master-stroke of 1560 opened the way for Knox's second and more profound contribution to the English Reformation, since the influences which thereafter flowed between the two kingdoms were by no means one-sided. Moreover, this convergence meant that the overseas western world would at last be pervaded by a British Protestantism more broadly based, and more securely linked to Reformed beliefs, than the original Anglican Settlement of Elizabeth. In defending the latter politically, the Queen had changed its future religious environment and alliances more radically than she or any Elizabethan could realise.

13 The Residual Problems

The Anglican Church

THE ELIZABETHAN SETTLEMENT was less a pacification than a compromise between contending forces which Elizabeth and her Stuart successors failed to reconcile. The gradual consolidation of an Anglican Church must nevertheless be numbered among the achievements of this versatile age. As a Christian body it was neither created nor re-created by the Statutes of Supremacy and Uniformity, and even when the Queen died its full potential was still hard to discern. By then Richard Hooker's *Laws of Ecclesiastical Polity*[1] had gone far to accomplish such a feat of prophecy, but the Church had not yet achieved that poise between Protestant and Catholic ideals which Hooker desired to see. In its spiritual realities it had hitherto been not merely a Protestant, but in remarkable degree a Puritan Church. And scarcely had it begun to understand Hooker's dream when the miscalculations of its ill-chosen leaders involved it in well-nigh fatal disaster.

Between the accession of Elizabeth and the Civil Wars the Church of England became in many respects well adapted to its place and period. It proved less socially and intellectually oppressive than most churches of that day. By the limited standards of the period it allowed very considerable freedom for experiment and speculation. Born in years of internal tension, growing to maturity amid cultural ferment and alongside a great national literature, it had little chance to relapse into the dull pietism which beset some state-churches. While gratifying the general demand for a centralised Church coterminous with the nation, it also left room for some real divergences of outlook. It could produce a few saints; it could not merely tolerate but foster a number of geniuses. It could find work for individualists more easily than either Rome or Geneva; even among its clergy it could admit John Donne and Robert Herrick as well as Nicholas Ferrar and George Herbert. Since the days of Edward VI its devotional appeal had never been limited to the educated classes and, though it was slow to convert certain remote areas of the kingdom, its hold upon the people steadily strengthened and its Prayer Book became widely loved. Alongside its disappointing failures it inevitably made some progress in the tasks of practical reform, for both in Catholic and in Protestant countries organised religion now manifested a growing spirit of integrity, consistency, devotion and discipline. In England, if reforms owed much to Puritan idealism and agitation, some of them must also be credited to the bishops and their officials, whose assiduity becomes more apparent as we familiarise ourselves with hitherto unknown archives in the diocesan registries. Here we see officialdom striving to ensure regular services, audible reading and at least quarterly sermons, to provide complete church furniture, to enforce peaceable and reverent behaviour by the laity, to remove superstitious objects and customs.

The chief problem before the Elizabethan bishops was the education of clergy, and several set a praiseworthy example by the examinations and other modes of pressure which they applied.[2] Their efforts, together with the growing influx of graduates, the rise of public literacy, the increasing plenitude of books on all subjects, had made a real impact on the clergy by the middle of the reign. The bishops continued to complain about their poor latinity, but the book-lists of many country parsons suggest that both general and scriptural knowledge were expanding in consonance with the growing opportunities of the period. The proportion of graduates varied greatly from one area to another, but everywhere it grew. In the diocese of Worcester it was nineteen per cent in 1560, twenty-three per cent in 1580, fifty-two per cent in 1620 and eighty-four per cent in 1640. This seems to represent a more typical growth than that in the favoured diocese of Oxford, where in the same period the figures increase from thirty-eight per cent in 1560 to ninety-six per cent in 1640.[3] From the outset of the Reformation—and this would also have happened had England remained Catholic—the old fringe of disreputable and criminous clerks had been gradually falling away. Elizabethan England at least attained Sir Thomas More's modest ambition—a less numerous but more respectable clergy.

Concerning the Elizabethan bishops, we generalise and moralise at our peril.[4] They ranged from near-saints to worldly courtiers. Most had middle-class origins and, in an age of climbers, few wholly freed themselves from the habits of social ambition. Several were nepotists, who strained the resources of their sees in order to establish their children in the charmed circle of county families. A few obtained preferment by methods little short of simony. Yet alongside such behaviour, even the less admirable contrived to appear devout and to achieve a minimum respectability. While the bishops remained dutiful servants of the monarchy, they resided in their dioceses to a greater extent than did their medieval predecessors. Few held high office under the

Crown, and their secular duties resembled those of justices of the peace rather than those of ambassadors or officers of state. Amid many enemies and still more dangerous friends they did their duty by Church and country. It would be pleasant to record that their ability and wisdom improved along with those of their clergy, but in fact the team which served Charles I was weaker than that which served Elizabeth at any part of her reign.

The darkest aspects of the Anglican Church resulted from its failure to solve the financial problems which so gravely impaired its efficiency and its morale. These material cares, recently depicted with fine scholarship by Mr. Hill,[5] deserve a more detailed treatment than we can here attempt, for they had hitherto been underweighted by less realistic historians. They sprang from a fundamental inconsistency in the outlook of the official and moneyed classes. The new religious emphases lay heavily upon preaching. This fact and the rising standards of public education demanded a more learned ministry, which demanded in turn a larger, more buoyant financial provision in order to attract the ablest men and to maintain their standards in an age of steady inflation. This need obtained widespread recognition, but it disposed few laymen to make financial sacrifices. Their knowledge that the Church had already sustained great material losses did not cure their itch to exploit its resources. Like her brother and her father Elizabeth often granted long and favourable leases of episcopal lands to officials and courtiers. The bishops were constrained to accept these unfavourable bargains through their own need for royal favours and for popularity among influential laymen. Again, an ill-considered parliamentary Act of 1549[6] had exempted various classes of former tithe-payers, and had made tithes more difficult to collect. In any case, while they could be assessed on agricultural produce, no one could seriously pretend to estimate the 'new' wealth born of rising trade and industry; hence in the cities the continued payment of personal tithe depended upon the elastic consciences of the payers. To this problem the common law courts now proceeded to contribute; having asserted their right to a share in the tithe-cases, these courts refused to enforce clerical claims except where formal contracts could be produced.

Meanwhile, the gentry who had succeeded the monks as holders of impropriated benefices continued to allow vicars only the small tithes or, in unendowed vicarages, to pay them meagre stipends. The stingy squire who paid and treated his vicar as a superior servant and who neglected his share in the church repairs was far from universal, yet he was not uncommon. The Reformation brought into the landed classes many small men, who could not begin to emulate the old barons and bishops as patrons. A process which was otherwise politically and even socially beneficial did not thereby help to repair the endowment of the Church. Sometimes the impropriator had little to spare and saw no reason to be generous over what was in essence a business deal, for impropriated livings continued to be freely bought and sold by laymen. In 1603 these benefices were estimated by the bishops to number 3,849 out of a total of about 9,284.[7] As we have seen, the economic experiences of the parish clergy varied most widely. There nevertheless remained too many livings incapable of supporting men dedicated to study and preaching rather than to farming or some other remunerative sideline. Again, as the bishops never tired of saying, poverty diminished the standing of the Church in a materialist world. It was not so much absolute indigence as failure to keep pace with rising lay standards which prejudiced careers in the Church. In several of the richer and more Puritan towns preachers were independently maintained by the corporations at high salaries. On the other hand it was not unknown for prosperous laymen to make hypocritical reference to the spiritual benefits of clerical austerity, while both White Kennett and Sir Thomas Wilson wondered whether Elizabeth deliberately kept the clergy poor in order to preserve their utter dependence on the Crown.[8] She was not in fact wholly oblivious to the political importance of a preaching clergy, and in 1599 she endowed four stipendiary preachers with annual incomes of £50 each in order to maintain the Settlement in semi-Catholic Lancashire. But this gesture strained her limited generosity, and it was not followed up in other unreliable areas. While James I realised more clearly the common interest which should have bound together Church and Crown, by his time it had become almost impossible to dip into the pockets of ungenerous and impecunious laymen. In due course Archbishop Laud made vigorous efforts to recover impropriations and force the citizens of London to pay tithe,[9] but he had gathered little beyond some additional hatred by the time his rule collapsed. Even after the Restoration no radical reform was forthcoming, and the crisis of endowments lingered on to be partially solved by piecemeal augmentations and by Queen Anne's Bounty. That there remained poor incumbents, and gross inequities as between one incumbent and another, should not be blamed purely upon our medieval and Tudor ancestors, since under more favourable circumstances later generations have continued to tolerate so much of the muddle and injustice bequeathed to the national Church by the past. This sombre story serves as one of many reminders that the Reformation had very real limits upon its power to reform, yet we should view with scepticism those theories which blame a supposed Protestant deprecation of good works. Protestantism even at its most uncompromising never disbelieved in good works; it merely disbelieved that they availed to justify or save the doer. If our Elizabethans lacked generosity toward the Church, in the field of secular charity—including education—good works continued to abound. Moreover, those who truly believed in Protestant religion were loudest in their condemnation of covetous impropriators and exploiting courtiers. Elizabethan and Jacobean Puritans understood well enough that the further spoliation of the Church must end by injuring religion itself. Whereas at least some of the financial scandals of the medieval Church had arisen from actual abuses of Catholic doctrine, those of the Anglican Church cannot accurately be dignified by theological explanations, for they were the patent offspring of Mammon.

The Catholics

OF the external threats presented to the Settlement that of Catholicism remained insignificant for a decade. It then assumed menacing proportions between 1569 and 1588, yet was largely contained by the end of the reign.[10] When in the summer of 1559 Elizabeth's commissioners toured the provinces, they found an insignificant number of Catholic clergy venturing to refuse the oath of Supremacy.[11] Men as conservative as Robert Parkyn continued in their benefices till death removed them. During the first years some of the more nominal conformists may have been saying masses in secret to groups of Catholics, yet little open defiance appeared. When at last in 1569 a Catholic-feudal rebellion arose, it completely failed to engage more than a small section of northern England and did not even come near to capturing York. Until the papal bull of 1570 excommunicated Elizabeth and urged her subjects to depose her, Catholic recusancy scarcely existed upon any measurable scale. English Catholicism was re-created during the last three decades of the reign by the adventurous labours of the Seminarists and Jesuits. Their work was rendered vastly more difficult by the violence of the bull which the Pope issued in direct contravention of Philip's cautious advice. Inevitably the Seminarists were declared traitors by English law, and when one of them was captured, the magistrates commonly asked him: 'If the Pope and the King of Spain landed in England, for whom would you fight?' Even the most resolute found the question difficult, for how many Englishmen would accept conversion at the point of the Spanish pike or risk seeing in their own country the horrors of the French Wars of Religion? Seen as individuals, these missionaries are true heroes and martyrs, yet the fact remains that they were sent by superiors and rulers with every intention of using their work as a basis for the forcible imposition of a foreign Catholic monarch upon England. The practical difficulty before the government was to distinguish between the small minority of Catholics which concerted murder-plots against the Queen, and the great majority which wanted somehow to combine the two loyalties and which duly demonstrated its political allegiance to Elizabeth during the Armada year. Caught between the millstones of State and Papacy a steady stream of priests suffered with admirable fortitude the atrocious deaths of traitors.

During the eighties and nineties under missionary influence the number of recusants grew apace in certain areas of England; they were devoted people prepared to risk imprisonment and the theoretically overwhelming but slackly enforced fines imposed by the Statute of 1581.[12] Except in Lancashire,[13] these open Catholics constituted a very small part of the population. For Yorkshire we happen to possess a census of recusants compiled in 1604 with exceptional thoroughness and care.[14] Their numbers had of late shown a sudden increase, because of their hopes that the new King would inaugurate a policy of toleration. In this large area, which contained several of the major Catholic districts in England, the recusants achieved a total of less than 3,500 in a population of more then 300,000. Even this small figure contained several hundred people who attended the Anglican matins and evensong but who refused to communicate. In most parts of England there must also have existed a fringe of sympathisers, deterred from open defiance by the fear of fines; yet since Tudor officialdom did not compile psychological surveys, no one can pretend to estimate their number. There seems, however, no reason to suppose that these so-called church-papists remained very numerous toward the end of the reign. The new English Catholicism developed a certain aristocratic distinction and background. The priests, its creators, sprang from gentle families which sent their sons abroad to be trained in Cardinal Allen's colleges or by the Jesuits. Returning on the perilous 'English Mission' they passed in disguise from one country house to another, these being the chief places of concealment in a countryside where all newcomers were conspicuous.[15] Accordingly, a large part of their converts came from the families, servants and tenants of Catholic squires.

The greater dangers presented by the Counter-Reformation did not, however, lie in recusancy but in the assassination-plots directed against the Queen and in the threat of a foreign invasion which would tempt English Catholics to desert their national allegiance. For many years one of Cecil's recurring nightmares might appropriately have appeared in diagrammatic form—a map of western Europe, with one arrow stretching from Spain to Ireland, a second from Ireland to Lancashire and a third from Lancashire to London.[16] Yet thanks in large part to the immense preoccupations and the naval weakness of Spain this diagram never developed into military fact. English Catholicism looked, in short, more formidable than it was, and its adherents suffered accordingly. Already identified in patriotic Elizabethan minds with foreign powers, it had to attempt the reconversion of England from bases in enemy territory and in league with conspiracy against the only possible English government. The devotion of its laity and the heroism of its priesthood, great as they were, could not accomplish an impossible task.

Puritanism: A Brief Anatomy

WHEREAS the Catholics were dangerous to Elizabeth through external forces, the Puritan problem remained internal, not only to English society but to the English Church itself.[17] And that Puritanism contained heavier explosive charges than Catholicism, the history of the seventeenth century was to demonstrate. Since its inception the term has been used in various senses. If we narrow it to Separatism and Presbyterianism, it lacks any formidable content until after 1640. The earlier Separatists like Robert Harrison, Robert Browne and John Penry represented, together with the congregations in London and Norwich, a minute element in the religious life of their own day. Cartwright's Presbyterianism and the Marprelate Tracts occupied only one short period of Elizabeth's reign, and the former attained no serious renewal until the era of the Civil Wars. Most modern historians have recognised the essential unity of a greater phenomenon by giving the term Puritanism a far wider scope. This was, wrote Trevelyan, 'the religion of all those who wished either to purify the usage of the established Church from the taint of popery, or to worship separately by forms so purified'. At least since the eighteenth century, such wide definitions have been common because they are useful and significant. When Daniel Neal and Benjamin Brook compiled their immense biographical collections of the great Puritans, they were very largely writing about Calvinistic clergymen of the Anglican Church.[18]

If we so define the phenomenon, it seems most inaccurate to see in the reign of Elizabeth a conflict between 'Anglicanism' and 'Puritanism'. Parker and Jewel were in very real senses forerunners of the 'balanced' Anglicanism of Hooker, yet even so the vast majority of Elizabethan Englishmen who cared deeply about religion were either Roman Catholics or Anglican Puritans. Until 1600 or later that spirituality within the Anglican Church which could reasonably be described as non-Puritan remained rather exiguous. Even Archbishop Whitgift, who so fiercely disciplined Puritan mislikers of the surplice, did not differ from them upon the essential points of theology. He was a strict Calvinist, who upbraided Cartwright himself for venturing to say that the doctrine of free will was 'not repugnant to salvation'.[19] In 1595–6 Peter Baro, the French Lady Margaret professor at Cambridge, taught that Christ died for all men and that human free will had a rôle to play in salvation. Further attacks on Calvin had already been made by Baro's pupil William Barrett.[20] The outraged authorities of Calvinist Cambridge fell with wrath upon these anticipators of Arminius, and if Whitgift prevented their entire humiliation, he also made it clear at this time that he too disagreed with their liberalism. His Lambeth Articles of 1595 do very little to temper the most rigorous predestinatory doctrine. The change of front in the leadership of the Church scarcely began until 1599, when Whitgift, aged and incapable, virtually assigned the Primate's functions to Richard Bancroft, Bishop of London. The latter now demonstrated his broader sympathies by ordering the London clergy to march in Peter Baro's funeral procession. At the Hampton Court Conference in 1604 it was Bancroft who successfully opposed Puritan efforts to attach Whitgift's Lambeth Articles to the Thirty-nine Articles as part of the official summary of belief. These events, following upon the reception of Hooker's great work, mark the undermining of the Anglo-Puritan dominance and the recovery of a medial tradition, which eschewed the rigours of orthodox Calvinism, deprecated bibliolatry, stressed the rôle of reason in interpreting the Christian Faith and resisted the demands for changes in liturgy, church-government and the Articles. It should be stressed that this movement was not simply based upon the new liberal tendencies in continental Protestant theology. To a certain extent it may also be regarded as a restatement of our own *via media*, adumbrated long ago by the Henrician and Edwardian moderates and always recoverable from Cranmer's Prayer Book, especially as modified by Elizabeth in 1559.

In itself the retention of bishops in no way impugned the Puritan character of the Elizabethan Church. Despite Martin Marprelate neither Calvin nor Knox had denounced the episcopal office, while on the other side Hooker supported it with no trace of fanaticism. He even denied the necessity of episcopal ordination. Matthew Parker apart, all the important earlier Elizabethan bishops had been Marian exiles, having strong ties with Geneva, Zürich and Strassburg. It was the Genevan spirit which dominated Cambridge and fired the minds of the young clergymen poured out by that university into the parishes during Elizabeth's reign. The real Protestantising of the clergy did not take place in 1559, or by subsequent resignations or deprivations. It took the form of a steady influx of Puritan recruits, apparently speeded by the high average age of the beneficed clergy in 1559. This factor had been produced in its turn by the surplus of unemployed clerics and the consequently small number of ordinations during the crisis of the Reformation.

Throughout Elizabethan England Puritan preachers dominated the pulpits, even though many of them were intermittently engaged in disputes with their bishops. As their sermons show, their preaching ability and their numbers had no equivalent in pre-Reformation or mid-Tudor England. In London were Edward Dering and Henry Smith, at Norwich John More, in Suffolk John Knewstub, in Essex Richard Rogers, in Kent Dudley

Fenner, in Sussex Thomas Underdown, in Leicestershire Anthony Gilby and Arthur Hildersham, in north Oxfordshire John Dod, in Yorkshire Giles Wigginton, Edmund Bunney, John Favour and several others. And in Cambridge itself the young men could model their styles on the great master, William Perkins.[21] These are merely a small selection from the more obvious names. The same outlook can be traced in the wills of many obscure clerics who did not preserve or publish their sermons. Many held for a time the well-paid office of lecturer or town-preacher in one or other of the little Genevas created by Puritan magistrates. Though, as we have seen, new forces took shape among the Jacobean and Caroline divines, this sober Puritan tradition continued strong inside the Church, and not a few of its traits can be observed even in men whose theological principles would entitle them to be called Arminians. It became a most pervasive spirit, and even at the height of Laud's career the Church of England did not begin to look like a Church of the Counter-Reformation. Puritanism in our sense was never limited to Nonconformists; it was a powerful element in the origins of the Anglican Church and it was first through that Church that it won its abiding rôle in the life and outlook of the nation. To the present writer, as to most Anglicans, it would seem clear that Archbishops Laud and Neile brought some valid if not very profound criticisms against their Puritan adversaries. Armed with more statesmanship they might have manœuvred the Church without disaster into a more latitudinarian position, one with scope and tolerance for all except extremists. Yet it remains a gross misuse of terminology to call their party Anglican and to begrudge that label to their opponents, or to their Puritan predecessors, Archbishops Grindal and Hutton. Puritanism belonged to the mainstream of the Reformation. From the outset the national Church took its stand upon the principles of the Reformation, and among its early members the Puritans bulk very large indeed.

In more recent times the distinction and the peculiar Englishness of the Anglican Church has arisen, not from the claim of any one of its groups to special insight but from its success as an experiment in practical toleration and co-operation between varying schools of thought. In the very occasional need to enforce this experiment has lain the chief justification for a measure of state-control. Charles I understood this ideal as dimly as most of his subjects. He also failed to grasp the already historic function of Puritanism within the English Church, and in his reign the monarchy declined into an instrument of the Laudian minority-group. Today English Christians are still seeking to mitigate the more untoward effects of that chain-reaction which, after a series of bitter blows and counter-blows, culminated in the Clarendon Code and a more decisive cleavage between Anglicans and Nonconformists.

To assess the true character of the Puritan movement inside and outside the Church we must free our minds from the present popular use of the term, deriving in large part from satire directed against Victorian religious hypocrisy. That by any modern standards the actual movement had some critical weaknesses would hardly be denied, yet it has often suffered unduly at the hands of doctrinaire critics who have fixed their gaze upon some unrepresentative aspect of a large and complicated phenomenon. The characteristics of Puritanism which I now attempt to summarise are based to a minimal extent upon my private judgement, but rather upon detailed and documented surveys by Professor Knappen and other scholars profoundly acquainted with Puritan sermons, pamphlets, social treatises and devotional works.

This has been called a clerical movement, yet its clergy were far more closely controlled by laymen than were those of the Middle Ages. It aspired to bring lay and clerical society closer together and to abolish the dual standard sanctioned by the medieval Church. In England it always enjoyed heavy support among the gentry and substantial merchants. Even the venturesome Presbyterian classis-movement of 1582–9 was heavily backed by lay congregations which encouraged their incumbents to set aside the Prayer Book.[22] To the end of Elizabeth's reign it can be said to have commanded a majority in the House of Commons. Its active lay leaders stood among the most influential men in the land—Sir Francis Knollys, Sir Walter Mildmay, Ambrose Dudley, Earl of Warwick, Sir Francis Walsingham and Robert Beale. The Queen's devout cousin, Henry Hastings, Earl of Huntingdon, Lord President of the Council in the North, stood at the centre of the great web of Puritanism in the Midlands and the northern counties. Puritans were patronised by self-interested politicians from the Earl of Leicester downwards. Cecil, it is true, seems accounted a lost leader by the godly; his attitude to religious zeal became ever more suspicious and coloured by erastianism, yet even Cecil protected several important Puritans and was very far from wanting to see Whitgift domineering over scrupulous ministers.

During the present century the rôle of Puritanism among the laity has been given a fresh interpretation by Max Weber and Tawney. At all events when read incautiously, the latter's *Religion and the Rise of Capitalism* has tended to disseminate the image of the Puritan as a ruthless man of business, justifying the profit-motive by his 'doctrine of stewardship' and regarding even economic opportunity as a trust or stewardship reposed by God in the elect. The present writer is one of those who find it impossible to accept this image as characteristic of the movement. Comparatively late in its history Puritanism did indeed help to produce a few writers capable of thinking in some such terms. Yet even if the business world, where Puritanism made so many converts, sometimes rationalised itself religiously in this way, we need not for a moment ascribe the development of its economic practices and principles to Puritanism.

As Tawney himself reminds us, Catholic bankers were the leading figures in the sixteenth-century world of business, while the creative centres of modern big-scale finance—Antwerp, Lyons, Augsburg, Genoa and Venice—were all in Catholic countries. And centuries earlier, while Dante had put the Cahorsine money-lenders in hell, Pope Innocent IV, with far greater prescience, had called them *Romanae ecclesiae filii speciales.*[23] It might also be pleaded that even the doctrine of stewardship looks less repulsive in the context of seventeenth-century pioneering expansion than it is apt to look in modern eyes. Yet the fact remains that such ideas are utterly unrepresentative of classical Puritanism and even of Puritan economic theory. Looking at the whole movement we see an essentially other-worldly religion, dominated not only by an almost morbid moral sensitivity but by a real distrust of 'modern' capitalist tendencies. In his detailed survey of Tudor Puritanism Dr. Knappen proved this point beyond much doubt, while more recently another learned survey of English Protestant thought between 1570 and 1640 has concluded that such thought stood utterly opposed to the whole spirit of capitalist enterprise.[24] During this period the Puritans showed themselves to have inherited the tradition of Latimer and Hales; they were more outspoken than any group in their denunciation of usury, economic greed and social injustice. With these sins they classed the covetous behaviour of the laymen responsible for the economic and social servitude of the clergy. Puritan theory derives chiefly from clerical writers with small reason to feel complacent over modern tendencies. Again, the whole Puritan century ending at the Restoration can boast a good record of generosity, beneficence and public spirit. Professor Jordan's researches[25] have gone far to justify Arthur Hildersham's claim (*c.* 1635) that more money had been put into English hospitals, charities, colleges and schools during the last sixty years than in any previous century. These gifts were admittedly made in an inflated currency, and the London merchants, by far the biggest Puritan givers, may possibly have been sacrificing less than their generous Catholic grandfathers. Yet broadly considered, the Reformation appears to have made men neither more nor less generous; it simply deflected gifts from the Church to other charitable objects. The image conjured up by too narrow a concentration upon economic theorists may best be redefined by studying a wide selection of real Puritans. Among the host of such corrective figures one might begin with the dedicated organiser of the Presbyterian underground, John Field[26]; with the severe but generous Huntingdon; with Sir Walter Mildmay, founder of that Puritan seminary Emmanuel College; with Richard Greenham, the charitable, unworldly rector of Dry Drayton; or with the diarist Lady Margaret Hoby, immersed in prayer, beneficence and morose self-examination at Hackness.[27]

If 'progressive' economic theory cannot be accepted as a norm of

Puritanism, neither can particular theories of government or of church-government.[28] There were Episcopalian, Presbyterian and Congregationalist Puritans. Some showed themselves political opportunists, ready to clutch for the support of any powerful man, whatever his ulterior motives. If certain Puritans made heroic colonists or successfully resisted autocratic governments, this may have been due less to Puritan political theory than to their religiously disciplined personalities, to their training in ecclesiastical and social cohesion and in the last resort to the fact that their antagonists forced such rôles upon them. Throughout the world of that day local circumstances so often inspired the political thought and action of churchmen. It remains highly improbable that a political movement remotely like the one headed by Pym and Hampden could ever have developed in a Catholic society. Milton could not have put forth his magnificent plea for freedom of thought and publication except at the culmination of a long Puritan attack upon royal and prelatical authority. Yet without minimising the religious elements of the so-called Puritan Revolution, we should all nowadays acknowledge the immense weight of its secular causes.

How much positive generalisation dare we then apply to the social and political effects of English Puritanism? We might reasonably claim that it flourished most as a social religion among townsmen, that it required a modicum of education, thoughtfulness and independence of spirit, again that in time it helped to produce minds passionately addicted to certain limited yet important notions of civic and personal freedom. It taught a man to stand on his own feet and put a useful stock of biblical texts in his head. Despite some exceptions like the Levellers, Puritans seldom accepted democratic egalitarianism in lay life. But however they defined the Church, they accorded it an authority of its own, and their clerics at least were anti-erastian. For them the Church had its own social rules, and they believed that within it a man's standing should depend less upon worldly rank than upon spiritual gifts and moral repute.

Today many historians would consider the political achievement of Puritanism in terms far more concrete than these, in terms almost expressible by statistics and maps. Puritanism took an important share in bringing into line those areas of western England, Wales and the North which had been slowest to accept the implications of Tudor government and Protestant religion.[29] Contemporaries felt no doubt that in these 'dark corners of the land' the religious and political tasks were closely interrelated. 'Where preaching wanteth, obedience faileth', wrote Archbishop Grindal to Elizabeth, and he went on to instance the parish of Halifax, which 'by continual preaching had been better instructed than the rest' and hence in 1569 stood 'ready to bring 3 or 4,000 men into the field to serve you against the said rebels'.[30] Like John Wesley in later times, the Puritans saw that the diffusion of ideas could not be left to supine and conservative incumbents but depended in no small part on a supply of trained preachers, in many cases itinerant. Upon a truly astonishing scale, successful London merchants provided preachers, schools and charities in their provincial birthplaces, especially in Lancashire, Yorkshire and the Marches of Wales.[31] Even while Puritanism seemed to be creating division, in another and deeper sense it was uniting the kingdom.

When we have finished our efforts to modernise and secularise Puritanism, it remains an obstinately religious phenomenon, and its common characteristics must be sought in its religious teachings. It had no system of mysticism. In so far as it placed any emphasis upon religious 'experiences', these were simple and communicable; they gave no reason for founding esoteric communities or for solitary withdrawal. Worldly problems it tended to reduce to moral problems; to goodness it subordinated aesthetic and intellectual values. While it taught strict sobriety and moderation in all things, it did not, as popularly imagined, devote special attention to sexual morality. As for the deliberate mortification of the flesh, this savoured of Rome and was usually taken by Puritan writers to be the outcome and the source of spiritual pride.[32] The basis of moral life, like that of religious belief, was to be sought in the Bible, which Puritans exalted not merely above the Church in general but above all contemporary Protestant churches. Puritan theologians insisted not only that General Councils could err but that even the pronouncements of Luther and Calvin could not be taken as final. To this limited degree they were exponents of a belief in the progressive self-revelation of God to man. Their over-emphasis upon the Old Testament has been commonly exaggerated, and they were not guilty of fundamentalism in the sense of attaching equal authority to all parts of the Bible. They saw that even the New Testament contained disharmonies and that certain of its passages must be controlled by others more important. In general they took those passages as normative which described and regulated the life of the young Christian churches.[33]

Puritanism may have seemed 'non-Anglican' to patriots (as well as to verbalists) because it continued to entertain a close regard for foreign Reformation movements, because its theologians so frequently cited 'the best Reformed churches' in support of ideas disapproved by the monarch and by insular conservatives. Nevertheless, its internationalism did not entail a wholesale acceptance of the new non-religious currents of knowledge. Most, though not all, of its champions tended to distrust abstract learning and scientific curiosity.[34] Except in so far as it broadly encouraged mental independence and individualism, one can hardly follow the contention that Puritanism should be numbered among the ancestors of the scientific and philosophical triumphs of the seventeenth century. Its enthusiasm for education remained immense, however restricted in purpose. It aspired to create Bible-reading laymen and women; equally, it aimed to produce a highly educated clergy, to achieve a new situation where even obscure ministers could preach effectively and act as genuine spiritual pastors to the most intelligent of their flocks. Preaching had above all to be 'plain'; it had to deliver the message with an absence of rhetorical and literary flourishes. Puritans thought that the future of the Church lay with a clergy distinguished not by miraculous sacramental functions but by a new fervour, a superior intellectual equipment, a power to communicate. This ambition did not, however, presuppose a return to the old, narrow, clerical *esprit de corps*. The main purpose of the new cleric was to impart zeal to laymen, making them able to join in selecting their own ministers, to examine their own spiritual lives, to lead family prayers, to read godly books and take part in ecclesiastical administration. On all sides 'zeal' became the watchword.[35]

We have hitherto concentrated chiefly upon the creative aspects of the Puritan movement. These were unduly stifled by Elizabeth; she erected her barriers at the wrong points and by excessive suspicion failed to elicit for her national Church many of the gifts which a controlled Puritanism might have bestowed. Yet she did right to prevent the monopolising of that Church by the Puritan spirit, just as Charles I did wrong in allowing its Laudian enemies to attempt a counter-monopoly. The complete triumph of Puritanism would have submerged other religious values developing within Anglicanism. It would also have imposed an undue strain upon that large proportion of the English people who were willing to worship in church but not to embrace so intense and so disciplined a religious life. A national church cannot become a club for religious athletes. And while Puritanism promoted some forms of freedom, it unquestionably limited others. At all events until the period of the Civil Wars, very few of its adherents approached a broad conception of religious toleration. Though they accorded liberty of conscience and worship to other 'moderate' Protestants, their attitude toward their Roman Catholic adversaries remained implacable, even when less desperate political circumstances should have suggested a more humane and more Christian approach. In becoming the heirs of Calvin they had dropped the gentler tradition of Melanchthon.

Over the social failings of Puritanism modern observers agree more readily than over its religious limitations. Many would criticise its excessive contempt for the medieval past, its insensitivity toward sacramental values, its inordinate concern with predestinarian dogma and with supposed assurances of personal salvation, its fussy rejection of externals so modest as the surplice, the marriage-ring, the sign of the cross in baptism. For the present writer such criticisms, however valid, are somewhat overshadowed by a profounder though more debatable matter. Colet, Luther, Calvin and the English

Puritans display in turn that growing tendency among the critics of Catholicism—the tendency to turn from the veneration of many saints to the veneration of the great Saint. Some ignorant things have been said against Pauline Christianity, and it might be presumptuous for any Christian to attack the Reformers on account of the intensity with which they studied St. Paul. It nevertheless remains possible, and most tempting for intelligent and systematic minds, to dwell too exclusively upon Paul's wonderful presentation of the Gospel, to hang too devoutly upon his lightest word. A wholly unsuperstitious Christianity must centre its gaze not upon a man, not even upon this supremely dedicated man, but upon the Son of Man chiefly revealed in the Four Gospels. To this rotund proposition the Reformers would no doubt have added a fervent Amen; and they would have contended that this was precisely the aim of their Reformation. Yet it might not be impertinent to ask them, and in particular the English Puritans, whether their practical emphases were so Christocentric as their basic principles demanded. Attempting to summarise the approach of the large body of Elizabethan Puritan writers, Knappen[36] has written that they show 'a surprising lack of Christological thought . . . it is true, the Four Gospels do not appear to have attracted them particularly . . . certainly the person of Christ figures very little in their literature'. These are the hard misgivings which every reader of Puritan literature must sometimes have felt, but the final word should perhaps await a still fuller investigation of the theological content of Puritan writings. If it be true that the Puritan ideal was less involved with the person of Christ than it should have been, this does not of course mean that it had failed to differentiate itself from the popular cults of earlier centuries. If it taught men to see Christ through the eyes of St. Paul instead of through a cloud of minor saints, gilded legends and plain myths, this surely marked a growth in the fullness of knowledge. Then as now, Christians gave but limited time and mental energy to their religion and, if their minds were for ever clouded by the swarms of sparrows, they were unlikely to soar with the eagles. And let us frankly add that the Puritan Reformers of Tudor and Stuart England were not the only intelligent Christians who have found it more congenial to weave philosophical theology around the Epistles than to follow Paul himself and be drawn into the spirit of Jesus. As in our century, so in theirs, how many could truly say, or even in the secret places of the heart aspired to say, 'I live, yet not I, but Christ liveth in me'?

14 An Epilogue

The Origins of Religious Toleration

THE EFFECTS of the English Reformation upon the growth of religious toleration and the ideal of religious liberty were discussed over thirty years ago by Professor J. W. Allen and, in much greater detail, by Professor W. K. Jordan. To their admirable work few additions of substance have since been made, and here we can expand but slightly upon a few of the issues raised by their researches.[1] We have already witnessed the intolerance of 'moderate' Reformers toward Anabaptist beliefs. Amid a movement initially based upon the claims of the individual conscience, such attitudes look to us as obnoxious as their converse—mass hysteria against the Catholic religion amongst Englishmen over-excited by the menace of political Catholicism. The least critical admirer of the Reformation could not ignore the magnitude of these divergences from modern Christian and indeed from modern western norms, and he could only palliate them by reference to that genuine fear of spiritual, social and political chaos which beset our Tudor ancestors. Such emotions had not a little in common with those felt in earlier years by pious Catholics in the face of heresy, yet among Protestants they can hardly claim the same degree of rational consistency. The interest of the subject does not, however, cease at this point. From the first there had also existed in Protestant thought—in Zwingli, Melanchthon and Bucer, as well as among the Anabaptists—a more liberal tradition, which John Frith was perhaps the first to echo in England. When Frith claimed that no one interpretation of the presence in the eucharist should be made obligatory, when Starkey acknowledged that some current beliefs and observances could be regarded as *adiaphora*, then at least the seeds of a doctrine of toleration had begun to grow in English minds.

Amid English Reformation writings we can trace one series of toleration-manifestoes related to Zwingli and to Anabaptism. *The Sum of Scripture*, condemned by Archbishop Warham in 1530, asserts that true Christianity has nothing to do with persecution, that 'the secular sword belongeth not to

Christ's Kingdom'. In 1547 *A Brief and Plain Declaration* disclaims Anabaptism yet declares that the doctrine of Jesus was peace and that Christians seeking to establish the Kingdom of God on earth must only employ the weapons of the Spirit. A lost Anabaptist work, which happens to be described in detail by John Knox, dismissed the whole concept of persecution as belonging to the Old Testament and being utterly foreign to the nature of Christianity.[2] Similar notions began also to dawn upon thinkers otherwise violently opposed to Anabaptism. George Joye cited history to show the powerlessness of persecution to resist the truth. Thomas Starkey deprecated the excessive reliance placed by Church and State upon law and legal coercion. We cannot, he says in effect, make virtuous men by these mechanisms. Anticlericals like St. German countenanced the preservation of religious order by the temporal power but they also attacked the whole basis of ecclesiastical persecution. One of them, the ex-friar and London mercer Henry Brinklow, went still further and claimed that since faith is a gift of God, no man should be put to death for lack of it. True Christians cannot, in his view, desire to persecute for heresy; even the temporal power should, as in Germany, banish heretics rather than burn them. This same moderation of the traditional penalty was proposed some years later (*A New Dialogue*, 1548; *A Preservative*, 1551) by William Turner, physician to Protector Somerset and later dean of Wells. This able Puritan individualist describes heresy as 'no material thing that we must fight withall, but ghostly'. It is therefore 'most meet that we should fight with the sword of God's word and with a spiritual fire against them, else we are like to profit but little in our business'.[3] John Foxe also stood staunchly among those who bade the Church rely upon its spiritual weapons. Under Elizabeth he strove hard to save Anabaptists from the fire, and he enunciated a sweeping doctrine of tolerance even toward Catholics, whose doctrines he detested with every fibre of his being.[4] Thomas Cranmer would not go so far, yet he persecuted only a few extremists, used Catholics with gentleness and showed unexampled latitude in allowing liberty of worship to foreign Protestants.

When considering ideas of toleration amid the first generation of English Reformers it would be anachronistic to envisage a kindly Renaissance humanism fighting against an obscurantist Protestant biblicism. During this part of the story the chief hero is not Erasmus of Rotterdam but the New Testament itself. After all, the notion was bound to occur at least to some of these diligent Bible-readers that Christ and his Apostles nowhere envisaged or advocated the winning of human hearts through juridical persecution and physical duress. Many must indeed have noted this fact, but all too few drew the practical conclusions which seem to us so obvious.

A good many Elizabethan writers and parliamentary speakers[5] advocated religious toleration and its corollary, the simplification of doctrine. Of the theorists the most distinguished were laymen, like the engineer and prospector Jacobus Acontius, the jurist Alberico Gentilis and Edwin Sandys, a son of the Archbishop and a pupil of Hooker.[6] Acontius, the most far-sighted of all, even contrived to remain *persona grata* with the Queen while publishing views on religious liberty which flouted the standards of Catholic and Protestant states alike. He regarded all forms of persecution as springing from the sin of personal arrogance, and in his bold relativism he denied that absolute truth could be ensured by any doctrinal system or any Church. And though as a Protestant he looked upon the Bible as the one certain guide to faith, Acontius rejected as naïve the prevalent notion that free minds would come to interpret it uniformly. His outlook, obviously deriving something from Renaissance scepticism, remained alive in Elizabethan England and can thenceforth be claimed as one of the many pillars of tolerationist theory. In the complex minds of the Queen and her great minister it found answering chords.

Neither Elizabeth nor Burghley wanted to wage a religious persecution, and it remains broadly true that they avoided anything resembling one for over a decade, in fact until subversive political Catholicism forced their hands. In the world of these *politiques* some hard practical considerations had replaced the old Augustinian-Thomist concept of heresy as a sin worthy of capital punishment. From the time when the European states took responsibility for religious order from the hands of the Church Universal, the ancient sanctions were doomed. Hooker had to defend the Elizabethan Settlement on religious grounds, but even he was bound to regard the Anglican Church as merely one of those which together comprised the Catholic Church, and he freely admitted that men could attain salvation under the tutelage of Rome. In 1601 Bancroft made real efforts to arrange a compromise whereby Catholics would obtain a large measure of toleration in return for their rejection of the Papal claim to depose princes. Again, when we are tempted to view Arminianism as prone to renew religious persecution, we should recall that this movement arose as a protest against Calvinist intolerance and that its later persecuting tendency displayed its weak dependence on the State and involved it in ruin. While the Reformation was slow to produce genuine tolerance among its devotees, it soon destroyed the more solid psychological bases for religious persecution. Once Catholic Christendom had been succeeded by a multiplicity of national churches and dissenting groups, persecution also began to occasion practical disadvantages which could be seen, intermittently at least, to outweigh the advantages of uniformity. Such situations inevitably led to practical experiments in toleration, and where it was proved that such toleration could subsist without disaster, the more positive ideals of religious liberty were bound sooner or later to make their appeal. At varying rates most of the peoples bought their freedom.

The price in terms of spiritual confusion often proved high, for history is usually a hard bargainer with men.

The Complexity of the English Reformation

In this account we have displayed the English Reformation as essentially complex in its causes, its progress and its consequences. We have observed conflicts between King and Pope, Church and State, common lawyers and canon lawyers, laymen and clerics, ecclesiastical and lay landowners, citizens and bishops. We have witnessed many ideological clashes on church government and finance, clerical privilege, Church–State relations, the rôle of ecclesiastical law, the theologies of the eucharist, justification and grace. But above all we have learned to view the movement as a process of Protestantisation among the English people, a process not always favoured by the State, a process exerting a mass of direct and indirect influences not only upon English history but upon the whole of western civilisation. For the present writer the unifying theme lies in a change of viewpoint concerning the nature and functions of religion, both in the individual and in society. Yet athwart the Reformation struggles, and greatly complicating their outcome, ran a series of cross-currents—the old agrarian and social discontents of the peasantry, the threat of a Spanish hegemony over Europe, the secularisation of culture, the impact of the printing press, the rise of prices which dislocated State finance and all sorts of customary payments and relationships between men. Above all, in England as in the Netherlands, Protestantism became at last inextricably involved with the national self-assertion of a people fighting for its place in a new European and extra-European order.

We have dealt with worldly forces and spiritual forces; most commonly have we been dealing with mixtures of the two and with the rationalisation of self-interest. We have seen that the Reformation left unaffected few aspects of our national life, whether religious, intellectual, social, economic or political. It ended by producing not one English religion but a series of English religions, all of them claiming a primeval authenticity. But from the outset it completely transcended the bounds of ecclesiastical history. So ubiquitous were its influences that we cannot begin intelligently to speculate on the courses which our history would have taken in its absence. The English Reformation ranks as one of those many causal phenomena beginning relatively far back in our national history and destroying in advance all attempts to 'explain' the present by mere reference to recent history.

Those factors which made possible and effective the revolutionary behaviour of Henry VIII might in themselves form the subject of a major work of scholarship. Even had he not quarrelled over his divorce with the Habsburg-controlled Papacy, he could scarcely have avoided a major series of politico-religious conflicts. For many years genuine abuses had sprung from the outworn administrative and disciplinary systems of the Church. They had been magnified not merely by the conduct of avaricious and mundane clergymen but also by lay jealousy and malice. The Crown did not need to whip up anticlerical feeling; its task was to canalise, even to restrain such feeling. Anticlericalism probably owed less to the actual faults of the clergy than to a gradual shift in the attitude of lay society and to the growth of its literacy and intellectual resilience, its wealth, its political power. A multitude of nagging testamentary and tithe causes, lay resentment against the moral jurisdiction and the heavy probate fees of the church courts, the rise of lay education, humanist biblical criticism, Erasmian ridicule, the declining reputation of the Roman Curia, the survival of Lollardy and neo-Lollard anticlerical opinion, the inveterate anticlericalism of the common lawyers, the long-remembered scandal of Richard Hunne, the colourful but disastrous experiment with Thomas Wolsey; all these influences and many more had created before the meeting of the Reformation Parliament an atmosphere little short of explosive. They did not in themselves entail a Protestant Reformation, but they could hardly have resulted in less than a series of radical readjustments between England and Rome, still more between Church and State, most inevitably of all between the clerical order and lay society. Henry VIII became involved in these matters without wanting a religious Reformation and without at first realising the enormous powers which the anticlericalism of his subjects had placed in his hands. His intervention nevertheless ended by producing religious results, because it pushed England out of step with the continental Reformation movements, began new sequences of insular events and so helped to confer a unique character upon the English Reformation.

In the field of religion many weaknesses of the late medieval Church were plainly apparent to intelligent but orthodox contemporaries. Though we should beware of exaggerating their importance in ordinary custom-ridden minds, we find heavy support from the sources when we refuse to see them through the pre-Raphaelite spectacles of our grandfathers. Scholastic religion, having overestimated its powers, had ended in disharmony, irrelevance and discredit. Beliefs of marginal authenticity, especially those relating to purgatory and saint-worship, had been suffered in everyday practice to occupy central places in the Christian life. The professional education of parish priests was criticised as quite inadequate by numerous writers of unquestioned Catholic orthodoxy, and its character was reflected in the paucity of direct religious teaching outside the larger towns. With certain notable exceptions monasticism was uninspired; it shed little spiritual light into the world outside the cloister and its amassing of appropriated benefices hampered the didactic functions of the Church. Again, when ordination was so little selective, a small fringe of disreputable clerics was bound to accumulate and to taint the moral reputation of the priesthood. The authority of the latter had come to depend in too great a degree upon its sacramental functions, too little upon the moral and intellectual pre-eminence of clergymen in society. The finest aspects of late medieval religious life, mysticism and the related *devotio moderna* tended to be too demanding and esoteric for ordinary people, whereas the popular cult-religion—John Myrc's world of flying demons and saintly thaumaturges—seemed to the sophisticated both childish and unduly directed to the raising of money.

At least by the year 1500 the fostering of a sound middle way of devotion between these two extremes should have become the chief aim of the Church, yet in England more than in most countries such a development was inhibited by the old anti-Lollard suspicions against religious literature in the vernacular and especially against biblical translation. Our bishops, in these matters among the most cautious and unimaginative in Europe, were mostly civil servants, often educated in the Roman law and always busied by secular duties; they tended to think of the Church in terms of jurisdiction rather than in terms of religious education. Even the more intelligent and spiritually-minded, like John Fisher, failed to perceive that a shifting lay outlook demanded new methods, and they tended merely to be shocked when, to put the matter crudely in our modern terms, they found the gentry and merchants of the Renaissance age less docile than the illiterate barons and villeins of a former world.

In the atmosphere of the sixteenth century it had become more difficult to soothe lay curiosity by an ecclesiastically-processed version of the Faith. Nevertheless, in the first instance it was a group of intellectual clerics, some of them friars, who discovered Luther and introduced his concepts into both English universities. This movement soon found lay supporters, both in the international world of the merchants and among members of the former Lollard groups of London and south-eastern England. A new and incomparably powerful weapon came to hand in Tyndale's New Testament, itself made possible through the protection afforded to Tyndale (and to subsequent translators) by an astute confederacy of businessmen in London and Antwerp. The force of this new appeal to the laity resided less in Luther's doctrine of the priesthood of all believers than in the fact that Lutheranism, enormously aided by the printers, placed the primary evidences of the Christian Faith in the hands of laymen. The gulf so revealed between the Church of St. Paul and that of Cardinal Wolsey supplied the clinching argument for radical revisions both of theology and of institutions. Neither in England nor elsewhere was the existing establishment organised to guide, control and survive a general study of the Primitive Church. By the same token many who felt called to study it were unqualified to do so intelligently. There followed an unpleasant clash between the Reformers, too often arrogant in their newfound knowledge, and the bishops, who showed too little enthusiasm for common-sense reforms but placed only a half-hearted reliance on the faggot and the dungeon. The State was left as *deus ex machina*.

To critical people in search of positive beliefs Lutheranism offered a seductive solution. It streamlined the teaching of the New Testament around the doctrine of Justification by Faith Alone, a belief which abruptly demolished the need for the cult-religion and for a whole mass of hoary observances. Anglican and Catholic writers have seldom given full weight to the intrinsic attractiveness of these ideas to many minds of that century; however much repetition and overstatement may since have staled them, they lacked nothing in freshness and vitality for many of our best Tudor minds. Whatever its merits and demerits, the rise of Protestantism was based upon a positive evangel; we deceive ourselves if we describe the process in terms of drab negation or attribute its success merely to the shortcomings of contemporary Catholicism.

Meanwhile, Henry VIII carried the great conservative bulk of the nation with him in his dual action—the severance of England from the Roman jurisdiction and the curtailment of the wealth and privileges enjoyed by the English Church. Having initiated these processes he found himself confronted by the unwelcome demand for a third revolution, embracing Lutheran doctrine and based upon the presentation of the Bible in Protestant dress by Tyndale and Tyndale's followers. Despite his strong character and doctrinal conservatism Henry opposed these developments neither so passionately nor so consistently as historians have often supposed. His new Archbishop had strong sympathies with the Lutherans. In Thomas Cromwell the King found an administrative virtuoso capable of executing the immense technical tasks involved in the subjugation of the Church, yet he also allowed Cromwell scope to develop ideas more radical than his own. The minister organised the first great barrage of press-propaganda in English history, and his publicists not only defended the royal policy but anticipated several of the basic concepts of the Anglican *via media*. Still more important, Cromwell took the lead in making the English Bible public property in further versions by Coverdale and other English Protestants. The sale of Bibles, and free access to them in the churches, proved an event of primary importance in the history of the Reformation; it was just as irreversible as the dispersal of the monastic lands, and in the long run more revolutionary in its implications.

If Henry had foreseen the ultimate political dangers of Calvinist Protestantism, he might have been prompted to thrust aside his scruples and adopt as his State-religion a fully-fledged Lutheranism, with its veneration for the godly prince. Yet whether this step would have exorcised more radical creeds or merely paved the way for their advent, we can only conjecture. In the event, he attempted from 1539 to re-assert Catholic doctrine, but his efforts were spasmodic and ineffective. That the Reformation had already become far more than any mere act of state can be seen from that most crucial yet little-observed episode in the social history of the English Reformation—the conversion of a solid minority amongst the upper and middle classes to Protestant opinions, even while those opinions were still discouraged by the King. Judging by scattered evidence, including the religious phraseology in wills, this process had begun to acquire momentum before 1540 and was not arrested by the Six Articles persecution. Moreover, it had certainly gained a strong if cautious following within the Court. The future Duke of Somerset exemplified this process, while the King himself ran counter to the spirit of his own statutes in allowing his young heir to be educated by men of the new religious outlook. These quiet advances of Protestantism during Henry's last years account for the ease with which Somerset established it as the official religion from the beginning of the new reign. His championship, followed by that of Northumberland, gave it an invaluable breathing-space of more than six years, during which it spread and consolidated itself beyond the possibility of extinction by any machinery available to Tudor governments. By the end of Edward's reign it had taken full advantage of the old basis of proletarian heresy and had penetrated deeply into the working classes of south-eastern England, which supplied the great majority of the Protestant martyrs under Mary.

The Edwardian years display a rough poetic justice. The seizure of chantries and church goods marred the public image of the Reformation in the eyes of many people. The fund of social idealism amongst the Reformers, deeply impressive on paper and in the pulpit, availed little at this stage to check the profiteering which it so vociferously denounced. On the other side, Cranmer's accomplished liturgical work survived persecution to afford a solid basis for Elizabeth's resumption of the Edwardian experiment. More than any other factor this work gave a distinctive and unique flavour to the national Church. Cranmer bequeathed to the latter a liturgy too politically and devotionally attractive to be displaced by Calvinist or other continental models; he also preserved some Catholic elements, which half a century later attained a new importance when Anglicanism sought to broaden its scope.

While Cranmer and Ridley showed that Englishmen could read the Bible and the Fathers and then do some theological thinking on their own account, Hooper used his longer continental associations to found a Puritan tradition with its roots in Zürich and Geneva. So far as foreign influences are concerned—and the most patriotic English churchman could not deny their immense importance—the reign of Edward VI saw a major reorientation. Before its close the direct influence of Wittenberg had decisively waned and in the main the foreign pressures were coming from Swiss sources and increasingly from Calvin's Geneva. In the event they came in two waves. Protestant scholars and refugees from the severities of Charles V—who at this point made his second great contribution to the English Reformation—flooded into Edwardian England. Some were welcomed to key-positions in the universities, while others provided a public exhibition of Reformed religion in the heart of London. Amongst these men the close disciples of Luther were a negligible element. The second wave arrived a decade later with the return to England of the Marian exiles, who had been repulsed by Lutheran Germany but welcomed at Geneva, Zürich, Strassburg, Frankfurt and other centres where consubstantiation and prince-worship were not regarded as passports to respectability. In these foreign backgrounds Ponet, Knox and Goodman evolved anti-monarchical theories of politics more advanced then those about to emanate from the Huguenots. The immensely important change from prince-worship to 'civil courage', the change which made the Puritan attitude to authority so very different from that of Henry VIII's subjects, had begun both among the martyrs at home and among the English exiles on the continent.

Even while Mary was burning Englishmen for rejecting transubstantiation, Protestant theology began to lose interest in this old bone of contention and transferred its attentions to the more modish disputes over grace and predestination arising from the favourite themes of Calvin. Another sign of change in late Edwardian and Marian England was the rise of surreptitious sects organised on a congregational basis. Apart from the licensed model of the Foreigners' Church at the Austin Friars, the first examples came from the Anabaptists, who began to attract a following of native converts in London and in Kent. The supposition that the Marian martyrs contained more than a handful of such sectaries we have seen to be based on no solid grounds. Yet even Anglicans, both in their secret church in Marian London and at their various centres abroad, gained some interesting experience of congregational organisation and hence of self-reliance during the Marian persecution. Here again we observe an interesting tributary to the stream of Elizabethan Puritanism.

Its reputation badly compromised by Northumberland, the Reformation derived unexpected support from the blunders of Queen Mary. At first she incurred hatred through her Spanish marriage, but in the end the fires of Smithfield did not fail to damn her cause, at all events in London and the south-east, where for the most part the drama was enacted and where public opinion had to be respected by any successful English government. Equally important, the conduct of the eminent clerical martyrs raised the sagging moral status of the Protestant cause. Public opinion cannot, however, be regarded as homogeneous throughout mid-Tudor England, and we should be wise to abandon simplifying statements as to what 'the Englishman' thought concerning all these vicissitudes. During this long crisis there were slow-moving areas and swift-moving areas, yet whereas Protestantism appealed to the latter, Mary failed to enlist the positive enthusiasm of the former. Our new knowledge of the Marian North gives no hint that she aroused its still conservative society from the torpor into which the failure of its previous reactions and its lack of spiritual leaders had plunged it. And even in these remoter provinces there is clear evidence both of an advancing Protestantism and of a proletarian heresy still owing something to the old Lollard tradition.

If the Reformation were ever to be checked, a Catholic riposte was now due or overdue, yet it did not even begin to materialise in Marian England. The type of spirituality we associate with the Counter-Reformation remained conspicuously absent. Though Loyola was an older man than Calvin, and his contemporary in the University of Paris, his movement struck England with the seminary priests a quarter of a century after the initial impact of Calvinism. In view of the short time available, it might be ungenerous to ascribe this failure to Reginald Pole. Yet he showed no grasp of missionary methods, while his general mismanagement of the reaction illustrates both his personal lack of 'instinct' and the stultifying effect of long exile upon its victims. By contrast, English Protestantism could count itself fortunate to avoid the latter fate, for Mary's early death meant that most of the 800 Protestant exiles spent four years or less abroad—a period long enough to broaden and sharpen their minds, yet not so long as to deprive them of a sense of the realities at home. Even the intrigues and brawls between Coxians and Knoxians at Frankfurt did something to fit them for the work ahead and to keep alive the Anglican tradition.

The critical events which followed Elizabeth's accession sprang chiefly from the political acumen of these returning exiles, yet the nature of the Settlement and of the early Anglican Church was deeply affected by certain background factors, to which as yet we have had little chance to refer. While at this time Protestantism inspired only a minority of the nation, so did Catholicism. A fair amount of evidence shows the existence of a third factor comprised of secularism, relative indifference to religion, weariness of doctrinal contentions, obsession with peace and security. It is hard to resist the impression that this third force exerted at least as much weight as all the religious impulses in sanctioning the Elizabethan Settlement and in guaranteeing its stability against pressures from enthusiasts on the left and on the right. This mundane phenomenon should not be too roughly criticised by historians of religion. To some extent it represented the nation's instinct for material self-preservation, yet it was not wholly a negative reaction against the perils of religious fanaticism. Something more creative than mere disillusion or self-interest was also coming to birth in English society. The later acts of the drama we have described were enacted upon a shifting platform of European and of national culture.[7] The Copernican enlargement of the universe, the transoceanic discovery of non-Christian civilisations, the increasing dominance of society by its former middle orders with the resultant substitution of the family-man for chivalric and monastic models, these and many other forces were now swiftly reshaping the mental contours of educated society throughout the West.

The belief that English humanism declined after the execution of Thomas More has lately been revealed as fictitious by scholars like Bush and Caspari.[8] But the label 'humanism' with its classical, Italian and Erasmian connotations seems quite inadequate to express the whole of this tidal movement, the direction and depth of which can best be ascertained by examining the intellectual interests, not of great or even eminent minds, but of ordinary readers and writers in Tudor England. Provincial surveys undertaken by the present author suggest a striking mental development among such people around the mid-century.[9] Before about 1550–1560 the interests of these literate provincial Englishmen relate overwhelmingly to religion and to the Church; lay writers remain relatively few and the whole scene is still dominated by the professional interests of clergymen. Thereafter a dramatic broadening and diversification becomes apparent. Both laymen and clerics are now concerned with science, medicine, natural history, poetry, genealogy, history, the law, social and economic problems. Religious writing and publication do not necessarily decline in bulk, but they occupy a far smaller share of an enormously swelling output. In England as elsewhere, this powerful upgrowth of lay interests and lay writers occurred for reasons largely independent of the Reformation. Puritan zeal failed to retard it and it developed apace around and even within the Puritan mind. While it cooled the atmosphere, it also complicated the intellectual and spiritual situation of the educated man. In Sir Thomas Browne's famous metaphor he had now become an Amphibian, able to swim in more than one distinct element. This new situation may well be regarded as marking the end of the Middle Ages, yet in time it also caused the teachings of Luther and even Calvin to seem less than complete answers to the questioning of humanity.

While the *dénouement* of the Reformation under Elizabeth and the early Stuarts cannot properly be understood without reference to this mighty underlying change, the first stages of the Anglican Settlement were shaped by narrower and more immediate influences. Those exiles most under

Genevan influence did not return in time to share in the political bargaining of 1559, the parties to which were the Queen herself and the Prayer Book exiles. The latter stood as far to the left as users of the Prayer Book could possibly stand; they too venerated Calvin and had shown themselves prepared to revise the 1552 Book in a Protestant sense. In the event Elizabeth compelled them to revise it in a conservative direction. Ere long Genevan and other forms of radicalism attempted to pull the Anglican Church in their direction, yet their efforts were inhibited not merely by the conservative tastes of the Queen but by erastianism and secularism, above all by the fear of disunity in the face of Spain and political Catholicism. As the insensitivity of the Spanish Tudor had made the Elizabethan Settlement possible, so the fear of Philip ended by consolidating that Settlement and by checking for several decades the fissiparous tendencies within English Protestantism.

Nevertheless, the Puritan movement maintained its integrity and critical spirit, even when it was directing from within the otherwise meagre spiritual life of the Elizabethan Church. Though Separatist and Presbyterian tendencies never gained many followers under Elizabeth, Puritanism had only to be mishandled in the succeeding period of relative international tranquillity, in order to be driven anew into restless tendencies and to be turned at last against the monarchy itself. I have been concerned somewhat to defend Puritanism against its detractors. Britons who respect their own historic achievements can scarcely do otherwise, for Puritanism entered our bone and sinew; it gave an immense access of strength and discipline to our nation in the days of its grandeur. I should nevertheless regard it as a force more suited to pervade than to dominate the English spirit, for the latter was proceeding toward types of creativity and freedom incompatible with full-fledged Genevan patterns of intellectual and social discipline. Within the narrower fields of theology the hitherto Anglo-Puritan Church began before 1600 to produce non-Puritan ways of thought. The reconciliation of these so-called Arminian ideas with the dominant Puritan tenor of English life demanded a degree of statesmanship greater than that possessed by the Stuart kings and a more genuinely latitudinarian temper than that of William Laud and his associates.

The material results of the English Reformation will certainly form the subject of further local and regional researches, pending which most generalisation should be regarded as tentative. In the present state of knowledge we can scarcely assign to these material results a commanding place in the economic and social history of Tudor England. The rapid dispersal of monastic lands amongst a host of purchasers helped to endow younger sons who might otherwise have remained landless, and it contributed beyond doubt to that remarkable increase in the number of landed families observable throughout England from the mid-century. There seems every reason to distrust the once popular image of easy-going monkish landlords undergoing replacement by rack-renting squires. We have seen that strong forces operated against the prevalence of either of these stylised characters. Rising rents and fines must be seen against a background of population-pressure and monetary inflation, concerning which contemporary analysis was often mistaken or insensitive. While aggrieved tenants did not lack legal remedies, they should in general have been well able to absorb these additional costs, since as producers and sellers of foodstuffs they were among the biggest beneficiaries from the inflationary process. Here further research should proceed with an open mind and in the full realisation that the economic impacts of the Reformation will prove almost impossible to disentangle from a host of independent factors—debasement, inflation, enclosure and the pressure of rising population upon relatively static production.

We have also attempted by concrete examples to display the decreasing appreciation and care which Tudor parishioners showed for the chantries and other institutions added by late medieval piety to the endowment of parish life in England. Here there lay an important field for reform and even for reconversion to changed uses, yet mere legal confiscation could not be justified by pleas of superstitious usage. The Edwardian government of self-styled Protestants, morally degenerating and financially bankrupt, was in no posture to rehabilitate parochial ministration, charity and education. In particular, the debt of English education to Henry VIII proved more substantial than its debt to his son, whose name was undeservedly attached to the grammar schools he refounded. Nevertheless, it now seems unlikely that substantial damage accrued to English schools, while the spate of new schools and of charitable benefactions in general effectively delivers Tudor and Stuart Protestantism from sweeping charges of neglect toward the young and the poor. If good works were channelled to a decreasing extent through the Church, the change was inevitable in an age when laymen had come to abound in administrative knowledge and experience. This tendency we may already have exaggerated, since the Anglican Church, and later the other denominations, continued to play a very considerable rôle in education and charitable endeavour. A change more certainly apparent during the century which followed the reign of Henry VIII lies in the exiguous part of the national wealth now expended upon ecclesiastical buildings, or upon the fine arts in the service of the Church.

Ironically enough, the Crown might be regarded as—next to the Church—the greatest material loser by the processes of dissolution. Henry VIII and his son's ministers undertook these steps during a period of heavily mounting costs and inflexible taxation. The consequent sale and dispersal of ecclesiastical lands ensured the final economic demotion of the Church, while the Crown merely surmounted a dangerous crisis without achieving economic stability. The kings of Spain, who continued exploiting the taxable capacity of a swollen Church, benefited more than the kings of England, who seized a great share of ecclesiastical wealth only to lose most of it within little more than a decade.[10] This loss gradually brought the Crown into competition with its accomplice in secularisation and successor in ownership—a class far more numerous, more critical, more wealthy, more indestructible than the neo-feudalists of the fifteenth century. In contrast with this depressive effect on government, the change brought stimulus to the national economy. Whereas in seventeenth-century Spain, economists constantly regretted their lack of a middle class with creative habits of investment, in England the gradual growth of a more fluid and productive economy was apparently promoted by these alterations in land-ownership and class-structure. A free market in land, exploitation of the land, rising manufactures, expanding internal and overseas trade, increasing population, these are interrelated developments which displaced the domestic balance of power and enhanced the rôle of England in that enormous world now being revealed to European enterprise. The contributions of the Reformation to this complex will never be assessed with any sort of precision, yet one finds it impossible to doubt that the laicising of landed capital was a vastly more potent factor for change than any support which late Protestant economic theory may have given to an already long-established capitalist ethic. In sum, it is probably safe to suppose that throughout the economic field the English Reformation did little more than accentuate trends of theory and practice already operative at its outset and by no means dependent upon its support.

Confusion has usually resulted from attempts to denounce or to justify essentially religious movements by reference to the non-religious phenomena accompanying them. When the Reformation is being debated in terms of religious and ethical values, its political, economic and social background, which sprang in large part from a pre-existent order, should be introduced into the debate with restraint and discrimination. When, for example, French historians deplore the supposed impoverishment inflicted by the English Reformation upon the peasantry, it is legitimate to ask them whether the lot of the French peasantry was more equitable under Louis XIV than that of its English counterpart under Queen Anne. The worlds of religion and economics were never closely geared together. It is certain that Catholic principles did not prevent the subjects of Henry VIII from buying monastic lands, and it is questionable whether at any stage the practices or codes of Protestant landlords and businessmen can be distinguished ethically from those of their Catholic counterparts. Again, it would be less than rational to impugn the religious opinions of Cranmer or Hooper because they failed to control the desperate financial policies of Northumberland. With an equal lack of good sense one might blame the horrors of the Fourth Crusade upon

Innocent III or condemn the Counter-Reformation by reference to the cruel persecutions of Louis XIV. In short, the Reformation has been too often distorted, its worldly effects misrepresented, by all sorts of doctrinaires, anachronists and wishful thinkers, both sacred and profane by inspiration. But perhaps we are all nowadays learning to move more cautiously within these difficult borderlands between religious and secular history. If not, it seems high time we began!

Toward a Longer Perspective

LOOKING back on the foregoing narrative with such impartiality as I can command, my first reflection concerns its incompleteness. My examination of the Elizabethan *dénouement* has been all too brief; at the tragic yet strangely fruitful divisions of the seventeenth century I have given no more than a few glances, though they stand among the more direct results of the English Reformation. The growth of Presbyterianism and of the Congregationalist, Baptist, Quaker and other denominations during the central decades of that century might almost be regarded as a second English Reformation. This explosion of the Puritan movement passed outside the religious field and shattered beyond repair the dream of an authoritarian orthodoxy in Church and State which had in no small measure survived into the Protestant world. The fact that changes of this type tended to occur first in Protestant countries suggests that the Reformation of the sixteenth century was an early if involuntary stage in the rise of societies which permit a multiplicity of religions, liberty of choice to the individual and freedom of worship even to minor and unpopular sects. To us this outcome looks far more inevitable than it did even to the most far-seeing and liberal of the original Reformers. But in the longer run, even those countries where the Counter-Reformation succeeded could not resist the tide of toleration; having suffered much for their hesitancy they at last followed suit. And it might have been predicted that Spain, the grand eccentric of the European family, would form the sole exception, albeit a partial, intermittent and precarious one. Elsewhere the spirits of the dead Anabaptists could look down upon a nineteenth-century world where their demand for freedom had at last been met.

Could we embark in detail upon the English aspects of this second Reformation, there would be no final resting-place in 1662 or in 1688, for long afterwards, even down to our own day, further sequels continue to illuminate the nature and the immense potentialities of the events we have described. The pietist, humanist and scientific trends of the eighteenth century all made their impacts upon the Protestant mind and, especially in Britain, kept it lively. What do they know of the Reformation who have not met John Wesley and his friends or who have not sensed the solid and devout beneficence of late Georgian England? On the one hand, the Methodist and Evangelical movements sprang almost directly from spiritual impulses initiated by the Reformers; on the other, Protestant beliefs made interesting combinations with the secular thought of the Age of Reason. This latter phase has been harshly regarded by modern Protestant theologians; like most attempts to integrate revealed Christianity and 'modern' discovery, it had its blind alleys and its sub-Christian implications. Yet it had this saving grace—that it was not a new orthodoxy imposed by churches and states as binding upon their members. It might indeed have been disastrous had English Christians failed to take seriously Newton's universe and the philosophical thinking in which it became clothed. They could no more ignore these developments than their predecessors could have ignored scholasticism or humanism. If the Protestant churches in England paid a price for joining the hurly-burly of a new free world of thought, they also gained immeasurable benefits; in the long run they acquired new vistas, more humility, more self-knowledge from these astringent experiences.

Another sequel to the rise of English Protestantism was its capacity for expansion, both in territories mainly populated by Britons and among hitherto non-Christian peoples. The English and Scottish Reformations came to resemble an intense source of light projected across time and falling upon great screens of space. From one viewpoint this process can be regarded as an ideological function of imperialism, yet it could also display in abundance the finest Christian missionary qualities.

British Protestantism, it is true, also fell for a time into selfish and hypocritical company, which stifled its social liberalism, made it dissociate spiritual from physical well-being and greatly diminished its influence throughout the urban working-classes. If it proved slow to denounce slavery, it took even longer to denounce child-labour and sub-human industrial conditions at home. Despite such failures at home and abroad, Anglicanism and the major Nonconformist churches assumed the status of world-religions. For better or worse, British Protestantism placed its ineradicable stamp upon the image of Britain throughout the world. Most strikingly it showed its capacity to give birth to self-governing churches, even as secular imperialism created self-governing dominions. Today, as the ties of Empire and Commonwealth tend to loosen, men of many nations continue to use Thomas Cranmer's Prayer Book—or adaptations of it—and to owe deep if unconscious debts to a host of Tudor and Stuart Englishmen. Yet while religion became a major factor in our transoceanic enterprises, it failed to fulfil its initial promise to draw us more closely to the continent of Europe. Whatever view may be taken of the solidity of the bridges built by medieval churchmen across the narrow seas, it is certainly true that until quite recent days Protestant churchmen did far too little to promote understanding between the nations of Europe.

Upon North America, however, our Reformation made a reverberating impact, and for the mid-twentieth century its chief living significance might well be thought to lie in the United States. There many churches, both British and continental, have together created a profoundly Protestant culture far overflowing the bounds of religious life, a culture which has demonstrated more successfully than its European equivalents that even an exaggerated concern for material production and consumption need not destroy churchgoing, manifest devotion and social generosity. Within this culture the churches originating in England and Scotland have played the predominant part, thanks largely to the former intellectual ascendancy and westward expansion of New England. In world history the New England colonies take a most prominent place among those many social and political experiments heavily coloured by the Reformation. It has become a commonplace among American sociologists that this Puritan heritage, held steady by the churches which derive directly from its tradition, continues to play a striking rôle in the moral and didactic attitudes of the American people. That often fruitful, often dangerous idealism which sees persons, peoples and governments in stark antitheses of good and evil has been widely attributed to this persistent tradition. Certainly, it is far from fanciful to see here the re-entry of Puritanism, diluted and half-secularised, upon a new and enormous plane of world affairs. Within the same gigantic society, still in process of self-creation, the tradition of the English Reformation may well merge most fruitfully with the Lutheran and Calvinist revivals which had their origins in nineteenth-century Europe. Perhaps in the United States rather than in Europe will a re-grouping of the split forces of the Reformation come to shape the future of Christianity and even to embark upon the long task of reconciliation with the Catholic world. Whatever the event, if we seek the relevance of the English Reformation to the problems of our own century, we should be wise to let our thoughts flow freely outside the British Isles.

In our own age common prudence suggests that the rivalries of Christian churches should be limited to friendly debate. With most of the world still awaiting conversion and with anti-Christian forces growing ever stronger, we can no longer afford to waste our energies in recriminations, in winning converts from one another or even in duplication of effort. One purpose of historiography is to free men from the dead hand of history. If he entertains any practical objectives in the study of the Reformation, the Christian historian may legitimately hope to close at least some of the old rifts by explaining them with a due blend of sympathy and of hard-headed realism. In so doing, he can also underline the obvious truth that none of the parties to the original disputes had anything like a monopoly of virtue, of good sense, of charity, of understanding in the Faith. In the English-speaking world, a better comprehension of doctrine and of history has enormously narrowed the gap between the Anglican-Episcopalian Churches and those of the other leading Protestant denominations. The proposed reunion of Anglicans and Methodists in Britain would represent an even greater triumph for maturity than the creation in 1925 of the United Church of Canada by the former Congregational, Methodist and Presbyterian churches of that country. Everywhere attractive vistas of reunion, close collaboration and common worship seem to lie ahead.

Even between Protestants and Catholics a host of sensible experiments in co-operation need not await doctrinal *rapprochement*. In this seventh decade of our century one would need to be blind not to observe here a new spirit at work on both sides. As never before, the Catholic world is making efforts to understand the situation of non-Catholic Christianity, while throughout the Protestant world there is growing an appreciation not merely for Catholic virtues as seen in individuals but for that magnificent capacity to produce holiness shown by Catholicism throughout the ages. In his own small academic sphere the writer (who has constant occasion to work with Catholic historians) can testify to the surprising growth of charity and understanding which has developed during the last thirty years. Convinced Christians are willy-nilly in some degree denominational partisans, yet today we are all becoming less guilty of conscious and half-conscious attempts to strain or to expurgate the facts of the great controversial age of the Reformation. There appears at least a striking tendency among professional historians and serious students to respect and accommodate historical facts, however unpalatable to their various confessional outlooks. This in itself is a remarkable advance for the cause of Truth. In time even the writers of cheap proselytising literature will find it possible—indeed more effective—to follow the trend.

This much said, it would be idle to deny that some of the barriers between Protestants and Catholics remain formidable, and only facile optimism would forecast any dramatic approaches in our time toward doctrinal agreement or institutional integration. When we have finished bewailing the greed, folly and fanaticism of the sixteenth century, the Reformation still stands in mountainous bulk across the landscapes of western Christianity. It concerned most vital issues which still live to perplex and divide us. Even today some of the principles which it sought to establish could neither be conscientiously abandoned by the Protestant Churches nor be conceded by the Catholic Church without an utter abnegation of its historic claims. The later liberalising, the variety and contradictions of Protestant thought have in some senses led the two still further apart. For all their impressive façades of bishops, convocations, moderators, assemblies, boards and synods, the Protestant Churches have become different in kind from the Church of Rome. Despite the growing urge to unity, only a dwindling fragment of their members desire to see anything approaching uniformity of belief and practice. The weight of their own ecclesiastical traditions presses lightly upon most intelligent Protestants, and few are disposed to grovel before the Thirty-nine Articles or the Westminster Confession, remarkable as these may have been in their day and generation. To many even the venerable early creeds may no longer seem adequate summaries of basic Christian belief. Some, like the present writer, find one of the more fruitful concepts of the Reformation in the doctrine of *adiaphora*, or 'things indifferent'. Extending this they would maintain that all the Christian churches have shipped more ballast than the New Testament sources will justify, that the quality of a man's faith does not depend upon the number of propositions he can swallow, that philosophic and imaginative theology (Thomist, Calvinist, modern teutonic or any other) should never again be allowed to leave its proper plane of hypothesis and make itself binding or even officially recommended.

It might well be contended that even the Reformers erred through their inability to throw off the vainglorious scholastic spirit, to avoid rebuilding, all too high above the documents, the exciting but insecure towers of ratiocination. If in this dark life we need credal formularies, let them at least be clear, short and simple; let them try to be truly representative of the teaching and living of Jesus; above all, let them impose as little as possible of any man's corrupt and arrogant imagination. Imperfectly as the Reformers executed their task, too swiftly as they froze the living things in their minds, this desire to free man's image of God from anthropomorphism and marginal cults, to envisage the magnitude and the uniqueness of Christ's sacrifice, to cast aside misleading unessentials and accretions, to bring men nearer in love to the real person of the Founder, this type of aspiration lies at the heart of their message for our own century. As the best of them sought in humility to recover the ever-living Word made Flesh, so we and our successors can continue the search in still greater humility, without any illusion that our own attempts will be specially privileged or successful. When they talk of God, or of the Son of God, fallen creatures and visible churches should at least be tentative. It needed Christ himself to interpret the world of the Spirit in the lame words of men.

REFERENCES

Where essential, references are made below to primary sources, but it would have been inappropriate (and prodigal of space) to attempt reference to such sources for the more routine passages and the 'accepted' facts. Hence I have often cited secondary authorities where these provide useful ranges of reference to the primary sources. Apart from indicating my chief authorities, the notes are also designed to provide bibliographical guidance on many topics. Unless otherwise stated, Arabic numerals refer to pages, and Roman numerals to volumes. Dates and places of publication are given only when they may prove vital: e.g., for recent, rare, old or foreign publications.

Common Abbreviations

A.P.C.	*Acts of the Privy Council*, ed. J. R. Dasent
Dixon	R. W. Dixon, *History of the Church of England*
D.N.B.	*Dictionary of National Biography*
Dugmore	C. W. Dugmore, *The Mass and the English Reformers*
E.H.R.	*English Historical Review*
Foxe	J. Foxe, *Acts and Monuments*, ed. Cattley and Townsend
Garrett	C. H. Garrett, *The Marian Exiles*
Gee and Hardy	H. Gee and W. J. Hardy, *Documents Illustrative of English Church History*
Hill	J. E. C. Hill, *Economic Problems of the Church*
Hughes	P. Hughes, *The Reformation in England*
J.E.H.	*Journal of Ecclesiastical History*
Knappen	M. M. Knappen, *Tudor Puritanism* (Chicago, 1939)
L. & P.	*Letters and Papers of Henry VIII*, ed. Brewer, Gairdner and Brodie
Lollards and Protestants	A. G. Dickens, *Lollards and Protestants in the Diocese of York*
O.D.C.C.	*Oxford Dictionary of the Christian Church*, ed. F. L. Cross
Pol. Hist. Eng.	*Political History of England*, ed. W. Hunt and R. L. Poole [most references are to vol. vi, by A. F. Pollard]
Ridley	J. Ridley, *Thomas Cranmer* (1962)
Span. Cal.	*Calendar of State Papers, Spanish*
S.T.C.	*Short Title Catalogue . . . 1475–1640*, ed. A. W. Pollard and G. R. Redgrave
T.R.H.S.	*Transactions of the Royal Historical Society*
Tudor Bibliog.	*Bibliography of British History, Tudor Period*, ed. C. Read (1959)
V.C.H.	*Victoria County History*
Ven. Cal.	*Calendar of State Papers, Venetian*

CHAPTER 1, PAGES 1–21

1. Durham University Library, Cosin MS v.v. 19
2. B. M. Sloane MS 1584
3. A sympathetic sketch of the popular religion is in H. Maynard Smith, *Pre-Reformation England*, ch. iii, iv
4. *The Pilgrimage of Robert Langton*, ed. E. M. Blackie (Cambridge, Mass., 1924)
5. *Visitations of the Diocese of Norwich*, ed. A. Jessopp (*Camden Soc.*, 2 ser., xliii); see 320 for refs.; C. E. Woodruff in *Archaeologia Cantiana*, xliv, 13–32
6. Sir T. More, *English Works* (edn. 1557), 337–8
7. For the Parkyn MSS and my commentaries, see *Tudor Treatises* (*Yorks. Archaeol. Soc., Record Ser.*, cxxv), 18ff
8. Printed in *ibid.*, 67–88
9. Printed in *E.H.R.*, lxii, 58–83
10. Letters printed in *Transactions, Hunter Archaeol. Soc.*, vi, pt. 6, 280–4
11. Bodleian MS Eng. Poet. e. 59; compare the present writer in *Bodleian Library Record*, iv, no. 2, 67ff
12. P. Janelle, *L'Angleterre Catholique à la Veille du Schisme* (Paris, 1935), 13ff
13. *Dialogue concerning Heresyes* (1528) in *Works* (1557), 233–4, but compare 186; P. Janelle, *op. cit.*, 17
14. See references in E. F. Jacob, *The Fifteenth Century* (*Oxford History of England*), 663ff., and J. W. Adamson in *The Library*, 4 ser., x, 163ff
15. Compare G. G. Coulton, *Art and the Reformation*, ch. xix, xx
16. *The First Churchwardens' Book of Louth*, ed. R. C. Dudding, 181. Compare *V.C.H., London*, i, 238
17. *York Mystery Plays*, ed. L. Toulmin Smith, *Introduction*; A. C. Cawley, *The Wakefield Pageants in the Towneley Cycle* (1958); T. Wright, *Chester Plays* (*Shakespeare Soc.*, 1843). Other refs. in H. Maynard Smith, *op. cit.*, 141–9
18. *Lollards and Protestants*, 232; J. Strype, *Ecclesiastical Memorials*, iii (2), 390–92
19. See on these rewards the instructions for a parish priest in B. M. Harleian MS 4172, fos. 8v–9. This and other authorities are cited by E. G. Ashby, *Some Aspects of Parish Life in the City of London from 1429 to 1529* (London M.A. thesis, 1951), 315ff. Further recent discussion in *Journal of Theological Studies*, new ser., xiv (April 1963), 229
20. H. Maynard Smith, *op. cit.*, ch. i, gives a good account of Henry's will and obsequies
21. C. C. Butterworth, *The English Primers, 1529–1545*, ch. i, gives detail on earlier versions
22. *A Relation of the Island of England* (*Camden Soc.*, 1 ser., xxxvii), 23
23. Select bibliography on mysticism in *O.D.C.C.*, 936; on the *devotio moderna*, *ibid.*, 394
24. On the English mystics see D. Knowles, *The English Mystical Tradition* (1961); on Hilton, Helen Gardner in *Essays and Studies, English Association*, xxii, 103ff
25. *Clifford Letters of the Sixteenth Century*, ed. A. G. Dickens (*Surtees Soc.*, clxxii), 68–9
26. Trinity College, Cambridge, MS 1160. I was mistaken in doubting Methley's

terminal date; I am informed by Fr. Andrew Gray that the official Carthusian *cartae* give 1528

27. Pembroke College, Cambridge, MS 221
28. *To Hew Heremyte* (P.R.O., SP 1/239, fos. 266–7v) is printed (inaccurately) in E. M. Nugent, *The Thought and Culture of the English Renaissance*, 388ff
29. Lincoln Cathedral Library, MS A. 6, 8
30. M. Chauncy, *Historia Aliquot Martyrum* (Mainz, 1550) was translated anonymously as *The History of the Sufferings of Eighteen Carthusians* (1890)
31. D. Knowles, *The Religious Orders in England*, iii, 368–9
32. *The Spiritual Exercises of a Dominican Friar*, ed. C. Kirchberger (1929)
33. G. Sitwell in *The Month*, April 1959, 218ff; O. de Veghel, *Benoit de Canfield* (Rome, 1949); H. Bremond, *A Literary History of Religious Thought in France*, ii, 111–26
34. D. Knowles, *The English Mystical Tradition*, ch. ix

CHAPTER 2, PAGES 22–37

This chapter is lightly annotated, since fuller references appear in the present writer's 'Heresy and the Origins of English Protestantism' in *Britain and the Netherlands*, ii, ed. J. S. Bromley and E. H. Kossman (1964), 47–66. On earlier Lollardy reference should now be made to M. E. Aston in *Past and Present*, xvii, 1–44, and to J. A. F. Thomson, *The Later Lollards 1414–1520* (1965).

1. Most recent interpretation in K. B. McFarlane, *John Wycliffe and the Beginnings of English Nonconformity*. Detail and refs. in H. B. Workman, *John Wyclif*
2. On its development see e.g. H. S. Cronin in *E.H.R.*, xxii, 292–304; M. Deanesly, *The Lollard Bible*; V. H. H. Green, *Bishop Reginald Pecock*. J. Gairdner, *Lollardy and the Reformation* is useful for the 15th century, but greatly underestimates Tudor Lollardy
3. J. F. Mozley, *John Foxe and his Book* successfully defends Foxe against S. R. Maitland and Gairdner. A short summary of Foxe's Lollard material is in Hughes, i, 127–33
4. *Lollards and Protestants* gives refs. for this and the subsequent passages on York diocese
5. Registers &c. listed in *Britain and the Netherlands*, ii, 51–3
6. W. H. Summers, *The Lollards of the Chiltern Hills* (1906)
7. *V.C.H. London*, i, 234–8; *L. & P.*, iv (2), nos. 4029–30; J. Strype, *Ecclesiastical Memorials*, i (1), 113–34; (2), 50–62. A conspectus of Lollardy in London is given in the thesis by E. G. Ashby (note 19 to ch. 1 above), ch. ix
8. Foxe, iv, 181–2, 722–3; v, 647–54; Warham's Register, Lambeth Palace Library MS 1108, fos. 164–81; *British Magazine*, xxiii–xxv *passim*
9. Foxe, iv, 213; *V.C.H.*, *Berkshire*, ii, 21
10. Foxe, iv, 557–8
11. J. Fines, 'Heresy Trials in the Diocese of Coventry and Lichfield' in *J.E.H.*, xiv, 160–74

12. E. E. Reynolds, *St. John Fisher*, 120
13. Foxe, iv, 208–14
14. J. Strype, *op. cit.*, i (2), 54–5
15. Foxe, iv, 584
16. *Lollards and Protestants*, 24–7
17. *Original Letters*, i (*Parker Soc.*, 1846), 221
18. C. Sturge, *Cuthbert Tunstal*, 362–3
19. *Erasmi Epistolae*, ed. P. S. Allen, v. 292
20. D. Wilkins, *Concilia*, iii, 804–7
21. E.g., *S.T.C.*, nos. 15225, 20036, 24045, 25588, 25590–91. See M. Aston in *History*, xlix, 149ff

CHAPTER 3, PAGES 38-58

1. *The Register or Chronicle of Butley Priory*, ed. A. G. Dickens, 58–9
2. A. F. Pollard, *Wolsey*, 308–12
3. M. Kelly, *Canterbury Jurisdiction and Influence during the Episcopate of William Warham, 1503–1532* (Cambridge Ph.D. thesis, 1963)
4. E. Cavendish, *The Life and Death of Cardinal Wolsey*, ed. R. S. Sylvester (*Early English Text Soc.*, no. 243), 90, 116
5. *A Sermon of Cuthbert Byshop of Duresme* (1539); compare C. Sturge, *Cuthbert Tunstal*, 193. For an anti-papal sermon of 1516 see *L. & P.*, ii, no. 2692
6. E. Hall, *Henry VIII*, ed. C. Whibley, ii, 95
7. J. J. Scarisbrick, 'Clerical Taxation in England, 1485–1547', in *J.E.H.*, xi, 41–54
8. *Letters of Richard Fox, 1486–1527*, ed. P. S. and H. M. Allen, 93, 97
9. The education and background of the bishops is treated at length by L. B. Smith, *Tudor Prelates and Politics* and by J. J. Scarisbrick, *The Conservative Episcopate in England, 1529–1535* (Cambridge Ph.D. thesis, 1955)
10. *Clifford Letters of the Sixteenth Century* (*Surtees Soc.*, clxxii), 42–4 gives refs.
11. Cited with other relevant More passages in Hughes, i, 86ff
12. *L'Angleterre Catholique à la Veille du Schisme*, 33–6
13. *Sermo Exhortatorius Cancellarii Eboracensis* (W. de Worde, *c.* 1510). Hughes briefly describes the book, which the present writer proposes to reprint
14. E. L. Cutts, *Parish Priests and their People*, 146, but I have not checked this computation by reference to the York records; Margaret Roper, *The Secular Clergy of the Diocese of Lincoln* (Oxford B.Litt. thesis, 1962), 76
15. P. Heath, *The Parish Clergy in England, 1450–1530* (London M.A. thesis, 1961), 115–19; I am also indebted to this thesis for other points on the clergy in the subsequent paragraphs
16. G. R. Elton, *Star Chamber Stories*, ch. vi
17. A. Hamilton Thompson, *The English Clergy*, 115–16
18. Refs. in H. Maynard Smith, *Pre-Reformation England*, 34–5

19. These figures sent me by Mr. Heath are somewhat more precise then those given in his thesis (note 15 above). Latimer says this (*Sermons*, Everyman edn., 85) of vicars with 12 to 14 marks a year
20. H. Ellis, *Original Letters*, 3 ser., ii, 338; 'exile': meagre, poor
21. Borthwick Institute, York: Diocesan Records, R.VII.G.600
22. A. G. Dickens in *Proceedings, Cambridge Antiquarian Soc.*, xlii, 21–9
23. J. Bale, *Yet a Course at the Romyshe Foxe* (1543), 364
24. D. Knowles and R. N. Hadcock, *Medieval Religious Houses*, 364
25. The figures in Hughes, i, 40 involve an average of four inhabitants, but they seem based on the unreliable calculations of F. A. Gasquet, *Henry VIII and the English Monasteries*, ii, 23–4, 237, 322–3
26. *Register of Butley Priory* (note 1 above), app. i
27. Hughes, i, 44: on the poverty of most nunneries, *ibid.*, i, 71
28. A. Savine, *English Monasteries on the Eve of the Dissolution*, 287
29. *Visitations of the Diocese of Lincoln*, ed. A. Hamilton Thompson (*Lincoln Record Soc.*, xxxiii–v–vii)
30. See above, note 5 to ch. 1
31. *Collectanea Anglo-Premonstratensia*, ed. F. A. Gasquet (*Camden Soc.*, 3 ser., vi, x, xii)
32. *Yorks. Archaeol. Journal*, xvi, 446–7
33. For a little-known example of a 'bad' house, Marton Priory, Yorks., see J. S. Purvis in *ibid.*, xxxv, 393–403
34. A. G. Little, *The Greyfriars in Oxford* (*Oxford Hist. Soc.*, xx), 54
35. D. Knowles, *The Religious Orders in England*, iii, is now the standard work both on the state of the Tudor monasteries and on the process of their dissolution. On William More, see *ibid.*, ch. ix
36. I. S. Leadam in *T.R.H.S.*, vii, viii, and in *The Domesday of Enclosures*, especially i, 48–9. Compare the cases of depopulation by monasteries cited by M. Beresford, *The Lost Villages of England*, index, under 'monasteries as depopulators'
37. *Utopia* (Everyman edn.), 24
38. Called *Rede me and be not wrothe* by some misguided literary histories, and attributed to William Roy. See the passage printed by R. H. Tawney and E. Power, *Tudor Economic Documents*, iii, 20–21
39. *Select Cases . . . in the Star Chamber*, ii (*Selden Soc.*, xxv), pp. xciiff
40. *Register of Butley Priory* (note 1 above), 16, 50
41. E.g., *L. & P.*, x, nos. 716, 858, 916; xiii (2), no. 306
42. A. Savine, *op. cit.*, 238
43. D. Knowles, *op. cit.*, iii, 212ff
44. See above, note 30 to ch. 1

CHAPTER 4, PAGES 59–82

1. For a conspectus of modern Luther studies, see E. G. Rupp, *The Righteousness of God*

2. For the implications of Luther's justificatory teaching, see J. S. Whale, *The Protestant Tradition*, pt. i; on its impact upon English Reformers, see E. G. Rupp, *The English Protestant Tradition*, ch. viii
3. Refs. in W. K. Jordan, *The Development of Religious Toleration in England*, i, 327–8
4. For a succinct account of the connection: J. Mackinnon, *The Origins of the Reformation*, 348ff, but compare E. G. Rupp, *The Righteousness of God*, 88ff
5. J. Colet, *Exposition of St. Paul's Epistle to the Romans*, trans. J. H. Lupton (1873), has valuable introduction. E. W. Hunt, *Dean Colet and his Theology* (S.P.C.K., 1956) amplifies this. Lupton's *Life of John Colet* (1887) is still of value
6. H. A. Enno van Gelder, *The Two Reformations of the 16th Century*, trans. J. F. Finlay (The Hague, 1961). The present writer is fully in accord with the criticisms made by G. R. Elton in *Journal of Theological Studies*, new ser., xiv (1), 222–6
7. Foxe, v, 415–16. For references to the dates which follow, see C. S. Meyer in *J.E.H.*, ix, 173–87
8. J. A. Muller, *Stephen Gardiner*, 14, 342, n. 6
9. On Barnes, see E. G. Rupp, *The English Protestant Tradition*, 31–46
10. *L. & P.*, iv (1), no. 1962; *Greyfriars Chron.* (*Camden Soc.*, 1 ser., liii), 33
11. *L. & P.*, iv (3), no. 6385: the same letter in which he denounces Gonville Hall as a centre of heresy
12. W. A. Clebsch (see above, p. vii) is now obligatory reading on the theology of Tyndale and other early leaders. J. F. Mozley, *William Tyndale* (1937), is scholarly but rather uncritical. To the authorities given by them add J. G. Møller in *J.E.H.*, xiv, 50ff
13. *Lollards and Protestants*, 131–7
14. Dixon, i, 413–14, from Alesius and Foxe
15. W. Tyndale, *Obedience of a Christian Man* in *Doctrinal Treatises* (*Parker Soc.*, 1848), 255
16. On Roy and Jerome Barlow, see E. G. Rupp, *op. cit*, 52ff, and above, note 38 to ch. 3
17. C. C. Butterworth and A. G. Chester, *George Joye, 1495?–1553* (Philadelphia and O.U.P., 1962); see also J. F. Mozley, *Coverdale and his Bibles*, 42ff. The latter work remains standard for Coverdale himself. On *The Supper of the Lord*, see W. D. J. Cargill Thompson in *Harvard Theological Review*, liii, 47–76
18. Foxe, v, 421ff and app. 6
19. Foxe, v, 1–16. Foxe edited *The Whole Works of W. Tyndall, John Frith and Doctor Barnes* (1572). Clebsch, *op. cit.*, ch. vi–viii, best covers Frith's life and theology
20. On adiaphorism in Melanchthon and in the English writers, see W. G. Zeeveld, *Foundations of Tudor Policy*, especially 137ff
21. Foxe, iv, 619–56; Tout in *D.N.B.*; Rupp, *op. cit.*, 22–31; C. Sturge, *Cuthbert Tunstal*, 137–9
22. On Stafford see C. H. and T. Cooper, *Athenae Cantabrigienses*, i, 39; H. Maynard Smith, *Henry VIII and the Reformation*, 259–60; H. C. Porter,

Reformation and Reaction in Tudor Cambridge, 42
23. *Span. Cal.*, iv (1), 349–50

CHAPTER 5, PAGES 83–108

1. Erastianism: the ascendancy of State over Church in ecclesiastical affairs, so called after the Swiss theologian Thomas Erastus (1524–83)
2. Brief bibliography in *O.D.C.C.*, 863; best edn. of *Defensor Pacis*, ed. C. W. Previté-Orton; summaries in G. H. Sabine, *Hist. of Political Theory*, ch. xv, and in E. Armstrong, *Italian Studies*, 59–72. See also commentary by C. W. Previté-Orton in *Proc. British Academy*, xxi, 137–84
3. G. Barraclough, *Papal Provisions*; W. T. Waugh in *E.H.R.*, xxxvii, 173ff, and in *History*, viii, 289; further refs. in *O.D.C.C.*, 1095, 1118–19, and by G. L. Harriss in *Past and Present*, xxv, 15ff
4. Refs. in *O.D.C.C.*, 1213; add I. D. Thornley in *Tudor Studies presented to A. F. Pollard*, 182–207
5. Ed. D. M. Brodie (1948)
6. D. Wilkins, *Concilia*, iii, 651; J. H. Lupton, *Life of John Colet*, 293ff; M. Kelly, *Canterbury Jurisdiction and Influence* (see above, note 3 to ch. iii), 110ff
7. A. F. Pollard, *Wolsey*, 31ff, helped by E. Jeffries Davis in *E.H.R.*, xxx, 477ff, gave the first tolerable account. A. Ogle, *The Tragedy of the Lollards' Tower* largely replaces earlier surveys, though it needs corrections from S. F. C. Milsom in *E.H.R.*, lxxvi, 80–82
8. *Hist. of the English Church in the Sixteenth Century*, ch. iii
9. *V.C.H., London*, i, 236ff, 247ff
10. *E.H.R.*, xxx, 481
11. Chapuys, 13 Dec. 1529 in *Span. Cal., 1529–30*, 367; E. Hall, *Henry VIII*, ed. C. Whibley, ii, 163ff
12. *Ibid.*, ii, 225ff
13. F. Le Van Baumer, *The Early Tudor Theory of Kingship* (New Haven, 1940), ch. iii, and the same author in *American Historical Review*, xlii, 631ff
14. Fish was incorporated by Foxe, iv, 659ff. Modern edns. by J. M. Cowper in *Early Eng. Text Soc.*, extra ser., xiii, and by E. Arber in *English Scholar's Library*, no. 4
15. The writs themselves mention church-reform (Rymer, *Foedera*, xiv, 302). For some of the points which follow, see G. W. O. Woodward in *Schweizer Beiträge zur Allgemeinen Geschichte*, Band 16 (1958), 56ff
16. Detail in A. F. Pollard, *op. cit.*, ch. vi. The lead taken by More in the attack on Wolsey cannot be doubted: see *ibid.*, 256, n. 3, and R. W. Chambers, *Thomas More* (edn. 1963), 230–31
17. I owe this point, which seems unnoticed by the commentators, to Dr. Woodward
18. J. J. Scarisbrick in *Cambridge Historical Journal*, xii, 22ff. M. Kelly (above, note 6), 225ff, suggests the possible modification mentioned below
19. *The Letters of Stephen Gardiner*, ed. J. A. Muller, 392

20. The large literature on the divorce can be approached through G. Mattingly, *Catherine of Aragon*. Useful summaries in Hughes, i, 156ff, and in A. F. Pollard, *Henry VIII*, 173ff
21. *L. & P.*, v, no. 45
22. J. J. Scarisbrick, 'Henry VIII and the Vatican Library' in *Bibliothèque d'Humanisme et Renaissance*, xxiv, 211–16

CHAPTER 6, PAGES 109–138

1. Select bibliography in A. G. Dickens, *Thomas Cromwell and the English Reformation*, 185ff; note especially the contributions by G. R. Elton
2. On these writers, see W. G. Zeeveld, *Foundations of Tudor Policy*; F. Le Van Baumer, *The Early Tudor Theory of Kingship*, and the latter again (on Starkey and Marsiglio) in *Politica*, ii, 188–205
3. *D.N.B.*, Marshall, William; *L. & P.*, vii, no. 423
4. Refs. to the familiar statutes which follow are in all standard accounts. The chief relevant passages are reprinted in, e.g., Gee and Hardy; J. R. Tanner, *Tudor Constitutional Documents*; G. R. Elton, *The Tudor Constitution*
5. Detail in G. R. Elton, *The Tudor Revolution in Government*, 76ff
6. Compare G. R. Elton in *E.H.R.*, lxvi, 507–34, and J. P. Cooper in *ibid.*, lxxii, 616–41
7. Printed, Gee and Hardy, 145–53
8. D. Wilkins, *Concilia*, iii, 746
9. On this and sequel: M. Kelly in *T.R.H.S.*, 5 ser., xv, 97ff
10. Printed in Gee and Hardy, 154–76
11. E. Hall, *Henry VIII*, ed. Whibley, ii, 209–12
12. G. R. Elton in *E.H.R.*, lxvi, 174–97; R. Koebner in *Bulletin of the Institute of Historical Research*, xxvi, 29–52; G. L. Harriss in *Past and Present*, xxv, 9–12
13. Dickens, *op. cit.*, 142ff summarises *S.T.C.*, no. 292
14. G. W. O. Woodward; see note 15 to ch. 5, above
15. Other examples in Woodward, *op. cit.*, 65
16. Ed. J. Caley and J. Hunter (1810–34); chief commentary, A. Savine, *English Monasteries on the Eve of the Dissolution*
17. F. C. Dietz, *English Government Finance, 1485–1558* (*Univ. of Illinois Studies*, ix, no. 3), 80–82, 138
18. I. D. Thornley in *E.H.R.*, xxxii, 556ff.; G. R. Elton, *The Tudor Constitution*, 59ff
19. R. W. Chambers, *Thomas More* remains the best life, but it sees the age only through More's eyes, and endows him with a supernatural consistency
20. *Span. Cal.*, iv (2), nos. 1130 (p. 813), 1133 (p. 821). Chapuys should always be regarded with great caution, but he had no motive for fabricating these communications
21. On the neo-feudal conspiracy, see refs. in G. Mattingly, *Catherine of Aragon*, 328

22. M. H. and R. Dodds, *The Pilgrimage of Grace and the Exeter Conspiracy*. On Abbot Cooke, below, see J. E. Paul in *Bulletin of the Institute of Historical Research*, xxxiii, no. 87, 115–21. Dodds, *op. cit.*, ably handles the material in *L. & P.*, yet seriously idealises the Pilgrimage. For a summary of causes see R. R. Reid, *The King's Council in the North*, 121ff. For Bigod's rebellion see *Lollards and Protestants*, 90–113, and for generalisation A. G. Dickens, *Thomas Cromwell*, 95–102
23. M. H. and R. Dodds, *op. cit.*, i, 139
24. *E.H.R.*, v, 335–6
25. M. H. and R. Dodds, *op. cit.*, i, 347–8, 383, discusses this and other divisions of opinion
26. *Lollards and Protestants*, 126–31
27. Zeeveld, *op. cit.*, 232–3
28. J. C. Cox, *The Parish Registers of England*, especially 1–4, 236–8
29. On the subsequent passages see J. F. Mozley, *Coverdale and his Bibles*; A. W. Pollard, *Records of the English Bible*; J. Isaacs in *The Bible in its Ancient and English Versions*, ed. H. W. Robinson, 146–95
30. *L. & P.*, v, no. 221
31. In 1583 by Dr. William Fulke, who may have received it from Coverdale: see J. F. Mozley, *op. cit.*, 112–13
32. On Rogers see Foxe, vi, 596
33. *L. & P.*, xiv (2), no. 214
34. Castillon's report on a conversation with Cromwell, printed in A. W. Pollard, *op. cit.*, 249–51; compare *L. & P.*, xiii (2), no. 1163
35. J. F. Mozley, *op. cit.*, 214ff
36. *L. & P.*, xiv (2), no. 1086, printed in A. W. Pollard, *op. cit.*, 236–7
37. *State Papers of Henry VIII*, i, 589–90
38. *D.N.B.*, Taverner, Richard; on his Bible see J. F. Mozley, *op. cit.*, 347–8
39. On Gardiner's plea for latinisation see *ibid.*, 273–6, and A. W. Pollard, *op. cit.*, 272–5
40. I cite the 'Great Bible' as reprinted in *The English Hexapla* (1841)

CHAPTER 7, PAGES 136–166

1. *Register of Butley Priory* (note 1 to ch. 3 above), 67
2. *L. & P.*, vii, no. 1355. Already in 1532, Henry had dissolved Christchurch, Aldgate, without Papal authorisation; see E. Jeffries Davis in *T.R.H.S.*, 4 ser., viii, 127-50
3. R. B. Merriman, *Life and Letters of Thomas Cromwell*, ii, 265
4. R. Ehrenberg, *Capital and Finance in the Age of the Renaissance*, 108
5. Best account by D. Knowles, *The Religious Orders in England*, iii, pt. 3
6. *Sermons* (*Parker Soc.*, 1844), 123
7. Spelman's *History and Fate of Sacrilege* was written *c.* 1633, published 1698
8. E. Hall, *Henry VIII*, ed. C. Whibley, ii, 268
9. G. W. O. Woodward in *E.H.R.*, lxxvi, 385–401
10. G. A. J. Hodgett in *J.E.H.*, xiii, 195–202

11. Full account in W. C. Richardson, *History of the Court of Augmentations* (Baton Rouge, 1961)
12. On pensions see A. G. Dickens in *E.H.R.*, lv, 412ff., and G. A. J. Hodgett in *Lincoln Record Society*, liii, pp. xvii–xix. G. Baskerville, *English Monks and the Dissolution of the Monasteries*, has valuable information but seems in general to convey an over-optimistic view. His best work is in the detailed articles, e.g. in *Surrey Archaeological Collections*, xlvii, 12–28; *Essays in History presented to R. L. Poole*, 436–65
13. Refs. to York diocesan records in A. G. Dickens, *The Marian Reaction in the Diocese of York*, ii, 16–17
14. *Ibid.*, ii, 17–19
15. *Yorks. Archaeol. Journal*, xix, 100–4
16. Baskerville, *op. cit.*, 242–3, but see G. A. J. Hodgett in *J.E.H.*, xiii, 201
17. Described by the present writer in *E.H.R.*, lv, 384–412
18. J. Hunter, *South Yorkshire*, ii, 274–6
19. A. Savine, *English Monasteries on the Eve of the Dissolution*, 100
20. N. R. Ker, *Medieval Libraries of Great Britain*, pp. xiff; N. R. Ker in *The Library*, 4 ser., xxiii, 7ff
21. E. Jeffries Davis, 'The Transformation of London', in *Tudor Studies presented to A. F. Pollard*, 287–314
22. For Henry VIII's schemes, see *L. & P.*, xiv (1), nos. 868, 1189–90; xiv (2), nos. 429–30; Dixon, ii, 221–6; *King Henry the Eighth's Scheme of Bishopricks*, ed. H. Cole (1838)
23. D. Knowles, *op. cit.*, iii, 389–92
24. A. F. Leach, *The Schools of Medieval England*, 311ff
25. *Complaynt of Roderyck Mors* (*Early Eng. Text Soc.*, extra ser., xxii), 9, 33
26. Ed. E. Lamond, 85
27. *Sermons* (*Parker Soc.*, 1844), 63–5, 247–9, etc.
28. M. Beresford, *The Lost Villages of England*, 166
29. *Discourse of the Common Weal*, ed. E. Lamond, 19
30. H. R. Trevor-Roper, *The Gentry, 1540–1640* (*Econ. Hist. Review Supplement*, i)
31. E. Kerridge in *Econ. Hist. Review*, 2 ser., vi, 16–34
32. Mary E. Finch, *The Wealth of Five Northamptonshire Families* (*Northamptonshire Record Soc.*, xix), 165–9
33. A. Simpson, *The Wealth of the Gentry, 1540–1660* (1961)
34. E.g., *York Civic Records*, vi (*Yorks. Archaeol. Soc. Record Ser.*, cxii), 17; present writer in *V.C.H.*, *City of York*, 132–3
35. In H. A. L. Fisher, *Pol. Hist. Eng.*, v, app. ii
36. On the subsequent passages see especially H. J. Habakkuk, 'The Market for Monastic Property', in *Econ. Hist. Review*, 2 ser., x, 362–80
37. S. B. Liljegren, *The Fall of the Monasteries* (Lund, 1924), 85
38. R. B. Smith, *A Study of Landed Income and Social Structure in the West Riding of Yorkshire in the Period 1535–46* (Leeds Ph.D. thesis, 1962)
39. Joan Thirsk, *Fenland Farming in the Sixteenth Century* (Univ. of Leicester, 1953)
40. W. G. Hoskins, *The Midland Peasant*, 141

41. G. A. J. Hodgett, *The Dissolution of the Monasteries in Lincolnshire* (London M.A. thesis, 1947)
42. Joyce Youings, *Devon Monastic Lands: Calendar of Particulars for Grants* (*Devon and Cornwall Record Soc.*, new ser., i)
43. S. T. Bindoff, *Tudor England*, 124–7
44. R. B. Smith, *op. cit.*, 174ff
45. A. L. Rowse, *Tudor Cornwall*, 222
46. *D.N.B.*, York, Sir John; *Select Cases in the Court of Requests* (*Selden Soc.*, xii), 198ff, 201ff
47. F. G. Emmison, *Tudor Secretary* (1961), ch. xiv, especially 269–70
48. Ed. A. G. Dickens in *Bedfordshire Hist. Record Soc.*, xxxvi, 38ff
49. On Harrington see not only R. H. Tawney in *Proc. British Academy*, xxvii, 199ff, but the criticism by C. B. Macpherson in *Past and Present*, no. 17 (April 1960)
50. Based mainly on *The Visitation of Yorkshire . . . 1584–5 . . . and 1612*, ed. J. Foster (1875)
51. *Harleian Soc.*, xii
52. *Ibid.*, xliii
53. *Ibid.*, l, li, lii, lv
54. *Ibid.*, xiii, xiv
55. *Ibid.*, lxvi
56. A. L. Rowse, *op. cit.*, 212; 'spry' is a form of 'spray', i.e. branch

CHAPTER 8, PAGES 167–196

1. Refs. to primary authorities for the whole of Cranmer's career are in Ridley
2. *Ibid.*, 148–51
3. R. B. Merriman, *Life and Letters of Thomas Cromwell*, ii, 128–31
4. Modern lives by Honor McCusker (Bryn Mawr, 1942) and Jesse W. Harris (Urbana, 1949)
5. Listed by W. T. Davies, *A Bibliography of John Bale* [Oxford, 1940]
6. *Illustrium Majoris Britanniae Scriptorum*, &c. (1548–9; 1557–9); also *Index Britanniae Scriptorum*, ed. Poole and Bateson (1902)
7. See *Summary Catalogue of Western MSS in the Bodleian Library*, nos. 3429, 3460, 27635–6
8. In Bale's *Select Works* (*Parker Soc.*, 1849), 1ff, 136ff
9. *L. & P.*, xiv (1), no. 47
10. *Kynge Johan* (*Camden Soc.*, 1 ser., ii). Nicholas Udall, the 'Father of English Comedy', was also a notable Protestant publicist
11. On Starkey and Morison see W. G. Zeeveld, *Foundations of Tudor Policy*; *Early Eng. Text Soc.*, extra ser., xii and xxxii; F. Le Van Baumer, as cited above, note 13 to ch. 5. On Taverner see *D.N.B.*; J. F. Mozley, *Coverdale and his Bibles*, 347–8
12. On Lambert see Foxe, v, 181ff; comment in Ridley, 94–5, 174–6; Dugmore, 177–81

13. P. Janelle, *Obedience in Church and State*; my summary is also based on that in Hughes, i, 337–41
14. On Cromwell's foreign policy see R. B. Merriman, *op. cit.*, i, 213–41
15. Compare G. Constant, *The Reformation in England*, i, 404ff; text in C. Hardwick, *History of the Articles of Religion* (1890), 237–58
16. Text in C. Lloyd, *Formularies of Faith* (1825), 21–212. On the accompanying circumstances the modern authorities seem most inconsistent and the whole affair needs further investigation
17. Detail in Dixon, ii, 251ff. On the later career of Barnes, see *D.N.B.*; E. G. Rupp, *The English Protestant Tradition*, ch. ii, vi; J. A. Muller, *Stephen Gardiner*, ch. xiii
18. Summarised in Dixon, ii, 233–4; G. Burnet, *History of the Reformation*, ed. N. Pocock, i, 438
19. W. G. Zeeveld, *op. cit.*, 152–6
20. Gee and Hardy, 269–81
21. C. H. Smyth, *Cranmer and the Reformation under Edward VI*, ch. x; his dating is accepted by E. C. Ratcliff, 'The Liturgical Work of Archbishop Cranmer', in *J.E.H.*, vii, 194
22. Refs. to the prymers in H. Maynard Smith, *Henry VIII and the Reformation*, 394–9
23. Detail in Dixon, ii, 328–33
24. On these attacks see Ridley, 186 and ch. xv: the chief source is Morice's *Anecdotes*, printed in *Narratives of the Reformation* (*Camden Soc.*, 1 ser., lxxvii): see 251–9
25. *The King's Book*, as reprinted by the Church Historical Society in 1932, amounts to little more than the text in C. Lloyd, *op. cit.*, 213ff. On the doctrine of the Church see 69ff as well as 31–7; on the mass see 163–5 as well as 50–57. On the circumstances see D. Wilkins, *Concilia*, iii, 868, and J. A. Muller, *The Letters of Stephen Gardiner*, 259. A longer summary is in H. Maynard Smith, *Henry VIII and the Reformation*, 375–80
26. On Cranmer's development see C. H. Smyth, *op. cit.*, 48–66, and Dugmore, ch. v–viii; note criticisms by T. M. Parker in *Journal of Theological Studies*, new ser., xii, 132–46, and Dugmore's rejoinder in *ibid.*, xiv, 227–34. Further refs. in Ridley, especially 168–70, 252–4, 280–83. Smyth's term 'Suvermerianism' has not proved acceptable to theologians. On Cranmer's adaptation of Justus Jonas, see F. A. Gasquet and E. Bishop, *Edward VI and the Book of Common Prayer*, 129–31. On Gardiner's view, mentioned below, see Dugmore, ch. viii, and on Tunstall's, *ibid.*, 152–4
27. Ed. C. S. Cobb in *Alcuin Club Collections*, xviii
28. H. Maynard Smith, *op. cit.*, 403–4
29. They were published 1547. A reprint was ed. by J. Griffiths (1859)
30. J. F. Mozley, *op. cit.*, ch. xiii, gives further detail
31. *Narratives of the Reformation* (note 24 above), 349–51
32. Mozley, *op. cit.*, 284
33. See Mozley, *op. cit.*, 265–9, for an attempt to reconcile Foxe's details with those given in 1547 by William Palmer

34. Fuller account in *Lollards and Protestants*, 171–2, 215–18
35. *Ibid.*, 172
36. *Ibid.*, 149–50
37. *Ibid.*, 114–31
38. E. Hall, *Henry VIII*, ed. C. Whibley, ii, 285–6
39. *Ricart's Kalendar* (*Camden Soc.*, 2 ser., v), 55; *L. & P.*, xiv (1), no. 184. On Bristol in 1533 see *L. & P.*, vi, nos. 796, 799, 873
40. An account of Edward's education and friends is in Hester W. Chapman, *The Last Tudor King*
41. On these cases see E. Trollope in *Assoc. Archit. Soc. Rep.*, vi (1862), 117ff; *Lollards and Protestants*, 33–4
42. Above, note 8
43. For Surrey's fall, see E. Casady, *Henry Howard, Earl of Surrey* (New York, 1938), ch. ix

CHAPTER 9, PAGES 197–229

1. Short Calvin bibliographies in *O.D.C.C.* 220 and in B. Hall, *John Calvin* (Historical Association, G.33), 38–9
2. On the early influence of Calvin, see C. D. Cremeans, *The Reception of Calvinist Thought in England* (Urbana, 1949), 29–40
3. On all these events, see A. F. Pollard, *Pol. Hist. Eng.*, vi, ch. i; and Pollard in *D.N.B.*, Seymour, Edward
4. Ridley, 262–3
5. *Ibid.*, 265ff; Dixon, ii, 423ff
6. *Pol. Hist. Eng.*, vi, 16
7. A. F. Pollard in *D.N.B.*, Seymour, Edward, and in *England under Protector Somerset*
8. 1 Edward VI cap. 14 in Gee and Hardy, 328–57; good comments in *Pol. Hist. Eng.*, vi, 18–20
9. 37 Henry VIII cap. 4
10. *A.P.C., 1550–1552*, 74; an example of a free chapel in *Suffolk Institute of Archaeology, Proc.*, xii, 33; Dixon, ii, 381–2, lists colleges, etc.
11. For a list (incomplete) of printed chantry surveys see *Tudor Bibliog.*, 180; additions in *E.H.R.*, lv, 413, n. 3; and in *Texts and Calendars*, ed. E. L. C. Mullins (Royal Hist. Soc.), 561, s.v. chantry certificates
12. Printed in *Surtees Soc.*, xci, xcii
13. W. Camden, *Britannia* (edn. 1753), i, p. ccxxx
14. Above, note 10 to ch. 1
15. *Suffolk Institute of Archaeology, Proc.*, xii, 30–71 *passim*
16. *Somerset Record Soc.*, ii; index gives refs. to these places
17. Details in *Lollards and Protestants*, 207
18. *Transactions, Bristol and Gloucester Arch. Soc.*, viii, 253
19. *A.P.C., 1547–1550*, 193, 195
20. A. G. Dickens in *Yorks. Arch. Journal*, xxxvi, 164ff
21. *Oxfordshire Record Soc.*, i, 3, 5

22. *Oxfordshire Record Soc.*, i, 42
23. Figures based on the histories of hospitals in *V.C.H.*, *Yorks.*, iii
24. *Surtees Soc.*, xci, 175
25. *Ibid.*, xcii, 400
26. *V.C.H.*, *Cumberland*, ii, 55
27. *Surtees Soc.*, xci, 61
28. *Oxfordshire Record Soc.*, i, 14–16
29. *Shropshire Arch. and Nat. Hist. Soc.*, 3 ser., x, 269–392; *Surtees Soc.*, xci, xcii
30. Joan Simon in *British Journal of Educational Studies*, iii, no. 2, 127ff; iv, no. 1, 32ff
31. Based on P. J. Wallis and W. E. Tate, *A Register of Old Yorks. Grammar Schools*, *Univ. of Leeds Inst. of Education, Researches and Studies*, no. 13
32. Cited by N. Wood, *The Reformation and English Education*, 181–2
33. *Surtees Soc.*, xci, 192
34. *Oxfordshire Record Soc.*, i, 23
35. *V.C.H.*, *Lancs.*, ii, 46
36. *Oxfordshire Record Soc.*, i, pp. xvi–xvii
37. A. G. Dickens in *Yorks. Arch. Journal*, xxxiv, 151ff
38. *Yorks. Star Chamber Proceedings*, ii (*Yorks. Archaeol. Soc. Record Ser.*, xlv), 13–36
39. *York Civic Records*, v (*ibid.*, cx), *passim*
40. *Oxfordshire Record Soc.*, i, 44; the communicants were earlier, probably in error, numbered 460 (*ibid.*, 22)
41. *Ibid.*, 19–20; *Shropshire Arch. and Nat. Hist. Soc.*, 3 ser., x, 327–8; *Surtees Soc.*, xci, p. xiv; xcii, p. vii
42. Refs. in Dixon, ii, 381–2
43. Following analysis based on A. Hamilton Thompson, *The English Clergy*, 78ff
44. B.M. Add. MS 5813, ed. A. G. Dickens in *Tudor Treatises* (*Yorks. Archaeol. Soc. Record Ser.*, cxxv), 89–142
45. *Ibid.*, 126–7
46. Ed. A. G. Dickens in *Yorks. Arch. Journal*, xxxvii, 376ff
47. G. Burnet, *History of the Reformation*, ed. Pocock, v. 197–217, prints the bishops' replies
48. Dugmore, 124–5
49. The literature on the Prayer Book is extensive: see *Tudor Bibliog.*, 165–8. F. Procter, revised H. W. Frere, *A New Hist. of the Book of Common Prayer* is a serviceable general account. See also F. E. Brightman, *The English Rite*; E. C. Ratcliff, *The Book of Common Prayer*; E. C. Ratcliff in *J.E.H.*, vii, 189–203; Dugmore, ch. vi, vii; T. M. Parker, *The English Reformation*, ch. vii, viii; the chapters (ii and iii) respectively by Dugmore and Parker in *The English Prayer Books 1549–1662* (S.P.C.K. for Alcuin Club, 1963). For the Edwardian Acts of Uniformity, see Gee and Hardy, 358ff, 369ff
50. Procter and Frere, *op. cit.*, 50–52
51. Dugmore, 130
52. F. Rose-Troup, *The Western Rebellion of 1549*; A. L. Rowse, *Tudor Cornwall*, 262ff

53. F. W. Russell, *Kett's Rebellion in Norfolk* (1859) is still indispensable; good modern analysis in S. T. Bindoff, *Ket's Rebellion* (Historical Association, G.12)
54. See note 37 above
55. *John Bon and Mast Person*, reprinted in *Tudor Tracts*, ed. A. F. Pollard, 159–99
56. On this Ipswich group see the present writer in *Notes and Queries*, Dec. 1954, 513; *S.T.C.*, nos. 18055–6, 20661–3; Foxe, v, 254; viii, 223–5, 598–600
57. Sig. Aiii, Bi
58. Summarised by Dugmore, 120–23; compare *S.T.C.*, nos. 24162–6
59. Several obscure pamphlets are summarised but in some cases misdated by an anonymous writer in *Church Quarterly Review*, xxxv (1892–3), 33–68; for examples of liberalism see pp. 44–5, 49. On Turner see above, 323
60. *S.T.C.*, nos. 2419–2700: see note 13 to ch. 12 below
61. The fullest account of this group is by Whitney R. D. Jones, *Contemporary Opinion upon the Economic and Social Aspects of the Commonwealth, 1529–59* (Cardiff M.A. thesis, 1963). See for brief account G. R. Elton, *England under the Tudors*, 185–7. Lives of Latimer by H. S. Darby (1953) and by A. G. Chester (Philadelphia, 1954). The continuity from Cromwell was noticed by H. R. Trevor-Roper, *Historical Essays*, 89. On Robert Crowley see J. W. Allen, *A History of Political Thought in the Sixteenth Century*, 138ff
62. D. S. Bailey, *Thomas Becon and the Reformation of the Church in England*: on what follows see especially pp. 81–2, 97, 120
63. E.g. *Greyfriars' Chronicle* (*Camden Soc.*, 1 ser., liii), 55, 57, 63
64. B.M. Harleian MS 425, fo. 124ff printed in *Narratives of the Reformation* (*Camden Soc.*, 1 ser., lxxvii), 71–84
65. Ridley, 298–9
66. *Ibid.*, 302–3
67. *Pol. Hist. Eng.*, vi, 45–6

CHAPTER 10, PAGES 230–258

1. *Pol. Hist. Eng.*, vi, ch. iii; G. Scott Thompson, *Lords Lieutenants in the Sixteenth Century*, 24ff; W. C. Richardson, *History of the Court of Augmentations*, ch. vi
2. Ridley, 327–30. On foreign refugees, see *Tudor Bibliog.*, 163–5
3. *Cal. Pat. Edw. VI*, iii, 317
4. C. Hopf, *Martin Bucer and the English Reformation*; H. Eells, *Martin Bucer* (New Haven, 1931); *Tudor Bibliog.*, nos. 2124, 2127
5. Cited by E. G. Rupp in *New Cambridge Modern History*, ii, 111
6. *D.N.B.*, Utenhove, John. On Glastonbury, see Dixon, iii, 236, 427
7. Modern sketch and brief bibliog. of Knox in J. D. Mackie, *John Knox* (Historical Association, G.20)
8. On Bradford and Marsh see *V.C.H.*, *Lancashire*, ii, 48; on the schemes for itinerant preachers, see J. E. C. Hill in *T.R.H.S.*, 5 ser., xiii, 79ff

9. G. H. Williams, *The Radical Reformation* (1962); E. A. Payne in *New Cambridge Modern History*, ii, 119–33; also *Tudor Bibliog.*, no. 1795
10. G. H. Williams, *op. cit.*, ch. xiii
11. *Original Letters* (*Parker Soc.*, 1846–7), 65–6; *A Lesson of the Incarnation of Christ* in *Later Writings of John Hooper* (*Parker Soc.*, 1852), 1–18
12. Williams, *op. cit.*, 780, gives titles
13. D. Wilkins, *Concilia*, iv, 42–3. Michael Thombe was apparently a German. A John Thombe, previously a subject of the Emperor, was naturalised in June 1549 (*Huguenot Soc.*, viii, 232)
14. D. Wilkins, *op. cit.*, iv, 44–5. Note also the Unitarian priest John Ashton in *ibid.*, 41
15. On the Family of Love see also *Tudor Bibliog.*, nos. 2469, 2471–2; E. B. Bax, *Rise and Fall of the Anabaptists*, 338ff; G. H. Williams, *op. cit.*, 788ff
16. *Ibid.*, 781; C. Burrage, *The Early English Dissenters*, i, 57–60
17. Dixon, iii, 207–12; G. H. Williams, *op. cit.*, 781; C. Burrage, *op. cit.*, i, 50–53
18. Foxe, vii, 306–18
19. *Writings of John Bradford, Letters, Treatises, etc.* (*Parker Soc.*, 1853), 128–31, 194–8. Compare also his *Defence of Election* in *Writings of John Bradford, Sermons, Meditations, etc.* (*Parker Soc.*, 1848), 307–30; and Dixon, iv, 300–3
20. On Bucer in Cambridge see H. C. Porter, *Reformation and Reaction in Tudor Cambridge*, 51–67
21. Knappen, 91–5, from à Lasco's *Forma ac Ratio*
22. On the Ordinal: Ridley, 307–8; E. C. Ratcliff in *J.E.H.*, vii, 201
23. C. Sturge, *Cuthbert Tunstal*, 281–96
24. C. Hopf in *Journal of Theological Studies*, xliv, 194–9; *Writings of John Bradford, Letters, Treatises, etc.*, 373–93; Ridley, 308–10, 313–15; Knappen, 82–9
25. F. D. Price, 'Gloucester Diocese under Bishop Hooper' in *Trans. Bristol and Gloucester Arch. Soc.*, lx, 51–151; J. Gairdner in *E.H.R.*, xix, 98–121; on Hooper's social liberalism see Knappen, 406–8
26. Price, *op. cit.*, 82–3
27. *Hist. MSS Comm.*, *Cecil*, i, 107, dated 2 Feb. 1553
28. A. G. Dickens, *Robert Holgate* (*St. Anthony's Hall Publications*, viii)
29. Printed in *Alcuin Club Collections*, xv, 310ff
30. Dickens, *op. cit.*, 24–5, and in *E.H.R.*, lii, 428ff; lvi, 450ff
31. H. Machyn, *Diary* (*Camden Soc.*, 1 ser., xlii), 8; *Greyfriars' Chronicle* (*ibid.*, liii), 70
32. 2 & 3 Edw. VI cap. 21; *Lords' Journals*, i, 343
33. Hilda Grieve in *T.R.H.S.*, 4 ser., xxii, 142–3; G. Baskerville in *E.H.R.*, xlviii, 44; E. L. C. Mullins, *The Effects of the Marian and Elizabethan Religious Settlements upon the Clergy of London* (London M.A. thesis, 1948), 122; R. B. Walker, *A History of the Reformation in the Archdeaconries of Lincoln and Stow* (Liverpool Ph.D. thesis, 1959), 217–19
34. A. G. Dickens, *The Marian Reaction in the Diocese of York*, i (*St. Anthony's Hall Publications*, xi), 14–15
35. H. Grieve, *op. cit.*, 150, 159

36. F. W. Brooks in *Journal of the British Archaeological Association*, 3 ser., x, 23–37
37. See Hill, 108–13. For a general account of the economic background, see A. Tindal Hart, *The Country Priest in English History*, ch. vii
38. Refs. in Dugmore, 150–56
39. *Ibid.*, 158–9
40. On the Second Prayer Book, see again refs. in note 49 to ch. 9 above
41. Ratcliff, *op. cit.*, 200–1
42. Dugmore, 163–72
43. Gee and Hardy, 369–72
44. On these events and on the *Reformatio Legum* below, see L. T. Dibdin and C. E. Chadwyck-Healey, *English Church Law and Divorce*; related refs. in *Tudor Bibliog.*, 211–12; a convenient edn. is *The Reformation of the Ecclesiastical Laws*, ed. E. Cardwell (1850). On its revival see J. E. Neale, *Elizabeth I and her Parliaments*, i, 194ff. On the heresy clauses, see Ridley, 333-4
45. The Forty-two Articles are discussed in all standard commentaries on the Thirty-nine; see *Tudor Bibliog.*, nos. 1922–3, 1936 and bibliog. in *O.D.C.C.*, 1349
46. Compare W. R. Matthews, *The Thirty-Nine Articles* (1961)
47. C. Hardwick, *A History of the Articles of Religion*, *passim*
48. Dugmore, 172–3; T. M. Parker in *Journal of Theological Studies*, new ser., xii, 136
49. *A.P.C., 1550–1552*, 228
50. Printed in *Surtees Soc.*, xcvii, 4ff
51. For typical surveys in print, see *Surtees Soc.*, xcvii; *Alcuin Club Collections*, vi, vii, ix, xx, xxiii; H. B. Walters, *London Churches at the Reformation*
52. *Somerset Record Soc.*, iv, 218
53. *A.P.C., 1552–1554*, 218
54. Antonio Guaras, *The Accession of Queen Mary*, ed. R. Garnett (1892), 81
55. *Ven. Cal.*, v, 346
56. Cited by J. A. Froude, *History of England*, iv, 362, from the State Papers Domestic
57. *Discourse of the Common Weal*, ed. E. Lamond, 21–2
58. For Northumberland's conspiracy see *Pol. Hist. Eng.*, vi, ch. v
59. 'The Life and Death of Sir Nicholas Throckmorton', a verse-biography in B.M. Add. MS 58541: the passage is on fo. 137v (old ref., p. 272). Throckmorton, later implicated in Wyatt's revolt, escaped through the unusual independence of a jury
60. C. Wriothesley, *Chronicle*, ii (*Camden Soc.*, 2 ser., xx), 90–91

CHAPTER 11, PAGES 259–282

1. *Pol. Hist. Eng.*, vi, 97–8
2. J. E. Neale, *The Elizabethan House of Commons*, 286–8; *Elizabeth I and her Parliaments*, i, 21–9. On the character of Mary's government, see especially

E. H. Harbison, *Rival Ambassadors at the Court of Queen Mary* (Princeton, 1940)

3. E.g., *A.P.C.*, *1552–1554*, 373, 375, 387, 389, 391, 395, 426, etc. I used D. M. Loades, *Popular Subversion and Government Security in England during the Reign of Mary I* (Cambridge Ph.D. thesis, 1961). He has since published *Two Tudor Conspiracies* (Cambridge, 1965)
4. *Ven. Cal.*, v. 560
5. D. M. Loades, *Popular Subversion*, ch. vii
6. Revolt and resultant punishments best treated by *ibid.*, ch. viii–x. Most informative contemporary narrative: John Proctor's, reprinted in *Tudor Tracts*, ed. A. F. Pollard, 199–257
7. *Greyfriars' Chronicle* (*Camden Soc.*, 1 ser., liii), 87
8. *Ven. Cal.*, v, 556
9. *Ibid.*, vi, 1074–5
10. *Ibid.*, vi, 1018
11. *Papiers d'Etat du Cardinal de Granvelle*, ed. C. Weiss (*Documents inédits sur l'histoire de France*, Paris, 1841–52), iv, 432–3
12. *Pol. Hist. Eng.*, vi, 130
13. On Cecil's position: C. Read, *Mr. Secretary Cecil and Queen Elizabeth*, 108ff
14. On responsibility for the persecution, and its statistics, see J. H. Blunt, *The Reformation of the Church of England*, ii, 220ff. See also H. E. Malden in *T.R.H.S.*, 2 ser., ii, 61–76, and *Pol. Hist. Eng.*, vi, 133–4, 153–7
15. Cited by J. H. Blunt, *op. cit.*, ii, 245n. The remarks to Philpot are in Foxe, vii, 645, 647
16. H. C. Lea, *History of the Inquisition of Spain*, ii, 49–50
17. J. H. Blunt, *op. cit.*, 245ff, possibly exaggerates Spanish influence. Dixon, iv, 339–43, tries unconvincingly to exculpate the Spaniards
18. Cited by J. A. Froude, *History of England*, vi, 99
19. J. Strype, *Ecclesiastical Memorials*, iii (2), 554–6. It gives places and numbers, but not names
20. C. H. Smyth, *Cranmer and the Reformation under Edward VI*, 3
21. *Pol. Hist. Eng.*, vi, 157
22. Strype, *op. cit.*, iii (2), 133–5; on Bentham see also Garrett, 86–7. Compare Renard's report that 'plusieurs . . . se sont voulu voluntairement mettre au feug sur le bûche à costé de ceulx que l'on brusloit' (*Papiers d'Etat du Cardinal de Granvelle*, iv, 404)
23. Foxe, vi, 596
24. W. J. Brown, *Life of Rowland Taylor* (1959)
25. Foxe, vi, 676–8
26. Ridley, ch. xxv, discusses and documents the final episode
27. Foxe, vii, 423
28. J. Strype, *Matthew Parker* (1821), i, 65–6
29. Garrett, 142–3, 288–9
30. *A.P.C.*, *1556–1558*, 119; compare *ibid.*, 102, 148, 169; J. Strype, *Ecclesiastical Memorials*, iii (2), 413–14
31. *A.P.C.*, *1554–1556*, 169

32. *A.P.C., 1554-1556*, 115-59 *passim*; Foxe, viii, 151
33. Described in D. M. Loades, *op. cit.*, 163-7
34. *Ibid.*, 171-7. At Ipswich the pamphleteers Peter Moone and John Ramsey were involved
35. Foxe, viii, 393-7; *A.P.C., 1554-1556*, 310, 312, 318; *1556-1558*, 18, 129-30, 142, 215
36. *Ibid.*, 336
37. H. N. Birt, *The Elizabethan Settlement*, 510, cites B.M. Harleian MS 4992, fo. 7
38. On the London congregation see Foxe, viii, 384, 444-61, 558-60; J. Strype, *op. cit.*, iii (2), 132-5; Knappen, 159-62
39. Foxe, viii, 450-51
40. Foxe, viii, 384. We cannot necessarily equate Cuthbert Simpson with 'one Simson' (Dixon, iii, 209) associated with the Freewillers of Bocking. The latter may, e.g., have been John Simson (Foxe, vii, 330). The charges against Cuthbert Simpson indicate nothing beyond Anglicanism, and the surname was common enough
41. J. Strype, *op. cit.*, iii (2), 132
42. Foxe, viii, 584-90
43. Foxe, viii, 384; Garrett, 176, 262
44. Foxe, vii, 738
45. On Colchester see Foxe, viii, 382-93
46. Foxe, viii, 556-7. The names and other references to heresy there show that this Stoke was involved, not Stoke-by-Clare. Compare, e.g., Foxe, vii, 382; viii, 389
47. Foxe, viii, 562-6; on Marsh see *ibid.*, vii, 39-68
48. Lincoln Diocesan Records, Vj.13, fos. 158b, 162b
49. Foxe, viii, 598-600
50. *Lollards and Protestants*, 223-35
51. Detail in A. G. Dickens, *The Marian Reaction in the Diocese of York*, i, 6-8
52. *Ibid.*, i, 9-21
53. Foxe, vi, 439
54. Dickens, *op. cit.*, ii, 23-9
55. Refs. in *Lollards and Protestants*, 213-14
56. The only full account of the restorations is in D. Knowles, *The Religious Orders in England*, iii, ch. xxxiv
57. The relevant passages are printed and fully discussed only by J. H. Crehan, 'St. Ignatius and Cardinal Pole' in *Archivum Historicum Societatis Iesu*, xxv (1956), 72-98. Loyola, who showed great insight into the priorities, died in 1556, and his successor Lainez was less pressing.
58. *Greyfriars' Chronicle*, 95; on processions see also *ibid.*, 94, 97
59. Cited in *Pol. Hist. Eng.*, vi, 172, n. 3
60. Cited by J. A. Froude, *op. cit.*, vi, 84

CHAPTER 12, PAGES 283–306

1. C. H. Garrett is indispensable for the scholarly biographies of the exiles, but she seems curiously hostile toward them, and has some debatable general conclusions. A. B. Hinds, *The Making of the England of Elizabeth* (1895), was a pioneering essay. Knappen, ch. vi, has the best short account of Frankfurt. Other works listed in *Tudor Bibliog.*, 182–3
2. Statistics in Garrett, 40–42
3. The names which follow are all in *D.N.B.*, supplemented by Garrett
4. Garrett, 1–29, 58–9
5. *Ibid.*, 11
6. *Ibid.*, 50–52
7. *Ibid.*, 49–50
8. Hinds, *op. cit.*, 44, cites Lever and Sandys to similar effect
9. Fuller summary in J. W. Allen, *History of Political Thought in the Sixteenth Century*, 118ff
10. On these two see *ibid.*, 106–18
11. Knappen, 142
12. On the Geneva version see *The Bible in its Ancient and English Versions*, ed. H. W. Robinson, 181–9
13. See above, note 60 to ch. 9; also 'Metrical Psalters' in *O.D.C.C.*, 895, and refs. there
14. P. Collinson in *J.E.H.*, ix, 188–208, replaces all previous investigations. A convenient modern edition is that by E. Arber, 1908
15. *Ibid.*, 44–9
16. *Ibid.*, 50–51
17. See Knappen, 117, 127–8
18. *A Brief Discourse*, ed. Arber, 76–80, gives the letter and Calvin's reply
19. Knappen, 154ff; Hinds, *op. cit.*, 47–65
20. *A Brief Discourse*, 150
21. Garrett, 22
22. On the rise of congregational principles, see Knappen, ch. viii
23. *Ibid.*, 137; W. M. Southgate, 'The Marian Exiles and the Influence of John Calvin', in *History*, xxvii, 148–52
24. The subsequent section is chiefly based on J. E. Neale, *Elizabeth I and her Parliaments*, pt. i
25. *Span. Cal.*, *1558–1567*, 39
26. J. E. Neale, *op. cit.*, 35ff
27. *Pol. Hist. Eng.*, vi, 179
28. *Span. Cal.*, *1558–1567*, 7
29. *Ibid.*, 37; *Pol. Hist. Eng.*, vi, 180 n. 2
30. Dugmore, 213–14
31. *Pol. Hist. Eng.*, vi, 182ff., gives details
32. *Span. Cal.*, *1558–1567*, 25
33. C. G. Bayne, in *E.H.R.*, xxiii, 455ff, 643ff
34. J. Strype, *Annals of the Reformation* (1820–40), i (2), 408

35. E.g. Dugmore, 209ff
36. J. E. Neale, *op. cit.*, 57–8
37. *Ibid.*, 58. Further Protestant names have now been recovered
38. C. Read, *Mr. Secretary Cecil and Queen Elizabeth*, 130
39. *D.N.B.*, Guest, Edmund; on his later rôle, see Dugmore, 213–14, 223–5
40. *Zürich Letters* (*Parker Soc.*, 1842), 11
41. J. E. Neale, *op. cit.*, 74–5; 1 Eliz. cap. 19
42. *Correspondence of Matthew Parker* (*Parker Soc.*, 1853), 66
43. Gee and Hardy, 442–57
44. Cited by D. L. Keir, *Constitutional History of Modern Britain*, 81
45. *Correspondence of Matthew Parker*, 65
46. Gee and Hardy, 458–66

CHAPTER 13, PAGES 307–321

1. Books i–iv, 1594; Book v, 1597
2. Good examples in *Lincoln Episcopal Records* (*Lincoln Record Soc.*, ii; see p. xii) and in *The State of the Church* (*ibid.*, xxiii; see pp. xviii ff)
3. Miss D. M. Barratt's figures, cited by Hill, 207
4. Broad picture in A. L. Rowse, *The England of Elizabeth*, 407ff, and in Hill, especially ch. i–ii. Some recent works on individual prelates: V. J. K. Brook, *A Life of Archbishop Parker* (1962) and *Whitgift and the English Church* (1957); W. M. Southgate, *John Jewel and the Problem of Doctrinal Authority* (Cambridge, Mass., 1962); S. B. Babbage, *Puritanism and Richard Bancroft* (1962); J. E. Booty, *John Jewel as Apologist of the Church of England* (1963)
5. The rest of this section is largely based on Hill
6. *Ibid.*, 91
7. *Ibid.*, 144–5
8. *Ibid.*, 215. Compare Sandys on the lack of preachers, especially in the North, in J. Strype, *Annals of the Reformation*, iii (2), 69–70
9. Hill, ch. xii
10. For the large literature on English Catholicism under Elizabeth see *Tudor Bibliog.*, 189ff. In addition, note Hughes, iii, 239ff, recent articles in *Recusant History* and *The Month*, and recent volumes of the Catholic Record Society. There are also several important theses, some of them cited below, note 12. An interesting general review is that by J. Bossy in *Past and Present*, xxi, 39ff. A most important recent work is A. C. F. Beales, *Education under Penalty* (1963), which ranges widely and has an excellent bibliography
11. Probably about 200 were deprived. Birt and Pollen have argued for a larger figure, and have supposed unexplained disappearances of clerics during the subsequent years to have been the results of resignation by Catholics (refs. in J. B. Black, *The Reign of Elizabeth*, 17 note). In some cases this may be true, but we should beware of straining this negative evidence, especially when it contradicts the submissive character of the Tudor parish clergy

12. On the slack enforcement of the £20 per month fine, see F. X. Walker, *The Implementation of the Elizabethan Statutes against Recusants* (London Ph.D. thesis, 1961); M. O'Dwyer, *Catholic Recusants in Essex* (London M.A. thesis, 1960), ch. vii; J. E. Paul, *The Hampshire Recusants in the Reign of Elizabeth* (Southampton Ph.D. thesis), ch. xi. See also M. O'Dwyer in *The Month*, July 1958, 28ff
13. On Lancashire recusancy see J. S. Leatherbarrow, *The Lancashire Elizabethan Recusants* (*Chetham Soc.*, cx), and comment by A. L. Rowse, *op. cit.*, 440ff
14. On Yorkshire recusancy see, e.g., the present writer in *Yorks. Arch. Journal*, xxxv, 157ff; xxxvii, 24ff, and (with J. A. Newton) in *ibid.*, xxxviii, 524ff; H. Aveling, *Post-Reformation Catholicism in East Yorkshire* (*East Yorks. Local Hist. Soc.*, 1960); *Northern Catholics* (1966); A. C. Southern in *Biographical Studies*, ii (1953), 135ff
15. Many of the best examples are in H. Foley, *Records of the English Province of the Society of Jesus* (7 vols., 1877–84)
16. Compare *Lord Burghley's Map of Lancashire, 1590* in *Catholic Record Society, Miscellanea*, iv, 162–222
17. Subsequent generalisation largely based on Knappen. Also especially relevant are P. Collinson, *The Elizabethan Puritan Movement* (1967) and A. F. Scott Pearson, *Thomas Cartwright and Elizabethan Puritanism.* In general see *Tudor Bibliog.*, 200ff and add, e.g., H. C. Porter (see note 20 below); P. Collinson (see notes 22, 26 below); R. A. Marchant, *The Puritans and the Church Courts in the Diocese of York* (1960); S. J. Knox, *Walter Travers* (1962); Claire Cross, *The Puritan Earl* (1966); J. A. Newton, *Puritanism in the Diocese of York, 1603–40* (London Ph.D. thesis, 1955). C. H. and K. George, *The Protestant Mind of the English Reformation* (Princeton, 1961) is a broad intellectual survey
18. D. Neal, *The History of the Puritans* (1732–8, etc.); B. Brook, *The Lives of the Puritans* (1813)
19. C. H. and K. George, *op. cit.*, 66
20. H. C. Porter, *Reformation and Reaction in Tudor Cambridge*, ch. xv–xvii
21. Knappen, 387ff; H. C. Porter, *op. cit.*, ch. xii; R. A. Marchant, *op. cit.*, 222–318, has voluminous biographical material on northern Puritan clergy
22. P. Collinson, *The Puritan Classical Movement in the Reign of Elizabeth I* (London Ph.D. thesis, 1957)
23. R. H. Tawney, *Religion and the Rise of Capitalism* (Pelican edn., 1938), 43, 260
24. C. H. and K. George, *op. cit.*, 144–73
25. W. K. Jordan, *Philanthropy in England* (1959), especially ch. vi; *The Charities of London* (1960); *The Charities of Rural England* (1961). Note points by L. Stone in *E.H.R.*, lxxvii, 327–9, and by other reviewers there cited
26. See important essay by P. Collinson in *Elizabethan Government and Society, Essays Presented to Sir John Neale*, 127–62
27. On Mildmay, see Knappen, 469ff; on Greenham, *ibid.*, 382ff; on Huntingdon, M. C. Cross in *Trans. Leicestershire Archaeol. Soc.*, xxxvi, 6–21; on Lady Hoby, *Diary of Lady Margaret Hoby*, ed. D. M. Meads
28. Knappen, 333ff
29. Important article by J. E. C. Hill in *T.R.H.S.*, 5 ser., xiii, 77–102
30. J. Strype, *Grindal* (1821), 562

31. This emerges from Jordan's work, note 25 above; see references in J. E. C. Hill, *op. cit.*, 94ff
32. Knappen, ch. xxiii, corrects popular misconceptions on asceticism in Puritan thought
33. *Ibid.*, 355–60
34. *Ibid.*, ch. xxvi
35. *Ibid.*, 348ff
36. *Ibid.*, 376

CHAPTER 14, PAGES 322–340

1. J. W. Allen, *A History of Political Thought in the Sixteenth Century*, pt. ii, ch. ix, compare also pt. i, ch. v; W. K. Jordan, *The Development of Religious Toleration in England*, i. A. G. Dickens in Congregational Historical Society, xx, 58–73.
2. For these three works see W. K. Jordan, *op. cit.*, 57ff, 66ff, 74ff
3. On Brinklow see *ibid.*, 61ff, and on Turner, *ibid.*, 72ff
4. Article, as yet unpublished, by V. N. Olsen, 'John Foxe the Martyrologist and Toleration'
5. Examples of tolerationist speeches in Parliament: J. W. Allen, *op. cit.*, 231, 237–8
6. On Acontius and Gentilis see W. K. Jordan, *op. cit.*, 303ff. On Sandys, *ibid*, 367ff, and Allen, *op. cit.*, 241ff
7. American writers have taken the lead in this approach, e.g. P. H. Kocher, *Science and Religion in Elizabethan England* (San Marino, 1953); F. R. Johnson, *Astronomical Thought in Renaissance England* (Baltimore, 1937). Another pertinent approach: L. B. Wright, *Middle Class Culture in Elizabethan England* (Chapel Hill, 1935)
8. D. Bush, *The Renaissance and English Humanism* (Toronto, 1939), 73–9; F. Caspari, *Humanism and the Social Order in Tudor England*, 133
9. A. G. Dickens in *T.R.H.S.*, 5 ser., xiii, 49–76
10. J. H. Elliott in *Past and Present*, xx, 52–75

INDEX